LORD JIM

~~~~~~

RIVERSIDE EDITIONS

RIVERSIDE EDITIONS

UNDER THE GENERAL EDITORSHIP OF

Gordon N. Ray

LORD JIM

JOSEPH CONRAD

*It is certain my conviction gains infinitely, the
moment another soul will believe in it.*—NOVALIS

WITH AN INTRODUCTION BY

MORTON DAUWEN ZABEL

THE UNIVERSITY OF CHICAGO

HOUGHTON MIFFLIN COMPANY

Joseph Conrad: 1857–1924

(Jozef Teodor Konrad Nalecz Korzeniowski)

LORD JIM was first published in serial form in *Blackwood's Magazine*, October 1899–November 1900, and in book form in 1900

goes against the norms of society.

motivated by strong feelings.

The text of *Lord Jim* is that of the authorized edition published by J. M. Dent and Sons, Ltd., London, and by Doubleday and Company, New York .

INTRODUCTION

By Morton Dauwen Zabel

I

Lord Jim was begun in May 1898, while Conrad was still involved in the long struggle with the book that occupied him severely and unsuccessfully for three years before it was abandoned and which only after another twenty years became the novel published in 1920 as *The Rescue*. That beginning at Pent Farm in Kent in the spring of 1898 was hardly more than tentative, and by Conrad's own account without anticipation of the long novel that was to issue from it. The manuscript was laid aside for the writing of "Youth" in June; was resumed briefly in December but was again put aside for the writing of "Heart of Darkness"; was taken up in earnest once more in September 1899; and was completed on July 16, 1900, nine months after its fourteen-month serialization had begun in *Blackwood's Magazine*.

> The end of *L. J.* has been pulled off with a steady drag of 21 hours [Conrad wrote Galsworthy a few days later]. I sent wife and child out of the house (to London) and sat down at 9 A.M. with a desperate resolve to be done with it. Now and then I took a walk round the house, out at one door in at the other. Ten-minute meals. A great hush. Cigarette ends growing into a mound similar to a cairn over a dead hero. Moon rose over the barn, looked in at the window and climbed out of sight. Dawn broke, brightened. I put the lamp out and went on, with the morning breeze blowing the sheets of MS. all over the room. Sun rose. I wrote the last word and went into the dining-room. Six o'clock I shared a piece of cold chicken with Escamillo (who was very miserable and in want of sympathy, having missed the child dreadfully all day).[1] Felt very well, only sleepy: had a bath at seven and at 1.30 was on my way to London.

[1] Escamillo: the Conrads' dog.

The tale was Conrad's fourth novel, his fifth book, and the ordeal that went into its making had already, even at that early point in his literary career, become a familiar, expected, and incurable experience with him. *Blackwood's*, the sympathetic *"Maga"* which at this period played an important and encouraging part in Conrad's progress, had contracted for the serialization of the book after having published "Karain," "Youth," and "Heart of Darkness"; [2] and it was largely on that incentive that he returned to the manuscript begun a year earlier — "my first thought was of a short story, concerned only with the pilgrim ship episode; nothing more" — but with which, "after writing a few pages," he had "become discontented and . . . laid them aside for a time." *The Rescue*, at first provisionally titled *The Rescuer*, having meanwhile proved wholly baffling in spite of being under contract to the *Illustrated London News* and to S. S. McClure in America, was finally given up in despair as a lost cause, not to be resumed until 1916. William Blackwood's encouragement came as a token of salvation to Conrad in these straits; he never forgot the debt he owed him for having supported him at this distracted moment of his career. The role of *Blackwood's* was in fact of major value to Conrad during his three-year association with the Edinburgh magazine. It took him, at the height of his early powers, away from the intractable subject and baffled labor of *The Rescue* and spurred him to write three tales that originated in the most intimate sources of his personal history and imagination; it helped him to achieve, by the end of his first six years of professional authorship, the basis of dramatic method and artistry, as well as the mastery of a radical subject in his lifework, that were to serve him in his finest tales of the next two decades.

Yet neither the drama nor the art of *Lord Jim* came easily, even after they had already been tested in the two remarkable stories that had preceded the writing of the novel. "I don't know how to thank you for all you say in your critical letter anent *Lord Jim*,"

---

[2] "Karain: A Memory" in November 1897; "Youth" in September 1898; "Heart of Darkness" in February–April 1899. *Lord Jim* was serialized October 1899–November 1900. Letters quoted here are taken from G. Jean-Aubry's *Joseph Conrad: Life and Letters* (1927) except where otherwise noted. Those to Edward Garnett are quoted from his *Letters from Conrad 1895 to 1924* in its English edition (London: Nonesuch Press, n.d., c. 1928) rather than from its American edition (Indianapolis: Bobbs-Merrill Co., 1928).

Conrad wrote on November 9, 1899, to Edward Garnett, his first literary friend and editor, who had written him about the first numbers of the serial. "Of the faults you point out I've been aware all along, but that the thing had any good at all in it I vow and declare I was ignorant. The faults are mine and the good (since you say there is some good in it) comes from devil knows whence. Well! As long as it *is* there." And a few days later, on November 13th: "*Jim's* dragging his slow length along — *après* — *nous verrons*. Annihilation perhaps. I repeat: *Nous verrons!*" "Too wretched for words," he repeated on November 19th; and a month earlier, on October 12th, he had wailed to another friend, E. L. Sanderson: "I am at it day after day, and I want all day, every minute of a day, to produce a beggarly tale of words or perhaps to produce nothing at all. And when that is finished (I thought it would be so on the first of this month, — but no fear!) I must go on, even go on at once and drag out of myself another 20,000 words, if the boy is to have his milk and I my beer . . . and if the world is not absolutely to come to an end. And after I have written and have been paid, I shall have the satisfaction of knowing that I can't allow myself the relaxation of being ill more than three days under the penalty of starvation: nor the luxury of going off the hooks altogether without playing the part of a thief regarding various confiding persons, whose desire to serve me was greater than their wisdom."

Even after the end of the tale was in sight he remained doubtful of its success. "*Vous me mettez du coeur au ventre*," he wrote Cunninghame Graham in March 1900, in response to his admiration, "though I can't possibly agree to your praises of *Jim*." And after the book was published in its completed form on October 15th and Garnett had written him a sympathetic criticism of it, Conrad replied on November 12th:

> Yes! you've put your finger on the plague spot. The division of the book into two parts which is the basis of your criticism demonstrates to me once more your amazing insight; and your analysis of the effect of the book puts into words precisely and suggestively the dumb thoughts of every reader — and my own.

And he went on to admit problems in the novel which he had encountered in the writing and which have taxed the attention and sympathy of its readers ever since:

Such is indeed the effect of the book; the effect which you can name and others can only feel. I admit I stood for a great triumph and I have only succeeded in giving myself utterly away. Nobody'll see it, but you have detected me falling back into my lump of clay I had been lugging up from the bottom of the pit, with the idea of breathing big life into it. And all I have done was to let it fall with a silly crash.

For what is fundamentally wrong with the book — the cause and the effect — is want of power. I do not mean the "power" of reviewers' jargon. I mean the want of illuminating imagination. I wanted to obtain a sort of lurid light out [of] the very events. You know what I have done — alas! I haven't been strong enough to breathe the right sort of life into my clay — the *revealing* life.

I've been satanically ambitious, but there's nothing of a devil in me, worse luck. The *Outcast* is a heap of sand, the *Nigger* a splash of water, *Jim* a lump of clay. . . . This time I am only very bruised, very sore, very humiliated.

This is the effect of the book upon me; the intimate and personal effect. Humiliation. Not extinction. Not yet. . . .

The vein, the tone, and the reaction had already become an inevitable part of Conrad's experience in the writing of his books. It was thus that he looked back in 1900 on the achievement that had even then won him his high place in the esteem of his fellow-craftsmen and in the art of modern English fiction. Henry James was one of the first to write him an enthusiastic letter on receiving *Lord Jim*, but much as this heartened Conrad some of his doubts about the novel persisted for many years, long after it had become one of the most popular and widely acclaimed of his tales. When he wrote his "Author's Note" for it in 1917 he recalled the strictures of some of its early critics: that "the work starting as a short story had got beyond the writer's control"; that, concerning Marlow's part in the narrative, "no man could have been expected to talk all that time, and other men to listen so long"; that " 'it [was] all so morbid.' " And though he allowed, on the question "whether this was not the book of mine I liked best," that "i don't go so far as to feel grieved and annoyed by the preference some people give to my Lord Jim," he was still defensive about the truth and sincerity of the story. Yet he succeeded in putting his finger on the point and theme that have given *Lord Jim* its rank and value among his works. "The acute consciousness of lost honour": it was thus that he defined its subject. "Such a consciousness may be wrong, or it may be right, or it may be condemned as artificial," he said; "and, perhaps, my Jim is not a type of wide commonness." "But," he continued:

> I can safely assure my readers that he is not the product of coldly perverted thinking. He's not a figure of Northern Mists either. One sunny morning in the commonplace surroundings of an Eastern roadstead, I saw his form pass by — appealing — significant — under a cloud — perfectly silent. Which is as it should be. It was for me, with all the sympathy of which I was capable, to seek fit words for his meaning. He was "one of us."

II

The steps — conscious or unconscious, sometimes deliberate, more often accidental — by which a writer arrives at his essential subject vary greatly. It is only after the radical theme of his work is established that we are able to define the logic or inevitability by which it asserted itself, and to speculate on the origins or impulses from which it emerged. It may be taken as a general rule that every author of confirmed talent strikes his central preoccupation at a fairly early age, yet allowance must be made for those in whom the grasp is slow to assert itself and mastery a matter of delayed assurance, uncertain emergence, and deceptive hazards. Some novelists — Turgenev, Tolstoy, Proust — may show their subject at the outset but approach it by reconnoitering stages and oblique attack; others — Balzac or Melville — will resort to extravagant or fanciful means to outline a drama which they will only gradually define in accurate detail and full-bodied form; others still — Hawthorne, Henry James, in our own time Joyce, Forster, Hemingway, Faulkner — use the slighter narrative forms to establish themes which must wait their period of gestation before arriving at mature substance and expression. But against these there are always the cases of talent which springs into full and recognizable stature virtually (if never quite literally) at an initial stroke: Jane Austen with the first version of *Pride and Prejudice* at twenty-two, Dickens with the *Pickwick Papers* or Thomas Mann with *Buddenbrooks* at twenty-five. Conrad's is a case of this order but it presents some unusual features.

He did not begin to write until he was past thirty. His first novel, *Almayer's Folly*, was published in 1895 when he was thirty-seven. His entire career in literature falls in his middle and later life. He came to writing with his temper confirmed, his sense of experience established, his characteristic subject ineradicably lodged in his mind and imagination. It first comes to us clearly announced on the first page of his first book. Almayer, "leaning with both his elbows on the balustrade of the verandah" of his "new but already decaying house" above the swirling waters of the River Pantai in up-country Borneo, appears in the opening sentences of his history as the embodiment of a long-pondered idea. The "dream" that possesses him is already a portent of the doom, the "folly," that will claim and condemn him, as it will claim so many other men in Conrad's future tales:

> . . . he went on looking fixedly at the great river that flowed — indifferent and hurried — before his eyes. He liked to look at it about the time of sunset; perhaps because at that time the sinking sun would spread a glowing gold tinge on the waters of the Pantai, and Almayer's thoughts were often busy with gold; gold he had failed to secure; gold the others had secured — dishonestly, of course — or gold he meant to secure yet. . . . He absorbed himself in his dream of wealth and power away from this coast where he had dwelt for so many years, forgetting the bitterness of toil and strife in the vision of a great and splendid reward. . . . he would grow young again, he would forget the twenty-five years of heartbreaking struggle on this coast where he felt like a prisoner. All this was nearly within his reach. . . .

The dream, the gold, the flight, the fame: they declare themselves as the terms of his fate, with only, at that early moment of his tale, the screaming voice of his native wife behind him in the house — "Kaspar! Makan!" — to sound the warning that hovers in the background, startling him "from his dream of splendid future into the unpleasant realities of the present hour." The opening lines of Willems' history in *An Outcast of the Islands* are equally prophetic:

> When he stepped off the straight and narrow path of his peculiar honesty, it was with an inward assertion of unflinching resolve to fall back again into the monotonous but safe stride of virtue as soon as his little excursion into the wayside quagmires had produced the desired effect. . . . he was unable to conceive that the

moral significance of any act of his could interfere with the very nature of things. . . . It is a fine thing to be a providence, and to be told so on every day of one's life. It gives one a feeling of enormously remote superiority, and Willems revelled in it. . . .

Scarcely a story in Conrad's first years of authorship — "Karain," "An Outpost of Progress," "The Return," "Youth," "Heart of Darkness" — is without some comparable suggestion of the subject thus launched in his first two books. The conviction or delusion of a special destiny, an arbitrary assumption of superiority to common experience, a secret sense of the personal fate: it is these that possess his men, but invariably with a hint, covert or explicit, that this conviction will soon find itself at odds with the rough justice of fortune, the implacable or impersonal lines of life that disregard a man's idea of his own character or endowment and that will impose on him a test of reality for which youthful expectation, egotistic self-regard, or reckless self-law has little prepared him. *Nostromo*, *The Secret Agent*, *Under Western Eyes*, *Victory*, *The Shadow-Line*, and *The Rescue* were to present variations on the theme in the future. When Conrad wrote "The Secret Sharer" in 1909 he gave the idea one of its most concise and explicit definitions: "I wondered how far I should turn out faithful to that ideal conception of one's own personality every man sets up for himself secretly."

Inevitably the subject was bound to seek its total realization in a particular book. When Conrad, with four years of professional authorship behind him, set about the writing of his fourth novel in 1898, the moment for its first full presentation had arrived. *Lord Jim* is the book that gave it its ordained opportunity, the novel in which Conrad's central moral problem was to be most typically established and achieved. It is not without reason that *Lord Jim* has always held a special rank among his works. It provides the key to a drama he made unmistakably his own. In many respects it still remains his most fully representative, his most expressly Conradian, tale.

Such a subject, repeatedly recurred to, tenaciously held in the grip of sympathy and imagination, inevitably issues from acutely intimate sources in a writer's nature. There is every evidence in Conrad's tales, letters, and memoirs to encourage us to trace it to his own personality — to the roots of character which, however long he may have remained unconscious of them, declared themselves in his mature manhood as the sources of his emotional and moral life, as of the art that was ultimately to issue from them by way of the transforming imagination. He himself is explicit on their relevance to his career and fiction. His personal statements, not to mention the overt and often excessive tendency to self-analysis and self-dramatization that runs through much of his work, can make us believe that few authors show so close a relationship between the creations of their imagination and the facts of their personal constitution and history.

Such comparison is however hazardous: it is likely to fail in taking sufficient account of the intervening imagination and what it makes of the personal substance in which it works. Meanwhile there is evidence that the Jim of Conrad's novel was, like many other figures throughout his tales, suggested by an original.

There was a Jim Lingard in Conrad's past, a nephew of the Captain Tom Lingard who gave him the like-named character in *Almayer's Folly*, *An Outcast of the Islands*, and *The Rescue*. Jim had served on his uncle's ship and was later set up by him as a trader in Berouw. He was called "Tuan Jim" by the natives of the East, "Lord Jim" by the officers of the ship *Vidar*, "thanks to the swaggering manner he assumed," when Conrad served as mate on that ship in 1887–88. He married a half-Chinese Malay woman. Several incidents of his history are close to those of the fictional hero's. If nothing more, his name and title stuck in Conrad's mind, though his surname was dropped. He evidently had no connection with the other man Conrad said he saw "one sunny morning in the commonplace surroundings of an Eastern roadstead"; a teller of tales seldom adheres to a single model. But it appears that the memory of these two men — one known fairly closely, the other only by a glimpse — fused with certain experiences of his own in Conrad's imagination, and that he was further spurred by what he had learned or heard of other European adventurers in the East of those days, when the imperial ventures of Europe brought so many men out of England, Holland, and other western countries into the kingdoms and ports of the Orient.

James Brooke was one of them: the English sailor and trader who became Rajah of Sarawak in 1841, devoted himself to his Bornean people, fought the pirates and Bornean princes who threatened them, jealously defended his sovereignty to the English authorities and his enemies in Parliament, became a hero of

Sarawak as Jim became one in Patusan, "gave Sarawak security, justice, and prosperity," died in 1868, and became the legendary hero of a series of chronicles of his career that were published between 1846 and 1876 and in after-years. Conrad's reading of these books remains unestablished, though there is fair evidence that he knew Brooke's history closely. But no reading was necessary for him to have heard during his Eastern sojourns of the fabled hero of one of the most stirring legends of the East in the Nineteenth Century. Conrad's country of Patusan was named from the Patusan on the Sakarran River where Brooke wiped out a nest of pirates in August 1844; the histories of Patusan and Sarawak show other similarities; so do the names of characters who figure in them.

The "pilgrim ship episode" from which the novel stems is even more closely documented. An old steamer called the *Jeddah* did in fact sail from Singapore for Jeddah, the port of Mecca, in the summer of 1880, with some nine hundred Moslem pilgrims aboard. On the night of August 7th she was abandoned by all her officers except one during stormy weather that overtook her near Cape Gardafui near the mouth of the Red Sea. The pilgrims were left to their fate in what was evidently an attempt on the part of her owners, the captain and a Singapore Arab, to collect the heavy insurance they had taken out. The *Jeddah* was towed to Aden, the same port reached by the deserters in their lifeboat. There was an inquiry in Aden and later a detailed investigation in Singapore. The news of the event became common knowledge among the seamen of the East and was remembered by some of them more than forty years later.[3]

The "hearsay," "fragments of autobiography," "hints of things that really happened and of people that really existed," that habit-

---

[3] The events and characters that figure among the source suggestions of *Lord Jim* are most fully given in John Dozier Gordan's *Joseph Conrad: The Making of a Novelist* (Cambridge: Harvard University Press, 1940), Chapter II, "The Four Sources," especially pp. 57–74. Two letters on the *Jeddah* in the London *Times Literary Supplement*, September 6 and October 11, 1923, are notably relevant. Other discussion is given in G. Jean-Aubry's *Joseph Conrad: Life and Letters* (New York: Doubleday, 1927), I, pp. 97–98, and in his *Vie de Conrad* (Paris: Gallimard, 1947), translated as *The Sea Dreamer* (New York: Doubleday, 1957), pp. 239–40 and *passim*. For a sidelight on the pilgrim ship episode, see "Tuan Jim," by P. Elphinstone, in *Turnstile 1* (London: Turnstile Press, 1948), pp. 225–29. Further details will appear in Jocelyn Baines's biographical study of Conrad, to be published in 1958.

ually played their part in the shaping of Conrad's tales played their
part here, and they combined to animate what is of greater importance generally in his work — the treatment of what he called
the "subjects of which a writer of tales is more or less conscious
within himself." Here it was not a case, as he said of "Heart of
Darkness," of using "experience pushed a little (and only very
little) beyond the actual facts of the case," in order to bring it
"home to the minds and bosoms of the readers." Nor was it a
case of the "need of slight dramatization" — "very slight" — to
"make the thing actual," as in "a piece of strict autobiography"
like *The Shadow-Line*. Once the character of Jim was established
in the first three chapters; once the pilgrim ship episode had
served as "a good starting-point" for "a free and wandering tale,"
another purpose than the documentary or even the dramatic took
over the story. That purpose Conrad also named in his "Author's
Note." It was the depiction of "the whole 'sentiment of existence'
in a simple and sensitive character" caught in "the acute consciousness of lost honour."

For the portrayal of such a "sentiment" no given model could
possibly serve adequately, whether the Jim Lingard of the *Vidar*
or the James Brooke of Sarawak. The fate of the Jim whom
Conrad created, once launched on its devious, elusive, "wandering" course, was inevitably destined, given Conrad's propensity to
moral interrogation and analysis, to include the fates of many
other men, the judgments and commitments of all on whom it
impinged — that "community of mankind" which "knits together
the loneliness of innumerable hearts . . . in dreams, in joy, in sorrow, in aspirations, in illusions, in hope, in fear," and which "binds
men to each other," and "binds together all humanity." Conrad
had already taken this "community" as the province of his imaginative and moral vision. He had so defined it in his "preface" to
The Nigger of the "Narcissus" late in 1897. More than *The
Nigger* with its community of seamen on their ship; more than any
of his earlier tales, *Lord Jim* was to become a tale of the common
fate and shared experience of a whole host of characters — men of
many kinds and races, men of the sea and of the ports and nations:
English, Malay, Chinese, French, Dutch, German, Portuguese,
Italian, Australian, Arab, Moslem, Swiss, Scandinavian, American.
Conrad's conception of the moral community of human life — its
"solidarity" as he insisted on calling it — was now to take on the

widest possible dimensions. And the test to which his hero was to be subjected produced a tale not only "free and wandering" but one that, whatever Conrad felt to be its broken continuity and "want of power," was finally to show its own kind of dramatic coherence; a psychological and moral coherence, moreover, in which the scattered, disparate, and melodramatic elements of Jim's story will seek their eventual synthesis and unity.

III

A tale so conceived — focused in an individual but expanding to a wide periphery of life and experience — is likely to call for more than a hero. It calls for an interpreter who will see the hero in the setting of the world which is to test, judge, condemn, or redeem him. The novelist himself may so serve, but Conrad's way was otherwise. When Jim, in Chapter IV, stands facing the Court of Inquiry which represents the moral judgment of mankind that has called him to the bar of justice, his eyes, "wandering in the intervals of his answers," find themselves resting "upon a white man" who sits "apart from the others, with his face worn and clouded, but with quiet eyes that [glance] straight, interested and clear." Answering the court but tempted to cry "What's the good of this! what's the good!" he sees that the glance of the man is not "the fascinated stare of the others." It is "an act of intelligent voli-tion." Jim, between two questions, forgets himself so far as to find "leisure for a thought." "This fellow," runs the thought, "looks at me as though he could see somebody or something past my shoulder." He, who has come to doubt "whether he would ever again speak out as long as he lived," notes that the man seems "aware of his hopeless difficulty." His agony has met the response of another's eyes. Marlow has entered the tale.

It is uncertain just when the character of Marlow took shape in Conrad's mind. The two stories in which he first appears — "Youth" in 1898, "Heart of Darkness" in 1899 — preceded the completion of *Lord Jim*. There is no exact evidence to show that when Conrad sketched the opening episodes of his novel in the spring of 1898 Marlow figured in his plan. Created in these three tales of 1898–1900, he was not to reappear in Conrad's pages until twelve years later when, under certain radical changes of personality and a more arbitrary participation, he becomes the narrator of a large part of *Chance*.

That he filled a need of Conrad's imagination at this decisive stage of his development — became a necessary *persona* of his thought as well as a salient agent of his drama — is a notable fact of Conrad's creative life. It is of course a generally recognized feature of Conrad's kind of tale-telling that it needs and so frequently uses the voice of a narrator. Early stories like "Karain," "The Idiots," "The Lagoon," "Youth," "Heart of Darkness," and "Falk" use first-personal narration; there is a hovering "I" in *The Nigger*; Dr. Kennedy tells the tale of "Amy Foster"; the heroes of "Il Conde" and "The Secret Sharer" relate their strange encounters; the old professor in Geneva interprets the Russian drama of *Under Western Eyes*; Davidson contributes to *Victory*; even *Nostromo* resorts to interludes of intimate disclosure. When, in such cases, a detached or external witness serves to convey the drama he does so to evoke a dimension of sympathy, response, or intimate appeal, yet he is likely to remain incidental, sometimes abstract, impersonal, the exponent of an extra-dramatic or superior point of vantage. When Marlow takes on the role his part becomes essential, vital, a mode of commitment and participation. He becomes — notably in his first three appearances — more than a narrator. He becomes the secret sharer of the lives in which chance, curiosity, or compassion has compelled him to participate. In *Lord Jim* he becomes the recorder of Jim's fate in the latent conscience of all the men it touches. It is he who recognizes Jim as "one of us."

That such an intermediary became necessary to Conrad is evident in more than the use he makes of Marlow. It declares itself in what we come to know of his constitution as a man of imagination and of the habitual workings of his dramatic sense and emotion. The tradition of the "told story," the yarn or saga of maritime tradition, was apparently — against whatever protests he may have raised — firmly rooted in his mind by the time he took up writing. The habit of listening to such tales, the instinct of alerting himself to the speaking voice, must have grown on him during his twenty years of sailing and of travel in the East. Whatever his taciturnity or reserve, his response to the lore of ships and ports seems to have been avid. The spawning yarns and legends that crowd *Lord Jim* show it. Such influences are bound to count in a writer's life. The verbal histrionics and eccentricities in Dickens; the club, mess, and smoking-room lingoes in Kipling; the bar, café, newsroom, and army talk of Hemingway; the Southern fable-making and vernacular folklore of Faulkner, obviously originate in a long-standing immersion in a given element of speech and language. No writer's method or style is born of thin air. Whatever its conscious shaping and styling, it issues from the speech, voice, and verbal processes to which he has become habituated.

We know little about the tale-telling, local folklore, or family conversation Conrad had around him in childhood. His language was doubtless given part of its characteristic bent there. (Several Polish students have examined that early environment and the role it played in shaping his sensibility.) But it may be taken as certain that his familiarity with the speech and tall talk of ships and seamen was a continuous experience during his years at sea. It appears as a prevalent feature of his tales — the cluster of men around a mahogany table where the bottles and glasses glisten in lamplight; the old friends yarning on the decks of yachts and yawls; the tilted chairs on Eastern verandahs; the rumors of the ports. It was likewise a feature of the sea-tales of Marryat and Cooper in which Conrad delighted. (In Marryat, whom he called "the enslaver of youth," he found a "natural glamour" of atmosphere that shows a "completely successful expression of an unartistic nature," an "irresistible power to reach the adventurous side in the character, not only of his own but of all nations." Of Cooper's world he said that Cooper "could hear its voice, he could understand its silence." When he wrote his tribute to these writers Conrad said that they had "shaped" the "life of the writer of this appreciation," and that he had "never regretted his surrender" to their spell.) [4]

There was evidently another factor that bent Conrad's art in this direction. His imagination, natively strong in visualizing impulse, also worked aurally. "To make you hear" was as urgent a clause in his artist's credo as its two cognate clauses, "to make you feel" and "to make you *see*," and it may have come first in his own need as it came first in his famous formula. [5] He was on occasion

---

[4] "Tales of the Sea," dated 1898, in *Notes on Life and Letters* (1921), pp. 53–57.

[5] In the "Preface" (1897) to *The Nigger of the "Narcissus."*

able to write in irony or detachment, as in *Typhoon, The Secret Agent*, or *Victory*, and so, but dint of severe manipulation and control of tone, to render his tale objectively. He could, with an even more strenuous formality, maintain a historical omniscience that spread his drama below him panoramically, as in *Nostromo*. Apparently such methods exacted torments of tact and discipline. Sometimes they imposed so complex and precarious a jugglery of his material — *Nostromo* is the notable case — that the informing voice of his pages falls into confusion or distraction. Even in such novels he will often be forced to find relief in first-personal interludes. The desperation of Conrad's creative ordeal with which his letters sound from first to last — not even Flaubert's *affres de l'art* are more painfully documented — seems to have sought confidence as a mere matter of sanity in the talking voice that sounded in the ear of his imagination and freed his fancy as little else could, thus releasing his language from the tension of impersonality and his thought from the strain that otherwise sought relief either in rhetoric or in redundant verbalizing.

But there was a further necessity behind the creation of Marlow, and it brings us even closer to understanding the kind of tale Conrad found most congenial. It is especially relevant to both "Heart of Darkness" and *Lord Jim*. The subject of *Lord Jim* is more than the "acute consciousness of lost honour"; more also than the test that overtakes the "ideal conception of one's own personality every man sets up for himself secretly." It is the workings of these in "the whole 'sentiment of existence' " in a sensitive character.

The themes are cognate. The principle of honor premises an external court of appeal and judgment. The ideal conception of one's own personality, unless it remains private or secretive to the point of that subjective nihilism which is a standing threat to Conrad's isolated, locked-in, or self-confining characters, aspires to the reflection of its image in human approval or recognition. Since Conrad was not the kind of dramatist who leaves honor to speak purely in terms of heroic selfhood or self-sufficiency; since the nihilism of the individual temperament could never, in a man of his intensely human needs, remain the hermetic solipsism it became in the aesthetic or metaphysical heroes of Huysmans, Villiers, and the early Proust; since, moreover, the passion for recognition early defined itself as an obsessive preoccupation in his characteristic men and women, the stories he shaped around such characters were compelled to deal in the double vision, the double focus, of two opposing standards of being and existence — that of the self, and that of the human or moral community to which the self appeals for the "reality of its own existence." The "illusion" of private or secret selfhood is compelled to escape its isolation or estrangement by an imperative moral necessity.

The terror the self then faces comes with its realization of what an illusory or romantic error has done to distort or betray its capacity for human relationship and communication. Illusion and fact, private dream and public judgment, appearance and reality, are suddenly thrown into violent collision. Their conflict may become so destructive as to threaten sanity itself. In extreme cases it can impel derangement or suicide. It is then that the dream becomes "the destructive element" — is abruptly transformed into a truth in which the dreamer finds he must swim or sink. The drama such crisis precipitates is a drama of mutual duplicities. It is the drama not merely of the alter ego — of the "other self" on which Conrad can lay exaggerated emphasis in a story like "The Secret Sharer." It is the drama of an even more radical human condition — not of the other but of the double self.

Its prevalence in modern literature is salient and widespread. To a theme as old as Oedipus, Orestes, and Hamlet, the writers of the past hundred years have applied every possible refinement of moral and psychic analysis. Pirandello, as I have elsewhere noted,[6] made the problem the central subject of his plays. Twice at least in *Six Characters in Search of an Author* the Father states and defines it:

> We have this illusion of being one person for all, of having a personality that is unique in all our acts. But it isn't true. We perceive this when, tragically perhaps, in something we do, we are, as it were, suspended, caught up in the air on a kind of hook. Then we perceive that all of us was not in that act, and that it would be an atrocious injustice to judge us by that action alone, as if all our existence were summed up in that one deed.

And again:

> Each one of us has within him a world of things, each man of us his own special world. And how can we ever come to an under-

[6] In *Craft and Character* (New York: The Viking Press, 1957), "Conrad in His Age," pp. 207–27.

standing if I put in the words I utter the sense and value of things as I see them, while you who listen to me must inevitably translate them according to the conception of things each one of you has within himself.

His words can be taken as an explicit statement of Jim's plight in Conrad's novel and of the plea he lays before the court of human justice when his crisis of lost honor overtakes and imperils him.

In that court Marlow becomes advocate and counsel. The circle of judgment that closes around the typical Conradian hero is likely to take in the widest possible range of moral positions. Conrad himself seems to have been conscious to the point of distraction of how varied, diverse, and contradictory such judgments can be. It became his concern in books like *Lord Jim*, *Nostromo*, *Under Western Eyes*, *Chance*, and *Victory* to show the diversity and contradiction of human judgment in their fullest complexity. It is thus that his drama of the individual widens until it comes to include the moral universe that surrounds him, with every factor of prejudice or self-interest, compassion or ruthlessness, human hostility or abstract justice, playing its part in the test that focuses in the victim. It is the world of political and nationalistic passions in *The Secret Agent* and *Under Western Eyes*; of social mores in *Chance*; of sea-brotherhood in *The Nigger of the "Narcissus."* In *Nostromo* it becomes the organism of a whole nation in crisis, where the lack of a specific personal center permits the tale to ramify into a complex dialectic of creeds and codes of conduct which seriously threatens its dramatic coherence. What such tales describe is the steadily widening periphery of Conrad's argument — its ambition toward a totality of effect and inclusiveness of relevance.

Conrad's own disrupted and diffused experience unquestionably played its part in his conception of this order of drama. His life was tossed from Poland to France, from Europe to the East; from the constriction of ships to the wayward fates of men and nations outside familiar bounds and laws; from the impulses of a youthful vanity or self-indulgence that shows itself in his early history as one of inordinate self-will and recklessness, to a later respect for the codes of class, craft, maritime service, and finally of an adoptive British allegiance whose sense of the forms of loyalty and tradition could exasperate born subjects of the Crown. His experience in physical and psychic distraction could hardly have missed playing its part in the products of his imagination. Such distraction, confusion, instability, is basic to all his greater tales. It can be taken as their native element, their essential *donnée*. Marlow comes forward as its mediator, its apologist and arbiter. He serves equally as counsel for Jim and for the larger humanity that is divided and threatened by a perilous disequilibrium of its moral and spiritual forces.

That disequilibrium is the external and objective reality in which men are fated to live. It is Stein's "destructive element" when Stein enters the tale to act as the higher counsel who adds his philosophic vision to Marlow's more intimate human sense of Jim's case. The man who "tries to climb out into the air as inexperienced people endeavour to do, he drowns — *nicht wahr?*" The man who refuses to admit the existence of the element — who, that is, remains "ignorant of life to the last, without ever having been made to see all it may contain of perfidy, of violence, and of terror" — is "fortunate." He is "disdained by destiny." [7] But the man condemned by the "dream" to face the problem of "how to be," and whose dream grants him the privilege and the peril of realizing the moral destiny to which mankind is assigned, is the one who must, inescapably and of necessity, "submit" himself and

---

[7] The phrases in these two sentences are quoted from a passage in *Typhoon* (1902) inevitable to any account of Conrad's central subject; they refer to Captain MacWhirr, the stolid Scottish captain of the *Nan-Shan*: "The sea . . . had never put itself out to startle the silent man, who seldom looked up, and wandered innocently over the waters with the only visible purpose of getting food, raiment, and house-room for three people ashore. Dirty weather he had known, of course. He had been made wet, uncomfortable, tired in the usual way, felt at the time and presently forgotten. So that upon the whole he had been justified in reporting fine weather at home. But he had never been given a glimpse of immeasurable strength and of immoderate wrath, the wrath that passes exhausted but never appeased — the wrath and fury of the passionate sea. He knew it existed, as we know that crime and abominations exist; he had heard of it as a peaceable citizen in a town hears of battles, famines, and floods, and yet knows nothing of what these things mean — though, indeed, he may have been mixed up in a street row, have gone without his dinner once, or been soaked to the skin in a shower. Captain MacWhirr had sailed over the surface of the oceans as some men go skimming over the years of existence to sink gently into a placid grave, ignorant of life to the last, without ever having been made to see all it may contain of perfidy, of violence, and of terror. There are on sea and land such men thus fortunate — or thus disdained by destiny or by the sea."

Other quotations in this Introduction are from *Lord Jim* unless otherwise indicated.

"with the exertions of [his] hands and feet in the water" make "the deep, deep sea" keep him up.

The Marlow of *Lord Jim* has already known both dream and destruction in his own experience. He has told of his encounters with them in "Youth" and "Heart of Darkness." He has crossed his "shadow-line." [8] The good and evil he has known have brought him out of youth and early manhood into the first years of mature age. He is already the "meditating Buddha" who told the tale of his journey into the African darkness, but no lotus flower of serene confidence in cosmic justice has been given him to bless his knowledge. Sympathy with the fate of men still contends with a skepticism of justice in his character. Disillusionment must still compete with an invincible curiosity and a tenacious confidence in the capacity of men to justify their survival in a world of baffling or destructive forces. It is as such a mediator, participant, counsel of appeal, that Marlow acts in *Lord Jim*. In playing his part he will call to witness every man who has shared, consciously or not, in Jim's fortunes, and in the judgment that is finally to be rendered on his character and fate.

IV

Far along in the novel — Chapter XXVIII — after Jim's last adventure in Patusan has begun, Marlow refers to the tale he unfolds as "this amazing Jim-myth." And some pages earlier — Chapter XXI — when he speaks of "going home," he says that he has come to feel himself "bound to [Jim] in the name of that doubt which is the inseparable part of our knowledge."

> We wander in our thousands over the face of the earth [he continues], the illustrious and the obscure . . . but it seems to me that for each of us going home must be like going to render an account. We return to face our superiors, our kindred, our friends . . . the spirit that dwells within the land . . . a mute friend, judge, and

---

[8] *The Shadow-Line*, Conrad's short novel of 1917, concentrates another motif that had been working in his fiction from its beginnings. Its four opening paragraphs define the theme of the "shadow-line warning one that the region of early youth, too, must be left behind," and apply closely not only to *Lord Jim* but to *Under Western Eyes*, *Chance*, *The Arrow of Gold*, and other works.

inspirer. . . . All this may seem to you sheer sentimentalism; and indeed very few of us have the will or the capacity to look consciously under the surface of familiar emotions. . . . But the fact remains that you must touch your reward with clean hands, lest it turn to dead leaves, to thorns, in your grasp. . . . Yes! few of us understand, but we all feel it though, and I say *all* without exception, because those who do not feel do not count.

Marlow's commentary provides many clues to Jim's drama and to Conrad's intention in shaping it. These two may be taken as particularly pointed. That drama will be, from its inception in Jim's youth in England throughout its far-reaching complications of chance, accident, rumor, flight, and nemesis in the East, a history of what may be called — with all the necessary caution induced by reckless or misapplied usage — a "mythic" animus and suggestion. Begun in the afflatus of an illusory ideal of fate, it will, as it progresses, enforce in all who become involved in it a symbolic — a compulsory, inculpating, or accusing — import. As Jim will seek his mirror-image of heroism in the recognition of others, so the others will, by offering themselves as reflecting or responding agents, share in his desire, whether to satisfy it or deny it. And when, once the image is shattered by disgrace, Jim meets a reflection not of what he desires but of what the harsh conditions of reality impose on him, those conditions in men or events will find their recording sensibility in his mind and conscience — in what he "feels."

Jim being natively inexpressive, inarticulate, or baffled by his confusions, it is Marlow who must stand by to adjudicate or interpret what the other characters — the Patna officers, the judges of the Inquiry, Brierly, the French lieutenant, Chester, Robinson, De Jongh, Stein, Dain Waris, Doramin, Jewel, Tamb' Itam, Gentleman Brown — contribute to the drama. But the essential meaning of the experience will remain centered in Jim. In him the myth of his destiny began. In him the larger human myth will seek its eventual focus and significance.

Such experience may be termed "mythic" in two senses — in its original abstract conception in the romantic or self-idealizing mind, and in its concrete moral extension when it becomes generalized, diffused, shared by all who touch it. The radical condition of myth lies in its power to impose and compel its value on all the lives it touches or comes to include. And since Jim never surrenders his native Englishman's ambition to "go home" and "render an account" of himself to the folk and country who gave him the conscience he lives by; since, moreover, the refuge of the outcast, derelict, or man "disdained by destiny" is denied him by the laws of his moral constitution, the symbolic import of his fate never releases his own conscience, any more than it exempts the conscience of others, from the imperatives of justice. Patusan, Jim finally believes, will give him his chance to exonerate himself in the eyes of mankind. But Patusan is only a surrogate-kingdom — a reflector in its turn of the conscience and rough justice of "home." It will be a man from home — Gentleman Brown — who will penetrate that kingdom with his "vein of subtle reference to their common blood, an assumption of common experience; a sickening suggestion of common guilt, of secret knowledge that was like a bond of their minds and of their hearts." He will thus breach the final citadel of Jim's honor. Brown's vicious malignity will become, by a last irony, the agent of the justice which has from the first been an animating passion of Jim's life. When Marlow speaks his final tribute to his hero he closes the tale by underscoring the myth in its widest relevance and enigmatic truth:

> Not in the wildest days of his boyish visions could he have seen the alluring shape of such an extraordinary success! For it may very well be that in the short moment of his last proud and un-flinching glance, he had beheld the face of that opportunity which, like an Eastern bride, had come veiled to his side. . . . He goes away from a living woman to celebrate his pitiless wedding with a shadowy ideal of conduct. . . . He is one of us — and have I not stood up once, like an evoked ghost, to answer for his eternal constancy?

Our first glimpse of Jim in the opening paragraph — "his manner displayed a kind of dogged self-assertion which had nothing aggressive in it. It seemed a necessity, and it was directed apparently as much at himself as at anybody else. He was spotlessly neat, apparelled in immaculate white from shoes to hat" — is echoed in the epitaph on the faithful bridegroom of an ideal.

For if, in Conrad's moral universe, it is the ideal which condemns men to illusion and to its consequences in defeat or humiliation, it is also the ideal which is a necessary condition of their salvation — of their loyalty to principle, their sense of capacity,

their consciousness of honor, their dedication to significant existence which permits them to escape the disdain of destiny. If, as
Mrs. Gould says in *Nostromo*, there is "something inherent in the
necessities of successful action which carrie[s] with it the moral
degradation of the idea," it is nevertheless action — even the act of
death — by which the validity of the idea is tested and proved.
That test is latent in Jim's character from the first. He is by nature
— Stein says it first, Marlow says it finally — "excessively romantic." But his romanticism is evidently of the kind that Conrad
could trace in his own temperament: "an inborn faculty."

> This in itself may be a curse, but, when disciplined by a sense
> of personal responsibility and a recognition of the hard facts of
> existence shared with the rest of mankind, becomes but a point of
> view from which the very shadows of life appear endowed with
> an internal glow. And such romanticism is not a sin. It is none
> the worse for the knowledge of truth. It only tries to make the
> best of it, hard as it may be; and in this hardness discovers a cer-
> tain beauty.[9]

The protest may be taken as a source of Conrad's essential
strength as character and as artist. He appears to have been quite
fully aware of why such protest was necessary to him and to his
salvation from the confusions of emotion and impulse that were
a lifelong threat to his personal stability, as they continued to be
a threat to his security as an artist. "One admires what one lacks,"
he confessed to Madame Poradowska in 1891. "That is why I
admire perseverance and fidelity and constancy." [10]

The informing idea of *Lord Jim*, like the dramatic structure,
method, and eventual logic of the book, may be taken as origi-
nating in this conception of character and conduct. It is that conception — enacted by Jim, transmitted by Marlow, defined by

---

[9] From the "Author's Note" to *Within the Tides*, written in 1920; included
in Conrad's *Prefaces to His Works* (1937), pp. 153–54.

[10] He continues: "And then I like to look on the good side of men, particularly if there is a suggestion of pathos in the situation. That completes
the affair from the artistic point of view, which is mine in this business."
Letter of August 26, 1891, in *Letters of Joseph Conrad to Marguerite Poradowska* (1940), pp. 33–34. This collection is one of the most valuable documents on Conrad's life; the letters throughout define the animus and ideas,
especially in the years 1890–95, by which Conrad approached his career in
literature.

Stein, brought to proof and catharsis in the drama of Patusan —
that gave Conrad his novel, as well as the language and process by
which the novel came to be written as it was.

V

The writing and effect of the book, on which Conrad expressed
his anxious doubts when he wrote to Garnett after its completion,
bring into characteristic combination the elements of his work.
However criticism may qualify the novel (and there are necessary
qualifications to be made), there is no mistaking the impulse that
shaped it and gave it the form and style that make it typical.

There is, to begin with, the fable from which it takes its incentive — a fable which may begin in abstract idea but which becomes
dramatic by necessity and eventually moral in import. There is a
character, rather than a purely external plot or arbitrary action, in
which the fable originates and from whose "sensitive" constitution
the action issues. There is a psychological capacity in that character — a psychic, obsessive, or neurotic bent — which prohibits
direct or objective portrayal and whose ordeal of self-realization,
rooted in the retributive, recriminatory, or expiatory workings
of conscience, demands presentation by the more realistic and in-
tricate means of indirection: by the empirical, cross-chronological,
cumulative, and incremental method of Conrad's typical drama.[11]
There is finally the world of external conditions — strokes of fate
or chance, warnings of outer circumstance, the accident on the
Patna, the Court of Inquiry, the pursuing rumors of disgrace, the

---

[11] The method, whose basis is suggested by Conrad in some of his "Author's Notes," has been analyzed by many students: by R. L. Mégroz in
Joseph Conrad's Mind and Method (1931); by Joseph Warren Beach in *The
Twentieth Century Novel* (1932); by Edward Crankshaw in *Joseph Conrad*
(1936); by Albert Guerard in *Joseph Conrad* (1947), and in many studies of
individual tales. Henry James, in his essay of 1914 on "The New Novel," included in his *Notes on Novelists* (1914), gave it a celebrated definition in
two sentences of his discussion of *Chance*: "the way to do a thing that shall
make it undergo most doing," and "a prolonged hovering flight of the subjective over the outstretched ground of the case exposed." An early and
classic account is given by Conrad's onetime collaborator, Ford Madox Hueffer [Ford] in his *Joseph Conrad* (1924), Part III, Chapter II, notably under
the headings "General Effect," "Impressionism," "Selection," "Surprise,"
"Style," "Structure."

meeting with Marlow, the meeting with Stein, the mission to Patusan, the entry of Brown, the catastrophe that ensues — which imposes the test of reality, the "knowledge of truth," a "recognition of the hard facts of existence shared with the rest of mankind," on the subjective illusion in which the drama centers.

Obviously these elements never came to Conrad, any more than they come to any man of strong imagination, carefully and consciously sorted out. They came to him joined, organic, fused, whole. Therein lay his privilege, as therein also lay his dangerously intimate identification with them and his painful struggle to control them and render them effective in words, events, and action — in the "hearing," "feeling," and "seeing" he took as his aesthetic imperatives. The writer of *Lord Jim* is the writer we come to know in Conrad's other books and tales. He is not a free agent or arbitrary inventor, not an artist of cool or detached control, not — in spite of the elaborate commentary that accompanies his tales — a lucid rationalizer of the men and events he portrays. He is preëminently a writer deeply involved in what he offers, who gives the effect of identifying himself, admittedly at the risk of a damaging intimacy or self-dramatization, in everything he presents. Yet it is necessary to say that the elements of the Conradian drama — fable, character, psychology, action, abstract principle — are identifiable as the constituents of all his best work. If they account for its weaknesses, they also define its strength. One by one they can be traced and analyzed in his major novels — in *Nostromo*, *The Secret Agent*, *Under Western Eyes*, as in the later and more questionable *Chance*, *Victory*, *The Shadow-Line*. *Lord Jim* offers them in something akin to the form of paradigm.

The man who appears in the opening pages of the novel is already a man caught in the grip of a fate which it will be the tale's long and devious task to make real to him and to us. He is Jim: not yet Tuan Jim or Lord Jim, but "just Jim — nothing more," the water-clerk and ship-chandler's agent, "very popular," "spotlessly neat," known in the ports of the East to possess "Ability in the abstract," who yet suddenly and repeatedly throws up his job and departs, "a seaman in exile from the sea," mysteriously retreating "towards the rising sun" and driven by a "keen perception of the Intolerable" to Bombay, to Calcutta, to Rangoon, to Penang, to Batavia, in successive flights from the respect and esteem of men. The novel begins typically *in medias res*. We have been introduced to an enigma that seizes our attention as it has caught the attention, casual or mystified, of the men of the East. We are not yet aware of the egotism that has already claimed and closed Jim's character and on which it will be Jewel, many years and many pages later, who pronounces her bitter judgment: "He has left me. . . . you always leave us — for your own ends." But the mystery that will culminate in that judgment is already set.

Presently we learn something of Jim's origins: his English birth, his "vocation for the sea," his apprenticeship on the training-ship, his "hope of a stirring life in a world of adventure" as "an example of devotion to duty, and as unflinching as a hero in a book." Then, without premonition, there cuts across his young life a warning. In a harbor accident his first chance to show his readiness for heroism calls him and is missed. "He stood still." The heroic moment is given to his mates. "Too late, youngster," says the captain. "Better luck next time. This will teach you to be smart." Jim, sensing but dismissing his lost opportunity, holds the bowman of the cutter that rescues old Symons in secret contempt — sees his prowess as "a pitiful display of vanity"; feels "angry with the brutal tumult of earth and sky for taking him unawares and checking unfairly a generous readiness for narrow escapes." "He had," he believes, "enlarged his knowledge more than those who had done the work. When all men flinched, then — he felt sure — he alone would know how to deal with the spurious menace of wind and seas. He knew what to think."

Jim's "next time" is not long in coming. Once in the East he has another "glimpse of the earnestness in the anger of the sea." Injured by a falling spar during a storm, he begins to feel in the sea, and in the impulse that drove him to pursue its "enticing, disenchanting, and enslaving" rewards, a possible enmity. "Imagination, the enemy of men, the father of all terrors," lays its uneasy hand on his Platonic conception of his destiny. For the first time he becomes infected by the obverse of his romantic impulse — by a secret disaffection, the contagious cynicism of his mates. Lying "many days stretched on his back, dazed, battered, hopeless, and tormented as if at the bottom of an abyss of unrest," he finds himself filled "with a despairing desire to escape at any cost." He is "secretly glad he had not to go on deck."

He suppresses his secret. This signal too is missed. But it plays its part when, once more ashore and wanting to get back home, he takes a berth on the rusty, disreputable *Patna*, manned by a mongrel crew, about to take her cargo of eight hundred pilgrims across the Indian Ocean to the Red Sea and Mecca. Already Jim's idealism has become corrupted by a lurking "disdain." He enters on his new adventure barely conscious that his innocence is contaminated by a deeper peril — a secret resolve not only to hold himself in reserve for higher honor but to save himself from danger at any cost.

The *Patna* becomes the instrument of his unsuspected destiny. In the superbly told chapters — II and III — in which she enters on her fateful voyage, Jim is launched in the course that will confirm the fate he has evaded. The ship steams ahead, as vulnerable in her rusty plates as in her renegade crew; the pilgrims huddle on her decks; Jim nurses his sense of superiority, his thoughts "full of valourous deeds":

> They were the best parts of life, its secret truth, its hidden reality. They had a gorgeous virility, the charm of vagueness, they passed before him with a heroic tread; they carried his soul away with them and made it drunk with the divine philtre of an unbounded confidence in itself. There was nothing he could not face.

Then, darting in on the dream, there comes in the silence of a calm sea and cloudless night the stroke of chance that spells his destiny — the drunken engineer suddenly pitching "down headfirst as though he had been clubbed from behind," the shuddering tremor of the ship, the "faint noise as of thunder," the "sharp hull driving on its way seem[ing] to rise a few inches in succession through its whole length" as if "the ship had steamed across a narrow belt of vibrating water and of humming air."

The swift line of the tale that Conrad started in the spring of 1898 "as a short story" has moved forward with the impetuosity of Jim's own conscious purpose and unchallenged desire. We turn the page. We begin Chapter IV. A "month or so" has passed. With it has passed, forever and irretrievably, any further possibility of Jim's existing in a forward-moving chronology of his days and expectations. The novel has deepened into another and more complex dimension — a baffling and horrified consciousness that secret dream has come into violent collision with public circumstance. Jim stands arraigned before the official Court of Inquiry in an Eastern port, sole culprit of a crew of renegades that have cut and run, attempting to explain and defend himself, struggling for the words that will account for his jump into the lifeboat that left the *Patna* to sink with her helpless pilgrims. He sees around him the eyes of the world fixed on him in the dock — the dreamer and romantic brought under the hard stare of an inquisition that wants neither dreams nor romance but "Facts!" ("They demanded facts from him, as if facts could explain anything!") It is then that he sees, among so many glances of hostility, curiosity, indifference, or official justice, the eyes of the "white man" that answer his baffled helplessness. "Strange," says Marlow long afterward, "this fatality that would cast the complexion of a flight upon all his acts, of impulsive unreflecting desertion — of a jump into the unknown."

The unknown has claimed him. Dream or appearance has become a reality to which his existence is now condemned. The sense of superiority that once isolated him by choice has resulted in a breach of trust and a "consciousness of lost honour" that isolates him in deed, fact, and moral incomprehension. In his desperation, as Marlow sees it, he does not want "a judge." He wants "an ally, a helper, an accomplice." In that appeal he stirs the minds who recognize his need. "It seemed to me," Marlow confesses, "I was being made to comprehend the Inconceivable — and I know of nothing to compare with the discomfort of such a sensation." [12]

> I was made to look at the convention that lurks in all truth and on the essential sincerity of falsehood. He appealed to all sides at once — to the side turned perpetually to the light of day, and to that side of us which, like the other hemisphere of the moon, exists stealthily in perpetual darkness, with only a fearful ashy light falling at times on the edge. He swayed me. I own to it, I own up. . . . the mystery of his attitude got hold of me as though he had been an individual in the forefront of his kind, as if the obscure

[12] Cf. André Gide, *Journal 1889–1939*, 23 février, 1930, p. 971: "Much interested by the relationship I discover between *Under Western Eyes* and *Lord Jim*. (I regret not having spoken of this with Conrad.) That *irresponsible* act of the hero, to redeem which his whole life is subsequently engaged. For the thing that leads to the heaviest responsibility is just the *irresponsibilities* in a life. How can one efface that act? There is no more pathetic subject for a novel, nor one that has been more stifled in our literature by belief in Boileau's rule: that the hero must remain, from one end to the other of a drama or a novel, 'such as he was first seen to be.'" Translated by Justin O'Brien, *The Journals of André Gide*, Vol. III (1949), pp. 94–95.

truth involved were momentous enough to affect mankind's conception of itself.

The drama of Jim's isolation has become also a drama of identifications. It centers in him: he becomes agent and exponent of "the classic tragic irony" whereby will be enacted "the incongruity and yet the effective identity between the constructive will and the destructive act"; and "the *ananke* or compelling principle fatally inherent in [his] acts" [13] will describe a line that extends from the missed opportunity on the training-ship, through the jump from the *Patna*, the flights from port to port, the upriver journey into Patusan, to the confrontation with Brown and the final expiation. Once Jim has met Marlow and his long effort of justification and recovery begins, it is conveyed by means of distorted chronology and incremental repetition that describe the ordeal to which his life is condemned. Retrospect and anticipation will bring commitment and intention, will and action, the conscious self and the unrealized identity, into a redeeming existence, the ironic fatality of "how to be." But there will attach to that continuously active irony the surrounding responses and shared recognitions of most of the other lives his destiny touches.

The renegades of the *Patna* who flee the Inquiry use him as scapegoat of their own cowardice. They leave implicit what becomes overt in the hostility of Chester, Cornelius, and Gentleman Brown. By Jim's measure they all stand indicted in crime, treachery, or evil. He is the "one of them" who "counts" because he exposes what they conceal, experiences what they evade, admits what they deny. The people of Patusan — Doramin, Dain Waris, the faithful Tamb' Itam, the passionate Jewel — see him in another light. His heroism in their kingdom has shown him in the heroic potentialities that have redeemed the kindom, as the kingdom has given Jim his chance to redeem himself. Where the men of evil respond to the side of him that "exists stealthily in perpetual darkness," the Patusans idolize him for the "light of day" he has brought to their people. But that is a response even more danger-

[13] Dorothy Van Ghent in *The English Novel: Form and Function* (1953), pp. 229–244, here 230–231, and, for quotations in the second paragraph following, pp. 241–42. This brilliant discussion of *Lord Jim* best suggests the classical and mythic analogues — notably the myths of Oedipus and Orestes — that apply to the novel, and defines their relevance to its moral and psychic content.

ous when it suffers betrayal. Faith, devotion, and love exact a stricter price than enmity and hatred.

Two characters earlier in the story have already acted to concentrate the drama of identities: the French lieutenant of the gunboat that towed the *Patna* to port, and Brierly, the assessor at the Court of Inquiry. The first does so by antithesis, the second by recognition. The Frenchman, example of sober and unquestioning servitude in his profession, crosses Marlow's path "one afternoon in Sydney," far from the Eastern ports where Jim is known. The salvaging of the *Patna* has receded to an indistinct memory in his lifelong line of duty. He has all but forgotten the name of the ship, though he boarded her and remained on her for thirty hours while she was being towed to port. ("You did!" Marlow exclaims; to which the lieutenant replies: "It was judged proper. . . . One has done one's possible.") Unconsciously "his witness measures Jim's failure by the painful difference of fact": Marlow, listening to his laconic recital, sees that "the French lieutenant's unconscious heroism is the heroism that Jim had made a conscious ideal." [14] Yet it is not strictly true, as has been argued, that he makes no connection between his own practised rectitude and Jim's jump from the ship. "Ah! The young, the young," he says compassionately before he parts from Marlow forever. "And after all, one does not die of it." "Die of what?" asks Marlow.

> Of being afraid [the lieutenant replies]. One is always afraid. . . . The fear, the fear — look you — it is always there. . . . Brave — you conceive — in the Service — one has got to be — the trade demands it. . . . *Eh bien!* Each of them — I say each of them, if he were an honest man — *bien entendu* — would confess that there is a point — there is a point — for the best of us — there is somewhere a point when you let go everything. . . . And you have got to live with that truth — do you see? Given a certain combination of circumstances, fear is sure to come. Abominable funk. . . . And even for those who do not believe this truth there is fear all the same — the fear of themselves. Absolutely so. Trust me.

The truth which the Frenchman's years of sober responsibility have vouchsafed him, though he himself has never been put to the crucial test of it, is one that Brierly has missed. When Brierly — "Big Brierly, the captain of the crack ship of the Blue Star

[14] Van Ghent, pp. 241–42.

Line," called by Marlow "*the* fortunate man of the earth" — serves as assessor at the Inquiry, "his self-satisfaction" shows "to the world a surface as hard as granite." But he is unprepared for what he witnesses there. His self-possession soon proves vulnerable; his role in the proceedings begins to undermine his confidence: "I feel like a fool all the time." Watching Jim under fire he asks "What's the use of it? . . . Nothing can save him. He's done for. . . . Why eat all that dirt?" When Marlow suggests that it costs money to run away his bitterness and shock break out violently: "Well, then, let him creep twenty feet underground and stay there! By heavens! *I* would." His success has made him as unprepared and unready as Jim's innocence. "Very soon after" Brierly is a suicide, "committ[ing] his reality and his sham together to the keeping of the sea."

It is thus, even at the cost of irrational violence and desperation, that Jim's case evokes its recognitions. This community in faith, betrayal, and expiation widens until it becomes a "common fate" — the moral universe that Jim has stirred to consciousness around him. It will be the final effect of his tale to suggest that his destiny — destructive but also redeeming — is the element in which men, fated equally to consciousness and corruptibility, are condemned to exist. The return to innocence is impossible — as impossible as the "clean slate" Jim once hoped to regain. "A clean slate, did he say?" asks Marlow. "As if the initial word of each our destiny were not graven in imperishable characters upon the face of a rock."

VI

Lord Jim is notable among modern novels — though far from exceptional among the greater — in resisting easy definition and critical conclusions. It dramatizes an ambiguity; its method and language are ambiguous; it insists on the "enigma" of its theme and hero; its final effect and import are elusive. The subject to which Conrad gave explicit expression (possibly a too explicit expression) in "The Secret Sharer" here undergoes a process of dilation that hovers like a threat over the pages. The exhaustive analysis and dialectic to which the drama is subjected at times has the effect of antagonizing not only concrete action but any valid form of moral and philosophic resolution. The uncertainty of Marlow, the paradoxes of Stein, the embarrassments of Jim ramify all parts of the tale. What becomes in "Heart of Darkness" a conscious duplicity, in *Nostromo* a deliberate dialectic, in *The Secret Agent* and *Chance* a tragic perplexity, in *The Arrow of Gold* and *The Rescue* a rhetorical evasion, here acts continuously to undermine the character and action in which the book centers. But these qualities are less likely to be baffling to a reader today than they may have been when *Lord Jim* appeared in 1900. The age that has read *The Idiot* and *The Possessed*, *The Sacred Fount* and *The Golden Bowl*, *The Magic Mountain*, *The Counterfeiters*, and *The Trial*, is no longer taken unawares by them. They have become part and substance of fiction in a time of deceiving appearance and treacherous existence, of standards in dissolution and intelligence in acute suspense before the fact of an all-informing instability and uncertainty.

That Conrad was involved, by temperament as much as by external experience, in such an instability is one of the first facts of his case and of his role in modern literature. It gave him the disturbed insight that makes *Nostromo*, *The Secret Agent*, and *Under Western Eyes* prophetic judgments on contemporary history. It gave him his central subject and method as an artist. "The artist descends within himself, and in that lonely region of stress and strife, if he be deserving and fortunate, he finds the terms of his appeal." Conrad was fully conscious of the peculiar sources of his talent when he wrote his credo, the more so when he went on to say that the artist's appeal "is made to our less obvious capacities: to that part of our nature which, because of the warlike conditions of existence, is necessarily kept out of sight within the more resisting and hard qualities."

The "detached observer" was inescapably at odds in his make-up with what Thomas Mann saw in him as "a very much engaged intelligence" that refused "to hang miserably in the air between contraries." [15] The principles to which he appealed as a personal need and which he engaged as mainsprings of his dramas — Fidelity, Honor, Sincerity, etc. — betray their capitalized abstraction when set against the actualities with which the dramas deal: self-deception, self-delusion, evasion, the baffled intelligence, the confused and exacerbated emotion, a profound skepticism of values and history. It must be asked how far this conflict keeps *Lord Jim* from achieving the force and stature Conrad struggled to give it

[15] Thomas Mann, "Conrad's *The Secret Agent*," in *Past Masters and Other Papers* (1933), pp. 231–247; here 246–47.

— how far they account for the "plague spot" of its divided action, the "want of power" or of "illuminating imagination" he remorsefully felt when the book was finished.

A good part of his reaction may be discounted as chronic mortification. He felt it on finishing many of his tales, more often the ones criticism has rated among his best than those it has relegated to minor or inferior status. A large share of the discussion of *Lord Jim* has, however, taken its clue from his own feeling about the book. Even some of its oldest and confirmed admirers have found its appeal weakening on long acquaintance.[16] More recent critics, even those who admit it to major rank among his works, have refined on Conrad's own complaints. The "continued exhibition of Jim's case" in the Patusan drama, "eked out to provide the substance of a novel" from the "Malayan exotic [material] of Conrad's earliest vein," is felt to have "no inevitability as that." [17] "The effect of muddlement" in Marlow is taken (unavoidably taken in part) as deriving from "Conrad's conception of the story" — from "a man who is ruminating to obscure the issue" rather than "to clarify it"; with the result that "the uncertainty which remains even at the end of the book as to what judgment we should pass on Jim," taken together with the "passages of imprecise rhetoric," demonstrates that Conrad's own "feelings are too deeply and too personally involved for him to stand above the bewilderment in which he places Marlow." [18] Which in turn recalls an earlier and more eminent judgment: that Conrad's "central obscurity" derives from the "constant discrepancies between his nearer and his further vision," between his "experiences" and "what lies beyond them." [19] Conrad's letter to Garnett in 1900

---

[16] E.g., Richard Curle, *Joseph Conrad and His Characters* (1957), pp. 246–47.
[17] F. R. Leavis, *The Great Tradition* (1948), pp. 189–90.
[18] Douglas Hewitt, *Conrad: A Reassessment* (1952), pp. 31–39; here 38–39.
[19] E. M. Forster, "Joseph Conrad: A Note" (1921), in *Abinger Harvest* (1936), pp. 134–38; here 137. The essay, a review of Conrad's *Notes on Life and Letters*, includes two notable passages: "These essays do suggest that he is misty in the middle as well as at the edges, that the secret casket of his genius contains a vapour rather than a jewel; and that we need not try to write him down philosophically, because there is, in this particular direction, nothing to write. No creed, in fact. Only opinions, and the right to throw them overboard when facts make them look absurd. Opinions held under the semblance of eternity, girt with the sea, crowned with the stars, and therefore easily mistaken for a creed." Also: "One realizes, more definitely, what a noble artist is here, what an austere character, by whose side most of our contemporary writers appear obsequious."

gives a personal authority to these reservations. By all the evidence of the book's form, structure, and quality we may take it that his writing of it anticipated whatever difficulties of attention and credulity its readers have since encountered in reading it.

The dramatic diffusion, the puzzled intelligence, the struggling movement, the disrupted chronology, the excess of surmise and commentary, the over-insistent paradox — these must be admitted. They seem as inevitable to the existence of the novel as the vision in which it originated or the desperate tenacity by which it was pushed to its conclusion. The question is: could a book like *Lord Jim* have been written on any other terms? It is easy enough to discount Conrad's minor tales and later rhetorical dramas. These are obviously the products either of a forced convention or of an exhausted inspiration. But it is impossible to discount or undervalue *Lord Jim* or the dozen other novels and tales that share its power. Such works are perhaps by definition imperfect. They issue from too intimate a source, too personal and urgent an impulse. They may miss the self-defining quality and controlled vision by which some works of profound originality justify themselves. But their very imperfection defines the sources of insight, ruthless inquisition, and unsparing tenacity out of which they grow. Measured by such qualities, *Lord Jim* is not only a passionate and noble book. It is one of the books that establish the basis of sincerity and moral capacity on which the highest achievement in modern fiction rests.

To read it today is to be reminded anew of how the power of an intensely dramatic and visual imagination may redeem the conflict, complexity, and struggle to which the moral vision of our century is committed. The great scenes of the book tether its perplexity and ambiguity to that saving realism. Its most powerful passages — the voyage of the *Patna*, the scenes at the Inquiry, Marlow's first meeting with Jim, his interview with the French lieutenant, the role of Stein, Marlow's last sight of Jim on the shore of Patusan, the coming of Brown, Jim's final surrender — are scenes not only unforgettable. They show the force and suggestive power that permit them to fly off from the story and take a longer lease on life in the symbolizing imagination. Innumerable smaller details add their effect: the ship striking the sunken hulk, the jump to the lifeboat, the dog in the crowd, the "clear tinkle of a teaspoon falling on the tesselated floor of the verandah," ringing out "like a tiny and silvery scream," the sea breaking on the Patusan coast as against a "sombre wall that seemed the very stronghold of the night." It is these that compel us to hear, feel, and see an experience that may become part of our conscious and unconscious lives. They act to perpetuate in the reader's mind and emotion the ordeal of a soul under test, and compel him to recognize that neither the soul nor the test are fantasies but part of a "visible world," an "invincible truth," and "a common fate" he has come to share. It is by enforcing that recognition that *Lord Jim* stands high among the modern novels that testify to "the reality of our existence," and shows its sincerity in a high ambition. No serious experience of the art of fiction can ignore its value or fail to see it as one of the books of our century that have set a mark and defined a standard.

CONRAD: A BIOGRAPHICAL SKETCH

Conrad's life falls into four phases or divisions which mark clearly defined stages in the progress that took him from his birth in Poland to his final thirty years in authorship and his achievement as an English-writing novelist. They served him as the framework of the personal drama of which he was vividly conscious throughout his career and which he recorded not only in his two books of autobiography — *The Mirror of the Sea* in 1906 and *A Personal Record* in 1912 — but repeatedly and consciously in the imaginative transformations of his works in fiction. That the events of his intimate history served him as matter for his art was a fact he frequently admitted: "the sustained invention of a really telling lie demands a talent which I do not possess," he once said, and again: "every novel contains an element of autobiography — and this can hardly be denied, since the creator can only express himself in his creation." And he defined that which is "truly fiction" as what is "truly imagined from hints of things that really happened and of people that really existed." But that such events were subjected to complex and elaborate translation in his tales is another fact of his case as a man of imagination for which due allowance must be made — and has not always been made, even by his most tactful biographers. Yet there can be no doubt that he took the four chapters of his history as faces of a destiny in which he came to see an ordained justice and logic, and they must remain basic to any account of his career. They comprise his first seventeen years in Poland, 1857-1874; his four years in southern France and the maritime apprenticeship he entered on there, 1874–1878; then his sixteen years at sea, 1878–1894; and finally the twenty-nine years of professional authorship which began in 1895 and ended with his death in 1924.

Conrad's life began in the Polish Ukraine, in the town of Berdyczew, where he was born in December, 1857, as Jozef Teodor Konrad Nalecz Korzeniowski, to Apollo Nalecz Korzeniowski and his wife Ewelina Bobrowska, both of them members of families of the old landed gentry who had long identified themselves with the cause of Polish nationalism and independence and who, from the time of the "crime of partition" which in the late Eighteenth Century had divided Poland between the rival powers of Russia, Prussia, and Austria, had contributed their heroism and sons to the national cause. Three of Conrad's uncles suffered death and exile in that cause — Robert Korzeniowski in the Polish rising against Russia in 1863, Hilary Korzeniowski in Siberian exile in 1873, Stefan Bobrowski in a duel with a political enemy in 1862. Conrad's father, a writer who had translated works of Shakespeare, Alfred de Vigny, and Victor Hugo into Polish, was also active in this resistance; he belonged to the "Red" or extremist wing of the Russian-banned Polish National Committee and caused serious doubts to the more conservative Bobrowski family when he courted their daughter. In October of 1862 he was arrested because of his part in framing the seditious mandate of his Committee against the Russian occupation and was sentenced to deportation in a remote northern province of Russia, the Government Vologda. His wife and five-year-old son were permitted to accompany him; and though the exile was presently shifted to a milder southern province near Kiev, the health of both of Conrad's parents was fatally undermined by their hardships, the mother dying in April, 1865, soon after returning to Poland with her son, the father in May, 1869, in Cracow, whose citizens gave him an honorary public funeral with national mourning (as, four years later, they were to confer the freedom of the city on his son in tribute to the father's sacrifice). Conrad found himself an orphan at the age of twelve.

The Bobrowskis now took him under their care and his devoted uncle, Tadeusz Bobrowski, became his guardian. His schooling had begun under private tutors and was later continued under his father's guidance during the years in Russia. He attended high school in Lemberg, Galicia, when his father was permitted to live there on returning from exile in 1868–69; and after the father's death he went briefly to the St. Anne High School in Cracow. His guardian then engaged a tutor for him, Adam Pulman, a student in the University of Cracow, whose instruction between 1870 and 1874 gave Conrad the only advanced schooling he received. By this time however Conrad found himself restlessly divided between his Polish allegiances, with the tragedy they had brought into his early years, and his ambition to seek a career for himself in western Europe, perhaps at sea. He had caught his first glimpse of the Mediterranean from the Lido at Venice when, in the summer of 1873, he had gone on a vacation trip with Mr. Pulman in Germany, Switzerland, and Italy. He now persuaded his uncle Tadeusz to arrange that he go to France to seek a new life, and it was presently settled that he travel to Marseilles to seek his fortune under the sponsorship of a wealthy banker and shipper there, M. Delestang. "In 1874 I got into a train in Cracow (Vienna Express) on my way to the sea," Conrad said to John Galsworthy forty years later, "as a man might get into a dream." When, not yet seventeen, he arrived in Marseilles in October of that year, the next chapter of his life opened to him.

It was to last for four years. Delestang and his wife took him into their circle; several other older friends — Victor Chodzk, a Pole, Richard Fecht, a German, and Baptistin Solary, a Frenchman — gave him help and advice. Between December 1874 and February 1877 Conrad made three voyages as an apprentice seaman on Delestang's ships to the West Indies. But he soon encountered other adventures. What precisely they were has fallen into question with the progress of recent research on this phase of Conrad's life. The account offered by his biographer, G. Jean-Aubry, and implicitly supported by Conrad not only in his letters but in *The Mirror of the Sea* and *A Personal Record*, as well as in the fictionized account of this episode in his novel of 1919, *The Arrow of Gold*, is that he became involved in the royalist activities of the strongly *légitimiste* Delestang circle; that with two other young royalist enthusiasts he bought a share in a small boat, a *tartane* or *balancelle* called the *Tremolino*, captained by an old Mediterranean seaman, Dominic Cervoni, and engaged in smuggling illegal arms across the water to the Gulf of Rosas in Spain for the armies that were attempting to restore Don Carlos to the Spanish throne; that he also became involved romantically with a woman of Marseilles, known to us only as the Doña Rita de Lastaola of *The Arrow of Gold*; that when he found himself challenged by a rival, an expatriate Southerner from America called Blunt, he engaged to fight a duel with him, was wounded, fell into disgrace, and was abandoned by his Marseilles friends; that his uncle Tadeusz hastened to him from Cracow, tried to persuade him to return to Poland, but was refused by Conrad who, rousing himself from his bed, found a berth on a British freighter, the *Mavis*, in Marseilles harbor, and so, after a voyage to the eastern Mediterranean, made his way to England. It now appears that this may have been in part a fiction, devised partly by Tadeusz Bobrowski, partly by Conrad himself, to disguise the facts: that the *Tremolino* was very dubiously connected with the Carlist cause, if at all, though it was involved in some kind of smuggling; that the money Conrad had spent on the boat and on various gambling ventures in Marseilles and Monte Carlo had landed him in serious debt; and that in these desperate straits he made an attempt on his life. His uncle, arriving from Cracow, did undertake to pay off his debts, inventing the story of the duel to conceal the attempted suicide and in his concern "with national honor to some extent." [1] It seems clear that Conrad found a berth on a British ship, and that he landed at Lowestoft in England in April 1878, where the next phase of his history awaited him, at the age of twenty.

Now began the sixteen years during which he sailed the seas, and by gradual stages advanced from the rank of common seaman to third mate, to second mate, and eventually, in 1886, to master. His voyages soon took him to the Mediterranean and to Australia, but during the early 1880's he began to reach the countries of the East, the Indian Ocean, the Malay peninsula, the East Indies, the China seas. He became familiar with the ports and peoples of the Eastern nations; he learned to know the men of Oriental tribes and castes, the subject races of the Western powers, exiles, outcasts, men of lost kingdoms, dispossessed princes, wastrels and adventurers, seasoned mariners and fortune-seeking Europeans. In 1886 he was naturalized as a British subject. In 1888-89, on the ship *Otago*, he held his first command on a voyage from Bangkok to Port Adelaide. In 1890, out of work in London, he found, through the help of distant relatives in Brussels, an assignment on a boat plying the Congo and thus came upon the harrowing adventure of the

---

[1] The evidence for this revised account of Conrad's Marseilles experiences comes from a letter, recently recovered, of his uncle Tadeusz Bobrowski to Stefan Buszczynski, of March 24, 1879, which has been published by Mr. Jocelyn Baines in the London *Times Literary Supplement*, December 6, 1957, p. 748, with further details given in Mr. Baines's article "The Affair in Marseilles," *The London Magazine*, November 1957, pp. 41–46, and in his new study of Conrad, London, 1958. See the "Addendum" included here.

African journey he was to dramatize in "Heart of Darkness." In 1891–93 the *Torrens* took him again to Australia. And in 1893–94 the *Adowa* took him on the aborted journey from London to Rouen and back to London that was to prove to be his final experience as a seaman. Now, alone again in London, he once more took up the manuscript of a story he had been working on desultorily for five years in the ports and ships of his travels. He saw it as his single possible chance at a new life, and in solitary London lodgings he sweated out the finishing of the tale. It became his first novel, *Almayer's Folly*, and when, through the interest of the firm's reader, Edward Garnett, it was published by T. Fisher Unwin in London in 1895, his career in literature began.

In 1896 Conrad married an Englishwoman, Jessie George; their first son, Borys, was born in 1898, a second, John Alexander, in 1906. They lived in a series of country homes, first in Essex, then in Kent, then in Bedfordshire, then again in Kent, finally, from 1919 onward, at Oswalds, in the village of Bishopsbourne, near Canterbury. They made a number of vacation trips to southern France, Corsica, and Italy; in the summer of 1914 they took a trip to Poland, Conrad's first in more than twenty years, and were almost caught there by the mobilization of the armies and interned for the duration of the war, their return to England in the late autumn being aided by the American ambassador at Vienna, Frederic C. Penfield. In the spring months of 1923 Conrad made his single trip to the United States and reaped the honors of his fame. Success had been slow in coming to him during the first twenty years of his painful struggle and acute hardship as a writer, but the publication of *Chance* in 1912–13 turned the tide and brought him not only popularity but financial comfort in his final decade. But these are the outward events of his last three decades. His life from 1895 onward is chiefly the history of the writing of his books; of the harassed ordeal that went into their making; of the critical esteem that came to him from his fellow-craftsmen but of the practical recognition that lagged for years; of the emerging powers that enabled him to write, during the fifteen years between 1897, when he published *The Nigger of the "Narcissus,"* and 1911, when he completed *Under Western Eyes*, the books of his greatest strength; and of the last decade in which his powers progressively waned and what he wrote came by way of aftermath and epilogue to his highest achievement. He was engaged in writing his final novel, the unfinished *Suspense*, a tale of Napoleonic history, when he died suddenly at Oswalds on August 3, 1924.

The record of Conrad's last three decades is thus primarily a record of the titles and dates of his books. *Almayer's Folly* of 1895 was quickly followed by *An Outcast of the Islands* in 1896; by *The Nigger of the "Narcissus"* in 1897; by his first book of short stories, *Tales of Unrest*, in 1898; and by *Lord Jim* in 1900. For several years at this point he collaborated with Ford Madox Hueffer [Ford], three books ensuing from this partnership, *The Inheritors* in 1901, *Romance* in 1903, and *The Nature of a Crime*, which did not appear until many years later. Meanwhile *Typhoon* was published in 1902; the great drama of South American history and politics, *Nostromo*, in 1904; *The Secret Agent* in 1907; *Under Western Eyes* in 1911; *Chance* in 1913; *Victory* in 1915. Collections of shorter tales also appeared. The finest was the volume that contained *Youth*, "Heart of Darkness," and "The End of the Tether" in 1902; the volume headed by *Typhoon* appeared in 1903; *A Set of Six* came out in 1908; *'Twixt Land and Sea*, which included "The Secret Sharer," in 1912; *Within the Tides* in 1915. During the War of 1914–18 Conrad wrote his memory of the first command on the *Otago* into the story called *The Shadow-Line* of 1917; *The Arrow of Gold* appeared in 1919; *The Rescue*, now finished after having been begun and abandoned twenty years earlier, came out in 1920; *The Rover*, a tale of Napoleonic France, in 1923. Like other novelists of his time, Conrad tried to write plays, but his only full-length drama, a version of *The Secret Agent*, had only a brief run in London in November 1922. His two autobiographical works, *The Mirror of the Sea* and *A Personal Record* (first called *Some Reminiscences*) had appeared in 1906 and 1912 respectively. After his death the unfinished *Suspense* was published in 1925, four stories called *Tales of Hearsay* also in 1925, and a final collection of essays, a sequel to the *Notes on Life and Letters* of 1921, came out as *Last Essays* in 1926. Conrad was buried at Canterbury, under an epitaph from Spenser which he had quoted on the title-page of *The Rover* in 1923:

> Sleep after toyle, port after stormie seas,
> Ease after warre, death after life, doth greatly please.

SELECTED BIBLIOGRAPHY

The best guidance to Conrad's books and other publications may, in the absence thus far of a systematic bibliography of his productions, be found in two accounts of private collections of his works: *A Conrad Memorial Library: The Collection of George T. Keating* (New York: Doubleday, Doran and Co., 1928), and in Thomas J. Wise's several indexes of his collection, privately printed as *A Bibliography of the Writings of Joseph Conrad*, second edition (London: 1921·), *A Conrad Library* (London: 1928), and *The Ashley Library*, Vol. XI (London: 1936). A valuable check-list of publications, serializations, and studies has recently been published as *Joseph Conrad at Mid-Century: Editions and Studies 1895–1955* by Kenneth A. Lohf and Eugene P. Sheehy (Minneapolis: University of Minnesota Press, 1957).

The major works of Conrad have been published since 1920 in a series of sets or collections by J. M. Dent and Sons, Ltd., in London, and by Doubleday and Company (formerly Doubleday, Page and Company, and Doubleday, Doran and Company) in New York, as well as in the first collective limited edition published by William Heinemann of London in twenty volumes in 1921–27. The text of *Lord Jim* used in the present edition, which shows only minor changes or incidental corrections of earlier English and American book editions, is taken from Conrad's "authorized and final" text as printed by J. M. Dent of London in its most recent printing, 1946– , which in turn reproduces the text of Dent's 22-volume Uniform Edition, 1923–28, as supervised by Conrad. The current Doubleday edition follows this text also, with very minor variants of spelling and punctuation.

BIOGRAPHY: The fullest accounts thus far published of Conrad's life are G. Jean-Aubry's *Joseph Conrad: Life and Letters*, still the largest collection of the letters (New York: Doubleday, 1927) and his *Vie de Conrad* (Paris: Gallimard, 1947), now translated by Helen Sebba as *The Sea Dreamer* and subtitled, but not to be accepted, as "a definitive biography of Joseph Conrad" (New York: Doubleday, 1957). Both these works are to be seriously supplemented and corrected in major respects by Jocelyn Baines's *Joseph Conrad*, to be published in London by Weidenfeld and Nicolson in 1958, some of whose details are anticipated by his study "The Affair in Marseilles" in *The London Magazine*,

November 1957, pp. 41–46, and by "The Young Conrad in Marseilles," *The Times Literary Supplement* (London), December 6, 1957, p. 748. They are also importantly supplemented by other collections of letters and by studies of partial aspects of Conrad's career: by the letters that appear in Richard Curle's *Conrad to a Friend* and *The Last Twelve Years of Joseph Conrad* (both New York: Doubleday, 1928); in *Letters from Joseph Conrad 1895–1924*, edited by Edward Garnett (London: Nonesuch Press; Indianapolis: Bobbs-Merrill Co., 1928); in Conrad's *Lettres françaises*, edited by G. Jean-Aubry (Paris: Gallimard, 1929); and in the valuable collection titled *Letters of Joseph Conrad to Marguerite Poradowska*, translated and edited by John A. Gee and Paul J. Sturm (New Haven: Yale University Press, 1940); and by the studies of *Joseph Conrad in the Congo* by G. Jean-Aubry (London: Bookman's Journal Office, 1926); of *The Polish Heritage of Joseph Conrad* by Gustav Morf, whose interpretative parts are to be taken with reservations (London: Sampson Low, Marston and Co.; New York: Richard R. Smith, n.d. but c. 1929); of *Joseph Conrad as I Knew Him* by Mrs. Jessie Conrad (New York: Doubleday, 1926) and her *Joseph Conrad and His Circle* (New York: E. P. Dutton and Co., 1935); of *Joseph Conrad: The Making of a Novelist*, an authoritative account of Conrad's life and books up to 1900, by John Dozier Gordan (Cambridge: Harvard University Press, 1940); and of *Conrad and His Contemporaries* by J. H. Retinger (London: Minerva Publishing Co., 1941).

CRITICISM: Criticism, interpretation, appreciation, and analysis of Conrad's writings are now voluminous, and may best be traced in their more specialized aspects in the check-list by Lohf and Sheehy (1957), named above. The more important items among them may be listed under three divisions: those that appeared before Conrad's death in 1924, those that appeared between 1924 and 1940, and those that have been published since 1940.

Among the earlier and pioneer studies the following, published before 1924, were in their time outstanding and still contain useful matter: Henry James's essay on "The New Novel" in his *Notes on Novelists* (New York: Charles Scribner's Sons, 1914); *Joseph Conrad: A Study*, the first book-length examination, by Richard Curle (New York: Doubleday, 1914); James Gibbon Huneker's essay "The Genius of Joseph Conrad" in his *Ivory, Apes and Peacocks* (New York: Charles Scribner's Sons, 1915); Wilson Follett's *Joseph Conrad: A Short Study* . . . (New York: Doubleday, 1915); Hugh Walpole's *Joseph Conrad* (London: Nisbet and Co., n.d., c. 1916); H. L. Mencken's essay "Joseph Conrad" in his *A Book of Prefaces* (New York: Alfred A. Knopf, 1917); Ruth M. Stauffer's *Joseph Conrad: His Romantic Realism* (Boston: Four Seas Co., 1922); and Ernst Bendz's

Joseph Conrad: An Appreciation (Gothenburg, Sweden: N. J. Gumpert, 1923).

Between 1924 and 1940 the leading studies were: Ford Madox [Hueffer] Ford's *Joseph Conrad: A Personal Remembrance* (Boston: Little, Brown and Co., 1924), which is supplemented by his *Return to Yesterday* (Philadelphia: J. B. Lippincott Co., 1932) and his *Portraits from Life* (Boston: Houghton Mifflin Co., 1937); Arthur Symons's *Notes on Joseph Conrad* (London: Myers and Co., 1925); R. L. Mégroz's *Joseph Conrad's Mind and Method* (London: Faber and Faber, 1931); Joseph Warren Beach's chapter on "Impressionism: Conrad" in his *The Twentieth Century Novel: Studies in Technique* (New York: Appleton-Century-Crofts, 1932); W. W. Bancroft's *Joseph Conrad: His Philosophy of Life* (Boston: Stratford Co., 1933); Edward Crankshaw's *Joseph Conrad: Some Aspects of the Art of the Novel* (London: John Lane, The Bodley Head, 1936); Raymond Las Vergnas's French study, *Joseph Conrad* (Paris: H. Didier, 1938); and David Daiches's *The Novel and the Modern World* (Chicago: University of Chicago Press, 1939). A number of interesting shorter studies also appeared in this period: E. M. Forster's "Joseph Conrad: A Note" of 1921, included in his *Abinger Harvest* (New York: Harcourt Brace and Co., 1936); Virginia Woolf's two essays, "Joseph Conrad," included in *The Common Reader* (New York: Harcourt, Brace and Co., 1925) and "Mr. Conrad: A Conversation," included in *The Captain's Death Bed and Other Essays* (New York: Harcourt Brace and Co., 1950); the tributes of the French critics — Gide, Valéry, Lenormand, Maurois, Fernandez, Jaloux, and others — who contributed to a special memorial number, "Hommage à Joseph Conrad," of *La Nouvelle Revue française* (Paris: December 1, 1924: Nouvelle série, CXXXV, pp. 649–806); Liam O'Flaherty's short essay *Joseph Conrad* (London: E. Lahr, n.d.); and Thomas Mann's preface "Joseph Conrad's *The Secret Agent*," first published as an introduction to the German translation of that novel (*Der Geheimagent*, c. 1926), collected in his *Die Forderung des Tages* (Berlin: S. Fischer Verlag, 1930), translated in his *Past Masters and Other Essays* (New York: Alfred A. Knopf, 1933). Among many Polish studies that appeared in these and later years by Grabowski, Dybowski, Grzegorozyk, Perlowski, Retinger, and others, the most important and readily available is Jozef Ujejski's *Joseph Conrad* in its French translation (Paris: Edgar Malfère, 1939).

Since 1940, when new critical approaches began to appear in the study and assessment of Conrad, some of the leading treatments have been: M. C. Bradbrook's *Joseph Conrad: Poland's English Genius* (Cambridge, England: Cambridge University Press; New York: Macmillan Co., 1941); Albert Guerard, Jr.'s *Joseph Conrad* (New York: New Directions, 1947), and his new *Joseph Conrad* (Harvard, 1958);

Walter F. Wright's *Romance and Tragedy in Joseph Conrad* (Lincoln: University of Nebraska Press, 1949); F. R. Leavis's study of 1941, incorporated in his *The Great Tradition* (New York: George W. Stewart, 1950); Oliver Warner's essay, *Joseph Conrad*, of 1950 and his book, *Joseph Conrad*, of 1951 (both London: Longman's Green and Co.); Douglas Hewitt's *Conrad: A Reassessment* (Cambridge, England: Bowes and Bowes, 1952); Paul L. Wiley's *Conrad's Measure of Man* (Madison: University of Wisconsin Press, 1954); Walter Allen's *Six Great English Novelists* (London: Hamish Hamilton, 1955); E. H. Visiak's *The Mirror of Conrad* (London: Werner Laurie, 1955); Thomas Moser's *Joseph Conrad: Achievement and Decline* (Cambridge: Harvard University Press, 1957); and Richard Curle's *Joseph Conrad and His Characters* (London: William Heinemann, 1957). Of innumerable shorter studies and essays, only a few may be mentioned here: Elizabeth Bowen's in her *Collected Impressions* (New York: Alfred A. Knopf, 1950); Robert Penn Warren's introduction to *Nostromo* (New York: The Modern Library, 1951); Dorothy Van Ghent's study of *Lord Jim* in *The English Novel: Form and Function* (New York: Rinehart and Co., 1953). Among studies by the present editor dating from 1940 are: "Conrad: Nel Mezzo del Cammin," *The New Republic*, December 23, 1940; "Conrad: The Secret Sharer," *The New Republic*, April 21, 1941; "Conrad in His Age," *The New Republic*, November 16, 1942; "Joseph Conrad: Chance and Recognition," *The Sewanee Review*, January-March, 1945; "Introduction" to *The Portable Conrad* (New York: Viking Press, 1947, 1957); "Introduction" to *The Nigger of the "Narcissus"* (New York: Harper and Bros., 1951); "Introduction" to *Under Western Eyes* (New York: New Directions, 1951); four essays — "Conrad: Chance and Recognition," "The East and the Sea," "The Threat to the West," "Conrad in His Age" — in his *Craft and Character* (New York: Viking Press, 1957); and introductions to *Tales of the East and West* by Joseph Conrad (New York: Hanover House, 1958), to *Youth: A Narrative and Two Other Stories*, and to *The Shadow-Line and Two Other Tales* (New York: Doubleday-Anchor Books, 1958-59).

An essential adjunct to the study of Conrad's art is the "Author's Notes" he wrote for the Heinemann collected edition of his works between 1917 and 1921, now assembled as *Conrad's Prefaces to His Works*, with an introduction by Edward Garnett (London: J. M. Dent and Sons, 1937). These "Author's Notes" are usually included in the current Dent and Doubleday editions of Conrad's works.

M. D. Z.

LORD JIM

To
Mr. and Mrs. G. F. W. Hope
with grateful affection
after many years
of friendship

CHAPTER I

He was an inch, perhaps two, under six feet, powerfully built, and he advanced straight at you with a slight stoop of the shoulders, head forward, and a fixed from-under stare which made you think of a charging bull. His voice was deep, loud, and his manner displayed a kind of dogged self-assertion which had nothing aggressive in it. It seemed a necessity, and it was directed apparently as much at himself as at anybody else. He was spotlessly neat, apparelled in immaculate white from shoes to hat, and in the various Eastern ports where he got his living as ship-chandler's water-clerk he was very popular.

A water-clerk need not pass an examination in anything under the sun, but he must have Ability in the abstract and demonstrate it practically. His work consists in racing under sail, steam, or oars against other water-clerks for any ship about to anchor, greeting her captain cheerily, forcing upon him a card — the business card of the ship-chandler — and on his first visit on shore piloting him firmly but without ostentation to a vast, cavern-like shop which is full of things that are eaten and drunk on board ship; where you can get everything to make her seaworthy and beautiful, from a set of chain-hooks for her cable to a book of gold-leaf for the carvings of her stern; and where her commander is received like a brother by a ship-chandler he has never seen before. There is a cool parlour, easy-chairs, bottles, cigars, writing implements, a copy of harbour regulations, and a warmth of welcome that melts the salt of a three months' passage out of a seaman's heart. The connection thus begun is kept up, as long as the ship remains in harbour, by the daily visits of the water-clerk. To the captain he is faithful like a friend and attentive like a son, with the patience of Job, the unselfish devotion of a woman, and the jollity of a boon companion. Later on the bill is sent in. It is a beautiful and humane occupation. Therefore good water-clerks are scarce. When a water-clerk who possesses Ability in the abstract has also the advantage of having been brought up to the sea, he is worth to his employer a lot of money and some humour-

5

ing. Jim had always good wages and as much humouring as would have bought the fidelity of a fiend. Nevertheless, with black ingratitude he would throw up the job suddenly and depart. To his employers the reasons he gave were obviously inadequate. They said "Confounded fool!" as soon as his back was turned. This was their criticism on his exquisite sensibility.

To the white men in the waterside business and to the captains of ships he was just Jim — nothing more. He had, of course, another name, but he was anxious that it should not be pronounced. His incognito, which had as many holes as a sieve, was not meant to hide a personality but a fact. When the fact broke through the incognito he would leave suddenly the seaport where he happened to be at the time and go to another — generally farther east. He kept to seaports because he was a seaman in exile from the sea, and had Ability in the abstract, which is good for no other work but that of a water-clerk. He retreated in good order towards the rising sun, and the fact followed him casually but inevitably. Thus in the course of years he was known successively in Bombay, in Calcutta, in Rangoon, in Penang, in Batavia — and in each of these halting-places was just Jim the water-clerk. Afterwards, when his keen perception of the Intolerable drove him away for good from seaports and white men, even into the virgin forest, the Malays of the jungle village, where he had elected to conceal his deplorable faculty, added a word to the monosyllable of his incognito. They called him Tuan Jim: as one might say — Lord Jim.

Originally he came from a parsonage. Many commanders of fine merchant-ships come from these abodes of piety and peace. Jim's father possessed such certain knowledge of the Unknowable as made for the righteousness of people in cottages without disturbing the ease of mind of those whom an unerring Providence enables to live in mansions. The little church on a hill had the mossy greyness of a rock seen through a ragged screen of leaves. It had stood there for centuries, but the trees around probably remembered the laying of the first stone. Below, the red front of the rectory gleamed with a warm tint in the midst of grass-plots, flower-beds, and fir-trees, with an orchard at the back, a paved stable-yard to the left, and the sloping glass of greenhouses tacked along a wall of bricks. The living had belonged to the family for generations; but Jim was one of five sons,

and when after a course of light holiday literature his vocation
for the sea had declared itself, he was sent at once to a "training-
ship for officers of the mercantile marine."

He learned there a little trigonometry and how to cross top-
gallant yards. He was generally liked. He had the third place in
navigation and pulled stroke in the first cutter. Having a steady
head with an excellent physique, he was very smart aloft. His
station was in the fore-top, and often from there he looked down,
with the contempt of a man destined to shine in the midst of dangers, at the peaceful multitude of roofs cut in two by the brown
tide of the stream, while scattered on the outskirts of the surrounding plain the factory chimneys rose perpendicular against
a grimy sky, each slender like a pencil, and belching out smoke
like a volcano. He could see the big ships departing, the broad-
beamed ferries constantly on the move, the little boats floating
far below his feet, with the hazy splendour of the sea in the distance, and the hope of a stirring life in the world of adventure.

On the lower deck in the babel of two hundred voices he would
forget himself, and beforehand live in his mind the sea-life of
light litérature. He saw himself saving people from sinking ships,
cutting away masts in a hurricane, swimming through a surf with
a line; or as a lonely castaway, barefooted and half naked, walking on uncovered reefs in search of shellfish to stave off starvation.
He confronted savages on tropical shores, quelled mutinies on the
high seas, and in a small boat upon the ocean kept up the hearts
of despairing men — always an example of devotion to duty, and
as unflinching as a hero in a book.

"Something's up. Come along."

He leaped to his feet. The boys were streaming up the ladders.
Above could be heard a great scurrying about and shouting, and
when he got through the hatchway he stood still — as if confounded.

It was the dusk of a winter's day. The gale had freshened since
noon, stopping the traffic on the river and now blew with the
strength of a hurricane in fitful bursts that boomed like salvoes
of great guns firing over the ocean. The rain slanted in sheets
that flicked and subsided, and between whiles Jim had threatening glimpses of the tumbling tide, the small craft jumbled and
tossing along the shore, the motionless buildings in the driving
mist, the broad ferryboats pitching ponderously at anchor, the

vast landing-stages heaving up and down and smothered in sprays. The next gust seemed to blow all this away. The air was full of flying water. There was a fierce purpose in the gale, a furious earnestness in the screech of the wind, in the brutal tumult of earth and sky, that seemed directed at him, and made him hold his breath in awe. He stood still. It seemed to him he was whirled around.

He was jostled. "Man the cutter!" Boys rushed past him. A coaster running in for shelter had crashed through a schooner at anchor, and one of the ship's instructors had seen the accident. A mob of boys clambered on the rails, clustered round the davits. "Collision. Just ahead of us. Mr. Symons saw it." A push made him stagger against the mizzen-mast, and he caught hold of a rope. The old training-ship chained to her moorings quivered all over, bowing gently head to wind, and with her scanty rigging humming in a deep bass the breathless song of her youth at sea. "Lower away!" He saw the boat, manned, drop swiftly below the rail, and rushed after her. He heard a splash. "Let go; clear the falls!" He leaned over. The river alongside seethed in frothy streaks. The cutter could be seen in the falling darkness under the spell of tide and wind, that for a moment held her bound, and tossing abreast of the ship. A yelling voice in her reached him faintly: "Keep stroke, you young whelps, if you want to save anybody! Keep stroke!" And suddenly she lifted high her bow, and, leaping with raised oars over a wave, broke the spell cast upon her by the wind and tide.

Jim felt his shoulder gripped firmly. "Too late, youngster." The captain of the ship laid a restraining hand on that boy, who seemed on the point of leaping overboard, and Jim looked up with the pain of conscious defeat in his eyes. The captain smiled sympathetically. "Better luck next time. This will teach you to be smart."

A shrill cheer greeted the cutter. She came dancing back half full of water, and with two exhausted men washing about on her bottom boards. The tumult and the menace of wind and sea now appeared very contemptible to Jim, increasing the regret of his awe at their inefficient menace. Now he knew what to think of it. It seemed to him he cared nothing for the gale. He could affront greater perils. He would do so — better than anybody. Not a particle of fear was left. Nevertheless he brooded apart that evening while the bowman of the cutter — a boy with a face like a girl's and big grey eyes — was the hero of the lower deck. Eager questioners crowded round him. He narrated: "I just saw his head bobbing, and I dashed my boat-hook in the water. It caught in his breeches and I nearly went overboard, as I thought I would, only old Symons let go the tiller and grabbed my legs — the boat nearly swamped. Old Symons is a fine old chap. I don't mind a bit him being grumpy with us. He swore at me all the time he held my leg, but that was only his way of telling me to stick to the boat-hook. Old Symons is awfully excitable — isn't he? No — not the little fair chap — the other, the big one with a beard. When we pulled him in he groaned, 'Oh, my leg! oh, my leg!' and turned up his eyes. Fancy such a big chap fainting like a girl. Would any of you fellows faint for a jab with a boat-hook? — I wouldn't. It went into his leg so far." He showed the boat-hook, which he had carried below for the purpose, and produced a sensation. "No, silly! It was not his flesh that held him — his breeches did. Lots of blood, of course."

Jim thought it a pitiful display of vanity. The gale had ministered into a heroism as spurious as its own pretence of terror. He felt angry with the brutal tumult of earth and sky for taking him unawares and checking unfairly a generous readiness for narrow escapes. Otherwise he was rather glad he had not gone into the cutter, since a lower achievement had served the turn. He had enlarged his knowledge more than those who had done the work. When all men flinched, then — he felt sure — he alone would know how to deal with the spurious menace of wind and seas. He knew what to think of it. Seen dispassionately, it seemed contemptible. He could detect no trace of emotion in himself, and the final effect of a staggering event was that, unnoticed and apart from the noisy crowd of boys, he exulted with fresh certitude in his avidity for adventure, and in a sense of many-sided courage.

CHAPTER II

AFTER two years of training he went to sea, and entering the regions so well known to his imagination, found them strangely barren of adventure. He made many voyages. He knew the magic monotony of existence between sky and water: he had to bear the criticism of men, the exactions of the sea, and the prosaic severity of the daily task that gives bread — but whose only reward is in the perfect love of the work. This reward eluded him. Yet he could not go back, because there is nothing more enticing, disenchanting, and enslaving than the life at sea. Besides, his prospects were good. He was gentlemanly, steady, tractable, with a thorough knowledge of his duties; and in time, when yet very young, he became chief mate of a fine ship, without ever having been tested by those events of the sea that show in the light of day the inner worth of a man, the edge of his temper, and the fibre of his stuff; that reveal the quality of his resistance and the secret truth of his pretences, not only to others but also to himself.

Only once in all that time he had again the glimpse of the earnestness in the anger of the sea. That truth is not so often made apparent as people might think. There are many shades in the danger of adventures and gales, and it is only now and then that there appears on the face of facts a sinister violence of intention — that indefinable something which forces it upon the mind and the heart of a man, that this complication of accidents or these elemental furies are coming at him with a purpose of malice, with a strength beyond control, with an unbridled cruelty that means to tear out of him his hope and his fear, the pain of his fatigue and his longing for rest: which means to smash, to destroy, to annihilate all he had seen, known, loved, enjoyed, or hated; all that is priceless and necessary — the sunshine, the memories, the future, — which means to sweep the whole precious world utterly away from his sight by the simple and appalling act of taking his life.

Jim, disabled by a falling spar at the beginning of a week of which his Scottish captain used to say afterwards, "Man! it's a pairfect meeracle to me how she lived through it!" spent many days stretched on his back, dazed, battered, hopeless, and tormented as if at the bottom of an abyss of unrest. He did not care what the end would be, and in his lucid moments overvalued his indifference. The danger, when not seen, has the imperfect vagueness of human thought. The fear grows shadowy; and Imagination, the enemy of men, the father of all terrors, unstimulated, sinks to rest in the dulness of exhausted emotion. Jim saw nothing but the disorder of his tossed cabin. He lay there battened down in the midst of a small devastation, and felt secretly glad he had not to go on deck. But now and again an uncontrollable rush of anguish would grip him bodily, make him gasp and writhe under the blankets, and then the unintelligent brutality of an existence liable to the agony of such sensations filled him with a despairing desire to escape at any cost. Then fine weather returned, and he thought no more about it.

His lameness, however, persisted, and when the ship arrived at an Eastern port he had to go to the hospital. His recovery was slow, and he was left behind.

There were only two other patients in the white men's ward: the purser of a gunboat, who had broken his leg falling down a hatchway; and a kind of railway contractor from a neighbouring province, afflicted by some mysterious tropical disease, who held the doctor for an ass, and indulged in secret debaucheries of patent medicine which his Tamil servant used to smuggle in with unwearied devotion. They told each other the story of their lives, played cards a little, or, yawning and in pyjamas, lounged through the day in easy-chairs without saying a word. The hospital stood on a hill, and a gentle breeze entering through the windows, always flung wide open, brought into the bare room the softness of the sky, the languor of the earth, the bewitching breath of the Eastern waters. There were perfumes in it, suggestions of infinite repose, the gift of endless dreams. Jim looked every day over the thickets of gardens, beyond the roofs of the town, over the fronds of palms growing on the shore, at that roadstead which is a thoroughfare to the East, — at the roadstead dotted by garlanded islets, lighted by festal sunshine, its ships like toys, its brilliant activity resembling a holiday pageant, with the eternal serenity of the Eastern sky overhead and the smiling peace of the Eastern seas possessing the space as far as the horizon.

Directly he could walk without a stick, he descended into the

town to look for some opportunity to get home. Nothing offered just then, and, while waiting, he associated naturally with
the men of his calling in the port. These were of two kinds. Some,
very few and seen there but seldom, led mysterious lives, had preserved an undefaced energy with the temper of buccaneers and
the eyes of dreamers. They appeared to live in a crazy maze of
plans, hopes, dangers, enterprises, ahead of civilisation, in the dark
places of the sea; and their death was the only event of their fantastic existence that seemed to have a reasonable certitude of
achievement. The majority were men who, like himself, thrown
there by some accident, had remained as officers of country ships.
They had now a horror of the home service, with its harder conditions, severer view of duty, and the hazard of stormy oceans.
They were attuned to the eternal peace of Eastern sky and sea.
They loved short passages, good deck-chairs, large native crews,
and the distinction of being white. They shuddered at the thought
of hard work, and led precariously easy lives, always on the verge
of dismissal, always on the verge of engagement, serving Chinamen, Arabs, half-castes — would have served the devil himself had
he made it easy enough. They talked everlastingly of turns of
luck: how So-and-so got charge of a boat on the coast of China
— a soft thing; how this one had an easy billet in Japan somewhere,
and that one was doing well in the Siamese navy; and in all they
said — in their actions, in their looks, in their persons — could be
detected the soft spot, the place of decay, the determination to
lounge safely through existence.

To Jim that gossiping crowd, viewed as seamen, seemed at
first more unsubstantial than so many shadows. But at length he
found a fascination in the sight of those men, in their appearance
of doing so well on such a small allowance of danger and toil.
In time, beside the original disdain there grew up slowly another
sentiment; and suddenly, giving up the idea of going home, he
took a berth as chief mate of the *Patna*.

The *Patna* was a local steamer as old as the hills, lean like a
greyhound, and eaten up with rust worse than a condemned
water-tank. She was owned by a Chinaman, chartered by an
Arab, and commanded by a sort of renegade New South Wales
German, very anxious to curse publicly his native country, but
who, apparently on the strength of Bismarck's victorious policy,
brutalised all those he was not afraid of, and wore a "blood-and-

iron" air, combined with a purple nose and a red moustache. After she had been painted outside and whitewashed inside, eight hundred pilgrims (more or less) were driven on board of her as she lay with steam up alongside a wooden jetty.

They streamed aboard over three gangways, they streamed in urged by faith and the hope of paradise, they streamed in with a continuous tramp and shuffle of bare feet, without a word, a murmur, or a look back; and when clear of confining rails spread on all sides over the deck, flowed forward and aft, overflowed down the yawning hatchways, filled the inner recesses of the ship — like water filling a cistern, like water flowing into crevices and crannies, like water rising silently even with the rim. Eight hundred men and women with faith and hopes, with affections and memories, they had collected there, coming from north and south and from the outskirts of the East, after treading the jungle paths, descending the rivers, coasting in praus along the shallows, crossing in small canoes from island to island, passing through suffering, meeting strange sights, beset by strange fears, upheld by one desire. They came from solitary huts in the wilderness, from populous campongs, from villages by the sea. At the call of an idea they had left their forests, their clearings, the protection of their rulers, their prosperity, their poverty, the surroundings of their youth and the graves of their fathers. They came covered with dust, with sweat, with grime, with rags — the strong men at the head of family parties, the lean old men pressing forward without hope of return; young boys with fearless eyes glancing curiously, shy little girls with tumbled long hair; the timid women muffled up and clasping to their breasts, wrapped in loose ends of soiled head-cloths, their sleeping babies, the unconscious pilgrims of an exacting belief.

"Look at dese cattle," said the German skipper to his new chief mate.

An Arab, the leader of that pious voyage, came last. He walked slowly aboard, handsome and grave in his white gown and large turban. A string of servants followed, loaded with his luggage; the *Patna* cast off and backed away from the wharf.

She was headed between two small islets, crossed obliquely the anchoring-ground of sailing-ships, swung through half a circle in the shadow of a hill, then ranged close to a ledge of foaming reefs. The Arab standing up aft, recited aloud the prayer of travellers by sea. He invoked the favour of the Most High upon that journey, implored His blessing on men's toil and on the secret purposes of their hearts; the steamer pounded in the dusk the calm water of the Strait; and far astern of the pilgrim ship a screwpile lighthouse, planted by unbelievers on a treacherous shoal, seemed to wink at her its eye of flame, as if in derision of her errand of faith.

She cleared the Strait, crossed the bay, continued on her way through the "One-degree" passage. She held on straight for the Red Sea under a serene sky, under a sky scorching and unclouded, enveloped in a fulgor of sunshine that killed all thought, oppressed the heart, withered all impulses of strength and energy. And under the sinister splendour of that sky the sea, blue and profound, remained still, without a stir, without a ripple, without a wrinkle — viscous, stagnant, dead. The *Patna*, with a slight hiss, passed over that plain luminous and smooth, unrolled a black ribbon of smoke across the sky, left behind her on the water a white ribbon of foam that vanished at once, like the phantom of a track drawn upon a lifeless sea by the phantom of a steamer.

Every morning the sun, as if keeping pace in his revolutions with the progress of the pilgrimage, emerged with a silent burst of light exactly at the same distance astern of the ship, caught up with her at noon, pouring the concentrated fire of his rays on the pious purposes of the men, glided past on his descent, and sank mysteriously into the sea evening after evening, preserving the same distance ahead of her advancing bows. The five whites on board lived amidships, isolated from the human cargo. The awnings covered the deck with a white roof from stem to stern, and a faint hum, a low murmur of sad voices, alone revealed the presence of a crowd of people upon the great blaze of the ocean. Such were the days, still, hot, heavy, disappearing one by one into the past, as if falling into an abyss for ever open in the wake of the ship; and the ship, lonely under a wisp of smoke, held on her steadfast way black and smouldering in a luminous immensity, as if scorched by a flame flicked at her from a heaven without pity.

The nights descended on her like a benediction.

CHAPTER III

A MARVELLOUS stillness pervaded the world, and the stars, together with the serenity of their rays, seemed to shed upon the earth the assurance of everlasting security. The young moon recurved, and shining low in the west, was like a slender shaving thrown up from a bar of gold, and the Arabian Sea, smooth and cool to the eye like a sheet of ice, extended its perfect level to the perfect circle of a dark horizon. The propeller turned without a check, as though its beat had been part of the scheme of a safe universe; and on each side of the *Patna* two deep folds of water, permanent and sombre on the unwrinkled shimmer, enclosed within their straight and diverging ridges a few white swirls of foam bursting in a low hiss, a few wavelets, a few ripples, a few undulations that, left behind, agitated the surface of the sea for an instant after the passage of the ship, subsided splashing gently, calmed down at last into the circular stillness of water and sky with the black speck of the moving hull remaining everlastingly in its centre.

Jim on the bridge was penetrated by the great certitude of unbounded safety and peace that could be read on the silent aspect of nature like the certitude of fostering love upon the placid tenderness of a mother's face. Below the roof of awnings, surrendered to the wisdom of white men and to their courage, trusting the power of their unbelief and the iron shell of their fire-ship, the pilgrims of an exacting faith slept on mats, on blankets, on bare planks, on every deck, in all the dark corners, wrapped in dyed cloths, muffled in soiled rags, with their heads resting on small bundles, with their faces pressed to bent forearms: the men, the women, the children; the old with the young, the decrepit with the lusty — all equal before sleep, death's brother.

A draught of air, fanned from forward by the speed of the ship, passed steadily through the long gloom between the high bulwarks, swept over the rows of prone bodies; a few dim flames in globe-lamps were hung short here and there under the ridge-poles, and in the blurred circles of light thrown down and trembling slightly to the unceasing vibration of the ship appeared a chin upturned, two closed eyelids, a dark hand with silver rings, a meagre limb draped in a torn covering, a head bent back, a naked foot, a throat bared and stretched as if offering itself to the knife. The well-to-do had made for their families shelters with heavy boxes and dusty mats; the poor reposed side by side with all they had on earth tied up in a rag under their heads; the lone old men slept, with drawn-up legs, upon their prayer-carpets, with their hands over their ears and one elbow on each side of the face; a father, his shoulders up and his knees under his forehead, dozed dejectedly by a boy who slept on his back with tousled hair and one arm commandingly extended; a woman covered from head to foot, like a corpse, with a piece of white sheeting, had a naked child in the hollow of each arm; the Arab's belongings, piled right aft, made a heavy mound of broken outlines, with a cargo-lamp swung above, and a great confusion of vague forms behind: gleams of paunchy brass pots, the foot-rest of a deck-chair, blades of spears, the straight scabbard of an old sword leaning against a heap of pillows, the spout of a tin coffee-pot. The patent log on the taffrail periodically rang a single tinkling stroke for every mile traversed on an errand of faith. Above the mass of sleepers a faint and patient sigh at times floated, the exhalation of a troubled dream; and short metallic clangs bursting out suddenly in the depths of the ship, the harsh scrape of a shovel, the violent slam of a furnace-door, exploded brutally, as if the men handling the mysterious things below had their breasts full of fierce anger: while the slim high hull of the steamer went on evenly ahead, without a sway of her bare masts, cleaving continuously the great calm of the waters under the inaccessible serenity of the sky.

Jim paced athwart, and his footsteps in the vast silence were loud to his own ears, as if echoed by the watchful stars: his eyes roaming about the line of the horizon, seemed to gaze hungrily into the unattainable, and did not see the shadow of the coming event. The only shadow on the sea was the shadow of the black smoke pouring heavily from the funnel its immense streamer, whose end was constantly dissolving in the air. Two Malays, silent and almost motionless, steered, one on each side of the wheel, whose brass rim shone fragmentarily in the oval of light thrown out by the binnacle. Now and then a hand, with black fingers alternately letting go and catching hold of revolving spokes, appeared in the illumined part; the links of wheel-chains ground heavily in the grooves of the barrel. Jim would glance at the compass, would glance around the unattainable horizon, would stretch himself till his joints cracked with a leisurely twist of the body, in the very excess of well-being; and, as if made audacious by the invincible aspect of the peace, he felt he cared for nothing that could happen to him to the end of his days. From time to time he glanced idly at a chart pegged out with four drawing-pins on a low three-legged table abaft the steering-gear case. The sheet of paper portraying the depths of the sea presented a shiny surface under the light of a bull's-eye lamp lashed to a stanchion, a surface as level and smooth as the glimmering surface of the waters. Parallel rulers with a pair of dividers reposed on it; the ship's position at last noon was marked with a small black cross, and the straight pencil-line drawn firmly as far as Perim figured the course of the ship — the path of souls towards the holy place, the promise of salvation, the reward of eternal life — while the pencil with its sharp end touching the Somali coast lay round and still like a naked ship's spar floating in the pool of a sheltered dock. "How steady she goes," thought Jim with wonder, with something like gratitude for this high peace of sea and sky. At such times his thoughts would be full of valorous deeds: he loved these dreams and the success of his imaginary achievements. They were the best parts of life, its secret truth, its hidden reality. They had a gorgeous virility, the charm of vagueness, they passed before him with a heroic tread; they carried his soul away with them and made it drunk with the divine philtre of an unbounded confidence in itself. There was nothing he could not face. He was so pleased with the idea that he smiled, keeping perfunctorily his eyes ahead; and when he happened to glance back he saw the white streak of the wake drawn as straight by the ship's keel upon the sea as the black line drawn by the pencil upon the chart.

The ash-buckets racketed, clanking up and down the stoke-hold ventilators, and this tin-pot clatter warned him the end of his watch was near. He sighed with content, with regret as well at having to part from that serenity which fostered the adventurous freedom of his thoughts. He was a little sleepy, too, and felt a pleasurable languor running through every limb as though all the blood in his body had turned to warm milk. His skipper had come up noiselessly, in pyjamas and with his sleeping-jacket flung wide open. Red of face, only half awake, the left eye partly closed, the right staring stupid and glassy, he hung his big head over the chart and scratched his ribs sleepily. There was something obscene in the sight of his naked flesh. His bared breast glistened soft and greasy as though he had sweated out his fat in his sleep. He pronounced a professional remark in a voice harsh and dead, resembling the rasping sound of a wood-file on the edge of a plank; the fold of his double chin hung like a bag triced up close under the hinge of his jaw. Jim started, and his answer was full of deference; but the odious and fleshy figure, as though seen for the first time in a revealing moment, fixed itself in his memory for ever as the incarnation of everything vile and base that lurks in the world we love: in our own hearts we trust for our salvation in the men that surround us, in the sights that fill our eyes, in the sounds that fill our ears, and in the air that fills our lungs.

The thin gold shaving of the moon floating slowly downwards had lost itself on the darkened surface of the waters, and the eternity beyond the sky seemed to come down nearer to the earth, with the augmented glitter of the stars, with the more profound sombreness in the lustre of the half-transparent dome covering the flat disc of an opaque sea. The ship moved so smoothly that her onward motion was imperceptible to the senses of men, as though she had been a crowded planet speeding through the dark spaces of ether behind the swarm of suns, in the appalling and calm solitudes awaiting the breath of future creations. "Hot is no name for it down below," said a voice.

Jim smiled without looking round. The skipper presented an unmoved breadth of back: it was the renegade's trick to appear pointedly unaware of your existence unless it suited his purpose to turn at you with a devouring glare before he let loose a torrent of foamy, abusive jargon that came like a gush from a sewer. Now he emitted only a sulky grunt; the second engineer at the head of the bridge-ladder, kneading with damp palms a dirty sweat-rag, unabashed, continued the tale of his complaints. The sailors had a good time of it up here, and what was the use of them in the world he would be blowed if he could see. The poor devils of engineers had to get the ship along anyhow, and they could very well do the rest too; by gosh they —— "Shut up" growled the German stolidly. "Oh yes! Shut up — and when anything goes

wrong you fly to us, don't you?" went on the other. He was
more than half cooked, he expected; but anyway, now, he did not
mind how much he sinned, because these last three days he had
passed through a fine course of training for the place where the
bad boys go when they die — b'gosh, he had — besides being made
jolly well deaf by the blasted racket below. The durned, compound, surface-condensing, rotten scrapheap rattled and banged
down there like an old deck-winch, only more so; and what made
him risk his life every night and day that God made amongst
the refuse of a breaking-up yard flying round at fifty-seven revolutions, was more than *he* could tell. He must have been born
reckless, b'gosh. He . . . "Where did you get drink?" inquired
the German, very savage, but motionless in the light of the binnacle, like a clumsy effigy of a man cut out of a block of fat.
Jim went on smiling at the retreating horizon; his heart was
full of generous impulses, and his thought was contemplating
his own superiority. "Drink!" repeated the engineer with ami-
able scorn: he was hanging on with both hands to the rail, a
shadowy figure with flexible legs. "Not from you, captain.
You're far too mean, b'gosh. You would let a good man die
sooner than give him a drop of shnaps. That's what you Ger-
mans call economy. Penny wise, pound foolish." He became sentimental. The chief had given him a four-finger nip about ten
o'clock — "only one, s'elp me!" — good old chief; but as to getting the old fraud out of his bunk — a five-ton crane couldn't do
it. Not it. Not to-night anyhow. He was sleeping sweetly like
a little child, with a bottle of prime brandy under his pillow.
From the thick throat of the commander of the *Patna* came a low
rumble, on which the sound of the word *schwein* fluttered high
and low like a capricious feather in a faint stir of air. He and
the chief engineer had been cronies for a good few years — serving the same jovial, crafty, old Chinaman, with horn-rimmed gog-
gles and strings of red silk plaited into the venerable grey hairs of
his pigtail. The quay-side opinion in the *Patna's* home-port was
that these two in the way of brazen peculation "had done together
pretty well everything you can think of." Outwardly they were
badly matched: one dull-eyed, malevolent, and of soft fleshy
curves; the other lean, all hollows, with a head long and bony like
the head of an old horse, with sunken cheeks, with sunken temples,
with an indifferent glazed glance of sunken eyes. He had been

stranded out East somewhere — in Canton, in Shanghai, or perhaps in Yokohama; he probably did not care to remember himself the exact locality, nor yet the cause of his shipwreck. He had
been, in mercy to his youth, kicked quietly out of his ship twenty
years ago or more, and it might have been so much worse for
him that the memory of the episode had in it hardly a trace of
misfortune. Then, steam navigation expanding in these seas and
men of his craft being scarce at first, he had "got on" after a sort.
He was eager to let strangers know in a dismal mumble that he
was "an old stager out here." When he moved a skeleton seemed
to sway loose in his clothes; his walk was mere wandering, and
he was given to wander thus around the engine-room skylight,
smoking, without relish, doctored tobacco in a brass bowl at the
end of a cherrywood stem four feet long, with the imbecile
gravity of a thinker evolving a system of philosophy from the
hazy glimpse of a truth. He was usually anything but free with
his private store of liquor; but on that night he had departed from
his principles, so that his second, a weak-headed child of Wap-
ping, what with the unexpectedness of the treat and the strength
of the stuff, had become very happy, cheeky, and talkative. The
fury of the New South Wales German was extreme; he puffed
like an exhaust-pipe, and Jim, faintly amused by the scene, was
impatient for the time when he could get below: the last ten minutes of the watch were irritating like a gun that hangs fire; those
men did not belong to the world of heroic adventure; they
weren't bad chaps though. Even the skipper himself . . . His
gorge rose at the mass of panting flesh from which issued gurgling mutters, a cloudy trickle of filthy expressions; but he was
too pleasurably languid to dislike actively this or any other thing.
The quality of these men did not matter; he rubbed shoulders
with them, but they could not touch him; he shared the air they
breathed, but he was different. . . . Would the skipper go for
the engineer? . . . The life was easy and he was too sure of
himself — too sure of himself to . . . The line dividing his meditation from a surreptitious doze on his feet was thinner than a
thread in a spider's web.

　　The second engineer was coming by easy transitions to the consideration of his finances and of his courage.

　　"Who's drunk? I? No, no, captain! That won't do. You
ought to know by this time the chief ain't free-hearted enough

to make a sparrow drunk, b'gosh. I've never been the worse for liquor in my life; the stuff ain't made yet that would make *me* drunk. I could drink liquid fire against your whisky peg for peg, b'gosh, and keep as cool as a cucumber. If I thought I was drunk I would jump overboard — do away with myself, b'gosh. I would! Straight! And I won't go off the bridge. Where do you expect me to take the air on a night like this, eh? On deck amongst that vermin down there? Likely — ain't it! And I am not afraid of anything you can do."

The German lifted two heavy fists to heaven and shook them a little without a word.

"I don't know what fear is," pursued the engineer, with the enthusiasm of sincere conviction. "I am not afraid of doing all the bloomin' work in this rotten hooker, b'gosh! And a jolly good thing for you that there are some of us about the world that aren't afraid of their lives, or where would you be — you and this old thing here with her plates like brown paper — brown paper, s'elp me? It's all very fine for you — you get a power of pieces out of her one way and another; but what about me — what do I get? A measly hundred and fifty dollars a month and find yourself. I wish to ask you respectfully — respectfully, mind — who wouldn't chuck a dratted job like this? 'Tain't safe, s'elp me, it ain't! Only I am one of them fearless fellows. . . ."

He let go the rail and made ample gestures as if demonstrating in the air the shape and extent of his valour; his thin voice darted in prolonged squeaks upon the sea, he tiptoed back and forth for the better emphasis of utterance, and suddenly pitched down head-first as though he had been clubbed from behind. He said "Damn!" as he tumbled; an instant of silence followed upon his screeching: Jim and the skipper staggered forward by common accord, and catching themselves up, stood very stiff and still gazing, amazed, at the undisturbed level of the sea. Then they looked upwards at the stars.

What had happened? The wheezy thump of the engines went on. Had the earth been checked in her course? They could not understand; and suddenly the calm sea, the sky without a cloud, appeared formidably insecure in their immobility, as it poised on the brow of yawning destruction. The engineer rebounded vertically full length and collapsed again into a vague heap. This heap said "What's that?" in the muffled accents of profound grief.

A faint noise as of thunder, of thunder infinitely remote, less than a sound, hardly more than a vibration, passed slowly, and the ship quivered in response, as if the thunder had growled deep down in the water. The eyes of the two Malays at the wheel glittered towards the white men, but their dark hands remained closed on the spokes. The sharp hull driving on its way seemed to rise a few inches in succession through its whole length, as though it had become pliable, and settled down again rigidly to its work of cleaving the smooth surface of the sea. Its quivering stopped, and the faint noise of thunder ceased all at once, as though the ship had steamed across a narrow belt of vibrating water and of humming air.

CHAPTER IV

A MONTH or so afterwards, when Jim, in answer to pointed questions, tried to tell honestly the truth of this experience, he said, speaking of the ship: "She went over whatever it was as easy as a snake crawling over a stick." The illustration was good: the questions were aiming at facts, and the official Inquiry was being held in the police court of an Eastern port. He stood elevated in the witness-box, with burning cheeks in a cool lofty room: the big framework of punkahs moved gently to and fro high above his head, and from below many eyes were looking at him out of dark faces, out of white faces, out of red faces, out of faces attentive, spellbound, as if all these people sitting in orderly rows upon narrow benches had been enslaved by the fascination of his voice. It was very loud, it rang startling in his own ears, it was the only sound audible in the world, for the terribly distinct questions that extorted his answers seemed to shape themselves in anguish and pain within his breast, — came to him poignant and silent like the terrible questioning of one's conscience. Outside the court the sun blazed — within was the wind of great punkahs that made you shiver, the shame that made you burn, the attentive eyes whose glance stabbed. The face of the presiding magistrate, clean shaved and impassible, looked at him deadly pale between the red faces of the two nautical assessors. The light of a broad window under the ceiling fell from above on the heads and shoulders of the three men, and they were fiercely distinct in the half-light of the big court-room where the audience seemed composed of staring shadows. They wanted facts. Facts! They demanded facts from him, as if facts could explain anything!

"After you had concluded you had collided with something floating awash, say a water-logged wreck, you were ordered by your captain to go forward and ascertain if there was any damage done. Did you think it likely from the force of the blow?" asked the assessor sitting to the left. He had a thin horseshoe beard, salient cheek-bones and with both elbows on the desk clasped his rugged hands before his face, looking at Jim with thoughtful blue eyes; the other, a heavy, scornful man, thrown back in his seat, his left arm extended full length, drummed delicately with his finger-tips on a blotting-pad: in the middle the magistrate upright in the roomy arm-chair, his head inclined slightly on the shoulder, had his arms crossed on his breast and a few flowers in a glass vase by the side of his inkstand.

"I did not," said Jim. "I was told to call no one and to make no noise for fear of creating a panic. I thought the precaution reasonable. I took one of the lamps that were hung under the awnings and went forward. After opening the forepeak hatch I heard splashing in there. I lowered then the lamp the whole drift of its lanyard, and saw that the forepeak was more than half full of water already. I knew then there must be a big hole below the waterline." He paused.

"Yes," said the big assessor, with a dreamy smile at the blotting-pad; his fingers played incessantly, touching the paper without noise.

"I did not think of danger just then. I might have been a little startled: all this happened in such a quiet way and so very suddenly. I knew there was no other bulkhead in the ship but the collision bulkhead separating the forepeak from the forehold. I went back to tell the captain. I came upon the second engineer getting up at the foot of the bridge-ladder: he seemed dazed, and told me he thought his left arm was broken; he had slipped on the top step when getting down while I was forward. He exclaimed, 'My God! That rotten bulkhead 'll give way in a minute, and the damned thing will go down under us like a lump of lead.' He pushed me away with his right arm and ran before me up the ladder, shouting as he climbed. His left arm hung by his side. I followed up in time to see the captain rush at him and knock him down flat on his back. He did not strike him again: he stood bending over him and speaking angrily but quite low. I fancy he was asking him why the devil he didn't go and stop the engines, instead of making a row about it on deck. I heard him say, 'Get up! Run! fly!' He swore also. The engineer slid down the starboard ladder and bolted round the skylight to the engine-room companion which was on the port-side. He moaned as he ran. . . ."

He spoke slowly; he remembered swiftly and with extreme vividness; he could have reproduced like an echo the moaning of the engineer for the better information of these men who wanted facts. After his first feeling of revolt he had come round to the view that only a meticulous precision of statement would bring out the true horror behind the appalling face of things. The facts those men were so eager to know had been visible, tangible, open to the senses, occupying their place in space and time, requiring for their existence a fourteen-hundred-ton steamer and twenty-seven minutes by the watch; they made a whole that had features, shades of expression, a complicated aspect that could be remembered by the eye, and something else besides, something invisible, a directing spirit of perdition that dwelt within, like a malevolent soul in a detestable body. He was anxious to make this clear. This had not been a common affair, everything in it had been of the utmost importance, and fortunately he remembered everything. He wanted to go on talking for truth's sake, perhaps for his own sake also; and while his utterance was deliberate, his mind positively flew round and round the serried circle of facts that had surged up all about him to cut him off from the rest of his kind: it was like a creature that, finding itself imprisoned within an enclosure of high stakes, dashes round and round, distracted in the night, trying to find a weak spot, a crevice, a place to scale, some opening through which it may squeeze itself and escape. This awful activity of mind made him hesitate at times in his speech. . . .

"The captain kept on moving here and there on the bridge; he seemed calm enough, only he stumbled several times; and once as

I stood speaking to him he walked right into me as though he had been stone-blind. He made no definite answer to what I had to tell. He mumbled to himself; all I heard of it were a few words that sounded like 'confounded steam!' and 'infernal steam!' — something about steam. I thought . . ."

He was becoming irrelevant; a question to the point cut short his speech, like a pang of pain, and he felt extremely discouraged and weary. He was coming to that, he was coming to that — and now, checked brutally, he had to answer by yes or no. He answered truthfully by a curt "Yes, I did;" and fair of face, big of frame, with young, gloomy eyes, he held his shoulders upright above the box while his soul writhed within him. He was made to answer another question so much to the point and so useless, then waited again. His mouth was tastelessly dry, as though he had been eating dust, then salt and bitter as after a drink of sea-water. He wiped his damp forehead, passed his tongue over parched lips, felt a shiver run down his back. The big assessor had dropped his eyelids, and drummed on without a sound, careless and mournful; the eyes of the other above the sunburnt, clasped fingers seemed to glow with kindliness; the magistrate had swayed forward; his pale face hovered near the flowers, and then dropping sideways over the arm of his chair, he rested his temple in the palm of his hand. The wind of the punkahs eddied down on the heads, on the dark-faced natives wound about in voluminous draperies, on the Europeans sitting together very hot and in drill suits that seemed to fit them as close as their skins, and holding their round pith hats on their knees; while gliding along the walls the court peons, buttoned tight in long white coats, flitted rapidly to and fro, running on bare toes, red-sashed, red turban on head, as noiseless as ghosts, and on the alert like so many retrievers.

Jim's eyes, wandering in the intervals of his answers, rested upon a white man who sat apart from the others, with his face worn and clouded, but with quiet eyes that glanced straight, interested and clear. Jim answered another question and was tempted to cry out, "What's the good of this! what's the good!" He tapped with his foot slightly, bit his lip, and looked away over the heads. He met the eyes of the white man. The glance directed at him was not the fascinated stare of the others. It was an act of intelligent volition. Jim between two questions forgot himself so

far as to find leisure for a thought. This fellow — ran the thought
— looks at me as though he could see somebody or something past
my shoulder. He had come across that man before — in the street
perhaps. He was positive he had never spoken to him. For days,
for many days, he had spoken to no one, but had held silent, inco-
herent, and endless converse with himself, like a prisoner alone
in his cell or like a wayfarer lost in a wilderness. At present he
was answering questions that did not matter though they had a
purpose, but he doubted whether he would ever again speak out
as long as he lived. The sound of his own truthful statements
confirmed his deliberate opinion that speech was of no use to him
any longer. That man there seemed to be aware of his hopeless
difficulty. Jim looked at him, then turned away resolutely, as
after a final parting.

And later on, many times, in distant parts of the world, Marlow
showed himself willing to remember Jim, to remember him at
length, in detail and audibly.

Perhaps it would be after dinner, on a verandah draped in
motionless foliage and crowned with flowers, in the deep dusk
speckled by fiery cigar-ends. The elongated bulk of each cane-
chair harboured a silent listener. Now and then a small red glow
would move abruptly, and expanding light up the fingers of a
languid hand, part of a face in profound repose, or flash a crimson gleam into a pair of pensive eyes overshadowed by a frag-
ment of an unruffled forehead; and with the very first word uttered Marlow's body, extended at rest in the seat, would become
very still, as though his spirit had winged its way back into the
lapse of time and were speaking through his lips from the past.

CHAPTER V

"Oh yes. I attended the inquiry," he would say, "and to this day I haven't left off wondering why I went. I am willing to believe each of us has a guardian angel, if you fellows will concede to me that each of us has a familiar devil as well. I want you to own up, because I don't like to feel exceptional in any way, and I know I have him — the devil, I mean. I haven't seen him, of course, but I go upon circumstantial evidence. He is there right enough, and, being malicious, he lets me in for that kind of thing. What kind of thing, you ask? Why, the inquiry thing, the yellow-dog thing — you wouldn't think a mangy, native tyke would be allowed to trip up people in the verandah of a magistrate's court, would you? — the kind of thing that by devious, unexpected, truly diabolical ways causes me to run up against men with soft spots, with hard spots, with hidden plague spots, by Jove! and loosens their tongues at the sight of me for their infernal confidences; as though, forsooth, I had no confidences to make to myself, as though — God help me! — I didn't have enough confidential information about myself to harrow my own soul till the end of my appointed time. And what I have done to be thus favoured I want to know. I declare I am as full of my own concerns as the next man, and I have as much memory as the average pilgrim in this valley, so you see I am not particularly fit to be a receptacle of confessions. Then why? Can't tell — unless it be to make time pass away after dinner. Charley, my dear chap, your dinner was extremely good, and in consequence these men here look upon a quiet rubber as a tumultuous occupation. They wallow in your good chairs and think to themselves, 'Hang exertion. Let that Marlow talk.'

"Talk! So be it. And it's easy enough to talk of Master Jim, after a good spread, two hundred feet above the sea-level, with a box of decent cigars handy, on a blessed evening of freshness and starlight that would make the best of us forget we are only on sufferance here and got to pick our way in cross lights, watching every precious minute and every irremediable step, trusting

we shall manage yet to go out decently in the end — but not so
sure of it after all — and with dashed little help to expect from
those we touch elbows with right and left. Of course there are
men here and there to whom the whole of life is like an after-
dinner hour with a cigar; easy, pleasant, empty, perhaps enliv-
ened by some fable of strife to be forgotten before the end is told
— before the end is told — even if there happens to be any end to it.

"My eyes met his for the first time at that inquiry. You must
know that everybody connected in any way with the sea was
there, because the affair had been notorious for days, ever since
that mysterious cable message came from Aden to start us all
cackling. I say mysterious, because it was so in a sense though
it contained a naked fact, about as naked and ugly as a fact can
well be. The whole waterside talked of nothing else. First thing
in the morning as I was dressing in my state-room, I would hear
through the bulkhead my Parsee Dubash jabbering about the
Patna with the steward, while he drank a cup of tea, by favour,
in the pantry. No sooner on shore I would meet some acquaintance, and the first remark would be, 'Did you ever hear of anything to beat this?' and according to his kind the man would smile
cynically, or look sad, or let out a swear or two. Complete strangers would accost each other familiarly, just for the sake of easing
their minds on the subject: every confounded loafer in the town
came in for a harvest of drinks over this affair: you heard of it
in the harbour office, at every ship-broker's, at your agent's, from
whites, from natives, from half-castes, from the very boatmen
squatting half-naked on the stone steps as you went up — by Jove!
There was some indignation, not a few jokes, and no end of dis-
cussions as to what had become of them, you know. This went
on for a couple of weeks or more, and the opinion that whatever
was mysterious in this affair would turn out to be tragic as well,
began to prevail, when one fine morning, as I was standing in the
shade by the steps of the harbour office, I perceived four men
walking towards me along the quay. I wondered for a while
where that queer lot had sprung from, and suddenly, I may say,
I shouted to myself, 'Here they are!'

"There they were, sure enough, three of them as large as life,
and one much larger of girth than any living man has a right to
be, just landed with a good breakfast inside of them from an
outward-bound Dale Line steamer that had come in about an hour
after sunrise. There could be no mistake; I spotted the jolly skip-

per of the *Patna* at the first glance: the fattest man in the whole
blessed tropical belt clear round that good old earth of ours.
Moreover, nine months or so before, I had come across him in
Samarang. His steamer was loading in the Roads, and he was
abusing the tyrannical institutions of the German empire, and
soaking himself in beer all day long and day after day in De
Jongh's back-shop, till De Jongh, who charged a guilder for every
bottle without as much as the quiver of an eyelid, would beckon
me aside, and, with his little leathery face all puckered up, declare confidentially, 'Business is business, but this man, captain, he
make me very sick. Tfui!'

"I was looking at him from the shade. He was hurrying on a
little in advance, and the sunlight beating on him brought out his
bulk in a startling way. He made me think of a trained baby elephant walking on hind-legs. He was extravagantly gorgeous
too — got up in a soiled sleeping-suit, bright green and deep
orange vertical stripes, with a pair of ragged straw slippers on his
bare feet, and somebody's castoff pith hat, very dirty and two
sizes too small for him, tied up with a manilla rope-yarn on the
top of his big head. You understand a man like that hasn't the
ghost of a chance when it comes to borrowing clothes. Very
well. On he came in hot haste, without a look right or left, passed
within three feet of me, and in the innocence of his heart went
on pelting upstairs in the harbour office to make his deposition,
or report, or whatever you like to call it.

"It appears he addressed himself in the first instance to the principal shipping-master. Archie Ruthvel had just come in, and,
as his story goes, was about to begin his arduous day by giving a
dressing-down to his chief clerk. Some of you might have known
him — an obliging little Portuguese half-caste with a miserably
skinny neck, and always on the hop to get something from the
shipmasters in the way of eatables — a piece of salt pork, a bag of
biscuits, a few potatoes, or what not. One voyage, I recollect,
I tipped him a live sheep out of the remnant of my sea-stock: not
that I wanted him to do anything for me — he couldn't, you
know — but because his childlike belief in the sacred right to
perquisites quite touched my heart. It was so strong as to be almost beautiful. The race — the two races rather — and the climate . . . However, never mind. I know where I have a friend
for life.

"Well, Ruthvel says he was giving him a severe lecture — on

official morality, I suppose — when he heard a kind of subdued commotion at his back, and turning his head he saw, in his own words, something round and enormous, resembling a sixteen-hundred-weight sugar-hogshead wrapped in striped flannelette, up-ended in the middle of the large floor space in the office. He declares he was so taken aback that for quite an appreciable time he did not realise the thing was alive, and sat still wondering for what purpose and by what means that object had been transported in front of his desk. The archway from the ante-room was crowded with punkah-pullers, sweepers, police peons, the coxswain and crew of the harbour steam-launch, all craning their necks and almost climbing on each other's backs. Quite a riot. By that time the fellow had managed to tug and jerk his hat clear of his head, and advanced with slight bows at Ruthvel, who told me the sight was so discomposing that for some time he listened quite unable to make out what that apparition wanted. It spoke in a voice harsh and lugubrious but intrepid, and little by little it dawned upon Archie that this was a development of the *Patna* case. He says that as soon as he understood who it was before him he felt quite unwell — Archie is so sympathetic and easily upset — but pulled himself together and shouted 'Stop! I can't listen to you. You must go to the Master Attendant. I can't possibly listen to you. Captain Elliot is the man you want to see. This way, this way.' He jumped up, ran round that long counter, pulled, shoved: the other let him, surprised but obedient at first, and only at the door of the private office some sort of animal instinct made him hang back and snort like a frightened bullock. 'Look here! what's up? Let go! Look here!' Archie flung open the door without knocking. 'The master of the *Patna*, sir,' he shouts. 'Go in, captain.' He saw the old man lift his head from some writing so sharp that his nose-nippers fell off, banged the door to, and fled to his desk, where he had some papers waiting for his signature: but he says the row that burst out in there was so awful that he couldn't collect his senses sufficiently to remember the spelling of his own name. Archie's the most sensitive shipping-master in the two hemispheres. He declares he felt as though he had thrown a man to a hungry lion. No doubt the noise was great. I heard it down below, and I have every reason to believe it was heard clear across the Esplanade as far as the band-stand. Old father Elliot had a great stock of words and could shout — and didn't mind who he shouted at either. He would have shouted at the Viceroy himself. As he used to tell me: 'I am as high as I can get; my pension is safe. I've a few pounds laid by, and if they don't like my notions of duty I would just as soon go home as not. I am an old man, and I have always spoken my mind. All I care for now is to see my girls married before I die.' He was a little crazy on that point. His three daughters were awfully nice, though they resemble him amazingly, and on the mornings he woke up with a gloomy view of their matrimonial prospects the office would read it in his eye and tremble, because, they said, he was sure to have somebody for breakfast. However, that morning he did not eat the renegade, but, if I may be allowed to carry on the metaphor, chewed him up very small, so to speak, and — ah! ejected him again.

"Thus in a very few moments I saw his monstrous bulk descend in haste and stand still on the outer steps. He had stopped close to me for the purpose of profound meditation: his large purple cheeks quivered. He was biting his thumb, and after a while noticed me with a sidelong vexed look. The other three chaps that had landed with him made a little group waiting at some distance. There was a sallow-faced, mean little chap with his arm in a sling, and a long individual in a blue flannel coat, as dry as a chip and no stouter than a broomstick, with drooping grey moustaches, who looked about him with an air of jaunty imbecility. The third was an upstanding, broad-shouldered youth, with his hands in his pockets, turning his back on the other two who appeared to be talking together earnestly. He stared across the empty Esplanade. A ramshackle gharry, all dust and venetian blinds, pulled up short opposite the group, and the driver, throwing up his right foot over his knee, gave himself up to the critical examination of his toes. The young chap, making no movement, not even stirring his head, just stared into the sunshine. This was my first view of Jim. He looked as unconcerned and unapproachable as only the young can look. There he stood, clean-limbed, clean-faced, firm on his feet, as promising a boy as the sun ever shone on; and, looking at him, knowing all he knew and a little more too, I was as angry as though I had detected him trying to get something out of me by false pretences. He had no business to look so sound. I thought to myself — well, if this sort can go wrong like that . . . and I felt as though I could fling down my hat and dance on it from sheer mortification, as I once saw the skipper of an Italian barque do because his duffer of a mate got into a mess with his anchors when making a flying moor in a roadstead full of ships. I asked myself, seeing him there apparently so much at ease — is he silly? is he callous? He seemed ready to start whistling a tune. And note, I did not care a rap about the behaviour of the other two. Their persons somehow fitted the tale that was public property, and was going to be the subject of an official inquiry. 'That old mad rogue upstairs called me a hound,' said the captain of the *Patna*. I can't tell whether he recognised me — I rather think he did; but at any rate our glances met. He glared — I smiled; hound was the very mildest epithet that had reached me through the open window. 'Did he?' I said from some strange inability to hold my tongue. He nodded, bit his thumb again, swore under his breath: then lifting his head and looking at me with sullen and passionate impudence — 'Bah! the Pacific is big, my friendt. You damned Englishmen can do your worst; I know where there's plenty of room for a man like me: I am well aguaindt in Apia, in Honolulu, in . . .' He paused reflectively, while without effort I could depict to myself the sort of people he was 'aguaindt' with in those places. I won't make a secret of it that I had been 'aguaindt' with not a few of that sort myself. There are times when a man must act as though life were equally sweet in any company. I've known such a time, and, what's more, I shan't now pretend to pull a long face over my necessity, because a good many of that bad company from want of moral — moral — what shall I say? — posture, or from some other equally profound cause, were twice as instructive and twenty times more amusing than the usual respectable thief of commerce you fellows ask to sit at your table without any real necessity — from habit, from cowardice, from good-nature, from a hundred sneaking and inadequate reasons.

" 'You Englishmen are all rogues,' went on my patriotic Flensborg or Stettin Australian. I really don't recollect now what decent little port on the shores of the Baltic was defiled by being the nest of that precious bird. 'What are you to shout? Eh? You tell me? You no better than other people, and that old rogue he make Gottam fuss with me.' His thick carcass trembled on its legs that were like a pair of pillars; it trembled from head to foot. 'That's what you English always make — make a tam' fuss — for any little thing, because I was not born in your tam' country. Take away my certificate. Take it. I don't want the certificate. A man like me don't want your verfluchte certificate. I shpit on it.' He spat. 'I vill an Amerigan citizen begome,' he cried, fretting and fuming and shuffling his feet as if to free his ankles from some invisible and mysterious grasp that would not let him get away from that spot. He made himself so warm that the top of his bullet head positively smoked. Nothing mysterious prevented me from going away: curiosity is the most obvious of sentiments, and it held me there to see the effect of a full information upon that young fellow who, hands in pockets, and turning his back upon the sidewalk, gazed across the grass-plots of the Esplanade at the yellow portico of the Malabar Hotel with the air of a man about to go for a walk as soon as his friend is ready. That's how he looked, and it was odious. I waited to see him overwhelmed, confounded, pierced through and through, squirming like an impaled beetle — and I was half afraid to see it too — if you understand what I mean. Nothing more awful than to watch a man who has been found out, not in a crime but in a more than criminal weakness. The commonest sort of fortitude prevents us from becoming criminals in a legal sense; it is from weakness unknown, but perhaps suspected, as in some parts of the world you suspect a deadly snake in every bush — from weakness that may lie hidden, watched or unwatched, prayed against or manfully scorned, repressed or maybe ignored more than half a lifetime, not one of us is safe. We are snared into doing things for which we get called names, and things for which we get hanged, and yet the spirit may well survive — survive the condemnations, survive the halter, by Jove! And there are things — they look small enough sometimes too — by which some of us are totally and completely undone. I watched the youngster there. I liked his appearance; I knew his appearance; he came from the right place; he was one of us. He stood there for all the parentage of his kind, for men and women by no means clever or amusing, but whose very existence is based upon honest faith, and upon the instinct of courage. I don't mean military courage, or civil courage, or any special kind of courage. I mean just that inborn ability to look temptations straight in the face — a readiness unintellectual enough, goodness knows, but without pose — a power of resistance, don't you see, ungracious if you like, but priceless — an unthinking and blessed stiffness before the outward and inward terrors, before the might of nature, and the seductive corruption of men — backed by a faith invulnerable to the strength of facts, to the contagion of example, to the solicitation of ideas. Hang ideas! They are tramps, vagabonds, knocking at the back-door of your mind, each taking a little of your substance, each carrying away some crumb of that belief in a few simple notions you must cling to if you want to live decently and would like to die easy!

"This has nothing to do with Jim, directly; only he was outwardly so typical of that good, stupid kind we like to feel marching right and left of us in life, of the kind that is not disturbed by the vagaries of intelligence and the perversions of — of nerves, let us say. He was the kind of fellow you would, on the strength of his looks, leave in charge of the deck — figuratively and professionally speaking. I say I would, and I ought to know. Haven't I turned out youngsters enough in my time, for the service of the Red Rag, to the craft of the sea, to the craft whose whole secret could be expressed in one short sentence, and yet must be driven afresh every day into young heads till it becomes the component part of every waking thought — till it is present in every dream of their young sleep! The sea has been good to me, but when I remember all these boys that passed through my hands, some grown up now and some drowned by this time, but all good stuff for the sea, I don't think I have done badly by it either. Were I to go home tomorrow, I bet that before two days passed over my head some sunburnt young chief mate would overtake me at some dock gateway or other, and a fresh deep voice speaking above my hat would ask: 'Don't you remember me, sir? Why! little So-and-so. Such and such a ship. It was my first voyage.' And I would remember a bewildered little shaver, no higher than the back of this chair, with a mother and perhaps a big sister on the quay, very quiet but too upset to wave their handkerchiefs at the ship that glides out gently between the pier-heads: or perhaps some decent middle-aged father who had come early with his boy to see him off, and stays all the morning because he is interested in the windlass apparently, and stays too long, and has got to scramble ashore at last with no time at all to say good-bye. The mud pilot on the poop sings out to me in a drawl, 'Hold her with the check line for a moment, Mister Mate. There's a gentleman wants to get shore. . . . Up with you, sir. Nearly got car-

ried off to Talcahuano, didn't you? Now's your time; easy does
it. . . . All right. Slack away again forward there.' The tugs,
smoking like the pit of perdition, get hold and churn the old river
into fury; the gentleman ashore is dusting his knees — the benevolent steward has shied his umbrella after him. All very proper.
He has offered his bit of sacrifice to the sea, and now he may go
home pretending he thinks nothing of it; and the little willing
victim shall be very sea-sick before next morning. By-and-by,
when he has learned all the little mysteries and the one great secret
of the craft, he shall be fit to live or die as the sea may decree;
and the man who had taken a hand in this fool game, in which the
sea wins every toss, will be pleased to have his back slapped by
a heavy young hand, and to hear a cheery sea-puppy voice: 'Do
you remember me, sir? The little So-and-so.'

"I tell you this is good; it tells you that once in your life at
least you had gone the right way to work. I have been thus
slapped, and I have winced, for the slap was heavy, and I have
glowed all day long and gone to bed feeling less lonely in the
world by virtue of that hearty thump. Don't I remember the little So-and-so's! I tell you I ought to know the right kind of
looks. I would have trusted the deck to that youngster on the
strength of a single glance, and gone to sleep with both eyes —
and, by Jove! it wouldn't have been safe. There are depths of
horror in that thought. He looked as genuine as a new sovereign,
but there was some infernal alloy in his metal. How much? The
least thing — the least drop of something rare and accursed; the
least drop! — but he made you — standing there with his don't-
care-hang air — he made you wonder whether perchance he were
nothing more rare than brass.

"I couldn't believe it. I tell you I wanted to see him squirm for
the honour of the craft. The other two no-account chaps spotted their captain, and began to move slowly towards us. They
chatted together as they strolled, and I did not care any more
than if they had not been visible to the naked eye. They grinned
at each other — might have been exchanging jokes, for all I know.
I saw that with one of them it was the case of a broken arm; and
as to the long individual with grey moustaches he was the chief
engineer, and in various ways a pretty notorious personality.
They were nobodies. They approached. The skipper gazed in
an inanimate way between his feet: he seemed to be swollen to

an unnatural size by some awful disease, by the mysterious action of an unknown poison. He lifted his head, saw the two before him waiting, opened his mouth with an extraordinary, sneering contortion of his puffed face — to speak to them, I suppose — and then a thought seemed to strike him. His thick, purplish lips came together without a sound, he went off in a resolute waddle to the gharry and began to jerk at the door-handle with such a blind brutality of impatience that I expected to see the whole concern overturned on its side, pony and all. The driver, shaken out of his meditation over the sole of his foot, displayed at once all the signs of intense terror, and held with both hands, looking round from his box at this vast carcass forcing its way into his conveyance. The little machine shook and rocked tumultuously, and the crimson nape of that lowered neck, the size of those straining thighs, the immense heaving of that dingy, striped green-and-orange back, the whole burrowing effort of that gaudy and sordid mass troubled one's sense of probability with a droll and fearsome effect, like one of those grotesque and distinct visions that scare and fascinate one in a fever. He disappeared. I half expected the roof to split in two, the little box on wheels to burst open in the manner of a ripe cotton-pod — but it only sank with a click of flattened springs, and suddenly one venetian blind rattled down. His shoulders reappeared, jammed in the small opening; his head hung out, distended and tossing like a captive balloon, perspiring, furious, spluttering. He reached for the gharry-wallah with vicious flourishes of a fist as dumpy and red as a lump of raw meat. He roared at him to be off, to go on. Where? Into the Pacific, perhaps. The driver lashed; the pony snorted, reared once, and darted off at a gallop. Where? To Apia? to Honolulu? He had 6,000 miles of tropical belt to disport himself in, and I did not hear the precise address. A snorting pony snatched him into 'ewigkeit' in the twinkling of an eye, and I never saw him again; and, what's more, I don't know of anybody that ever had a glimpse of him after he departed from my knowledge sitting inside a ramshackle little gharry that fled round the corner in a white smother of dust. He departed, disappeared, vanished, absconded; and absurdly enough it looked as though he had taken that gharry with him, for never again did I come across a sorrel pony with a slit ear and a lackadaisical Tamil driver afflicted by a sore foot. The Pacific is indeed big; but whether he found a place for a display of his talents in it or not, the fact remains he had flown into space like a witch on a broomstick. The little chap with his arm in a sling started to run after the carriage, bleating, 'Captain! I say, Captain! I sa-a-ay!' — but after a few steps stopped short, hung his head, and walked back slowly. At the sharp rattle of the wheels the young fellow spun round where he stood. He made no other movement, no gesture, no sign, and remained facing in the new direction after the gharry had swung out of sight.

"All this happened in much less time than it takes to tell, since I am trying to interpret for you into slow speech the instantaneous effect of visual impressions. Next moment the half-caste clerk, sent by Archie to look a little after the poor castaways of the *Patna*, came upon the scene. He ran out eager and bareheaded, looking right and left, and very full of his mission. It was doomed to be a failure as far as the principal person was concerned, but he approached the others with fussy importance, and, almost immediately, found himself involved in a violent altercation with the chap that carried his arm in a sling and who turned out to be extremely anxious for a row. He wasn't going to be ordered about — 'not he, b'gosh.' He wouldn't be terrified with a pack of lies by a cocky half-bred little quill-driver. He was not going to be bullied by 'no object of that sort,' if the story were true 'ever so!' He bawled his wish, his desire, his determination to go to bed. 'If you weren't a God-forsaken Portuguee,' I heard him yell, 'you would know that the hospital is the right place for me.' He pushed the fist of his sound arm under the other's nose; a crowd began to collect; the half-caste, flustered, but doing his best to appear dignified, tried to explain his intentions. I went away without waiting to see the end.

"But it so happened that I had a man in the hospital at the time, and going there to see about him the day before the opening of the Inquiry, I saw in the white men's ward that little chap tossing on his back, with his arm in splints, and quite light-headed. To my great surprise the other one, the long individual with drooping white moustache, had also found his way there. I remembered I had seen him slinking away during the quarrel, in a half prance, half shuffle, and trying very hard not to look scared. He was no stranger to the port, it seems, and in his distress was able to make tracks straight for Mariani's billiard-room and grog-shop near the bazaar. That unspeakable vagabond, Mariani, who had known the man and had ministered to his vices in one or two other places, kissed the ground, in a manner of speaking, before him, and shut him up with a supply of bottles in an upstairs room of his infamous hovel. It appears he was under some hazy apprehension as to his personal safety, and wished to be concealed. However, Mariani told me a long time after (when he came on board one day to dun my steward for the price of some cigars) that he would have done more for him without asking any questions, from gratitude for some unholy favour received very many years ago — as far as I could make out. He thumped twice his brawny chest, rolled enormous black and white eyes glistening with tears: 'Antonio never forget — Antonio never forget!' What was the precise nature of the immoral obligation I never learned, but be it what it may, he had every facility given him to remain under lock and key, with a chair, a table, a mattress in a corner, and a litter of fallen plaster on the floor, in an irrational state of funk, and keeping up his pecker with such tonics as Mariani dispensed. This lasted till the evening of the third day, when, after letting out a few horrible screams, he found himself compelled to seek safety in flight from a legion of centipedes. He burst the door open, made one leap for dear life down the crazy little stairway, landed bodily on Mariani's stomach, picked himself up, and bolted like a rabbit into the streets. The police plucked him off a garbage-heap in the early morning. At first he had a notion they were carrying him off to be hanged, and fought for liberty like a hero, but when I sat down by his bed he had been very quiet for two days. His lean bronzed head, with white moustaches, looked fine and calm on the pillow, like the head of a war-worn soldier with a childlike soul, had it not been for a hint of spectral alarm that lurked in the blank glitter of his glance, resembling a nondescript form of a terror crouching silently behind a pane of glass. He was so extremely calm, that I began to indulge in the eccentric hope of hearing something explanatory of the famous affair from his point of view. Why I longed to go grubbing into the deplorable details of an occurrence which, after all, concerned me no more than as a member of an obscure body of men held together by a community of inglorious toil and by fidelity to a certain standard of conduct, I can't explain. You may call it an unhealthy curi-

osity if you like; but I have a distinct notion I wished to find
something. Perhaps, unconsciously, I hoped I would find that
something, some profound and redeeming cause, some merciful
explanation, some convincing shadow of an excuse. I see well
enough now that I hoped for the impossible — for the laying of
what is the most obstinate ghost of man's creation, of the uneasy
doubt uprising like a mist, secret and gnawing like a worm, and
more chilling than the certitude of death — the doubt of the sovereign power enthroned in a fixed standard of conduct. It is the
hardest thing to stumble against; it is the thing that breeds yelling
panics and good little quiet villainies; it's the true shadow of calamity. Did I believe in a miracle? and why did I desire it so
ardently? Was it for my own sake that I wished to find some
shadow of an excuse for that young fellow whom I had never
seen before, but whose appearance alone added a touch of personal concern to the thoughts suggested by the knowledge of his
weakness — made it a thing of mystery and terror — like a hint
of a destructive fate ready for us all whose youth — in its day —
had resembled his youth? I fear that such was the secret motive
of my prying. I was, and no mistake, looking for a miracle. The
only thing that at this distance of time strikes me as miraculous
is the extent of my imbecility. I positively hoped to obtain from
that battered and shady invalid some exorcism against the ghost
of doubt. I must have been pretty desperate too, for, without a
loss of time, after a few indifferent and friendly sentences which
he answered with languid readiness, just as any decent sick man
would do, I produced the word *Patna* wrapped up in a delicate
question as in a wisp of floss silk. I was delicate selfishly; I did
not want to startle him; I had no solicitude for him; I was not
furious with him and sorry for him: his experience was of no importance, his redemption would have had no point for me. He
had grown old in minor iniquities, and could no longer inspire
aversion or pity. He repeated *Patna?* interrogatively, seemed to
make a short effort of memory and said: 'Quite right. I am an
old stager out here. I saw her go down.' I made ready to vent
my indignation at such a stupid lie, when he added smoothly,
'She was full of reptiles.'

"This made me pause. What did he mean? The unsteady phantom of terror behind his glassy eyes seemed to stand still and look
into mine wistfully. 'They turned me out of my bunk in the

middle watch to look at her sinking,' he pursued in a reflective tone. His voice sounded alarmingly strong all at once. I was sorry for my folly. There was no snowy-winged coif of a nursing sister to be seen flitting in the perspective of the ward; but away in the middle of a long row of empty iron bedsteads an accident case from some ship in the Roads sat up brown and gaunt with a white bandage set rakishly on the forehead. Suddenly my interesting invalid shot out an arm thin like a tentacle and clawed my shoulder. 'Only my eyes were good enough to see. I am famous for my eyesight. That's why they called me, I expect. None of them was quick enough to see her go, but they saw that she was gone right enough, and sang out together — like this.' . . . A wolfish howl searched the very recesses of my soul. 'Oh! make 'im dry up,' whined the accident case irritably. 'You don't believe me, I suppose,' went on the other, with an air of ineffable conceit. 'I tell you there are no such eyes as mine this side of the Persian Gulf. Look under the bed.'

"Of course I stooped instantly. I defy anybody not to have done so. 'What can you see?' he asked. 'Nothing,' I said, feeling awfully ashamed of myself. He scrutinised my face with wild and withering contempt. 'Just so,' he said, 'but if I were to look I could see — there's no eyes like mine, I tell you.' Again he clawed, pulling at me downwards in his eagerness to relieve himself by a confidential communication. 'Millions of pink toads. There's no eyes like mine. Millions of pink toads. It's worse than seeing a ship sink. I could look at sinking ships and smoke my pipe all day long. Why don't they give me back my pipe? I would get a smoke while I watched these toads. The ship was full of them. They've got to be watched, you know.' He winked facetiously. The perspiration dripped on him off my head, my drill coat clung to my wet back: the afternoon breeze swept impetuously over the row of bedsteads, the stiff folds of curtains stirred perpendicularly, rattling on brass rods, the covers of empty beds blew about noiselessly near the bare floor all along the line, and I shivered to the very marrow. The soft wind of the tropics played in that naked ward as bleak as a winter's gale in an old barn at home. 'Don't you let him start his hollering, mister,' hailed from afar the accident case in a distressed angry shout that came ringing between the walls like a quavering call down a tunnel. The clawing hand hauled at my shoulder; he leered at me knowingly. 'The

ship was full of them, you know, and we had to clear out on the
strict Q. T.,' he whispered with extreme rapidity. 'All pink. All
pink — as big as mastiffs, with an eye on the top of the head and
claws all round their ugly mouths. Ough! Ough!' Quick jerks as
of galvanic shocks disclosed under the flat coverlet the outlines
of meagre and agitated legs; he let go my shoulder and reached
after something in the air; his body trembled tensely like a released harp-string; and while I looked down, the spectral horror
in him broke through his glassy gaze. Instantly his face of an old
soldier, with its noble and calm outlines, became decomposed before my eyes by the corruption of stealthy cunning, of an abominable caution and of desperate fear. He restrained a cry — 'Ssh!
what are they doing now down there?' he asked, pointing to the
floor with fantastic precautions of voice and gesture, whose meaning, borne upon my mind in a lurid flash, made me very sick of
my cleverness. 'They are all asleep,' I answered, watching him
narrowly. That was it. That's what he wanted to hear; these
were the exact words that could calm him. He drew a long
breath. 'Ssh! Quiet, steady. I am an old stager out here. I know
them brutes. Bash in the head of the first that stirs. There's too
many of them, and she won't swim more than ten minutes.' He
panted again. 'Hurry up,' he yelled suddenly, and went on in a
steady scream: 'They are all awake — millions of them. They are
trampling on me! Wait! Oh, wait! I'll smash them in heaps like
flies. Wait for me! Help! H-e-elp!' An interminable and sustained howl completed my discomfiture. I saw in the distance the
accident case raise deplorably both his hands to his bandaged
head; a dresser, aproned to the chin, showed himself in the vista
of the ward, as if seen in the small end of a telescope. I confessed
myself fairly routed, and without more ado, stepping out through
one of the long windows, escaped into the outside gallery. The
howl pursued me like a vengeance. I turned into a deserted landing, and suddenly all became very still and quiet around me, and
I descended the bare and shiny staircase in a silence that enabled
me to compose my distracted thoughts. Down below I met one
of the resident surgeons who was crossing the courtyard and
stopped me. 'Been to see your man, Captain? I think we may let
him go to-morrow. These fools have no notion of taking care of
themselves, though. I say, we've got the chief engineer of that
pilgrim ship here. A curious case. D. T.'s of the worst kind. He

has been drinking hard in that Greek's or Italian's grog-shop for three days. What can you expect? Four bottles of that kind of brandy a day, I am told. Wonderful, if true. Sheeted with boiler-iron inside, I should think. The head, ah! the head, of course, gone, but the curious part is there's some sort of method in his raving. I am trying to find out. Most unusual — that thread of logic in such a delirium. Traditionally he ought to see snakes, but he doesn't. Good old tradition's at a discount nowadays. Eh! His — er — visions are batrachian. Ha! ha! No, seriously, I never remember being so interested in a case of jimjams before. He ought to be dead, don't you know, after such a festive experiment. Oh! he is a tough object. Four-and-twenty years of the tropics too. You ought really to take a peep at him. Noble-looking old boozer. Most extraordinary man I ever met — medically, of course. Won't you?'

"I had been all along exhibiting the usual polite signs of interest, but now assuming an air of regret I murmured of want of time, and shook hands in a hurry. 'I say,' he cried after me, 'he can't attend that inquiry. Is his evidence material, you think?'

" 'Not in the least,' I called back from the gateway."

CHAPTER VI

THE authorities were evidently of the same opinion. The inquiry was not adjourned. It was held on the appointed day to satisfy the law, and it was well attended because of its human interest, no doubt. There was no incertitude as to facts — as to the one material fact, I mean. How the *Patna* came by her hurt it was impossible to find out; the court did not expect to find out; and in the whole audience there was not a man who cared. Yet, as I've told you, all the sailors in the port attended, and the water-side business was fully represented. Whether they knew it or not, the interest that drew them there was purely psychological — the expectation of some essential disclosure as to the strength, the power, the horror, of human emotions. Naturally nothing of the

kind could be disclosed. The examination of the only man able
and willing to face it was beating futilely round the well-known
fact, and the play of questions upon it was as instructive as the
tapping with a hammer on an iron box, were the object to find
out what's inside. However, an official inquiry could not be any
other thing. Its object was not the fundamental why, but the
superficial how, of this affair.

"The young chap could have told them, and, though that very
thing was the thing that interested the audience, the questions put
to him necessarily led him away from what to me, for instance,
would have been the only truth worth knowing. You can't expect
the constituted authorities to inquire into the state of a man's soul
— or is it only of his liver? Their business was to come down upon
the consequences, and frankly, a casual police magistrate and two
nautical assessors are not much good for anything else. I don't
mean to imply these fellows were stupid. The magistrate was very
patient. One of the assessors was a sailing-ship skipper with a
reddish beard, and of a pious disposition. Brierly was the other.
Big Brierly. Some of you must have heard of Big Brierly — the
captain of the crack ship of the Blue Star line. That's the man.

"He seemed consumedly bored by the honour thrust upon him.
He had never in his life made a mistake, never had an accident,
never a mishap, never a check in his steady rise, and he seemed to
be one of those lucky fellows who know nothing of indecision,
much less of self-mistrust. At thirty-two he had one of the best
commands going in the Eastern trade — and, what's more, he
thought a lot of what he had. There was nothing like it in the
world, and I suppose if you had asked him point-blank he would
have confessed that in his opinion there was not such another
commander. The choice had fallen upon the right man. The rest
of mankind that did not command the sixteen-knot steel steamer
Ossa were rather poor creatures. He had saved lives at sea, had
rescued ships in distress, had a gold chronometer presented to him
by the underwriters, and a pair of binoculars with a suitable in-
scription from some foreign Government, in commemoration of
these services. He was acutely aware of his merits and of his
rewards. I liked him well enough, though some I know — meek,
friendly men at that — couldn't stand him at any price. I haven't
the slightest doubt he considered himself vastly my superior —
indeed, had you been Emperor of East and West, you could not

have ignored your inferiority in his presence — but I couldn't get
up any real sentiment of offence. He did not despise me for anything I could help, for anything I was — don't you know? I was
a negligible quantity simply because I was not *the* fortunate man
of the earth, not Montague Brierly in command of the *Ossa*, not
the owner of an inscribed gold chronometer and of silver-mounted
binoculars testifying to the excellence of my seamanship and to
my indomitable pluck; not possessed of an acute sense of my merits and of my rewards, besides the love and worship of a black
retriever, the most wonderful of its kind — for never was such a
man loved thus by such a dog. No doubt, to have all this forced
upon you was exasperating enough; but when I reflected that I
was associated in these fatal disadvantages with twelve hundred
millions of other more or less human beings, I found I could bear
my share of his good-natured and contemptuous pity for the sake
of something indefinite and attractive in the man. I have never
defined to myself this attraction, but there were moments when
I envied him. The sting of life could do no more to his com-
placent soul than the scratch of a pin to the smooth face of a rock.
This was enviable. As I looked at him flanking on one side the
unassuming pale-faced magistrate who presided at the inquiry, his
self-satisfaction presented to me and to the world a surface as
hard as granite. He committed suicide very soon after.

"No wonder Jim's case bored him, and while I thought with
something akin to fear of the immensity of his contempt for the
young man under examination, he was probably holding silent
inquiry into his own case. The verdict must have been of un-
mitigated guilt, and he took the secret of the evidence with him
in that leap into the sea. If I understand anything of men, the
matter was no doubt of the gravest import, one of those trifles
that awaken ideas — start into life some thought with which a
man unused to such a companionship finds it impossible to live.
I am in a position to know that it wasn't money, and it wasn't
drink, and it wasn't woman. He jumped overboard at sea barely
a week after the end of the inquiry, and less than three days after
leaving port on his outward passage; as though on that exact spot
in the midst of waters he had suddenly perceived the gates of the
other world flung open wide for his reception.

"Yet it was not a sudden impulse. His grey-headed mate, a
first-rate sailor and a nice old chap with strangers, but in his rela-

tions with his commander the surliest chief-officer I've ever seen, would tell the story with tears in his eyes. It appears that when he came on deck in the morning Brierly had been writing in the chart-room. 'It was ten minutes to four,' he said, 'and the middle watch was not relieved yet of course. He heard my voice on the bridge speaking to the second mate, and called me in. I was loth to go, and that's the truth, Captain Marlow — I couldn't stand poor Captain Brierly, I tell you with shame; we never know what a man is made of. He had been promoted over too many heads, not counting my own, and he had a damnable trick of making you feel small, nothing but by the way he said "Good morning." I never addressed him, sir, but on matters of duty, and then it was as much as I could do to keep a civil tongue in my head.' (He flattered himself there. I often wondered how Brierly could put up with his manners for more than half a voyage.) 'I've a wife and children,' he went on, 'and I had been ten years in the Company, always expecting the next command — more fool I. Says he, just like this: "Come in here, Mr. Jones," in that swagger voice of his — "Come in here, Mr. Jones." In I went. "We'll lay down her position," says he, stooping over the chart, a pair of dividers in hand. By the standing orders, the officer going off duty would have done that at the end of his watch. However, I said nothing, and looked on while he marked off the ship's position with a tiny cross and wrote the date and the time. I can see him this moment writing his neat figures: seventeen, eight, four A. M. The year would be written in red ink at the top of the chart. He never used his charts more than a year, Captain Brierly didn't. I've the chart now. When he had done he stands looking down at the mark he had made and smiling to himself, then looks up at me. "Thirty-two miles more as she goes," says he, "and then we shall be clear, and you may alter the course twenty degrees to the southward."

" 'We were passing to the north of the Hector Bank that voyage. I said, "All right, sir," wondering what he was fussing about, since I had to call him before altering the course anyhow. Just then eight bells were struck: we came out on the bridge, and the second mate before going off mentions in the usual way — "Seventy-one on the log." Captain Brierly looks at the compass and then all round. It was dark and clear, and all the stars were out as plain as on a frosty night in high latitudes. Suddenly he says with a sort of a little sigh: "I am going aft, and shall set the log at zero for you myself, so that there can be no mistake. Thirty-two miles more on this course and then you are safe. Let's see — the correction on the log is six per cent. additive; say, then, thirty by the dial to run, and you may come twenty degrees to starboard at once. No use losing any distance — is there?" I had never heard him talk so much at a stretch, and to no purpose as it seemed to me. I said nothing. He went down the ladder, and the dog, that was always at his heels whenever he moved, night or day, followed, sliding nose first, after him. I heard his boot-heels tap, tap on the after-deck, then he stopped and spoke to the dog — "Go back, Rover. On the bridge, boy! Go on — get." Then he calls out to me from the dark, "Shut that dog up in the chart-room, Mr. Jones — will you?"

" 'This was the last time I heard his voice, Captain Marlow. These are the last words he spoke in the hearing of any living human being, sir.' At this point the old chap's voice got quite unsteady. 'He was afraid the poor brute would jump after him, don't you see?' he pursued with a quaver. 'Yes, Captain Marlow. He set the log for me; he — would you believe it? — he put a drop of oil in it too. There was the oil-feeder where he left it near by. The boatswain's mate got the hose along aft to wash down at half-past five; by-and-by he knocks off and runs up on the bridge — "Will you please come aft, Mr. Jones," he says. "There's a funny thing. I don't like to touch it." It was Captain Brierly's gold chronometer watch carefully hung under the rail by its chain.

" 'As soon as my eyes fell on it something struck me, and I knew, sir. My legs got soft under me. It was as if I had seen him go over; and I could tell how far behind he was left too. The taffrail-log marked eighteen miles and three-quarters, and four iron belaying-pins were missing round the mainmast. Put them in his pockets to help him down, I suppose; but, Lord! what's four iron pins to a powerful man like Captain Brierly. Maybe his confidence in himself was just shook a bit at the last. That's the only sign of fluster he gave in his whole life, I should think; but I am ready to answer for him, that once over he did not try to swim a stroke, the same as he would have had pluck enough to keep up all day long on the bare chance had he fallen over-board accidentally. Yes, sir. He was second to none — if he said so himself, as I heard him once. He had written two letters in

the middle watch, one to the Company and the other to me. He
gave me a lot of instructions as to the passage — I had been in the
trade before he was out of his time — and no end of hints as to my
conduct with our people in Shanghai, so that I should keep the
command of the *Ossa*. He wrote like a father would to a favourite son, Captain Marlow, and I was five-and-twenty years his
senior and had tasted salt water before he was fairly breeched.
In his letter to the owners — it was left open for me to see — he
said that he had always done his duty by them — up to that moment — and even now he was not betraying their confidence, since
he was leaving the ship to as competent a seaman as could be
found — meaning me, sir, meaning me! He told them that if the
last act of his life didn't take away all his credit with them, they
would give weight to my faithful service and to his warm recommendation, when about to fill the vacancy made by his death.
And much more like this, sir. I couldn't believe my eyes. It made
me feel queer all over,' went on the old chap in great perturbation, and squashing something in the corner of his eye with the
end of a thumb as broad as a spatula. 'You would think, sir, he
had jumped overboard only to give an unlucky man a last show
to get on. What with the shock of him going in this awful rash
way, and thinking myself a made man by that chance, I was nearly
off my chump for a week. But no fear. The captain of the *Pelion*
was shifted into the *Ossa* — came aboard in Shanghai — a little pop-
injay, sir, in a grey check suit, with his hair parted in the middle.
"Aw — I am — aw — your new captain, Mister — mister — aw —
Jones." He was drowned in scent — fairly stunk with it, Captain
Marlow. I daresay it was the look I gave him that made him
stammer. He mumbled something about my natural disappointment — I had better know at once that his chief officer got the
promotion to the *Pelion* — he had nothing to do with it, of course
— supposed the office knew best — sorry. . . . Says I, "Don't you
mind old Jones, sir; damn his soul, he's used to it." I could see
directly I had shocked his delicate ear, and while we sat at our
first tiffin together he began to find fault in a nasty manner with
this and that in the ship. I never heard such a voice out of a
Punch and Judy show. I set my teeth hard, and glued my eyes
to my plate, and held my peace as long as I could; but at last I
had to say something: up he jumps tiptoeing, ruffling all his pretty
plumes, like a little fighting cock. "You'll find you have a differ-

ent person to deal with than the late Captain Brierly." "I've found it," says I, very glum, but pretending to be mighty busy with my steak. "You are an old ruffian, Mr. — aw — Jones; and what's more, you are known for an old ruffian in the employ," he squeaks at me. The damned bottle-washers stood about listening with their mouths stretched from ear to ear. "I may be a hard case," answers I, "but I ain't so far gone as to put up with the sight of you sitting in Captain Brierly's chair." With that I lay down my knife and fork. "You would like to sit in it yourself — that's where the shoe pinches," he sneers. I left the saloon, got my rags together, and was on the quay with all my dunnage about my feet before the stevedores had turned to again. Yes. Adrift — on shore — after ten years' service — and with a poor woman and four children six thousand miles off depending on my half-pay for every mouthful they ate. Yes, sir! I chucked it rather than hear Captain Brierly abused. He left me his night-glasses — here they are; and he wished me to take care of the dog — here he is. Hallo, Rover, poor boy. Where's the captain, Rover?' The dog looked up at us with mournful yellow eyes, gave one desolate bark, and crept under the table.

"All this was taking place, more than two years afterwards, on board that nautical ruin the *Fire-Queen* this Jones had got charge of — quite by a funny accident, too — from Matherson — mad Matherson they generally called him — the same who used to hang out in Haï-phong, you know, before the occupation days. The old chap snuffled on —

" 'Ay, sir, Captain Brierly will be remembered here, if there's no other place on earth. I wrote fully to his father and did not get a word in reply — neither Thank you, nor Go to the devil! — nothing! Perhaps they did not want to know.'

"The sight of that watery-eyed old Jones mopping his bald head with a red cotton handkerchief, the sorrowing yelp of the dog, the squalor of that flyblown cuddy which was the only shrine of his memory, threw a veil of inexpressibly mean pathos over Brierly's remembered figure, the posthumous revenge of fate for that belief in his own splendour which had almost cheated his life of its legitimate terrors. Almost! Perhaps wholly. Who can tell what flattering view he had induced himself to take of his own suicide?

" 'Why did he commit the rash act, Captain Marlow — can

you think?' asked Jones, pressing his palms together. 'Why? It
beats me! Why?' He slapped his low and wrinkled forehead.
'If he had been poor and old and in debt — and never a show —
or else mad. But he wasn't of the kind that goes mad, not he.
You trust me. What a mate don't know about his skipper isn't
worth knowing. Young, healthy, well off, no cares. . . . I sit
here sometimes thinking, thinking, till my head fairly begins to
buzz. There was some reason.'

" 'You may depend on it, Captain Jones,' said I, 'it wasn't anything that would have disturbed much either of us two,' I said;
and then, as if a light had been flashed into the muddle of his
brain, poor old Jones found a last word of amazing profundity.
He blew his nose, nodding at me dolefully: 'Ay, ay! neither you
nor I, sir, had ever thought so much of ourselves.'

"Of course the recollection of my last conversation with Brierly
is tinged with the knowledge of his end that followed so close
upon it. I spoke with him for the last time during the progress
of the inquiry. It was after the first adjournment, and he came
up with me in the street. He was in a state of irritation, which
I noticed with surprise, his usual behaviour when he condescended
to converse being perfectly cool, with a trace of amused tolerance, as if the existence of his interlocutor had been a rather
good joke. 'They caught me for that inquiry, you see,' he began, and for a while enlarged complainingly upon the inconven-
iences of daily attendance in court. 'And goodness knows how
long it will last. Three days, I suppose.' I heard him out in
silence; in my then opinion it was a way as good as another of
putting on side. 'What's the use of it? It is the stupidest set
out you can imagine,' he pursued, hotly. I remarked that there
was no option. He interrupted me with a sort of pent-up violence. 'I feel like a fool all the time.' I looked up at him. This
was going very far — for Brierly — when talking of Brierly. He
stopped short, and seizing the lappel of my coat, gave it a slight
tug. 'Why are we tormenting that young chap?' he asked. This
question chimed in so well to the tolling of a certain thought of
mine that, with the image of the absconding renegade in my
eye, I answered at once, 'Hanged if I know, unless it be that he
lets you.' I was astonished to see him fall into line, so to speak,
with that utterance, which ought to have been tolerably cryptic.
He said angrily, 'Why, yes. Can't he see that wretched skipper

of his has cleared out? What does he expect to happen? Nothing can save him. He's done for.' We walked on in silence a few steps. 'Why eat all that dirt?' he exclaimed, with an oriental energy of expression — about the only sort of energy you can find a trace of east of the fiftieth meridian. I wondered greatly at the direction of his thoughts, but now I strongly suspect it was strictly in character: at bottom poor Brierly must have been thinking of himself. I pointed out to him that the skipper of the *Patna* was known to have feathered his nest pretty well, and could procure almost anywhere the means of getting away. With Jim it was otherwise: the Government was keeping him in the Sailors' Home for the time being, and probably he hadn't a penny in his pocket to bless himself with. It costs some money to run away. 'Does it? Not always,' he said, with a bitter laugh, and to some further remark of mine — 'Well, then, let him creep twenty feet underground and stay there! By heavens! *I* would.' I don't know why his tone provoked me, and I said, 'There is a kind of courage in facing it out as he does, knowing very well that if he went away nobody would trouble to run after him.' 'Courage be hanged!' growled Brierly. 'That sort of courage is of no use to keep a man straight, and I don't care a snap for such courage. If you were to say it was a kind of cowardice now — of softness. I tell you what, I will put up two hundred rupees if you put up another hundred and undertake to make the beggar clear out early to-morrow morning. The fellow's a gentleman if he ain't fit to be touched — he will understand. He must! This infernal publicity is too shocking: there he sits while all these confounded natives, serangs, lascars, quartermasters, are giving evidence that's enough to burn a man to ashes with shame. This is abominable. Why, Marlow, don't you think, don't you feel, that this is abominable; don't you now — come — as a seaman? If he went away all this would stop at once.' Brierly said these words with a most unusual animation, and made as if to reach after his pocket-book. I restrained him, and declared coldly that the cowardice of these four men did not seem to me a matter of such great importance. 'And you call yourself a seaman, I suppose,' he pronounced, angrily. I said that's what I called myself, and I hoped I was too. He heard me out, and made a gesture with his big arm that seemed to deprive me of my individuality, to push me away into the crowd. 'The worst of it,' he said, 'is that all you fellows have no sense of dignity; you don't think enough of what you are supposed to be.'

"We had been walking slowly meantime, and now stopped opposite the harbour office, in sight of the very spot from which the immense captain of the *Patna* had vanished as utterly as a tiny feather blown away in a hurricane. I smiled. Brierly went on: 'This is a disgrace. We've got all kinds amongst us — some anointed scoundrels in the lot; but, hang it, we must preserve professional decency or we become no better than so many tinkers going about loose. We are trusted. Do you understand? — trusted! Frankly, I don't care a snap for all the pilgrims that ever came out of Asia, but a decent man would not have behaved like this to a full cargo of old rags in bales. We aren't an organised body of men, and the only thing that holds us together is just the name for that kind of decency. Such an affair destroys one's confidence. A man may go pretty near through his whole sea-life without any call to show a stiff upper lip. But when the call comes . . . Aha! . . . If I . . .'

"He broke off, and in a changed tone, 'I'll give you two hundred rupees now, Marlow, and you just talk to that chap. Confound him! I wish he had never come out here. Fact is, I rather think some of my people know his. The old man's a parson, and I remember now I met him once when staying with my cousin in Essex last year. If I am not mistaken, the old chap seemed rather to fancy his sailor son. Horrible. I can't do it myself — but you . . .'

"Thus, apropos of Jim, I had a glimpse of the real Brierly a few days before he committed his reality and his sham together to the keeping of the sea. Of course I declined to meddle. The tone of this last 'but you' (poor Brierly couldn't help it), that seemed to imply I was no more noticeable than an insect, caused me to look at the proposal with indignation, and on account of that provocation, or for some other reason, I became positive in my mind that the inquiry was a severe punishment to that Jim, and that his facing it — practically of his own free will — was a redeeming feature in his abominable case. I hadn't been so sure of it before. Brierly went off in a huff. At the time his state of mind was more of a mystery to me than it is now.

"Next day, coming into court late, I sat by myself. Of course I could not forget the conversation I had with Brierly, and now

I had them both under my eyes. The demeanour of one suggested gloomy impudence and of the other a contemptuous boredom; yet one attitude might not have been truer than the other,
and I was aware that one was not true. Brierly was not bored
— he was exasperated; and if so, then Jim might not have been
impudent. According to my theory he was not. I imagined
he was hopeless. Then it was that our glances met. They met,
and the look he gave me was discouraging of any intention
I might have had to speak to him. Upon either hypothesis
— insolence or despair — I felt I could be of no use to him. This
was the second day of the proceedings. Very soon after that
exchange of glances the inquiry was adjourned again to the
next day. The white men began to troop out at once. Jim
had been told to stand down some time before, and was able to
leave amongst the first. I saw his broad shoulders and his head
outlined in the light of the door, and while I made my way slowly
out talking with some one — some stranger who had addressed me
casually — I could see him from within the court-room resting
both elbows on the balustrade of the verandah and turning his
back on the small stream of people trickling down the few steps.
There was a murmur of voices and a shuffle of boots.

"The next case was that of assault and battery committed upon
a money-lender, I believe; and the defendant — a venerable villager with a straight white beard — sat on a mat just outside the
door with his sons, daughters, sons-in-law, their wives, and, I
should think, half the population of his village besides, squatting
or standing around him. A slim dark woman, with part of her
back and one black shoulder bared, and with a thin gold ring in
her nose, suddenly began to talk in a high-pitched, shrewish tone.
The man with me instinctively looked up at her. We were then
just through the door, passing behind Jim's burly back.

"Whether those villagers had brought the yellow dog with
them, I don't know. Anyhow, a dog was there, weaving himself
in and out amongst people's legs in that mute stealthy way native
dogs have and my companion stumbled over him. The dog leaped
away without a sound; the man, raising his voice a little, said with
a slow laugh, 'Look at that wretched cur,' and directly afterwards
we became separated by a lot of people pushing in. I stood back
for a moment against the wall while the stranger managed to get
down the steps and disappeared. I saw Jim spin round. He made

a step forward and barred my way. We were alone; he glared at me with an air of stubborn resolution. I became aware I was being held up, so to speak, as if in a wood. The verandah was empty by then, the noise and movement in court had ceased: a great silence fell upon the building, in which, somewhere far within, an oriental voice began to whine abjectly. The dog in the very act of trying to sneak in at the door, sat down hurriedly to hunt for fleas.

" 'Did you speak to me?' asked Jim very low, and bending forward, not so much towards me but at me, if you know what I mean. I said 'No' at once. Something in the sound of that quiet tone of his warned me to be on my defence. I watched him. It was very much like a meeting in a wood, only more uncertain in its issue, since he could possibly want neither my money nor my life — nothing that I could simply give up or defend with a clear conscience. 'You say you didn't,' he said, very sombre. 'But I heard.' 'Some mistake,' I protested, utterly at a loss, and never taking my eyes off him. To watch his face was like watching a darkening sky before a clap of thunder, shade upon shade imperceptibly coming on, the gloom growing mysteriously intense in the calm of maturing violence.

" 'As far as I know, I haven't opened my lips in your hearing,' I affirmed with perfect truth. I was getting a little angry, too, at the absurdity of this encounter. It strikes me now I have never in my life been so near a beating — I mean it literally; a beating with.fists. I suppose I had some hazy prescience of that eventuality being in the air. Not that he was actively threatening me. On the contrary, he was strangely passive — don't you know? but he was lowering, and, though not exceptionally big, he looked generally fit to demolish a wall. The most reassuring symptom I noticed was a kind of slow and ponderous hesitation, which I took as a tribute to the evident sincerity of my manner and of my tone. We faced each other. In the court the assault case was proceeding. I caught the words: 'Well — buffalo — stick — in the greatness of my fear. . . .'

" 'What did you mean by staring at me all the morning?' said Jim at last. He looked up and looked down again. 'Did you expect us all to sit with downcast eyes out of regard for your susceptibilities?' I retorted sharply. I was not going to submit meekly to any of his nonsense. He raised his eyes again, and this time

continued to look me straight in the face. 'No. That's all right,'
he pronounced with an air of deliberating with himself upon the
truth of this statement — 'that's all right. I am going through with
that. Only' — and there he spoke a little faster — 'I won't let any
man call me names outside this court. There was a fellow with
you. You spoke to him — oh, yes — I know; 'tis all very fine. You
spoke to him, but you meant me to hear. . . .'

"I assured him he was under some extraordinary delusion. I
had no conception how it came about. 'You thought I would be
afraid to resent this,' he said, with just a faint tinge of bitterness.
I was interested enough to discern the slightest shades of expression, but I was not in the least enlightened; yet I don't know what
in these words, or perhaps just the intonation of that phrase, induced me suddenly to make all possible allowances for him. I
ceased to be annoyed at my unexpected predicament. It was some
mistake on his part; he was blundering and I had an intuition that
the blunder was of an odious, of an unfortunate nature. I was
anxious to end this scene on grounds of decency, just as one is anxious to cut short some unprovoked and abominable confidence.
The funniest part was, that in the midst of all these considerations
of the higher order I was conscious of a certain trepidation as to
the possibility — nay, likelihood — of this encounter ending in
some disreputable brawl which could not possibly be explained,
and would make me ridiculous. I did not hanker after a three
days' celebrity as the man who got a black eye or something of
the sort from the mate of the *Patna*. He, in all probability, did
not care what he did, or at any rate would be fully justified in
his own eyes. It took no magician to see he was amazingly angry
about something, for all his quiet and even torpid demeanour.
I don't deny I was extremely desirous to pacify him at all costs,
had I only known what to do. But I didn't know, as you may well
imagine. It was blackness without a single gleam. We confronted
each other in silence. He hung fire for about fifteen seconds, then
made a step nearer, and I made ready to ward off a blow, though
I don't think I moved a muscle. 'If you were as big as two men
and as strong as six,' he said very softly, 'I would tell you what
I think of you. You . . .' 'Stop!' I exclaimed. This checked him
for a second. 'Before you tell me what you think of me,' I went
on, quickly, 'will you kindly tell me what it is I've said or done?'
During the pause that ensued he surveyed me with indignation,

while I made supernatural efforts of memory, in which I was hindered by the oriental voice within the court-room expostulating with impassioned volubility against a charge of falsehood. Then we spoke almost together. 'I will soon show you I am not,' he said, in a tone suggestive of a crisis. 'I declare I don't know,' I protested earnestly at the same time. He tried to crush me by the scorn of his glance. 'Now that you see I am not afraid you try to crawl out of it,' he said. 'Who's a cur now — hey?' Then, at last, I understood.

"He had been scanning my features as though looking for a place where he would plant his fist. 'I will allow no man,' . . . he mumbled, threateningly. It was, indeed, a hideous mistake; he had given himself away utterly. I can't give you an idea how shocked I was. I suppose he saw some reflection of my feelings in my face, because his expression changed just a little. 'Good God!' I stammered, 'you don't think I . . .' 'But I am sure I've heard,' he persisted, raising his voice for the first time since the beginning of this deplorable scene. Then with a shade of disdain he added, 'It wasn't you, then? Very well; I'll find the other.' 'Don't be a fool,' I cried in exasperation; 'it wasn't that at all.' 'I've heard,' he said again with an unshaken and sombre perseverance.

"There may be those who could have laughed at his pertinacity. I didn't. Oh, I didn't! There had never been a man so mercilessly shown up by his own natural impulse. A single word had stripped him of his discretion — of that discretion which is more necessary to the decencies of our inner being than clothing is to the decorum of our body. 'Don't be a fool,' I repeated. 'But the other man said it, you don't deny that?' he pronounced, distinctly, and looking in my face without flinching. 'No, I don't deny,' said I, returning his gaze. At last his eyes followed downwards the direction of my pointing finger. He appeared at first uncomprehending, then confounded, and at last amazed and scared as though a dog had been a monster and he had never seen a dog before. 'Nobody dreamt of insulting you,' I said.

"He contemplated the wretched animal, that moved no more than an effigy: it sat with ears pricked and its sharp muzzle pointed into the doorway, and suddenly snapped at a fly like a piece of mechanism.

"I looked at him. The red of his fair sunburnt complexion deepened suddenly under the down of his cheeks, invaded his forehead, spread to the roots of his curly hair. His ears became intensely crimson, and even the clear blue of his eyes was darkened many shades by the rush of blood to his head. His lips pouted a little, trembling as though he had been on the point of bursting into tears. I perceived he was incapable of pronouncing a word from the excess of his humiliation. From disappointment too — who knows? Perhaps he looked forward to that hammering he was going to give me for rehabilitation, for appeasement? Who can tell what relief he expected from this chance of a row? He was naïve enough to expect anything; but he had given himself away for nothing in this case. He had been frank with himself — let alone with me — in the wild hope of arriving in that way at some effective refutation, and the stars had been ironically unpropitious. He made an inarticulate noise in his throat like a man imperfectly stunned by a blow on the head. It was pitiful.

"I didn't catch up again with him till well outside the gate. I had even to trot a bit at the last, but when, out of breath at his elbow, I taxed him with running away, he said, 'Never!' and at once turned at bay. I explained I never meant to say he was running away from *me*. 'From no man — from not a single man on earth,' he affirmed with a stubborn mien. I forebore to point out the one obvious exception which would hold good for the bravest of us; I thought he would find out by himself very soon. He looked at me patiently while I was thinking of something to say, but I could find nothing on the spur of the moment, and he began to walk on. I kept up, and anxious not to lose him, I said hurriedly that I couldn't think of leaving him under a false impression of my — of my — I stammered. The stupidity of the phrase appalled me while I was trying to finish it, but the power of sentences has nothing to do with their sense or the logic of their construction. My idiotic mumble seemed to please him. He cut it short by saying, with courteous placidity that argued an immense power of self-control or else a wonderful elasticity of spirits — 'Altogether my mistake.' I marvelled greatly at this expression: he might have been alluding to some trifling occurrence. Hadn't he understood its deplorable meaning? 'You may well forgive me,' he continued, and went on a little moodily, 'All these staring people in court seemed such fools that — that it might have been as I supposed.'

"This opened suddenly a new view of him to my wonder. I looked at him curiously and met his unabashed and impenetrable eyes. 'I can't put up with this kind of thing,' he said, very simply, 'and I don't mean to. In court it's different; I've got to stand that — and I can do it too.'

"I don't pretend I understood him. The views he let me have of himself were like those glimpses through the shifting rents in a thick fog — bits of vivid and vanishing detail, giving no connected idea of the general aspect of a country. They fed one's curiosity without satisfying it; they were no good for purposes of orientation. Upon the whole he was misleading. That's how I summed him up to myself after he left me late in the evening. I had been staying at the Malabar House for a few days, and on my pressing invitation he dined with me there."

CHAPTER VII

"An outward-bound mail-boat had come in that afternoon, and the big dining-room of the hotel was more than half full of people with a hundred pounds round-the-world tickets in their pockets. There were married couples looking domesticated and bored with each other in the midst of their travels; there were small parties and large parties, and lone individuals dining solemnly or feasting boisterously, but all thinking, conversing, joking, or scowling as was their wont at home; and just as intelligently receptive of new impressions as their trunks upstairs. Henceforth they would be labelled as having passed through this and that place, and so would be their luggage. They would cherish this distinction of their persons, and preserve the gummed tickets on their portmanteaus as documentary evidence, as the only permanent trace of their improving enterprise. The dark-faced servants tripped without noise over the vast and polished floor; now and then a girl's laugh would be heard, as innocent and empty as her mind, or, in a sudden hush of crockery, a few words in an affected drawl from some wit embroidering for the benefit of a grinning tableful the last funny story of shipboard scandal. Two nomadic old maids, dressed up to kill, worked acrimoniously through the bill of fare, whispering to each other with faded lips, wooden-faced and bizarre, like two sumptuous scarecrows. A little wine opened Jim's heart and loosened his tongue. His appetite was good, too, I noticed. He seemed to have buried somewhere the opening episode of our acquaintance. It was like a thing of which there would be no more question in this world. And all the time I had before me these blue, boyish eyes looking straight into mine, this young face, these capable shoulders, the open bronzed forehead with a white line under the roots of clustering fair hair, this appearance appealing at sight to all my sympathies: this frank aspect, the artless smile, the youthful seriousness. He was of the right sort; he was one of us. He talked soberly, with a sort of composed unreserve, and with a quiet bearing that might have been the outcome of manly self-control, of impudence, of callousness, of a colossal unconsciousness, of a gigantic deception. Who can tell! From our tone we might have been discussing a third person, a football match, last year's weather. My mind floated in a sea of conjectures till the turn of the conversation enabled me, without being offensive, to remark that, upon the whole, this inquiry must have been pretty trying to him. He darted his arm across the tablecloth, and clutching my hand by the side of my plate, glared fixedly. I *was* startled. 'It must be awfully hard,' I stammered, confused by this display of speechless feeling. 'It is — hell,' he burst out in a muffled voice.

"This movement and these words caused two well-groomed male globe-trotters at a neighbouring table to look up in alarm from their iced pudding. I rose, and we passed into the front gallery for coffee and cigars.

"On little octagon tables candles burned in glass globes; clumps of stiff-leaved plants separated sets of cosy wicker chairs; and between the pairs of columns, whose reddish shafts caught in a long row the sheen from the tall windows, the night, glittering and sombre, seemed to hang like a splendid drapery. The riding lights of ships winked afar like setting stars, and the hills across the roadstead resembled rounded black masses of arrested thunderclouds.

" 'I couldn't clear out,' Jim began. 'The skipper did — that's all very well for him. I couldn't, and I wouldn't. They all got out of it in one way or another, but it wouldn't do for me.'

"I listened with concentrated attention, not daring to stir in my chair; I wanted to know — and to this day I don't know, I can only guess. He would be confident and depressed all in the same breath, as if some conviction of innate blamelessness had checked the truth writhing within him at every turn. He began by saying, in the tone in which a man would admit his inability to jump a twenty-foot wall, that he could never go home now; and this declaration recalled to my mind what Brierly had said, 'that the old parson in Essex seemed to fancy his sailor son not a little.'

"I can't tell you whether Jim knew he was especially 'fancied,' but the tone of his references to 'my Dad' was calculated to give me a notion that the good old rural dean was about the finest man that ever had been worried by the cares of a large family since the beginning of the world. This, though never stated, was implied with an anxiety that there should be no mistake about it, which was really very true and charming, but added a poignant sense of lives far off to the other elements of the story. 'He has seen it all in the home papers by this time,' said Jim. 'I can never face the poor old chap.' I did not dare to lift my eyes at this till I heard him add, 'I could never explain. He wouldn't understand.' Then I looked up. He was smoking reflectively, and after a moment, rousing himself, began to talk again. He discovered at once a desire that I should not confound him with his partners in — in crime, let us call it. He was not one of them; he was altogether of another sort. I gave no sign of dissent. I had no intention, for the sake of barren truth, to rob him of the smallest particle of any saving grace that would come in his way. I didn't know how much of it he believed himself. I didn't know what he was playing up to — if he was playing up to anything at all — and I suspect he did not know either; for it is my belief no man ever understands quite his own artful dodges to escape from the grim shadow of self-knowledge. I made no sound all the time he was wondering what he had better do after 'that stupid inquiry was over.'

"Apparently he shared Brierly's contemptuous opinion of these proceedings ordained by law. He would not know where to turn, he confessed, clearly thinking aloud rather than talking to me. Certificate gone, career broken, no money to get away, no work that he could obtain as far as he could see. At home he could perhaps get something; but it meant going to his people for help, and that he would not do. He saw nothing for it but ship before the mast — could get perhaps a quartermaster's billet in some steamer. Would do for a quartermaster. . . . 'Do you think you would?' I asked, pitilessly. He jumped up, and going to the stone balustrade looked out into the night. In a moment he was back, towering above my chair with his youthful face clouded yet by the pain of a conquered emotion. He had understood very well I did not doubt his ability to steer a ship. In a voice that quavered a bit he asked me, 'Why did I say that? I had been "no end kind" to him. I had not even laughed at him when' — here he began to mumble — 'that mistake, you know — made a confounded ass of myself.' I broke in by saying rather warmly that for me such a mistake was not a matter to laugh at. He sat down and drank deliberately some coffee, emptying the small cup to the last drop. 'That does not mean I admit for a moment the cap fitted,' he declared, distinctly. 'No?' I said. 'No,' he affirmed with quiet decision. 'Do you know what *you* would have done? Do you? And you don't think yourself' . . . he gulped something . . . 'you don't think yourself a — a — cur?'

"And with this — upon my honour! — he looked up at me inquisitively. It was a question it appears — a *bonâ-fide* question! However, he didn't wait for an answer. Before I could recover he went on, with his eyes straight before him, as if reading off something written on the body of the night. 'It is all in being ready. I wasn't; not — not then. I don't want to excuse myself; but I would like to explain — I would like somebody to understand — somebody — one person at least! You! Why not you?'

"It was solemn, and a little ridiculous, too, as they always are, those struggles of an individual trying to save from the fire his idea of what his moral identity should be, this precious notion of a convention, only one of the rules of the game, nothing more, but all the same so terribly effective by its assumption of unlimited power over natural instincts, by the awful penalties of its failure. He began his story quietly enough. On board that Dale Line steamer that had picked up these four floating in a boat upon the discreet sunset glow of the sea, they had been after the first day looked askance upon. The fat skipper told some story, the others had been silent, and at first it had been accepted. You don't cross-examine poor castaways you had the good luck to save, if not from cruel death, then at least from cruel suffering. Afterwards, with time to think it over, it might have struck the officers of the *Avondale* that there was 'something fishy' in the affair; but of course they would keep their doubts to themselves. They had picked up the captain, the mate, and two engineers of the steamer *Patna* sunk at sea, and that, very properly, was enough for them. I did not ask Jim about the nature of his feelings during the ten days he spent on board. From the way he narrated that part I was at liberty to infer he was partly stunned by the discovery he had made — the discovery about himself — and no doubt was at work trying to explain it away to the only man who was capable of appreciating all its tremendous magnitude. You must understand he did not try to minimise its importance. Of that I am sure; and therein lies his distinction. As to what sensations he experienced when he got ashore and heard the unforeseen conclusion of the tale in which he had taken such a pitiful part, he told me nothing of them, and it is difficult to imagine. I wonder whether he felt the ground cut from under his feet? I wonder? But no doubt he managed to get a fresh foothold very soon. He was ashore a whole fortnight waiting in the Sailors' Home, and as there were six or seven men staying there at the time, I had heard of him a little. Their languid opinion seemed to be that in addition to his other shortcomings, he was a sulky brute. He had passed these days on the verandah, buried in a long chair, and coming out of his place of sepulture only at meal-times or late at night, when he wandered on the quays all by himself, detached from his surroundings, irresolute and silent, like a ghost without a home to haunt. 'I don't think I've spoken three words to a living soul in all that time,' he said, making me very sorry for him; and directly he added, 'One of these fellows would have been sure to blurt out something I had made up my mind not to put up with, and I didn't want a row. No! Not then. I was too — too . . . I had no heart for it.' 'So that bulkhead held out after all,' I remarked, cheerfully. 'Yes,' he murmured, 'it held. And yet I swear to you I felt it bulge under my hand.' 'It's extraordinary what strains old iron will stand sometimes,' I said. Thrown back in his seat, his legs stiffly out and arms hanging down, he nodded slightly several times. You could not conceive a sadder spectacle. Suddenly he lifted his head; he sat up; he slapped his thigh. 'Ah!

what a chance missed! My God! what a chance missed!' he blazed out, but the ring of the last 'missed' resembled a cry wrung out by pain.

"He was silent again with a still, far-away look of fierce yearning after that missed distinction, with his nostrils for an instant dilated, sniffing the intoxicating breath of that wasted opportunity. If you think I was either surprised or shocked you do me an injustice in more ways than one! Ah, he was an imaginative beggar! He would give himself away; he would give himself up. I could see in his glance darted into the night all his inner being carried on, projected headlong into the fanciful realm of recklessly heroic aspirations. He had no leisure to regret what he had lost, he was so wholly and naturally concerned for what he had failed to obtain. He was very far away from me who watched him across three feet of space. With every instant he was penetrating deeper into the impossible world of romantic achievements. He got to the heart of it at last! A strange look of beatitude overspread his features, his eyes sparkled in the light of the candle burning between us; he positively smiled! He had penetrated to the very heart — to the very heart. It was an ecstatic smile that your faces — or mine either — will never wear, my dear boys. I whisked him back by saying, 'If you had stuck to the ship, you mean!'

"He turned upon me, his eyes suddenly amazed and full of pain, with a bewildered, startled, suffering face, as though he had tumbled down from a star. Neither you nor I will ever look like this on any man. He shuddered profoundly, as if a cold finger-tip had touched his heart. Last of all he sighed.

"I was not in a merciful mood. He provoked one by his contradictory indiscretions. 'It is unfortunate you didn't know beforehand!' I said with every unkind intention; but the perfidious shaft fell harmless — dropped at his feet like a spent arrow, as it were, and he did not think of picking it up. Perhaps he had not even seen it. Presently, lolling at ease, he said, 'Dash it all! I tell you it bulged. I was holding up my lamp along the angle-iron in the lower deck when a flake of rust as big as the palm of my hand fell off the plate, all of itself.' He passed his hand over his forehead. 'The thing stirred and jumped off like something alive while I was looking at it.' 'That made you feel pretty bad,' I observed, casually. 'Do you suppose,' he said, 'that I was thinking of myself, with a hundred and sixty people at my back, all fast asleep in that fore-'tween-deck alone — and more of them aft; more on the deck — sleeping — knowing nothing about it — three times as many as there were boats for, even if there had been time? I expected to see the iron open out as I stood there and the rush of water going over them as they lay. . . . What could I do — what?'

"I can easily picture him to myself in the peopled gloom of the cavernous place, with the light of the bulk-lamp falling on a small portion of the bulkhead that had the weight of the ocean on the other side, and the breathing of unconscious sleepers in his ears. I can see him glaring at the iron, startled by the falling rust, over-burdened by the knowledge of an imminent death. This, I gathered, was the second time he had been sent forward by that skipper of his, who, I rather think, wanted to keep him away from the bridge. He told me that his first impulse was to shout and straight away make all those people leap out of sleep into terror; but such an overwhelming sense of his helplessness came over him that he was not able to produce a sound. This is, I suppose, what people mean by the tongue cleaving to the roof of the mouth. 'Too dry,' was the concise expression he used in reference to this state. Without a sound, then, he scrambled out on deck through the number one hatch. A wind-sail rigged down there swung against him accidentally, and he remembered that the light touch of the canvas on his face nearly knocked him off the hatch-way ladder.

"He confessed that his knees wobbled a good deal as he stood on the foredeck looking at another sleeping crowd. The engines having been stopped by that time, the steam was blowing off. Its deep rumble made the whole night vibrate like a bass string. The ship trembled to it.

"He saw here and there a head lifted off a mat, a vague form uprise in sitting posture, listen sleepily for a moment, sink down again into the billowy confusion of boxes, steam-winches, ventilators. He was aware all these people did not know enough to take intelligent notice of that strange noise. The ship of iron, the men with white faces, all the sights, all the sounds, everything on board to that ignorant and pious multitude was strange alike, and as trustworthy as it would for ever remain incomprehensible. It occurred to him that the fact was fortunate. The idea of it was simply terrible.

"You must remember he believed, as any other man would have

done in his place, that the ship would go down at any moment; the bulging, rust-eaten plates that kept back the ocean, fatally must give way, all at once like an undermined dam, and let in a sudden and overwhelming flood. He stood still looking at these recumbent bodies, a doomed man aware of his fate, surveying the silent company of the dead. They *were* dead! Nothing could save them! There were boats enough for half of them perhaps, but there was no time. No time! No time! It did not seem worth while to open his lips, to stir hand or foot. Before he could shout three words, or make three steps, he would be floundering in a sea whitened awfully by the desperate struggles of human beings, clamorous with the distress of cries for help. There was no help. He imagined what would happen perfectly; he went through it all motionless by the hatchway with the lamp in his hand — he went through it to the very last harrowing detail. I think he went through it again while he was telling me these things he could not tell the court.

" 'I saw as clearly as I see you now that there was nothing I could do. It seemed to take all life out of my limbs. I thought I might just as well stand where I was and wait. I did not think I had many seconds . . .' Suddenly the steam ceased blowing off. The noise, he remarked, had been distracting, but the silence at once became intolerably oppressive.

" 'I thought I would choke before I got drowned,' he said.

"He protested he did not think of saving himself. The only distinct thought formed, vanishing, and reforming in his brain, was: eight hundred people and seven boats; eight hundred people and seven boats.

" 'Somebody was speaking aloud inside my head,' he said a little wildly. 'Eight hundred people and seven boats — and no time! Just think of it.' He leaned towards me across the little table, and I tried to avoid his stare. 'Do you think I was afraid of death?' he asked in a voice very fierce and low. He brought down his open hand with a bang that made the coffee-cups dance. 'I am ready to swear I was not — I was not. . . . By God — no!' He hitched himself upright and crossed his arms; his chin fell on his breast.

"The soft clashes of crockery reached us faintly through the high windows. There was a burst of voices, and several men came out in high good-humour into the gallery. They were exchanging jocular reminiscences of the donkeys in Cairo. A pale anxious youth stepping softly on long legs was being chaffed by a strutting and rubicund globe-trotter about his purchases in the bazaar. 'No, really — do you think I've been done to that extent?' he inquired very earnest and deliberate. The band moved away, dropping into chairs as they went; matches flared, illuminating for a second faces without the ghost of an expression and the flat glaze of white shirt-fronts; the hum of many conversations animated with the ardour of feasting sounded to me absurd and infinitely remote.

" 'Some of the crew were sleeping on the number one hatch within reach of my arm,' began Jim again.

"You must know they kept Kalashee watch in that ship, all hands sleeping through the night, and only the reliefs of quartermasters and look-out men being called. He was tempted to grip and shake the shoulder of the nearest lascar, but he didn't. Something held his arms down along his sides. He was not afraid — oh no! only he just couldn't — that's all. He was not afraid of death perhaps, but I'll tell you what, he was afraid of the emergency. His confounded imagination had evoked for him all the horrors of panic, the trampling rush, the pitiful screams, boats swamped — all the appalling incidents of a disaster at sea he had ever heard of. He might have been resigned to die but I suspect he wanted to die without added terrors, quietly, in a sort of peaceful trance. A certain readiness to perish is not so very rare, but it is seldom that you meet men whose souls, steeled in the impenetrable armour of resolution, are ready to fight a losing battle to the last, the desire of peace waxes stronger as hope declines, till at last it conquers the very desire of life. Which of us here has not observed this, or maybe experienced something of that feeling in his own person — this extreme weariness of emotions, the vanity of effort, the yearning for rest? Those striving with unreasonable forces know it well, — the shipwrecked castaways in boats, wanderers lost in a desert, men battling against the unthinking might of nature, or the stupid brutality of crowds."

CHAPTER VIII

〜〜

"How long he stood stock-still by the hatch expecting every moment to feel the ship dip under his feet and the rush of water to take him at the back and toss him like a chip, I cannot say. Not very long — two minutes perhaps. A couple of men he could not make out began to converse drowsily, and also, he could not tell where, he detected a curious noise of shuffling feet. Above these faint sounds there was that awful stillness preceding a catastrophe, that trying silence of the moment before the crash; then it came into his head that perhaps he would have time to rush along and cut all the lanyards of the gripes, so that the boats would float off as the ship went down.

"The *Patna* had a long bridge, and all the boats were up there, four on one side and three on the other — the smallest of them on the port-side and nearly abreast of the steering gear. He assured me, with evident anxiety to be believed, that he had been most careful to keep them ready for instant service. He knew his duty. I dare say he was a good enough mate as far as that went. 'I always believed in being prepared for the worst,' he commented, staring anxiously in my face. I nodded my approval of the sound principle, averting my eyes before the subtle unsoundness of the man.

"He started unsteadily to run. He had to step over legs, avoid stumbling against the heads. Suddenly some one caught hold of his coat from below, and a distressed voice spoke under his elbow. The light of the lamp he carried in his right hand fell upon an upturned dark face whose eyes entreated him together with the voice. He had picked up enough of the language to understand the word water, repeated several times in a tone of insistence, of prayer, almost of despair. He gave a jerk to get away, and felt an arm embrace his leg.

" 'The beggar clung to me like a drowning man,' he said, impressively. 'Water, water! What water did he mean? What did he know? As calmly as I could I ordered him to let go. He was stopping me, time was pressing, other men began to stir; I wanted

time — time to cut the boats adrift. He got hold of my hand now,
and I felt that he would begin to shout. It flashed upon me it was
enough to start a panic, and I hauled off with my free arm and
slung the lamp in his face. The glass jingled, the light went out,
but the blow made him let go, and I ran off — I wanted to get at
the boats; I wanted to get at the boats. He leaped after me from
behind. I turned on him. He would not keep quiet; he tried to
shout; I had half throttled him before I made out what he wanted.
He wanted some water — water to drink; they were on strict allowance, you know, and he had with him a young boy I had
noticed several times. His child was sick — and thirsty. He had
caught sight of me as I passed by, and was begging for a little
water. That's all. We were under the bridge, in the dark. He
kept on snatching at my wrists; there was no getting rid of him.
I dashed into my berth, grabbed my water-bottle, and thrust it
into his hands. He vanished. I didn't find out till then how much
I was in want of a drink myself.' He leaned on one elbow with
a hand over his eyes.

"I felt a creepy sensation all down my backbone; there was
something peculiar in all this. The fingers of the hand that shaded
his brow trembled slightly. He broke the short silence.

" 'These things happen only once to a man and . . . Ah! well!
When I got on the bridge at last the beggars were getting one
of the boats off the chocks. A boat! I was running up the ladder
when a heavy blow fell on my shoulder, just missing my head.
It didn't stop me, and the chief engineer — they had got him out
of his bunk by then — raised the boat-stretcher again. Somehow
I had no mind to be surprised at anything. All this seemed natural — and awful — and awful. I dodged that miserable maniac,
lifted him off the deck as though he had been a little child, and
he started whispering in my arms: "Don't! don't! I thought you
were one of them niggers." I flung him away, he skidded along
the bridge and knocked the legs from under the little chap — the
second. The skipper, busy about the boat, looked round and
came at me head down, growling like a wild beast. I flinched no
more than a stone. I was as solid standing there as this,' he tapped
lightly with his knuckles the wall beside his chair. 'It was as
though I had heard it all, seen it all, gone through it all twenty
times already. I wasn't afraid of them. I drew back my fist and
he stopped short, muttering —

" ' "Ah! it's you. Lend a hand quick."

" 'That's what he said. Quick! As if anybody could be quick
enough. Aren't you going to do something?' I asked. ' "Yes.
Clear out," he snarled over his shoulder.

" 'I don't think I understood then what he meant. The other
two had picked themselves up by that time, and they rushed together to the boat. They tramped, they wheezed, they shoved,
they cursed the boat, the ship, each other — cursed me. All in
mutters. I didn't move, I didn't speak. I watched the slant of
the ship. She was as still as if landed on the blocks in a dry dock
— only she was like this.' He held up his hand, palm under, the
tips of the fingers inclined downwards. 'Like this,' he repeated.
'I could see the line of the horizon before me, as clear as a bell,
above her stem-head; I could see the water far off there black
and sparkling, and still — still as a pond, deadly still, more still
than ever sea was before — more still than I could bear to look at.
Have you watched a ship floating head down, checked in sinking
by a sheet of old iron too rotten to stand being shored up. Have
you? Oh yes, shored up? I thought of that — I thought of every
mortal thing; but can you shore up a bulkhead in five minutes —
or in fifty for that matter? Where was I going to get men that
would go down below? And the timber — the timber! Would
you have had the courage to swing the maul for the first blow if
you had seen that bulkhead? Don't say you would: you had not
seen it; nobody would. Hang it — to do a thing like that you must
believe there is a chance, one in a thousand, at least, some ghost
of a chance; and you would not have believed. Nobody would
have believed. You think me a cur for standing there, but what
would you have done? What! You can't tell — nobody can tell.
One must have time to turn round. What would you have me do?
Where was the kindness in making crazy with fright all those
people I could not save single-handed — that nothing could save?
Look here! As true as I sit on this chair before you . . .'

"He drew quick breaths at every few words and shot quick
glances at my face, as though in his anguish he were watchful of
the effect. He was not speaking to me, he was only speaking before me, in a dispute with an invisible personality, an antagonistic
and inseparable partner of his existence — another possessor of his
soul. These were issues beyond the competency of a court of inquiry: it was a subtle and momentous quarrel as to the true essence

of life, and did not want a judge. He wanted an ally, a helper, an accomplice. I felt the risk I ran of being circumvented, blinded, decoyed, bullied, perhaps, into taking a definite part in a dispute impossible of decision if one had to be fair to all the phantoms in possession — to the reputable that had its claims and to the disreputable that had its exigencies. I can't explain to you who haven't seen him and who hear his words only at second hand the mixed nature of my feelings. It seemed to me I was being made to comprehend the Inconceivable — and I know of nothing to compare with the discomfort of such a sensation. I was made to look at the convention that lurks in all truth and on the essential sincerity of falsehood. He appealed to all sides at once — to the side turned perpetually to the light of day, and to that side of us which, like the other hemisphere of the moon, exists stealthily in perpetual darkness, with only a fearful ashy light falling at times on the edge. He swayed me. I own to it, I own up. The occasion was obscure, insignificant — what you will: a lost youngster, one in a million — but then he was one of us; an incident as completely devoid of importance as the flooding of an ant-heap, and yet the mystery of his attitude got hold of me as though he had been an individual in the forefront of his kind, as if the obscure truth involved were momentous enough to affect mankind's conception of itself. . . ."

Marlow paused to put new life into his expiring cheroot, seemed to forget all about the story, and abruptly began again.

"My fault of course. One has no business really to get interested. It's a weakness of mine. His was of another kind. My weakness consists in not having a discriminating eye for the incidental — for the externals — no eye for the hod of the rag-picker or the fine linen of the next man. Next man — that's it. I have met so many men," he pursued, with momentary sadness — "met them, too, with a certain — certain — impact, let us say; like this fellow, for instance — and in each case all I could see was merely the human being. A confounded democratic quality of vision which may be better than total blindness, but has been of no advantage to me, I can assure you. Men expect one to take into account their fine linen. But I never could get up any enthusiasm about these things. Oh! it's a failing; it's a failing; and then comes a soft evening; a lot of men too indolent for whist — and a story. . . ."

He paused again to wait for an encouraging remark perhaps, but nobody spoke; only the host, as if reluctantly performing a duty, murmured —

"You are so subtle, Marlow."

"Who? I?" said Marlow in a low voice. "Oh, no! But *he* was; and try as I may for the success of this yarn I am missing innumerable shades — they were so fine, so difficult to render in colourless words. Because he complicated matters by being so simple, too — the simplest poor devil! . . . By Jove! he was amazing. There he sat telling me that just as I saw him before my eyes he wouldn't be afraid to face anything — and believing in it, too. I tell you it was fabulously innocent and it was enormous, enormous! I watched him covertly, just as though I had suspected him of an intention to take a jolly good rise out of me. He was confident that, on the square, 'on the square, mind!' there was nothing he couldn't meet. Ever since he had been 'so high' — 'quite a little chap,' he had been preparing himself for all the difficulties that can beset one on land and water. He confessed proudly to this kind of foresight. He had been elaborating dangers and defences, expecting the worst, rehearsing his best. He must have led a most exalted existence. Can you fancy it? A succession of adventures, so much glory, such a victorious progress! and the deep sense of his sagacity crowning every day of his inner life. He forgot himself; his eyes shone; and with every word my heart, searched by the light of his absurdity, was growing heavier in my breast. I had no mind to laugh, and lest I should smile I made for myself a stolid face. He gave signs of irritation.

" 'It is always the unexpected that happens,' I said in a propitiatory tone. My obtuseness provoked him into a contemptuous 'Pshaw!' I suppose he meant that the unexpected couldn't touch him; nothing less than the unconceivable itself could get over his perfect state of preparation. He had been taken unawares — and he whispered to himself a malediction upon the waters and the firmament, upon the ship, upon the men. Everything had betrayed him! He had been tricked into that sort of high-minded resignation which prevented him lifting as much as his little finger, while these others who had a very clear perception of the actual necessity were tumbling against each other and sweating desperately over that boat business. Something had gone wrong there at the last moment. It appears that in their flurry they had contrived in some mysterious way to get the sliding bolt of the foremost boat-chock jammed tight, and forthwith had gone out of the remnants of their minds over the deadly nature of that accident. It must have been a pretty sight, the fierce industry of these beggars toiling on a motionless ship that floated quietly in the silence of a world asleep, fighting against time for the freeing of that boat, grovelling on all-fours, standing up in despair, tugging, pushing, snarling at each other venomously, ready to kill, ready to weep, and only kept from flying at each other's throats by the fear of death that stood silent behind them like an inflexible and cold-eyed taskmaster. Oh, yes! It must have been a pretty sight. He saw it all, he could talk about it with scorn and bitterness; he had a minute knowledge of it by means of some sixth sense, I conclude, because he swore to me he had remained apart without a glance at them and at the boat — without one single glance. And I believe him. I should think he was too busy watching the threatening slant of the ship, the suspended menace discovered in the midst of the most perfect security — fascinated by the sword hanging by a hair over his imaginative head.

"Nothing in the world moved before his eyes, and he could depict to himself without hindrance the sudden swing upwards of the dark sky-line, the sudden tilt up of the vast plain of the sea, the swift still rise, the brutal fling, the grasp of the abyss, the struggle without hope, the starlight closing over his head for ever like the vault of a tomb — the revolt of his young life — the black end. He could! By Jove! who couldn't? And you must remember he was a finished artist in that peculiar way, he was a gifted poor devil with the faculty of swift and forestalling vision. The sights it showed him had turned him into cold stone from the soles of his feet to the nape of his neck; but there was a hot dance of thoughts in his head, a dance of lame, blind, mute thoughts — a whirl of awful cripples. Didn't I tell you he confessed himself before me as though I had the power to bind and to loose? He burrowed deep, deep, in the hope of my absolution, which would have been of no good to him. This was one of those cases which no solemn deception can palliate, which no man can help; where his very Maker seems to abandon a sinner to his own devices.

"He stood on the starboard side of the bridge, as far as he could get from the struggle for the boat, which went on with the agitation of madness and the stealthiness of a conspiracy. The two

Malays had meantime remained holding to the wheel. Just picture
to yourselves the actors in that, thank God! unique, episode of
the sea, four beside themselves with fierce and secret exertions,
and three looking on in complete immobility, above the awnings
covering the profound ignorance of hundreds of human beings,
with their weariness, with their dreams, with their hopes, arrested,
held by an invisible hand on the brink of annihilation. For that
they were so, makes no doubt to me: given the state of the ship,
this was the deadliest possible description of accident that could
happen. These beggars by the boat had every reason to go distracted with funk. Frankly, had I been there I would not have
given as much as a counterfeit farthing for the ship's chance to
keep above water to the end of each successive second. And still
she floated! These sleeping pilgrims were destined to accomplish
their whole pilgrimage to the bitterness of some other end. It
was as if the Omnipotence whose mercy they confessed had
needed their humble testimony on earth for a while longer, and
had looked down to make a sign, 'Thou shalt not!' to the ocean.
Their escape would trouble me as a prodigiously inexplicable
event, did I not know how tough old iron can be — as tough
sometimes as the spirit of some men we meet now and then, worn
to a shadow and breasting the weight of life. Not in the least
wonder of these twenty minutes, to my mind, is the behaviour
of the two helmsmen. They were amongst the native batch of all
sorts brought over from Aden to give evidence at the inquiry.
One of them, labouring under intense bashfulness, was very
young, and with his smooth, yellow, cheery countenance looked
even younger than he was. I remember perfectly Brierly asking
him, through the interpreter, what he thought of it at the time,
and the interpreter, after a short colloquy, turning to the court
with an important air —

" 'He says he thought nothing.'

"The other with patient blinking eyes, a blue cotton handkerchief, faded with much washing, bound with a smart twist over
a lot of grey wisps, his face shrunk into grim hollows, his brown
skin made darker by a mesh of wrinkles, explained that he had
a knowledge of some evil thing befalling the ship, but there had
been no order; he could not remember an order; why should he
leave the helm? To some further questions he jerked back his
spare shoulders, and declared it never came into his mind then
that the white men were about to leave the ship through fear of

death. He did not believe it now. There might have been secret
reasons. He wagged his old chin knowingly. Aha! secret reasons.
He was a man of great experience, and he wanted *that* white Tuan
to know — he turned towards Brierly, who didn't raise his head —
that he had acquired a knowledge of many things by serving white
men on the sea for a great number of years — and, suddenly, with
shaky excitement he poured upon our spellbound attention a lot
of queer-sounding names, names of dead-and-gone skippers, names
of forgotten country ships, names of familiar and distorted sound,
as if the hand of dumb time had been at work on them for ages.
They stopped him at last. A silence fell upon the court, — a silence that remained unbroken for at least a minute, and passed
gently into a deep murmur. This episode was *the* sensation of the
second day's proceedings — affecting all the audience, affecting
everybody except Jim, who was sitting moodily at the end of the
first bench, and never looked up at this extraordinary and damn-
ing witness that seemed possessed of some mysterious theory of
defence.

"So these two lascars stuck to the helm of that ship without
steerage-way, where death would have found them if such had
been their destiny. The whites did not give them half a glance,
had probably forgotten their existence. Assuredly Jim did not
remember it. He remembered he could do nothing; he could do
nothing, now he was alone. There was nothing to do but to sink
with the ship. No use making a disturbance about it. Was there?
He waited upstanding, without a sound, stiffened in the idea of
some sort of heroic discretion. The first engineer ran cautiously
across the bridge to tug at his sleeve.

" 'Come·and help! For God's sake, come and help!'

"He ran back to the boat on the points of his toes, and returned
directly to worry at his sleeve, begging and cursing at the same
time.

" 'I believe he would have kissed my hands,' said Jim, savagely,
'and, next moment, he starts foaming and whispering in my face,
"If I had the time I would like to crack your skull for you." I
pushed him away. Suddenly he caught hold of me round the
neck. Damn him! I hit him. I hit out without looking. "Won't
you save your own life — you infernal coward?" he sobs. Coward! He called me an infernal coward! Ha! ha! ha! ha! He called
me — ha! ha! ha! . . .'

"He had thrown himself back and was shaking with laughter.

I had never in my life heard anything so bitter as that noise. It fell like a blight on all the merriment about donkeys, pyramids, bazaars, or what not. Along the whole dim length of the gallery the voices dropped, the pale blotches of faces turned our way with one accord, and the silence became so profound that the clear tinkle of a teaspoon falling on the tesselated floor of the verandah rang out like a tiny and silvery scream.

" 'You mustn't laugh like this, with all these people about,' I remonstrated. 'It isn't nice for them, you know.'

"He gave no sign of having heard at first, but after a while, with a stare that, missing me altogether, seemed to probe the heart of some awful vision, he muttered carelessly — 'Oh! they'll think I am drunk.'

"And after that you would have thought from his appearance he would never make a sound again. But — no fear! He could no more stop telling now than he could have stopped living by the mere exertion of his will."

CHAPTER IX

" 'I was saying to myself, "Sink — curse you! Sink!" ' These were the words with which he began again. He wanted it over. He was severely left alone, and he formulated in his head this address to the ship in a tone of imprecation, while at the same time he enjoyed the privilege of witnessing scenes — as far as I can judge — of low comedy. They were still at that bolt. The skipper was ordering. 'Get under and try to lift;' and the others naturally shirked. You understand that to be squeezed flat under the keel of a boat wasn't a desirable position to be caught in if the ship went down suddenly. 'Why don't you — you the strongest?' whined the little engineer. 'Gott-for-dam! I am too thick,' spluttered the skipper in despair. It was funny enough to make angels weep. They stood idle for a moment, and suddenly the chief engineer rushed again at Jim.

" 'Come and help, man! Are you mad to throw your only

chance away? Come and help, man! Man! Look there — look!'

"And at last Jim looked astern where the other pointed with maniacal insistence. He saw a silent black squall which had eaten up already one-third of the sky. You know how these squalls come up there about that time of the year. First you see a dark-ening of the horizon — no more; then a cloud rises opaque like a wall. A straight edge of vapour lined with sickly whitish gleams flies up from the southwest, swallowing the stars in whole con-stellations; its shadow flies over the waters, and confounds sea and sky into one abyss of obscurity. And all is still. No thunder, no wind, no sound; not a flicker of lightning. Then in the tenebrous immensity a livid arch appears; a swell or two like undulations of the very darkness run past, and suddenly, wind and rain strike together with a peculiar impetuosity as if they had burst through something solid. Such a cloud had come up while they weren't looking. They had just noticed it, and were perfectly justified in surmising that if in absolute stillness there was some chance for the ship to keep afloat a few minutes longer, the least disturbance of the sea would make an end of her instantly. Her first nod to the swell that precedes the burst of such a squall would be also her last, would become a plunge, would, so to speak, be prolonged into a long dive, down, down to the bottom. Hence these new capers of their fright, these new antics in which they displayed their extreme aversion to die.

" 'It was black, black,' pursued Jim with moody steadiness. 'It had sneaked upon us from behind. The infernal thing! I suppose there had been at the back of my head some hope yet. I don't know. But that was all over anyhow. It maddened me to see myself caught like this. I was angry, as though I had been trapped. I *was* trapped! The night was hot, too, I remember. Not a breath of air.'

"He remembered so well that, gasping in the chair, he seemed to sweat and choke before my eyes. No doubt it maddened him; it knocked him over afresh — in a manner of speaking — but it made him also remember that important purpose which had sent him rushing on that bridge only to slip clean out of his mind. He had intended to cut the life-boats clear of the ship. He whipped out his knife and went to work slashing as though he had seen nothing, had heard nothing, had known of no one on board. They thought him hopelessly wrong-headed and crazy, but dared not

protest noisily against this useless loss of time. When he had done
he returned to the very same spot from which he had started. The
chief was there, ready with a clutch at him to whisper close to
his head, scathingly, as though he wanted to bite his ear —

" 'You silly fool! do you think you'll get the ghost of a show
when all that lot of brutes is in the water? Why, they will batter
your head for you from these boats.'

"He wrung his hands, ignored, at Jim's elbow. The skipper kept
up a nervous shuffle in one place and mumbled, 'Hammer! hammer! Mein Gott! Get a hammer.'

"The little engineer whimpered like a child, but broken arm and
all, he turned out the least craven of the lot as it seems, and, actually, mustered enough pluck to run an errand to the engine-room.
No trifle it must be owned in fairness to him. Jim told me he
darted desperate looks like a cornered man, gave one low wail,
and dashed off. He was back instantly clambering, hammer in
hand, and without a pause flung himself at the bolt. The others
gave up Jim at once and ran off to assist. He heard the tap, tap of
the hammer, the sound of the released chock falling over. The
boat was clear. Only then he turned to look — only then. But he
kept his distance — he kept his distance. He wanted me to know
he had kept his distance; that there was nothing in common between him and these men — who had the hammer. Nothing whatever. It is more than probable he thought himself cut off from
them by a space that could not be traversed, by an obstacle that
could not be overcome, by a chasm without bottom. He was as
far as he could get from them — the whole breadth of the ship.

"His feet were glued to that remote spot and his eyes to their
indistinct group bowed together and swaying strangely in the
common torment of fear. A hand-lamp lashed to a stanchion above
a little table rigged· up on the bridge — the *Patna* had no chart-
room amidships — threw a light on their labouring shoulders, on
their arched and bobbing backs. They pushed at the bow of the
boat; they pushed out into the night; they pushed, and would no
more look back at him. They had given him up as if indeed he
had been too far, too hopelessly separated from themselves, to
be worth an appealing word, a glance, or a sign. They had no
leisure to look back upon his passive heroism, to feel the sting of
his abstention. The boat was heavy; they pushed at the bow with
no breath to spare for an encouraging word: but the turmoil of

terror that had scattered their self-control like chaff before the wind, converted their desperate exertions into a bit of fooling, upon my word fit for knockabout clowns in a farce. They pushed with their hands, with their heads, they pushed for dear life with all the weight of their bodies, they pushed with all the might of their souls — only no sooner had they succeeded in canting the stem clear of the davit than they would leave off like one man and start a wild scramble into her. As a natural consequence the boat would swing in abruptly, driving them back, helpless and jostling against each other. They would stand nonplussed for a while, exchanging in fierce whispers all the infamous names they could call to mind, and go at it again. Three times this occurred. He described it to me with morose thoughtfulness. He hadn't lost a single movement of that comic business. 'I loathed them. I hated them. I had to look at all that,' he said without emphasis, turning upon me a sombrely watchful glance. 'Was ever there any one so shamefully tried!'

"He took his head in his hands for a moment, like a man driven to distraction by some unspeakable outrage. These were things he could not explain to the court — and not even to me; but I would have been little fitted for the reception of his confidences had I not been able at times to understand the pauses between the words. In this assault upon his fortitude there was the jeering intention of a spiteful and vile vengeance; there was an element of burlesque in his ordeal — a degradation of funny grimaces in the approach of death or dishonour.

"He related facts which I have not forgotten, but at this distance of time I couldn't recall his very words: I only remember that he managed wonderfully to convey the brooding rancour of his mind into the bare recital of events. Twice, he told me, he shut his eyes in the certitude that the end was upon him already, and twice he had to open them again. Each time he noted the darkening of the great stillness. The shadow of the silent cloud had fallen upon the ship from the zenith, and seemed to have extinguished every sound of her teeming life. He could no longer hear the voices under the awnings. He told me that each time he closed his eyes a flash of thought showed him that crowd of bodies, laid out for death, as plain as daylight. When he opened them, it was to see the dim struggle of four men fighting like mad with a stubborn boat. 'They would fall back before it time after time, stand

swearing at each other, and suddenly make another rush in a
bunch. . . . Enough to make you die laughing,' he commented
with downcast eyes; then raising them for a moment to my face
with a dismal smile, 'I ought to have a merry life of it, by God!
for I shall see that funny sight a good many times yet before I die.'
His eyes fell again. 'See and hear. . . . See and hear,' he repeated
twice, at long intervals, filled by vacant staring.

"He roused himself.

" 'I made up my mind to keep my eyes shut,' he said, 'and I
couldn't. I couldn't, and I don't care who knows it. Let them go
through that kind of thing before they talk. Just let them — and do
better — that's all. The second time my eyelids flew open and my
mouth too. I had felt the ship move. She just dipped her bows —
and lifted them gently — and slow! everlastingly slow; and ever so
little. She hadn't done that much for days. The cloud had raced
ahead, and this first swell seemed to travel upon a sea of lead.
There was no life in that stir. It managed, though, to knock over
something in my head. What would you have done? You are sure
of yourself — aren't you? What would you do if you felt now —
this minute — the house here move, just move a little under your
chair. Leap! By heavens! you would take one spring from where
you sit and land in that clump of bushes yonder.'

"He flung his arm out at the night beyond the stone balustrade.
I held my peace. He looked at me very steadily, very severe.
There could be no mistake: I was being bullied now, and it be-
hoved me to make no sign lest by a gesture or a word I should
be drawn into a fatal admission about myself which would have
had some bearing on the case. I was not disposed to take any risk
of that sort. Don't forget I had him before me, and really he was
too much like one of us not to be dangerous. But if you want to
know I don't mind telling you that I did, with a rapid glance, esti-
mate the distance to the mass of denser blackness in the middle of
the grass-plot before the verandah. He exaggerated. I would have
landed short by several feet — and that's the only thing of which
I am fairly certain.

"The last moment had come, as he thought, and he did not
move. His feet remained glued to the planks if his thoughts were
knocking about loose in his head. It was at this moment, too, that
he saw one of the men around the boat step backwards suddenly,
clutch at the air with raised arms, totter and collapse. He didn't

exactly fall, he only slid gently into a sitting posture, all hunched up and with his shoulders propped against the side of the engine-room skylight. 'That was the donkey-man. A haggard, white-faced chap with a ragged moustache. Acted third engineer,' he explained.

" 'Dead,' I said. We had heard something of that in court.

" 'So they say,' he pronounced with sombre indifference. 'Of course I never knew. Weak heart. The man had been complaining of being out of sorts for some time before. Excitement. Over-exertion. Devil only knows. Ha! ha! ha! It was easy to see he did not want to die either. Droll, isn't it? May I be shot if he hadn't been fooled into killing himself! Fooled — neither more nor less. Fooled into it, by heavens! just as I . . . Ah! If he had only kept still; if he had only told them to go to the devil when they came to rush him out of his bunk because the ship was sinking! If he had only stood by with his hands in his pockets and called them names!'

"He got up, shook his fist, glared at me, and sat down.

" 'A chance missed, eh?' I murmured.

" 'Why don't you laugh?' he said. 'A joke hatched in hell. Weak heart! . . . I wish sometimes mine had been.'

"This irritated me. 'Do you?' I exclaimed with deep-rooted irony. 'Yes! Can't *you* understand?' he cried. 'I don't know what more you could wish for,' I said, angrily. He gave me an utterly uncomprehending glance. This shaft had also gone wide of the mark, and he was not the man to bother about stray arrows. Upon my word, he was too unsuspecting; he was not fair game. I was glad that my missile had been thrown away, — that he had not even heard the twang of the bow.

"Of course he could not know at the time the man was dead. The next minute — his last on board — was crowded with a tumult of events and sensations which beat about him like the sea upon a rock. I use the simile advisedly, because from his relation I am forced to believe he had preserved through it all a strange illusion of passiveness, as though he had not acted but had suffered himself to be handled by the infernal powers who had selected him for the victim of their practical joke. The first thing that came to him was the grinding surge of the heavy davits swinging out at last — a jar which seemed to enter his body from the deck through the soles of his feet, and travel up his spine to the crown of his

head. Then, the squall being very near now, another and a heavier swell lifted the passive hull in a threatening heave that checked
his breath, while his brain and his heart together were pierced as
with daggers by panic-stricken screams. 'Let go! For God's sake,
let go! Let go! She's going.' Following upon that the boat-falls
ripped through the blocks, and a lot of men began to talk in startled tones under the awnings. 'When these beggars did break out,
their yelps were enough to wake the dead,' he said. Next after the
splashing shock of the boat literally dropped in the water, came
the hollow noises of stamping and tumbling in her, mingled with
confused shouts: 'Unhook! Unhook! Shove! Unhook! Shove
for your life! Here's the squall down on us. . . .' He heard, high
above his head, the faint muttering of the wind; he heard below
his feet a cry of pain. A lost voice alongside started cursing a
swivel hook. The ship began to buzz fore and aft like a disturbed
hive, and, as quietly as he was telling me all of this — because just
then he was very quiet in attitude, in face, in voice — he went on
to say without the slightest warning as it were, 'I stumbled over
his legs.'

"This was the first I heard of his having moved at all. I could
not restrain a grunt of surprise. Something had started him off at
last, but of the exact moment, of the cause that tore him out of
his immobility, he knew no more than the uprooted tree knows of
the wind that laid it low. All this had come to him: the sounds, the
sights, the legs of the dead man — by Jove! The infernal joke was
being crammed devilishly down his throat, but — look you — he
was not going to admit of any sort of swallowing motion in his
gullet. It's extraordinary how he could cast upon you the spirit of
his illusion. I listened as if to a tale of black magic at work upon a
corpse.

" 'He went over sideways, very gently, and this is the last thing
I remember seeing on board,' he continued. 'I did not care what
he did. It looked as though he were picking himself up: I thought
he was picking himself up, of course: I expected him to bolt past
me over the rail and drop into the boat after the others. I could
hear them knocking about, down there, and a voice as if crying up
a shaft called out "George." Then three voices together raised a
yell. They came to me separately: one bleated, another screamed,
one howled. Ough!'

"He shivered a little, and I beheld him rise slowly as if a steady hand from above had been pulling him out of the chair by his hair. Up, slowly — to his full height, and when his knees had locked stiff the hand let him go, and he swayed a little on his feet. There was a suggestion of awful stillness in his face, in his movements, in his very voice when he said 'They shouted' — and involuntarily I pricked up my ears for the ghost of that shout that would be heard directly through the false effect of silence. 'There were eight hundred people in that ship,' he said, impaling me to the back of my seat with an awful blank stare. 'Eight hundred living people, and they were yelling after the one dead man to come down and be saved. "Jump, George! Jump! Oh, jump!" I stood by with my hand on the davit. I was very quiet. It had come over pitch dark. You could see neither sky nor sea. I heard the boat alongside go bump, bump, and not another sound down there for a while, but the ship under me was full of talking noises. Suddenly the skipper howled, "Mein Gott! The squall! The squall! Shove off!" With the first hiss of rain, and the first gust of wind, they screamed, "Jump, George! We'll catch you! Jump!" The ship began a slow plunge; the rain swept over her like a broken sea; my cap flew off my head; my breath was driven back into my throat. I heard as if I had been on the top of a tower another wild screech, "Geo-o-o-orge! Oh, jump!" She was going down, down, head first under me. . . .'

"He raised his hand deliberately to his face, and made picking motions with his fingers as though he had been bothered with cobwebs, and afterwards he blurted into the open palm for quite half a second before he blurted out —

" 'I had jumped . . .' He checked himself, averted his gaze. . . . 'It seems,' he added.

"His clear blue eyes turned to me with a piteous stare, and looking at him standing before me, dumfounded and hurt, I was oppressed by a sad sense of resigned wisdom, mingled with the amused and profound pity of an old man helpless before a childish disaster.

" 'Looks like it,' I muttered.

" 'I knew nothing about it till I looked up,' he explained, hastily. And that's possible, too. You had to listen to him as you would to a small boy in trouble. He didn't know. It had happened somehow. It would never happen again. He had landed partly on somebody and fallen across a thwart. He felt as though all his ribs on his left side must be broken; then he rolled over, and saw vaguely the ship he had deserted uprising above him, with the red sidelight glowing large in the rain like a fire on the brow of a hill seen through a mist. 'She seemed higher than a wall; she loomed like a cliff over the boat. . . . I wished I could die,' he cried. 'There was no going back. It was as if I had jumped into a well — into an everlasting deep hole. . . .' "

CHAPTER X

"HE LOCKED his fingers together and tore them apart. Nothing could be more true: he had indeed jumped into an everlasting deep hole. He had tumbled from a height he could never scale again. By that time the boat had gone driving forward past the bows. It was too dark just then for them to see each other, and, moreover, they were blinded and half drowned with rain. He told me it was like being swept by a flood through a cavern. They turned their backs to the squall; the skipper, it seems, got an oar over the stern to keep the boat before it, and for two or three minutes the end of the world had come through a deluge in a pitchy blackness. The sea hissed 'like twenty thousand kettles.' That's his simile, not mine. I fancy there was not much wind after the first gust; and he himself had admitted at the inquiry that the sea never got up that night to any extent. He crouched down in the bows and stole a furtive glance back. He saw just one yellow gleam of the masthead light high up and blurred like a last star ready to dissolve. 'It terrified me to see it still there,' he said. That's what he said. What terrified him was the thought that the drowning was not over yet. No doubt he wanted to be done with that abomination as quickly as possible. Nobody in the boat made a sound. In the dark she seemed to fly, but of course she could not have had much way. Then the shower swept ahead, and the great, distracting, hissing noise followed the rain into distance and died out. There was nothing to be heard then but the slight wash about the boat's sides. Somebody's teeth were chattering violently. A hand touched his back. A faint voice said, 'You there?' Another cried out, shakily, 'She's gone!' and they all stood up together to look astern. They saw no lights. All was black. A thin cold drizzle was driving into their faces. The boat lurched slightly. The teeth chattered faster, stopped, and began again twice before the man could master his shiver sufficiently to say, 'Ju-ju-st in ti-ti-me. . . . Brrrr.' He recognised the voice of the chief engineer saying surlily, 'I saw her go down. I happened to turn my head.' The wind had dropped almost completely.

"They watched in the dark with their heads half turned to windward as if expecting to hear cries. At first he was thankful the night had covered up the scene before his eyes, and then to know of it and yet to have seen and heard nothing appeared somehow the culminating-point of an awful misfortune. 'Strange, isn't it?' he murmured, interrupting himself in his disjointed narrative.

"It did not seem so strange to me. He must have had an unconscious conviction that the reality could not be half as bad, not half as anguishing, appalling, and vengeful as the created terror of his imagination. I believe that, in this first moment, his heart was wrung with all the suffering, that his soul knew the accumulated savour of all the fear, all the horror, all the despair of eight hundred human beings pounced upon in the night by a sudden and violent death, else why should he have said, 'It seemed to me that I must jump out of that accursed boat and swim back to see — half a mile — more — any distance — to the very spot . . .'? Why this impulse? Do you see the significance? Why back to the very spot? Why not drown alongside — if he meant drowning? why back to the very spot, to see — as if his imagination had to be soothed by the assurance that all was over before death could bring relief? I defy any one of you to offer another explanation. It was one of those bizarre and exciting glimpses through the fog. It was an extraordinary disclosure. He let it out as the most natural thing one could say. He fought down that impulse and then he became conscious of the silence. He mentioned this to me. A silence of the sea, of the sky, merged into one indefinite immensity still as death around these saved, palpitating lives. 'You might have heard a pin drop in the boat,' he said with a queer contraction of his lips, like a man trying to master his sensibilities while relating some extremely moving fact. A silence! God alone, who had willed him as he was, knows what he made of it in his heart. 'I didn't think any spot on earth could be so still,' he said. 'You couldn't distinguish the sea from the sky; there was nothing to see and nothing to hear. Not a glimmer, not a shape, not a sound. You could have believed that every bit of dry land had gone to the bottom; that every man on earth but I and these beggars in the boat had got drowned.' He leaned over the table with his knuckles propped amongst coffee-cups, liqueur-glasses, cigar-ends. 'I seemed to believe it. Everything was gone and — all was over . . .' he fetched a deep sigh . . . 'with me.' "

Marlow sat up abruptly and flung away his cheroot with force. It made a darting red trail like a toy rocket fired through the drapery of creepers. Nobody stirred.

"Hey, what do you think of it?" he cried with sudden animation. "Wasn't he true to himself, wasn't he? His saved life was over for want of ground under his feet, for want of sights for his eyes, for want of voices in his ears. Annihilation — hey! And all the time it was only a clouded sky, a sea that did not break, the air that did not stir. Only a night; only a silence.

"It lasted for a while, and then they were suddenly and unanimously moved to make a noise over their escape. 'I knew from the first she would go.' 'Not a minute too soon.' 'A narrow squeak, b'gosh!' He said nothing, but the breeze that had dropped came back, a gentle draught freshened steadily, and the sea joined its murmuring voice to this talkative reaction succeeding the dumb moments of awe. She was gone! She was gone! Not a doubt of it. Nobody could have helped. They repeated the same words over and over again as though they couldn't stop themselves. Never doubted she would go. The lights were gone. No mistake. The lights were gone. Couldn't expect anything else. She had to go. . . . He noticed that they talked as though they had left behind them nothing but an empty ship. They concluded she would not have been long when she once started. It seemed to cause them some sort of satisfaction. They assured each other that she couldn't have been long about it — 'Just shot down like a flat-iron.' The chief engineer declared that the masthead light at the moment of sinking seemed to drop 'like a lighted match you throw down.' At this the second laughed hysterically. 'I am g-g-glad, I am gla-a-a-d.' His teeth went on 'like an electric rattle,' said Jim, 'and all at once he began to cry. He wept and blubbered like a child, catching his breath and sobbing "Oh, dear!

oh, dear! oh, dear!" He would be quiet for a while and start suddenly, "Oh, my poor arm! oh, my poor a-a-a-arm!" I felt I could knock him down. Some of them sat in the stern-sheets. I could just make out their shapes. Voices came to me, mumble, mumble, grunt, grunt. All this seemed very hard to bear. I was cold, too. And I could do nothing. I thought that if I moved I would have to go over the side and . . .'

"His hand groped stealthily, came in contact with a liqueur-glass, and was withdrawn suddenly as if it had touched a red-hot coal. I pushed the bottle slightly. 'Won't you have some more?' I asked. He looked at me angrily. 'Don't you think I can tell you what there is to tell without screwing myself up?' he asked. The squad of globe-trotters had gone to bed. We were alone but for a vague white form erect in the shadow, that, being looked at, cringed forward, hesitated, backed away silently. It was getting late, but I did not hurry my guest.

"In the midst of his forlorn state he heard his companions begin to abuse some one. 'What kept you from jumping, you lunatic?' said a scolding voice. The chief engineer left the stern-sheets, and could be heard clambering forward as if with hostile intentions against 'the greatest idiot that ever was.' The skipper shouted with rasping effort offensive epithets from where he sat at the oars. He lifted his head at that uproar, and heard the name 'George,' while a hand in the dark struck him on the breast. 'What have you got to say for yourself, you fool?' queried somebody, with a sort of virtuous fury. 'They were after me,' he said. 'They were abusing me — abusing me . . . by the name of George.'

"He paused to stare, tried to smile, turned his eyes away and went on. 'That little second puts his head right under my nose, "Why, it's that blasted mate!" "What!" howls the skipper from the other end of the boat. "No!" shrieks the chief. And he, too, stopped to look at my face.'

"The wind had left the boat suddenly. The rain began to fall again, and the soft, uninterrupted, a little mysterious sound with which the sea receives a shower arose on all sides in the night. 'They were too taken aback to say anything more at first,' he narrated steadily, 'and what could I have to say to them?' He faltered for a moment, and made an effort to go on. 'They called me horrible names.' His voice, sinking to a whisper, now and then would leap up suddenly, hardened by the passion of scorn, as though he had been talking of secret abominations. 'Never mind what they called me,' he said, grimly. 'I could hear hate in their voices. A good thing, too. They could not forgive me for being in that boat. They hated it. It made them mad. . . .' He laughed short. . . . 'But it kept me from — Look! I was sitting with my arms crossed, on the gunwale! . . .' He perched himself smartly on the edge of the table and crossed his arms. . . . 'Like this — see? One little tilt backwards and I would have been gone — after the others. One little tilt — the least bit — the least bit.' He frowned, and tapping his forehead with the tip of his middle finger, 'It was there all the time,' he said, impressively. 'All the time — that notion. And the rain — cold, thick, cold as melted snow — colder — on my thin cotton clothes — I'll never be so cold again in my life, I know. And the sky was black, too — all black. Not a star, not a light anywhere. Nothing outside that confounded boat and those two yapping before me like a couple of mean mongrels at a tree'd thief. Yap! yap! What you doing here? You're a fine sort! Too much of a bloomin' gentleman to put his hand to it. Come out of your trance, did you? To sneak in? Did you? Yap! yap! You ain't fit to live! Yap! yap! Two of them together trying to out-bark each other. The other would bay from the stern through the rain — couldn't see him — couldn't make out — some of his filthy jargon. Yap! yap! Bow-ow-ow-ow-ow! Yap! yap! It was sweet to hear them; it kept me alive, I tell you. It has saved my life. At it they went, as if trying to drive me overboard with the noise! . . . I wonder you had pluck enough to jump. You ain't wanted here. If I had known who it was, I would have tipped you over — you skunk. What have you done with the other? Where did you get the pluck to jump — you coward? What's to prevent us three from firing you overboard? . . . They were out of breath; the shower passed away upon the sea. Then nothing. There was nothing round the boat, not even a sound. Wanted to see me overboard, did they? Upon my soul! I think they would have had their wish if they had only kept quiet. Fire me overboard! Would they? "Try," I said. "I would for twopence." "Too good for you," they screeched together. It was so dark that it was only when one or the other of them moved that I was quite sure of seeing him. By heavens! I only wish they had tried.'

"I couldn't help exclaiming, 'What an extraordinary affair!'

" 'Not bad — eh?' he said, as if in some sort astounded. They pretended to think I had done away with that donkey-man for some reason or other. Why should I? And how the devil was I to know? Didn't I get somehow into that boat? into that boat — I . . .' The muscles round his lips contracted into an unconscious grimace that tore through the mask of his usual expression — something violent, short-lived and illuminating like a twist of lightning that admits the eye for an instant into the secret convolutions of a cloud. 'I did. I was plainly there with them — wasn't I? Isn't it awful a man should be driven to do a thing like that — and be responsible? What did I know about their George they were howling after? I remembered I had seen him curled up on the deck. "Murdering coward!" the chief kept on calling me. He didn't seem able to remember any other two words. I didn't care, only his noise began to worry me. "Shut up," I said. At that he collected himself for a confounded screech. "You killed him. You killed him." "No," I shouted, "but I will kill you directly." I jumped up, and he fell backwards over a thwart with an awful loud thump. I don't know why. Too dark. Tried to step back, I suppose. I stood still facing aft, and the wretched little second began to whine, "You ain't going to hit a chap with a broken arm — and you call yourself a gentleman, too." I heard a heavy tramp — one — two — and wheezy grunting. The other beast was coming at me, clattering his oar over the stern. I saw him moving, big, big — as you see a man in a mist, in a dream. "Come on," I cried. I would have tumbled him over like a bale of shakings. He stopped, muttered to himself, and went back. Perhaps he had heard the wind. I didn't. It was the last heavy gust we had. He went back to his oar. I was sorry. I would have tried to — to . . .'

"He opened and closed his curved fingers, and his hands had an eager and cruel flutter. 'Steady, steady,' I murmured.

" 'Eh? What? I am not excited,' he remonstrated, awfully hurt, and with a convulsive jerk of his elbow knocked over the cognac-bottle. I started forward, scraping my chair. He bounced off the table as if a mine had been exploded behind his back, and half turned before he alighted, crouching on his feet to show me a startled pair of eyes and a face white about the nostrils. A look of intense annoyance succeeded. 'Awfully sorry. How clumsy of me!' he mumbled very vexed, while the pungent odour of spilt alcohol enveloped us suddenly with an atmosphere of a low drinking-bout in the cool, pure darkness of the night. The lights had been put out in the dining-hall; our candle glimmered solitary in the long gallery, and the columns had turned black from pediment to capital. On the vivid stars the high corner of the Harbour Office stood out distinct across the Esplanade, as though the sombre pile had glided nearer to see and hear.

"He assumed an air of indifference.

" 'I dare say I am less calm now than I was then. I was ready for anything. These were trifles. . . .'

" 'You had a lively time of it in that boat,' I remarked.

" 'I was ready,' he repeated. 'After the ship's lights had gone, anything might have happened in that boat — anything in the world — and the world no wiser. I felt this, and I was pleased. It was just dark enough, too. We were like men walled up quick in a roomy grave. No concern with anything on earth. Nobody to pass an opinion. Nothing mattered.' For the third time during this conversation he laughed harshly, but there was no one about to suspect him of being only drunk. 'No fear, no law, no sounds, no eyes — not even our own, till — till sunrise at least.'

"I was struck by the suggestive truth of his words. There is something peculiar in a small boat upon the wide sea. Over the lives borne from under the shadow of death there seems to fall the shadow of madness. When your ship fails you, your whole world seems to fail you; the world that made you, restrained you, taken care of you. It is as if the souls of men floating on an abyss and in touch with immensity had been set free for any excess of heroism, absurdity, or abomination. Of course, as with belief, thought, love, hate, conviction, or even the visual aspect of material things, there are as many shipwrecks as there are men, and in this one there was something abject which made the isolation more complete — there was a villainy of circumstances that cut these men off more completely from the rest of mankind, whose ideal of conduct had never undergone the trial of a fiendish and appalling joke. They were exasperated with him for being a half-hearted shirker: he focused on them his hatred of the whole thing; he would have liked to take a signal revenge for the abhorrent opportunity they had put in his way. Trust a boat on the high seas to bring out the Irrational that lurks at the bottom of every

thought, sentiment, sensation, emotion. It was part of the burlesque meanness pervading that particular disaster at sea that they
did not come to blows. It was all threats, all a terribly effective
feint, a sham from beginning to end, planned by the tremendous
disdain of the Dark Powers whose real terrors, always on the
verge of triumph, are perpetually foiled by the steadfastness of
men. I asked, after waiting for a while, 'Well, what happened?'
A futile question. I knew too much already to hope for the grace
of a single uplifting touch, for the favour of hinted madness,
of shadowed horror. 'Nothing,' he said. 'I meant business, but
they meant noise only. Nothing happened.'

"And the rising sun found him just as he had jumped up first
in the bows of the boat. What a persistence of readiness! He had
been holding the tiller in his hand, too, all the night. They had
dropped the rudder overboard while attempting to ship it, and
I suppose the tiller got kicked forward somehow while they were
rushing up and down that boat trying to do all sorts of things at
once so as to get clear of the side. It was a long heavy piece of
hard wood, and apparently he had been clutching it for six hours
or so. If you don't call that being ready! Can you imagine him,
silent and on his feet half the night, his face to the gusts of rain,
staring at sombre forms, watchful of vague movements, straining
his ears to catch rare low murmurs in the stern-sheets! Firmness
of courage or effort of fear? What do you think? And the endurance is undeniable, too. Six hours more or less on the defensive; six hours of alert immobility while the boat drove slowly
or floated arrested according to the caprice of the wind; while
the sea, calmed, slept at last; while the clouds passed above his
head; while the sky from an immensity lustreless and black, diminished to a sombre and lustrous vault, scintillated with a greater
brilliance, faded to the east, paled at the zenith; while the dark
shapes blotting the low stars astern got outlines, relief; became
shoulders, heads, faces, features, — confronted him with dreary
stares, had dishevelled hair, torn clothes, blinked red eyelids at
the white dawn. 'They looked as though they had been knocking about drunk in gutters for a week,' he described graphically;
and then he muttered something about the sunrise being of a kind
that foretells a calm day. You know that sailor habit of referring
to the weather in every connection. And on my side his few
mumbled words were enough to make me see the lower limb of

the sun clearing the line of the horizon, the tremble of a vast ripple running over all the visible expanse of the sea, as if the waters had shuddered, giving birth to the globe of light, while the last puff of the breeze would stir the air in a sigh of relief.

" 'They sat in the stern shoulder to shoulder, with the skipper in the middle, like three dirty owls, and stared at me,' I heard him say with an intention of hate that distilled a corrosive virtue into the commonplace words like a drop of powerful poison falling into a glass of water; but my thoughts dwelt upon that sunrise. I could imagine under the pellucid emptiness of the sky these four men imprisoned in the solitude of the sea, the lonely sun, regardless of the speck of life, ascending the clear curve of the heaven as if to gaze ardently from a greater height at his own splendour reflected in the still ocean. 'They called out to me from aft,' said Jim, 'as though we had been chums together. I heard them. They were begging me to be sensible and drop that "blooming piece of wood." Why *would* I carry on so? They hadn't done me any harm — had they? There had been no harm. . . . No harm!'

"His face crimsoned as though he could not get rid of the air in his lungs.

" 'No harm!' he burst out. 'I leave it to you. You can understand. Can't you? You see it — don't you? No harm! Good God! What more could they have done? Oh, yes, I know very well — I jumped. Certainly. I jumped! I told you I jumped; but I tell you they were too much for any man. It was their doing as plainly as if they had reached up with a boat-hook and pulled me over. Can't you see it? You must see it. Come. Speak — straight out.'

"His uneasy eyes fastened upon mine, questioned, begged, challenged, entreated. For the life of me I couldn't help murmuring, 'You've been tried.' 'More than is fair,' he caught up, swiftly. 'I wasn't given half a chance — with a gang like that. And now they were friendly — oh, so damnably friendly! Chums, shipmates. All in the same boat. Make the best of it. They hadn't meant anything. They didn't care a hang for George. George had gone back to his berth for something at the last moment and got caught. The man was a manifest fool. Very sad, of course. . . . Their eyes looked at me; their lips moved; they wagged their heads at the other end of the boat — three of them; they beckoned — to me. Why not? Hadn't I jumped? I said nothing.

There are no words for the sort of things I wanted to say. If I had opened my lips just then I would have simply howled like an animal. I was asking myself when I would wake up. They urged me aloud to come aft and hear quietly what the skipper had to say. We were sure to be picked up before the evening — right in the track of all the Canal traffic; there was smoke to the northwest now.

"'It gave me an awful shock to see this faint, faint blur, this low trail of brown mist through which you could see the boundary of sea and sky. I called out to them that I could hear very well where I was. The skipper started swearing, as hoarse as a crow. He wasn't going to talk at the top of his voice for *my* accommodation. "Are you afraid they will hear you on shore?" I asked. He glared as if he would have liked to claw me to pieces. The chief engineer advised him to humour me. He said I wasn't right in my head yet. The other rose astern, like a thick pillar of flesh — and talked — talked. . . .'

"Jim remained thoughtful. 'Well?' I said. 'What did I care what story they agreed to make up?' he cried, recklessly. 'They could tell what they jolly well liked. It was their business. I knew the story. Nothing they could make people believe could alter it for me. I let him talk, argue — talk, argue. He went on and on and on. Suddenly I felt my legs give way under me. I was sick, tired — tired to death. I let fall the tiller, turned my back on them, and sat down on the foremost thwart. I had enough. They called to me to know if I understood — wasn't it true, every word of it? It was true, by God! after their fashion. I did not turn my head. I heard them palavering together. 'The silly ass won't say anything.' "Oh, he understands well enough." "Let him be; he will be all right." "What can he do?" What could I do? Weren't we all in the same boat? I tried to be deaf. The smoke had disappeared to the northward. It was a dead calm. They had a drink from the water-breaker, and I drank, too. Afterwards they made a great business of spreading the boat-sail over the gunwales. Would I keep a look-out? They crept under, out of my sight, thank God! I felt weary, weary, done up, as if I hadn't had one hour's sleep since the day I was born. I couldn't see the water for the glitter of the sunshine. From time to time one of them would creep out, stand up to take a look all round, and get under again. I could hear spells of snoring below the sail. Some of them could sleep. One of them at least. I couldn't! All was light, light, and the boat seemed to be falling through it. Now and then I would feel quite surprised to find myself sitting on a thwart. . . .'

"He began to walk with measured steps to and fro before my chair, one hand in his trousers-pocket, his head bent thoughtfully, and his right arm at long intervals raised for a gesture that seemed to put out of his way an invisible intruder.

" 'I suppose you think I was going mad,' he began in a changed tone. 'And well you may, if you remember I had lost my cap. The sun crept all the way from east to west over my bare head, but that day I could not come to any harm, I suppose. The sun could not make me mad. . . .' His right arm put aside the idea of madness. . . . 'Neither could it kill me. . . .' Again his arm repulsed a shadow. . . . '*That* rested with me.'

" 'Did it?' I said, inexpressibly amazed at this new turn, and I looked at him with the same sort of feeling I might be fairly conceived to experience had he, after spinning round on his heel, presented an altogether new face.

" 'I didn't get brain fever, I did not drop dead either,' he went on. 'I didn't bother myself at all about the sun over my head. I was thinking as coolly as any man that ever sat thinking in the shade. That greasy beast of a skipper poked his big cropped head from under the canvas and screwed his fishy eyes up at me. "Donnerwetter! you will die," he growled, and drew in like a turtle. I had seen him. I had heard him. He didn't interrupt me. I was thinking just then that I wouldn't.'

"He tried to sound my thought with an attentive glance dropped on me in passing. 'Do you mean to say you had been deliberating with yourself whether you would die?' I asked in as impenetrable a tone as I could command. He nodded without stopping. 'Yes, it had come to that as I sat there alone,' he said. He passed on a few steps to the imaginary end of his beat, and when he flung round to come back both his hands were thrust deep into his pockets. He stopped short in front of my chair and looked down. 'Don't you believe it?' he inquired with tense curiosity. I was moved to make a solemn declaration of my readiness to believe implicitly anything he thought fit to tell me."

CHAPTER XI

~~~~~~

"HE HEARD me out with his head on one side, and I had another glimpse through a rent in the mist in which he moved and had his being. The dim candle spluttered within the ball of glass, and that was all I had to see him by; at his back was the dark night with the clear stars, whose distant glitter disposed in retreating planes lured the eye into the depths of a greater darkness; and yet a mysterious light seemed to show me his boyish head, as if in that moment the youth within him had, for a moment, gleamed and expired. 'You are an awful good sort to listen like this,' he said. 'It does me good. You don't know what it is to me. You don't' . . . words seemed to fail him. It was a distinct glimpse. He was a youngster of the sort you like to see about you; of the sort you like to imagine yourself to have been; of the sort whose appearance claims the fellowship of these illusions you had thought gone out, extinct, cold, and which, as if rekindled at the approach of another flame, give a flutter deep, deep down somewhere, give a flutter of light . . . of heat! . . . Yes; I had a glimpse of him then . . . and it was not the last of that kind. . . . 'You don't know what it is for a fellow in my position to be believed — make a clean breast of it to an elder man. It is so difficult — so awfully unfair — so hard to understand.'

"The mists were closing again. I don't know how old I appeared to him — and how much wise. Not half as old as I felt just then; not half as uselessly wise as I knew myself to be. Surely in no other craft as in that of the sea do the hearts of those already launched to sink or swim go out so much to the youth on the brink, looking with shining eyes upon that glitter of the vast surface which is only a reflection of his own glances full of fire. There is such magnificent vagueness in the expectations that had driven each of us to sea, such a glorious indefiniteness, such a beautiful greed of adventures that are their own and only reward! What we get — well, we won't talk of that; but can one of us restrain a smile? In no other kind of life is the illusion more wide of reality — in no other is the beginning *all* illusion — the disenchantment more swift — the subjugation more complete. Hadn't we all commenced with the same desire, ended with the same knowledge, carried the memory of the same cherished glamour through the sordid days of imprecation? What wonder that when some heavy prod gets home the bond is found to be close; that besides the fellowship of the craft there is felt the strength of a wider feeling — the feeling that binds a man to a child. He was there before me, believing that age and wisdom can find a remedy against the pain of truth, giving me a glimpse of himself as a young fellow in a scrape that is the very devil of a scrape, the sort of scrape greybeards wag at solemnly while they hide a smile. And he had been deliberating upon death — confound him! He had found *that* to meditate about because he thought he had saved his life, while all its glamour had gone with the ship in the night. What more natural! It was tragic enough and funny enough in all conscience to call aloud for compassion, and in what was I better than the rest of us to refuse him my pity? And even as I looked at him the mists rolled into the rent, and his voice spoke —

" 'I was so lost, you know. It was the sort of thing one does not expect to happen to one. It was not like a fight, for instance.'

" 'It was not,' I admitted. He appeared changed as if he had suddenly matured.

" 'One couldn't be sure,' he muttered.

" 'Ah! You were not sure,' I said, and was placated by the sound of a faint sigh that passed between us like the flight of a bird in the night.

" 'Well, I wasn't,' he said, courageously. 'It was something like that wretched story they made up. It was not a lie — but it wasn't truth all the same. It was something. . . . One knows a downright lie. There was not the thickness of a sheet of paper between the right and wrong of this affair.'

" 'How much more did you want?' I asked; but I think I spoke so low that he did not catch what I said. He had advanced his argument as though life had been a network of paths separated by chasms. His voice sounded reasonable.

" 'Suppose I had not — I mean to say, suppose I had stuck to the ship? Well. How much longer? Say a minute — half a minute. Come. In thirty seconds, as it seemed certain then, I would have been overboard; and do you think I would not have laid hold of the first thing that came in my way — oar, life-buoy, grating — anything? Wouldn't you?'

" 'And be saved,' I interjected.

" 'I would have meant to be,' he retorted. 'And that's more than I meant when I' . . . he shivered as if about to swallow some nauseous drug . . . 'jumped,' he pronounced with a convulsive effort, whose stress, as if propagated by the waves of the air, made my body stir a little in the chair. He fixed me with lowering eyes. 'Don't you believe me?' he cried. 'I swear! . . . Confound it! You got me here to talk, and . . . You must! . . . You said you would believe.' 'Of course I do,' I protested in a matter-of-fact tone which produced a calming effect. 'Forgive me,' he said. 'Of course I wouldn't have talked to you about all this if you had not been a gentleman. I ought to have known . . . I am — I am — a gentleman, too . . .' " 'Yes, yes,' I said, hastily. He was looking me squarely in the face and withdrew his gaze slowly. 'Now you understand why I didn't after all . . . didn't go out in that way. I wasn't going to be frightened at what I had done. And, anyhow, if I had stuck to the ship I would have done my best to be saved. Men have been known to float for hours — in the open sea — and be picked up not much the worse for it. I might have lasted it out better than many others. There's nothing the matter with *my* heart.' He withdrew his right fist from his pocket, and the blow he struck on his chest resounded like a muffled detonation in the night.

" 'No,' I said. He meditated, with his legs slightly apart and his chin sunk. 'A hair's-breadth,' he muttered. 'Not the breadth of a hair between this and that. And at the time . . .'

" 'It is difficult to see a hair at midnight,' I put in, a little viciously I fear. Don't you see what I mean by the solidarity of the craft? I was aggrieved against him, as though he had cheated me — me! — of a splendid opportunity to keep up the illusion of my beginnings, as though he had robbed our common life of the last spark of its glamour. 'And so you cleared out — at once.'

" 'Jumped,' he corrected me incisively. 'Jumped — mind!' he repeated, and I wondered at the evident but obscure intention. 'Well, yes! Perhaps I could not see then. But I had plenty of time and any amount of light in that boat. And I could think, too. Nobody would know, of course, but this did not make it any easier for me. You've got to believe that, too. I did not want all this talk. . . . No . . . Yes . . . I won't lie . . . I wanted it: it is the very thing I wanted — there. Do you think you or anybody could have made me if I . . . I am — I am not afraid to tell.

And I wasn't afraid to think either. I looked it in the face. I wasn't going to run away. At first — at night, if it hadn't been for these fellows I might have . . . No! by heavens! I was not going to give them that satisfaction. They had done enough. They made up a story, and believed it for all I know. But I knew the truth, and I would live it down — alone, with myself. I wasn't going to give in to such a beastly unfair thing. What did it prove after all? I was confoundedly cut up. Sick of life — to tell you the truth; but what would have been the good to shirk it — in — in — that way? That was not the way. I believe — I believe it would have — it would have ended — nothing.'

"He had been walking up and down, but with the last word he turned short at me.

" 'What do *you* believe?' he asked with violence. A pause ensued, and suddenly I felt myself overcome by a profound and hopeless fatigue, as though his voice had startled me out of a dream of wandering through empty spaces whose immensity had harassed my soul and exhausted my body.

" '. . . Would have ended nothing,' he muttered over me obstinately, after a little while. 'No! the proper thing was to face it out — alone for myself — wait for another chance — to find out . . .' "

CHAPTER XII

"ALL around everything was still as far as the ear could reach. The mist of his feelings shifted between us, as if disturbed by his struggles, and in the rifts of the immaterial veil he would appear to my staring eyes distinct of form and pregnant with vague appeal like a symbolic figure in a picture. The chill air of the night seemed to lie on my limbs as heavy as a slab of marble.

" 'I see,' I murmured, more to prove to myself that I could break my state of numbness than for any other reason.

" 'The *Avondale* picked us up just before sunset,' he remarked, moodily. 'Steamed right straight for us. We had only to sit and wait.'

"After a long interval, he said, 'They told their story.' And again there was that oppressive silence. 'Then only I knew what it was I had made up my mind to,' he added.

" 'You said nothing,' I whispered.

" 'What could I say?' he asked, in the same low tone. . . . 'Shock slight. Stopped the ship. Ascertained the damage. Took measures to get the boats out without creating a panic. As the first boat was lowered ship went down in a squall. Sank like lead. . . . What could be more clear' . . . he hung his head . . . 'and more awful?' His lips quivered while he looked straight into my eyes. 'I had jumped — hadn't I?' he asked, dismayed. 'That's what I had to live down. The story didn't matter.' . . . He clasped his hands for an instant, glanced right and left into the gloom: 'It was like cheating the dead,' he stammered.

" 'And there were no dead,' I said.

"He went away from me at this. That is the only way I can describe it. In a moment I saw his back close to the balustrade. He stood there for some time, as if admiring the purity and the peace of the night. Some flowering-shrub in the garden below spread its powerful scent through the damp air. He returned to me with hasty steps.

" 'And that did not matter,' he said, as stubbornly as you please.

" 'Perhaps not,' I admitted. I began to have a notion he was too much for me. After all, what did I know?

" 'Dead or not dead, I could not get clear,' he said. 'I had to live; hadn't I?'

" 'Well, yes — if you take it in that way,' I mumbled.

" 'I was glad, of course,' he threw out carelessly with his mind fixed on something else. 'The exposure,' he pronounced, slowly, and lifted his head. 'Do you know what was my first thought when I heard? I was relieved. I was relieved to learn that those shouts — did I tell you I had heard shouts? No? Well, I did. Shouts for help . . . blown along with the drizzle. Imagination I suppose. And yet I can hardly . . . How stupid. . . . The others did not. I asked them afterwards. They all said No. No? And I was hearing them even then! I might have known — but I didn't think — I only listened. Very faint screams — day after day. Then that little half-caste chap here came up and spoke to me. "The *Patna* . . . French gunboat . . . towed successfully to Aden . . . Investigation . . . Marine Office . . . Sailors' Home . . . arrangements made for your board and lodging!" I walked along with him, and I enjoyed the silence. So there had been no shouting. Imagination. I had to believe him. I could hear nothing any more. I wonder how long I could have stood it. It was getting worse, too . . . I mean — louder.'

"He fell into thought.

"'And I had heard nothing! Well — so be it. But the lights! The lights did go! We did not see them. They were not there. If they had been, I would have swam back — I would have gone back and shouted alongside — I would have begged them to take me on board. . . . I would have had my chance. . . . You doubt me? . . . How do you know how I felt? . . . What right have you to doubt? . . . I very nearly did it as it was — do you understand?' His voice fell. 'There was not a glimmer — not a glimmer,' he protested, mournfully. 'Don't you understand that if there had been, you would not have seen me here? You see me — and you doubt.'

"I shook my head negatively. This question of the lights being lost sight of when the boat could not have been more than a quarter of a mile from the ship was a matter for much discussion. Jim stuck to it that there was nothing to be seen after the first shower had cleared away; and the others had affirmed the same thing to the officers of the *Avondale*. Of course people shook their heads and smiled. One old skipper who sat near me in court tickled my ear with his white beard to murmur, 'Of course they would lie.' As a matter of fact nobody lied; not even the chief engineer with his story of the masthead light dropping like a match you throw down. Not consciously, at least. A man with his liver in such a state might very well have seen a floating spark in the corner of his eye when stealing a hurried glance over his shoulder. They had seen no light of any sort though they were well within range, and they could only explain this in one way: the ship had gone down. It was obvious and comforting. The foreseen fact coming so swiftly had justified their haste. No wonder they did not cast about for any other explanation. Yet the true one was very simple, and as soon as Brierly suggested it the court ceased to bother about the question. If you remember, the ship had been stopped and was lying with her head on the course steered through the night, with her stern canted high and her bows brought low down in the water through the filling of the fore-compartment. Being thus out of trim, when the squall struck her a little on the quarter, she swung head to wind as sharply as though she had been at anchor. By this change in her position all her lights were in a very few moments shut off from the boat to leeward. It may very well be that, had they been seen, they would have had the effect of a mute appeal — that their glimmer lost in the darkness of the cloud would have had the mysterious power of the human glance that can awaken the feelings of remorse and pity. It would have said, 'I am here — still here' . . . and what more can the eye of the most forsaken of human beings say? But she turned her back on them as if in disdain of their fate: she had swung round, burdened, to glare stubbornly at the new danger of the open sea which she so strangely survived to end her days in a breaking-up yard, as if it had been her recorded fate to die obscurely under the blows of many hammers. What were the various ends their destiny provided for the pilgrims I am unable to say; but the immediate future brought, at about nine o'clock next morning, a French gunboat homeward bound from Réunion. The report of her commander was public property. He had swept a little out of his course to ascertain what was the matter with that steamer floating dangerously by the head upon a still and hazy sea. There was an ensign, union down, flying at her main gaff (the serang had the sense to make a signal of distress at daylight); but the cooks were preparing the food in the cooking-boxes forward as usual. The decks were packed as close as a sheep-pen: there were people perched all along the rails, jammed on the bridge in a solid mass; hundreds of eyes stared, and not a sound was heard when the gunboat ranged abreast, as if all that multitude of lips had been sealed by a spell.

"The Frenchman hailed, could get no intelligible reply, and after ascertaining through his binoculars that the crowd on deck did not look plague-stricken, decided to send a boat. Two officers came on board, listened to the serang, tried to talk with the Arab, couldn't make head or tail of it: but of course the nature of the emergency was obvious enough. They were also very much struck by discovering a white man, dead and curled up peacefully on the bridge. '*Fort intrigués par ce cadavre,*' as I was informed a long time after by an elderly French lieutenant whom I came across one afternoon in Sydney, by the merest chance, in a sort of café, and who remembered the affair perfectly. Indeed this affair, I may notice in passing, had an extraordinary power

of defying the shortness of memories and the length of time: it
seemed to live, with a sort of uncanny vitality, in the minds of
men, on the tips of their tongues. I've had the questionable
pleasure of meeting it often, years afterwards, thousands of miles
away, emerging from the remotest possible talk, coming to the
surface of the most distant allusions. Has it not turned up to-
night between us? And I am the only seaman here. I am the only
one to whom it is a memory. And yet it has made its way out!
But if two men who, unknown to each other, knew of this affair
met accidentally on any spot of this earth, the thing would pop
up between them as sure as fate, before they parted. I had never
seen that Frenchman before, and at the end of an hour we had
done with each other for life: he did not seem particularly talkative either; he was a quiet, massive chap in a creased uniform sitting drowsily over a tumbler half full of some dark liquid. His
shoulder-straps were a bit tarnished, his clean-shaved cheeks were
large and sallow; he looked like a man who would be given to
taking snuff — don't you know? I won't say he did; but the habit
would have fitted that kind of man. It all began by his handing
me a number of *Home News*, which I didn't want, across the
marble table. I said, 'Merci.' We exchanged a few apparently
innocent remarks, and suddenly, before I knew how it had come
about, we were in the midst of it, and he was telling me how much
they had been 'intrigued by that corpse.' It turned out he had
been one of the boarding officers.

"In the establishment where we sat one could get a variety of
foreign drinks which were kept for the visiting naval officers,
and he took a sip of the dark medical-looking stuff, which probably was nothing more nasty than *cassis à l'eau*, and glancing
with one eye into the tumbler, shook his head slightly. '*Impossible de comprendre — vous concevez*,' he said, with a curious mixture of unconcern and thoughtfulness. I could very easily conceive how impossible it had been for them to understand. Nobody in the gunboat knew enough English to get hold of the
story as told by the serang. There was a good deal of noise, too,
round the two officers. 'They crowded upon us. There was a
circle round that dead man (*autour de ce mort*),' he described.
'One had to attend to the most pressing. These people were beginning to agitate themselves — *Parbleu!* A mob like that — don't
you see?' he interjected with philosophic indulgence. As to the

bulkhead, he had advised his commander that the safest thing was
to leave it alone, it was so villainous to look at. They got two
hawsers on board promptly (*en toute hâte*) and took the *Patna*
in tow — stern foremost at that — which, under the circumstances,
was not so foolish, since the rudder was too much out of the
water to be of any great use for steering, and this manœuvre
eased the strain on the bulkhead, whose state, he expounded with
stolid glibness, demanded the greatest care (*éxigeait les plus grands
ménagements*). I could not help thinking that my new acquaintance must have had a voice in most of these arrangements: he
looked a reliable officer, no longer very active, and he was seamanlike, too, in a way, though as he sat there, with his thick
fingers clasped lightly on his stomach, he reminded you of one of
those snuffy, quiet village priests, into whose ears are poured the
sins, the sufferings, the remorse of peasant generations, on whose
faces the placid and simple expression is like a veil thrown over
the mystery of pain and distress. He ought to have had a thread-
bare black *soutane* buttoned smoothly up to his ample chin, instead of a frockcoat with shoulder-straps and brass buttons. His
broad bosom heaved regularly while he went on telling me that
it had been the very devil of a job, as doubtless (*sans doute*) I
could figure to myself in my quality of a seaman (*en votre qualité
de marin*). At the end of the period he inclined his body slightly
towards me, and, pursing his shaved lips, allowed the air to escape with a gentle hiss. 'Luckily,' he continued, 'the sea was
level like this table, and there was no more wind than there is
here.' . . . The place struck me as indeed intolerably stuffy, and
very hot; my face burned as though I had been young enough to
be embarrassed and blushing. They had directed their course,
he pursued, to the nearest English port '*naturellement,*' where
their responsibility ceased '*Dieu merci.*' . . . He blew out his flat
cheeks a little. . . . 'Because, mind you (*notez bien*), all the
time of towing we had two quartermasters stationed with axes by
the hawsers, to cut as clear of our tow in case she . . .' He
fluttered downwards his heavy eyelids, making his meaning as
plain as possible. . . . 'What would you! One does what one can
(*on fait ce qu'on peut*),' and for a moment he managed to invest
his ponderous immobility with an air of resignation. 'Two quartermasters — thirty hours — always there. Two!' he repeated, lifting up his right hand a little, and exhibiting two fingers. This

was absolutely the first gesture I saw him make. It gave me the opportunity to 'note' a starred scar on the back of his hand — effect of a gunshot clearly; and, as if my sight had been made more acute by this discovery, I perceived also the seam of an old wound, beginning a little below the temple and going out of sight under the short grey hair at the side of his head — the graze of a spear or the cut of a sabre. He clasped his hands on his stomach again. 'I remained on board that — that — my memory is going (*s'en va*). Ah! Patt-nà. *C'est bien ça*. Patt-nà. *Merci*. It is droll how one forgets. I stayed on that ship thirty hours. . . .'

" 'You did!' I exclaimed. Still gazing at his hands, he pursed his lips a little, but this time made no hissing sound. 'It was judged proper,' he said, lifting his eyebrows dispassionately, 'that one of the officers should remain to keep an eye open (*pour ouvrir l'œil*)' . . . he sighed idly . . . 'and for communicating by signals with the towing ship — do you see? — and so on. For the rest, it was my opinion, too. We made our boats ready to drop over — and I also on that ship took measures. . . . *Enfin!* One has done one's possible. It was a delicate position. Thirty hours. They prepared me some food. As for the wine — go and whistle for it — not a drop.' In some extraordinary way, without any marked change in his inert attitude and in the placid expression of his face, he managed to convey the idea of profound disgust. 'I — you know — when it comes to eating without my glass of wine — I am nowhere.'

"I was afraid he would enlarge upon the grievance, for though he didn't stir a limb or twitch a feature, he made one aware how much he was irritated by the recollection. But he seemed to forget all about it. They delivered their charge to the 'port authorities,' as he expressed it. He was struck by the calmness with which it had been received. 'One might have thought they had such a droll find (*drôle de trouvaille*) brought them every day. You are extraordinary — you others,' he commented, with his back propped against the wall, and looking himself as incapable of an emotional display as a sack of meal. There happened to be a man-of-war and an Indian Marine steamer in the harbour at the time, and he did not conceal his admiration of the efficient manner in which the boats of these two ships cleared the *Patna* of her passengers. Indeed his torpid demeanour concealed nothing: it had that mysterious, almost miraculous, power of producing striking effects by means impossible of detection which is the last word of the highest art. 'Twenty-five minutes — watch in hand — twenty-five, no more.' . . . He unclasped and clasped again his fingers without removing his hands from his stomach, and made it infinitely more effective than if he had thrown up his arms to heaven in amazement. . . . 'All that lot (*tout ce monde*) on shore — with their little affairs — nobody left but a guard of seamen (*marins de l'État*) and that interesting corpse (*cet intéressant cadavre*). Twenty-five minutes.' . . . With downcast eyes and his head tilted slightly on one side he seemed to roll knowingly on his tongue the savour of a smart bit of work. He persuaded one without any further demonstration that his approval was eminently worth having, and resuming his hardly interrupted immobility, he went on to inform me that, being under orders to make the best of their way to Toulon, they left in two hours' time, 'so that (*de sorte que*) there are many things in this incident of my life (*dans cet épisode de ma vie*) which have remained obscure.' "

CHAPTER XIII

"AFTER these words, and without a change of attitude, he, so to speak, submitted himself passively to a state of silence. I kept him company; and suddenly, but not abruptly, as if the appointed time had arrived for his moderate and husky voice to come out of his immobility, he pronounced, '*Mon Dieu!* how the time passes!' Nothing could have been more commonplace than this remark; but its utterance coincided for me with a moment of vision. It's extraordinary how we go through life with eyes half shut, with dull ears, with dormant thoughts. Perhaps it's just as well; and it may be that it is this very dulness that makes life to the incalculable majority so supportable and so welcome. Nevertheless, there can be but few of us who had never known one of these rare moments of awakening when we see, hear, understand ever so much — everything — in a flash — before we fall back again into our agreeable somnolence. I raised my eyes when he spoke, and I saw him as though I had never seen him before. I saw his chin sunk on his breast, the clumsy folds of his coat, his clasped hands, his motionless pose, so curiously suggestive of his having been simply left there. Time had passed indeed: it had overtaken him and gone ahead. It had left him hopelessly behind with a few poor gifts: the iron-grey hair, the heavy fatigue of the tanned face, two scars, a pair of tarnished shoulder-straps; one of those steady, reliable men who are the raw material of great reputations, one of those uncounted lives that are buried without drums and trumpets under the foundations of monumental successes. 'I am now third lieutenant of the *Victorieuse*' (she was the flag-ship of the French Pacific squadron at the time), he said, detaching his shoulders from the wall a couple of inches to introduce himself. I bowed slightly on my side of the table, and told him I commanded a merchant vessel at present anchored in Rushcut-ters' Bay. He had 'remarked' her, — a pretty little craft. He was very civil about it in his impassive way. I even fancy he went the length of tilting his head in compliment as he repeated, breathing visibly the while, 'Ah, yes. A little craft painted black — very pretty — very pretty (*très coquet*).' After a time he twisted his body slowly to face the glass door on our right. 'A dull town (*triste ville*),' he observed, staring into the street. It was a bril-liant day; a southerly buster was raging, and we could see the passers-by, men and women, buffeted by the wind on the side-walks, the sunlit fronts of the houses across the road blurred by the tall whirls of dust. 'I descended on shore,' he said, 'to stretch my legs a little, but . . .' He didn't finish, and sank into the depths of his repose. 'Pray — tell me,' he began, coming up pon-derously, 'what was there at the bottom of this affair — precisely (*au juste*)? It is curious. That dead man, for instance — and so on.'

" 'There were living men, too,' I said; 'much more curious.'

" 'No doubt, no doubt,' he agreed half audibly, then, as if after mature consideration, murmured, 'Evidently.' I made no diffi-culty in communicating to him what had interested me most in this affair. It seemed as though he had a right to know: hadn't he spent thirty hours on board the *Patna* — had he not taken the succession, so to speak, had he not done 'his possible'? He lis-tened to me, looking more priest-like than ever, and with what —

probably on account of his downcast eyes — had the appearance of devout concentration. Once or twice he elevated his eyebrows (but without raising his eyelids), as one would say 'The devil!' Once he calmly exclaimed, 'Ah, bah!' under his breath, and when I had finished he pursed his lips in a deliberate way and emitted a sort of sorrowful whistle.

"In any one else it might have been an evidence of boredom, a sign of indifference; but he, in his occult way, managed to make his immobility appear profoundly responsive, and as full of valuable thoughts as an egg is of meat. What he said at last was nothing more than a 'very interesting,' pronounced politely, and not much above a whisper. Before I got over my disappointment he added, but as if speaking to himself, 'That's it. That *is* it.' His chin seemed to sink lower on his breast, his body to weigh heavier on his seat. I was about to ask him what he meant when a sort of preparatory tremor passed over his whole person, as a faint ripple may be seen upon stagnant water even before the wind is felt. 'And so that poor young man ran away along with the others,' he said, with grave tranquillity.

"I don't know what made me smile: it is the only genuine smile of mine I can remember in connection with Jim's affair. But somehow this simple statement of the matter sounded funny in French. . . . 'S'est enfui avec les autres,' had said the lieutenant. And suddenly I began to admire the discrimination of the man. He had made out the point at once: he did get hold of the only thing I cared about. I felt as though I were taking professional opinion on the case. His imperturbable and mature calmness was that of an expert in possession of the facts, and to whom one's perplexities are mere child's-play. 'Ah! The young, the young,' he said, indulgently. 'And after all, one does not die of it.' 'Die of what?' I asked, swiftly. 'Of being afraid.' He elucidated his meaning and sipped his drink.

"I perceived that the three last fingers of his wounded hand were stiff and could not move independently of each other, so that he took up his tumbler with an ungainly clutch. 'One is always afraid. One may talk, but . . .' He put down the glass awkwardly. . . . 'The fear, the fear — look you — it is always there.' . . . He touched his breast near a brass button on the very spot where Jim had given a thump to his own when protesting that there was nothing the matter with his heart. I suppose I made some sign of dissent, because he insisted, 'Yes! yes! One talks, one talks; this is all very fine; but at the end of the reckoning one is no cleverer than the next man — and no more brave. Brave! This is always to be seen. I have rolled my hump (*roulé ma bosse*),' he said, using the slang expression with imperturbable seriousness, 'in all parts of the world; I have known brave men — famous ones; *Allez!*' . . . He drank carelessly. . . . 'Brave — you conceive — in the Service — one has got to be — the trade demands it (*le métier veut ça*). Is it not so?' he appealed to me reasonably. '*Eh bien!* Each of them — I say each of them, if he were an honest man — *bien entendu* — would confess that there is a point — there is a point — for the best of us — there is somewhere a point when you let go everything (*vous lâchez tout*). And you have got to live with that truth — do you see? Given a certain combination of circumstances, fear is sure to come. Abominable funk (*un trac épouvantable*). And even for those who do not believe this truth there is fear all the same — the fear of themselves. Absolutely so. Trust me. Yes. Yes. . . . At my age one knows what one is talking about — *que diable!*' . . . He had delivered himself of all this as immovably as though he had been the mouthpiece of abstract wisdom, but at this point he heightened the effect of detachment by beginning to twirl his thumbs slowly. 'It's evident — *parbleu!*' he continued; 'for, make up your mind as much as you like, even a simple headache or a fit of indigestion (*un dérangement d'estomac*) is enough to . . . Take me, for instance — I have made my proofs. *Eh bien!* I, who am speaking to you, once . . .'

"He drained his glass and returned to his twirling. 'No, no; one does not die of it,' he pronounced, finally, and when I found he did not mean to proceed with the personal anecdote, I was extremely disappointed; the more so as it was not the sort of story, you know, one could very well press him for. I sat silent, and he too, as if nothing could please him better. Even his thumbs were still now. Suddenly his lips began to move. 'That is so,' he resumed, placidly. 'Man is born a coward (*L'homme est né poltron*). It is a difficulty — *parbleu!* It would be too easy otherwise. But habit — habit — necessity — do you see? — the eye of others — *voilà*. One puts up with it. And then the example of others who are no better than yourself, and yet make good countenance. . . .'

"His voice ceased.

" 'That young man — you will observe — had none of these inducements — at least at the moment,' I remarked.

"He raised his eyebrows forgivingly: 'I don't say; I don't say. The young man in question might have had the best dispositions — the best dispositions,' he repeated, wheezing a little.

" 'I am glad to see you taking a lenient view,' I said. 'His own feeling in the matter was — ah! — hopeful, and . . .'

"The shuffle of his feet under the table interrupted me. He drew up his heavy eyelids. Drew up, I say — no other expression can describe the steady deliberation of the act — and at last was disclosed completely to me. I was confronted by two narrow grey circlets, like two tiny steel rings around the profound blackness of the pupils. The sharp glance, coming from that massive body, gave a notion of extreme efficiency, like a razor-edge on a battle-axe. 'Pardon,' he said, punctiliously. His right hand went up, and he swayed forward. 'Allow me . . . I contended that one may get on knowing very well that one's courage does not come of itself (*ne vient pas tout seul*). There's nothing much in that to get upset about. One truth the more ought not to make life impossible. . . . But the honour — the honour, monsieur! . . . The honour . . . that is real — that is! And what life may be worth when' . . . he got on his feet with a ponderous impetuosity, as a startled ox might scramble up from the grass . . . 'when the honour is gone — *ah ça! par exemple* — I can offer no opinion. I can offer no opinion — because — monsieur — I know nothing of it.'

"I had risen, too, and, trying to throw infinite politeness into our attitudes, we faced each other mutely, like two china dogs on a mantelpiece. Hang the fellow! he had pricked the bubble. The blight of futility that lies in wait for men's speeches had fallen upon our conversation, and made it a thing of empty sounds. 'Very well,' I said, with a disconcerted smile, 'but couldn't it reduce itself to not being found out?' He made as if to retort readily, but when he spoke he had changed his mind. 'This, monsieur, is too fine for me — much above me — I don't think about it.' He bowed heavily over his cap, which he held before him by the peak, between the thumb and the forefinger of his wounded hand. I bowed, too. We bowed together: we scraped our feet at each other with much ceremony, while a dirty specimen of a waiter looked on critically, as though he had paid for the performance. 'Serviteur,' said the Frenchman. Another scrape. 'Monsieur' . . . 'Monsieur.' . . . The glass door swung behind his burly back. I saw the southerly buster get hold of him and drive him down wind with his hand to his head, his shoulders braced, and the tails of his coat blown hard against his legs.

"I sat down again alone and discouraged — discouraged about Jim's case. If you wonder that after more than three years it had preserved its actuality, you must know that I had seen him only very lately. I had come straight from Samarang, where I had loaded a cargo for Sydney: an utterly uninteresting bit of business, — what Charley here would call one of my rational transactions — and in Samarang I had seen something of Jim. He was then working for De Jongh, on my recommendation. Water-clerk. 'My representative afloat,' as De Jongh called him. You can't imagine a mode of life more barren of consolation, less capable of being invested with a spark of glamour — unless it be the business of an insurance canvasser. Little Bob Stanton — Charley here knew him well — had gone through that experience. The same who got drowned afterwards trying to save a lady's-maid in the *Sephora* disaster. A case of collision on a hazy morning off the Spanish coast you may remember. All the passengers had been packed tidily into the boats and shoved clear of the ship when Bob sheered alongside again and scrambled back on deck to fetch that girl. How she had been left behind I can't make out; anyhow, she had gone completely crazy — wouldn't leave the ship — held to the rail like grim death. The wrestling-match could be seen plainly from the boats; but poor Bob was the shortest chief mate in the merchant service, and the woman stood five feet ten in her shoes and was as strong as a horse, I've been told. So it went on, pull devil, pull baker, the wretched girl screaming all the time, and Bob letting out a yell now and then to warn his boat to keep well clear of the ship. One of the hands told me, hiding a smile at the recollection, 'It was for all the world, sir, like a naughty youngster fighting with his mother.' The same old chap said that 'At the last we could see that Mr. Stanton had given up hauling at the gal, and just stood by looking at her, watchful like. We thought afterwards he must 've been reckoning that, maybe, the rush of water would tear her away from the rail by and by and give him a show to save her. We daren't come alongside for our life; and after a bit the old ship went down all on a sudden with a lurch to starboard — plop. The suck in was something awful. We never saw anything alive or dead come up.' Poor Bob's spell of shore-life had been one of the complications of a love affair, I believe. He fondly hoped he had done with the sea for ever, and made sure he had got hold of all the bliss on earth, but it came to canvassing in the end. Some cousin of his in Liverpool put him up to it. He used to tell us his experiences in that line. He made us laugh till we cried, and, not altogether displeased at the effect, undersized and bearded to the waist like a gnome, he would tiptoe amongst us and say, 'It's all very well for you beggars to laugh, but my immortal soul was shrivelled down to the size of a parched pea after a week of that work.' I don't know how Jim's soul accommodated itself to the new conditions of his life — I was kept too busy in getting him something to do that would keep body and soul together — but I am pretty certain his adventurous fancy was suffering all the pangs of starvation. It had certainly nothing to feed upon in this new calling. It was distressing to see him at it, though he tackled it with a stubborn serenity for which I must give him full credit. I kept my eye on his shabby plodding with a sort of notion that it was a punishment for the heroics of his fancy — an expiation for his craving after more glamour than he could carry. He had loved too well to imagine himself a glorious racehorse, and now he was condemned to toil without honour like a costermonger's donkey. He did it very well. He shut himself in, put his head down, said never a word. Very well; very well indeed — except for certain fantastic and violent outbreaks, on the deplorable occasions when the irrepressible *Patna* case cropped up. Unfortunately that scandal of the Eastern seas would not die out. And this is the reason why I could never feel I had done with Jim for good.

"I sat thinking of him after the French lieutenant had left, not, however, in connection with De Jongh's cool and gloomy backshop, where we had hurriedly shaken hands not very long ago, but as I had seen him years before in the last flickers of the candle, alone with me in the long gallery of the Malabar House, with the chill and the darkness of the night at his back. The respectable sword of his country's law was suspended over his head. Tomorrow — or was it to-day? (midnight had slipped by long before we parted) — the marble-faced police magistrate, after distributing fines and terms of imprisonment in the assault-and-battery case, would take up the awful weapon and smite his bowed neck. Our communion in the night was uncommonly like a last vigil with a condemned man. He was guilty, too. He was guilty — as I had told myself repeatedly, guilty and done for; nevertheless, I wished to spare him the mere detail of a formal execution. I don't pretend to explain the reasons of my desire — I don't think I could; but if you haven't got a sort of notion by this time, then I must have been very obscure in my narrative, or you too sleepy to seize upon the sense of my words. I don't defend my morality. There was no morality in the impulse which induced me to lay before him Brierly's plan of evasion — I may call it — in all its primitive simplicity. There were the rupees — absolutely ready in my pocket and very much at his service. Oh! a loan; a loan of course — and if an introduction to a man (in Rangoon) who could put some work in his way . . . Why! with the greatest pleasure. I had pen, ink, and paper in my room on the first floor. And even while I was speaking I was impatient to begin the letter: day, month, year, 2:30 A. M. . . . for the sake of our old friendship I ask you to put some work in the way of Mr. James So-and-so, in whom, &c., &c. . . . I was even ready to write in that strain about him. If he had not enlisted my sympathies he had done better for himself — he had gone to the very fount and origin of that sentiment, he had reached the secret sensibility of my egoism. I am concealing nothing from you, because were I to do so my action would appear more unintelligible than any man's action has the right to be, and — in the second place — to-morrow you shall forget my sincerity along with the other lessons of the past. In this transaction, to speak grossly and precisely, I was the irreproachable man; but the subtle intentions of my immorality were defeated by the moral simplicity of the criminal. No doubt he was selfish, too, but his selfishness had a higher origin, a more lofty aim. I discovered that, say what I would, he was eager to go through the ceremony of execution; and I didn't say much, for I felt that in argument his youth would tell against me heavily: he believed where I had already ceased to doubt. There was something fine in the wildness of his unexpressed, hardly formulated hope. 'Clear out! Couldn't think of it,' he said, with a shake of the head. 'I make you an offer for which I neither demand nor expect any sort of gratitude,' I said; 'you shall repay the money when convenient, and . . .' 'Awfully good of you,' he muttered without looking up. I watched him narrowly: the

future must have appeared horribly uncertain to him; but he did
not falter, as though indeed there had been nothing wrong with
his heart. I felt angry — not for the first time that night. 'The
whole wretched business,' I said, 'is bitter enough, I should think,
for a man of your kind . . .' 'It is, it is,' he whispered twice, with
his eyes fixed on the floor. It was heartrending. He towered above
the light, and I could see the down on his cheek, the colour man-
tling warm under the smooth skin of his face. Believe me or not,
I say it was outrageously heartrending. It provoked me to brutality. 'Yes,' I said; 'and allow me to confess that I am totally
unable to imagine what advantage you can expect from this lick-
ing of the dregs.' 'Advantage!' he murmured out of his stillness.
'I am dashed if I do,' I said, enraged. 'I've been trying to tell you
all there is in it,' he went on, slowly, as if meditating something
unanswerable. 'But after all, it is *my* trouble.' I opened my mouth
to retort, and discovered suddenly that I'd lost all confidence in
myself; and it was as if he, too, had given me up, for he mumbled
like a man thinking half aloud. 'Went away . . . went into hos-
pitals. . . . Not one of them would face it. . . . They! . . .'
He moved his hand slightly to imply disdain. 'But I've got to get
over this thing, and I mustn't shirk any of it or . . . I won't shirk
any of it.' He was silent. He gazed as though he had been haunted.
His unconscious face reflected the passing expressions of scorn, of
despair, of resolution, — reflected them in turn, as a magic mirror
would reflect the gliding passage of unearthly shapes. He lived
surrounded by deceitful ghosts, by austere shades. 'Oh! nonsense,
my dear fellow,' I began. He had a movement of impatience.
'You don't seem to understand,' he said, incisively; then looking
at me without a wink, 'I may have jumped, but I don't run away.'
'I meant no offence,' I said; and added stupidly, 'Better men than
you have found it expedient to run, at times.' He coloured all
over, while in my confusion I half-choked myself with my own
tongue. 'Perhaps so,' he said at last; 'I am not good enough; I can't
afford it. I am bound to fight this thing down — I am fighting it
now.' I got out of my chair and felt stiff all over. The silence
was embarrassing, and to put an end to it I imagined nothing better
but to remark, 'I had no idea it was so late,' in an airy tone. . . .
'I daresay you have had enough of this,' he said, brusquely: 'and
to tell you the truth' — he began to look round for his hat — 'so
have I.'

"Well! he had refused this unique offer. He had struck aside my helping hand; he was ready to go now, and beyond the balustrade the night seemed to wait for him very still, as though he had been marked down for its prey. I heard his voice. 'Ah! here it is.' He had found his hat. For a few seconds we hung in the wind. 'What will you do after — after . . .' I asked very low. 'Go to the dogs as likely as not,' he answered in a gruff mutter. I had recovered my wits in a measure, and judged best to take it lightly. 'Pray remember,' I said, 'that I should like very much to see you again before you go.' 'I don't know what's to prevent you. The damned thing won't make me invisible,' he said with intense bitterness, — 'no such luck.' And then at the moment of taking leave he treated me to a ghastly muddle of dubious stammers and movements, to an awful display of hesitations. God forgive him — me! He had taken it into his fanciful head that I was likely to make some difficulty as to shaking hands. It was too awful for words. I believe I shouted suddenly at him as you would bellow to a man you saw about to walk over a cliff; I remember our voices being raised, the appearance of a miserable grin on his face, a crushing clutch on my hand, a nervous laugh. The candle spluttered out, and the thing was over at last, with a groan that floated up to me in the dark. He got himself away somehow. The night swallowed his form. He was a horrible bungler. Horrible. I heard the quick crunch-crunch of the gravel under his boots. He was running. Absolutely running, with nowhere to go to. And he was not yet four-and-twenty.'

CHAPTER XIV

"I slept little, hurried over my breakfast, and after a slight hesitation gave up my early morning visit to my ship. It was really very wrong of me, because, though my chief mate was an excellent man all round, he was the victim of such black imaginings that if he did not get a letter from his wife at the expected time he would go quite distracted with rage and jealousy, lose all grip on the work, quarrel with all hands, and either weep in his cabin or develop such a ferocity of temper as all but drove the crew to the verge of mutiny. The thing had always seemed inexplicable to me: they had been married thirteen years; I had a glimpse of her once, and, honestly, I couldn't conceive a man abandoned enough to plunge into sin for the sake of such an unattractive person. I don't know whether I have not done wrong by refraining from putting that view before poor Selvin: the man made a little hell on earth for himself, and I also suffered indirectly, but some sort of, no doubt, false delicacy prevented me. The marital relations of seamen would make an interesting subject, and I could tell you instances. . . . However, this is not the place, nor the time, and we are concerned with Jim — who was unmarried. If his imaginative conscience or his pride; if all the extravagant ghosts and austere shades that were the disastrous familiars of his youth would not let him run away from the block, I, who of course can't be suspected of such familiars, was irresistibly impelled to go and see his head roll off. I wended my way towards the court. I didn't hope to be very much impressed or edified, or interested or even frightened — though, as long as there is any life before one, a jolly good fright now and then is a salutary discipline. But neither did I expect to be so awfully depressed. The bitterness of his punishment was in its chill and mean atmosphere. The real significance of crime is in its being a breach of faith with the community of mankind, and from that point of view he was no mean traitor, but his execution was a hole-and-corner affair. There was no high scaffolding, no scarlet cloth (did they have scarlet cloth on Tower Hill? They should have had), no awe-stricken multitude to be horrified at his guilt and be moved to tears at his fate — no air of sombre retribution. There was, as I walked along, the clear sunshine, a brilliance too passionate to be consoling, the streets full of jumbled bits of colour like a damaged kaleidoscope: yellow, green, blue, dazzling white, the brown nudity of an undraped shoulder, a bullock-cart with a red canopy, a company of native infantry in a drab body with dark heads marching in dusty laced boots, a native policeman in a sombre uniform of scanty cut and belted in patent leather, who looked up at me with orientally pitiful eyes as though his migrating spirit were suffering exceedingly from that unforeseen — what d'ye call 'em? — avatar — incarnation. Under the shade of a lonely tree in the courtyard, the villagers connected with the assault case sat in a picturesque group, looking like a chromo-lithograph of a camp in a book of Eastern travel. One missed the obligatory thread of smoke in the fore-ground and the pack-animals grazing. A blank yellow wall rose behind overtopping the tree, reflecting the glare. The court-room was sombre, seemed more vast. High up in the dim space the punkahs were swaying short to and fro, to and fro. Here and there a draped figure, dwarfed by the bare walls, remained with-out stirring amongst the rows of empty benches, as if absorbed in pious meditation. The plaintiff, who had been beaten, an obese chocolate-coloured man with shaved head, one fat breast bare and a bright yellow caste-mark above the bridge of his nose, sat in pompous immobility: only his eyes glittered, rolling in the gloom, and the nostrils dilated and collapsed violently as he breathed. Brierly dropped into his seat looking done up, as though he had spent the night in sprinting on a cinder-track. The pious sailing-ship skipper appeared excited and made uneasy movements, as if restraining with difficulty an impulse to stand up and exhort us earnestly to prayer and repentance. The head of the magistrate, delicately pale under the neatly arranged hair, resembled the head of a hopeless invalid after he had been washed and brushed and propped up in bed. He moved aside the vase of flowers — a bunch of purple with a few pink blossoms on long stalks — and seizing in both hands a long sheet of bluish paper, ran his eye over it, propped his forearms on the edge of the desk, and began to read aloud in an even, distinct, and careless voice.

"By Jove! For all my foolishness about scaffolds and heads rolling off — I assure you it was infinitely worse than a beheading. A heavy sense of finality brooded over all this, unrelieved by the hope of rest and safety following the fall of the axe. These pro-ceedings had all the cold vengefulness of a death-sentence, had all the cruelty of a sentence of exile. This is how I looked at it that morning — and even now I seem to see an undeniable vestige of truth in that exaggerated view of a common occurrence. You may imagine how strongly I felt this at the time. Perhaps it is for that reason that I could not bring myself to admit the finality. The thing was always with me, I was always eager to take opin-ion on it, as though it had not been practically settled: individual opinion — international opinion — by Jove! That Frenchman's, for instance. His own country's pronouncement was uttered in the passionless and definite phraseology a machine would use, if machines could speak. The head of the magistrate was half hidden by the paper, his brow was like alabaster.

"There were several questions before the Court. The first as to whether the ship was in every respect fit and seaworthy for the voyage. The court found she was not. The next point, I remember, was, whether up to the time of the accident the ship had been navigated with proper and seamanlike care. They said Yes to that, goodness knows why, and then they declared that there was no evidence to show the exact cause of the accident. A floating derelict probably. I myself remember that a Norwegian barque bound out with a cargo of pitch-pine had been given up as missing about that time, and it was just the sort of craft that would capsize in a squall and float bottom up for months — a kind of maritime ghoul on the prowl to kill ships in the dark. Such wandering corpses are common enough in the North Atlantic, which is haunted by all the terrors of the sea, — fogs, icebergs, dead ships bent upon mischief, and long sinister gales that fasten upon one like a vampire till all the strength and the spirit and even hope are gone, and one feels like the empty shell of a man. But there — in those seas — the incident was rare enough to resemble a special arrangement of a malevolent providence, which, unless it had for its object the killing of a donkeyman and the bringing of worse than death upon Jim, appeared an utterly aimless piece of devilry. This view occurring to me took off my attention. For a time I was aware of the magistrate's voice as a sound merely; but in a moment it shaped itself into distinct words . . . 'in utter disregard of their plain duty,' it said. The next sentence escaped me somehow, and then . . . 'abandoning in the moment of danger the lives and property confided to their charge' . . . went on the voice evenly, and stopped. A pair of eyes under the white forehead shot darkly a glance above the edge of the paper. I looked for Jim hurriedly, as though I had expected him to disappear. He was very still — but he was there. He sat pink and fair and extremely attentive. 'Therefore, . . .' began the voice emphatically. He stared with parted lips, hanging upon the words of the man behind the desk. These came out into the stillness wafted on the wind made by the punkahs, and I, watching for their effect upon him, caught only the fragments of official language. . . . 'The Court . . . Gustav So-and-so master . . . native of Germany . . . James So-and-so . . . mate . . . certificates cancelled.'

A silence fell. The magistrate had dropped the paper, and leaning sideways on the arm of his chair, began to talk with Brierly
easily. People started to move out; others were pushing in, and
I also made for the door. Outside I stood still, and when Jim
passed me on his way to the gate, I caught at his arm and detained
him. The look he gave discomposed me, as though I had been
responsible for his state: he looked at me as if I had been the
embodied evil of life. 'It's all over,' I stammered. 'Yes,' he said,
thickly. 'And now let no man . . .' He jerked his arm out of
my grasp. I watched his back as he went away. It was a long
street, and he remained in sight for some time. He walked rather
slow, and straddling his legs a little, as if he had found it difficult
to keep a straight line. Just before I lost him I fancied he staggered a bit.

"'Man overboard,' said a deep voice behind me. Turning
round, I saw a fellow I knew slightly, a West Australian; Chester
was his name. He, too, had been looking after Jim. He was a man
with an immense girth of chest, a rugged, clean-shaved face of mahogany colour, and two blunt tufts of iron-grey, thick wiry hairs
on his upper lip. He had been pearler, wrecker, trader, whaler,
too, I believe; in his own words — anything and everything a man
may be at sea, but a pirate. The Pacific, north and south, was his
proper hunting-ground; but he had wandered so far afield looking for a cheap steamer to buy. Lately he had discovered — so
he said — a guano island somewhere, but its approaches were dangerous, and the anchorage, such as it was, could not be considered
safe, to say the least of it. 'As good as a gold-mine,' he would exclaim. 'Right bang in the middle of the Walpole Reefs, and if it's
true enough that you can get no holding-ground anywhere in less
than forty fathom, then what of that? There are the hurricanes,
too. But it's a first-rate thing. As good as a gold-mine — better! Yet
there's not a fool of them that will see it. I can't get a skipper or
a shipowner to go near the place. So I made up my mind to cart
the blessed stuff myself.' . . . This was what he required a
steamer for, and I knew he was just then negotiating enthusias-
tically with a Parsee firm for an old, brig-rigged, sea-anachronism
of ninety horse-power. We had met and spoken together several
times. He looked knowingly after Jim. 'Takes it to heart?' he
asked, scornfully. 'Very much,' I said. 'Then he's no good,' he
opined. 'What's all the to-do about? A bit of ass's skin. That

never yet made a man. You must see things exactly as they are —
if you don't, you may just as well give in at once. You will never
do anything in this world. Look at me. I made it a practice
never to take anything to heart.' 'Yes,' I said, 'you see things as
they are.' 'I wish I could see my partner coming along, that's
what I wish to see,' he said. 'Know my partner? Old Robinson.
Yes; *the* Robinson. Don't *you* know? The notorious Robinson.
The man who smuggled more opium and bagged more seals in
his time than any loose Johnny now alive. They say he used to
board the sealing-schooners up Alaska way when the fog was so
thick that the Lord God, He alone, could tell one man from another. Holy-Terror Robinson. That's the man. He is with me
in that guano thing. The best chance he ever came across in his
life.' He put his lips to my ear. 'Cannibal? — well, they used to
give him the name years and years ago. You remember the story?
A shipwreck on the west side of Stewart Island; that's right; seven
of them got ashore, and it seems they did not get on very well
together. Some men are too cantankerous for anything — don't
know how to make the best of a bad job — don't see things as they
are — as they *are*, my boy! And then what's the consequence?
Obvious! Trouble, trouble; as likely as not a knock on the head;
and serve 'em right, too. That sort is the most useful when it's
dead. The story goes that a boat of Her Majesty's ship *Wolverine*
found him kneeling on the kelp, naked as the day he was born,
and chanting some psalm-tune or other; light snow was falling at
the time. He waited till the boat was an oar's length from the
shore, and then up and away. They chased him for an hour up
and down the boulders, till a marine flung a stone that took him
behind the ear providentially and knocked him senseless. Alone?
Of course. But that's like that tale of sealing-schooners; the Lord
God knows the right and the wrong of that story. The cutter
did not investigate much. They wrapped him in a boat-cloak and
took him off as quick as they could, with a dark night coming on,
the weather threatening, and the ship firing recall guns every five
minutes. Three weeks afterwards he was as well as ever. He
didn't allow any fuss that was made on shore to upset him; he
just shut his lips tight, and let people screech. It was bad enough
to have lost his ship, and all he was worth besides, without paying attention to the hard names they called him. That's the man
for me.' He lifted his arm for a signal to some one down the

street. 'He's got a little money, so I had to let him into my thing.
Had to! It would have been sinful to throw away such a find,
and I was cleaned out myself. It cut me to the quick, but I could
see the matter just as it was, and if I *must* share — thinks I — with
any man, then give me Robinson. I left him at breakfast in the
hotel to come to court, because I've an idea. . . . Ah! Good
morning, Captain Robinson. . . . Friend of mine, Captain Robinson.'

"An emaciated patriarch in a suit of white drill, a solah topi
with a green-lined rim on a head trembling with age, joined us
after crossing the street in a trotting shuffle, and stood propped
with both hands on the handle of an umbrella. A white beard
with amber streaks hung lumpily down to his waist. He blinked
his creased eyelids at me in a bewildered way. 'How do you do?
how do you do?' he piped, amiably, and tottered. 'A little deaf,'
said Chester aside. 'Did you drag him over six thousand miles to
get a cheap steamer?' I asked. 'I would have taken him twice
round the world as soon as look at him,' said Chester with immense
energy. 'The steamer will be the making of us, my lad. Is it my
fault that every skipper and shipowner in the whole of blessed
Australasia turns out a blamed fool? Once I talked for three hours
to a man in Auckland. "Send a ship," I said, "send a ship. I'll
give you half of the first cargo for yourself, free gratis for nothing — just to make a good start." Says he, "I wouldn't do it if
there was no other place on earth to send a ship to." Perfect ass,
of course. Rocks, currents, no anchorage, sheer cliff to lay to,
no insurance company would take the risk, didn't see how he
could get loaded under three years. Ass! I nearly went on my
knees to him. "But look at the thing as it is," says I. "Damn rocks
and hurricanes. Look at it as it is. There's guano there, Queensland sugar-planters would fight for — fight for on the quay, I tell
you." . . . What can you do with a fool? . . . That's one of
your little jokes, Chester," he says. . . . Joke! I could have wept.
Ask Captain Robinson here. . . . And there was another ship-
owning fellow — a fat chap in a white waistcoat in Wellington,
who seemed to think I was up to some swindle or other. "I don't
know what sort of fool you're looking for," he says, "but I am
busy just now. Good morning." I longed to take him in my two
hands and smash him through the window of his own office. But
I didn't. I was as mild as a curate. "Think of it," says I. "*Do

think it over. I'll call to-morrow." He grunted something about being "out all day." On the stairs I felt ready to beat my head against the wall from vexation. Captain Robinson here can tell you. It was awful to think of all that lovely stuff lying waste under the sun — stuff that would send the sugar-cane shooting sky-high. The making of Queensland! The making of Queensland! And in Brisbane, where I went to have a last try, they gave me the name of a lunatic. Idiots! The only sensible man I came across was the cabman who drove me about. A broken-down swell he was, I fancy. Hey! Captain Robinson? You remember I told you about my cabby in Brisbane — don't you? The chap had a wonderful eye for things. He saw it all in a jiffy. It was a real pleasure to talk with him. One evening after a devil of a day amongst shipowners I felt so bad that, says I, "I must get drunk. Come along; I must get drunk, or I'll go mad." "I am your man," he says; "go ahead." I don't know what I would have done without him. Hey! Captain Robinson.'

"He poked the ribs of his partner. 'He! he! he!' laughed the Ancient, looked aimlessly down the street, then peered at me doubtfully with sad, dim pupils. . . . 'He! he! he!' . . . He leaned heavier on the umbrella, and dropped his gaze on the ground. I needn't tell you I had tried to get away several times, but Chester had foiled every attempt by simply catching hold of my coat. 'One minute. I've a notion.' 'What's your infernal notion?' I exploded at last. 'If you think I am going in with you . . .' 'No, no, my boy. Too late, if you wanted ever so much. We've got a steamer.' 'You've got the ghost of a steamer,' I said. 'Good enough for a start — there's no superior nonsense about us. Is there, Captain Robinson?' 'No! no! no!' croaked the old man without lifting his eyes, and the senile tremble of his head became almost fierce with determination. 'I understand you know that young chap,' said Chester, with a nod at the street from which Jim had disappeared long ago. 'He's been having grub with you in the Malabar last night — so I was told.'

"I said that was true, and after remarking that he, too, liked to live well and in style, only that, for the present, he had to be saving of every penny — 'none too many for the business! Isn't that so, Captain Robinson?' — he squared his shoulders and stroked his dumpy moustache, while the notorious Robinson, coughing at his side, clung more than ever to the handle of the umbrella, and seemed ready to subside passively into a heap of old bones. 'You see, the old chap has all the money,' whispered Chester, confidentially. 'I've been cleaned out trying to engineer the dratted thing. But wait a bit, wait a bit. The good time is coming.' . . . He seemed suddenly astonished at the signs of impatience I gave. 'Oh, crakee!' he cried; 'I am telling you of the biggest thing that ever was, and you . . .' 'I have an appointment,' I pleaded mildly. 'What of that?' he asked with genuine surprise; 'let it wait.' 'That's exactly what I am doing now,' I remarked; 'hadn't you better tell me what it is you want?' 'Buy twenty hotels like that,' he growled to himself; 'and every joker boarding in them, too — twenty times over.' He lifted his head smartly. 'I want that young chap.' 'I don't understand,' I said. 'He's no good, is he?' said Chester, crisply. 'I know nothing about it,' I protested. 'Why, you told me yourself he was taking it to heart,' argued Chester. 'Well, in my opinion a chap who . . . Anyhow, he can't be much good; but then you see I am on the look-out for somebody, and I've just got a thing that will suit him. I'll give him a job on my island.' He nodded significantly. 'I'm going to dump forty coolies there — if I've got to steal 'em. Somebody must work the stuff. Oh! I mean to act square: wooden shed, corrugated-iron roof — I know a man in Hobart who will take my bill at six months for the materials. I do. Honour bright. Then there's the water-supply. I'll have to fly round and get somebody to trust me for half-a-dozen second-hand iron tanks. Catch rain-water, hey? Let him take charge. Make him supreme boss over the coolies. Good idea, isn't it? What do you say?' 'There are whole years when not a drop of rain falls on Walpole,' I said, too amazed to laugh. He bit his lip and seemed bothered. 'Oh, well, I will fix up something for them — or land a supply. Hang it all! That's not the question.'

"I said nothing. I had a rapid vision of Jim perched on a shadowless rock, up to his knees in guano, with the screams of sea-birds in his ears, the incandescent ball of the sun above his head; the empty sky and the empty ocean all a-quiver, simmering together in the heat as far as the eye could reach. 'I wouldn't advise my worst enemy . . .' I began. 'What's the matter with you?' cried Chester; 'I mean to give him a good screw — that is, as soon as the thing is set going, of course. It's as easy as falling off a log. Simply nothing to do; two six-shooters in his belt. . . .

Surely he wouldn't be afraid of anything forty coolies could do —
with two six-shooters and he the only armed man, too! It's much
better than it looks. I want you to help me to talk him over.'
'No!' I shouted. Old Robinson lifted his bleared eyes dismally
for a moment, Chester looked at me with infinite contempt. 'So
you wouldn't advise him?' he uttered, slowly. 'Certainly not,' I
answered, as indignant as though he had requested me to help
murder somebody; 'moreover, I am sure he wouldn't. He is badly
cut up, but he isn't mad as far as I know.' 'He is no earthly good
for anything,' Chester mused aloud. 'He would just have done for
me. If you only could see a thing as it is, you would see it's the
very thing for him. And besides . . . Why! it's the most splendid, sure chance . . .' He got angry suddenly. 'I must have a
man. There! . . .' He stamped his foot and smiled unpleasantly.
'Anyhow, I could guarantee the island wouldn't sink under him —
and I believe he is a bit particular on that point.' 'Good morning,'
I said, curtly. He looked at me as though I had been an incomprehensible fool. . . . 'Must be moving, Captain Robinson,' he
yelled suddenly into the old man's ear. 'These Parsee Johnnies
are waiting for us to clinch the bargain.' He took his partner
under the arm with a firm grip, swung him round, and, unexpectedly, leered at me over his shoulder. 'I was trying to do him a
kindness,' he asserted, with an air and tone that made my blood
boil. 'Thank you for nothing — in his name,' I rejoined. 'Oh! you
are devilish smart,' he sneered; 'but you are like the rest of them.
Too much in the clouds. See what *you* will do with him.' 'I don't
know that I want to do anything with him.' 'Don't you?' he
spluttered; his grey moustache bristled with anger, and by his
side the notorious Robinson, propped on the umbrella, stood with
his back to me, as patient and still as a worn-out cab-horse. 'I
haven't found a guano island,' I said. 'It's my belief you wouldn't
know one if you were led right up to it by the hand,' he riposted
quickly; 'and in this world you've got to see a thing first, before
you can make use of it. Got to see it through and through at
that, neither more nor less.' 'And get others to see it, too,' I in-
sinuated, with a glance at the bowed back by his side. Chester
snorted at me. 'His eyes are right enough — don't you worry. He
ain't a puppy.' 'Oh, dear, no!' I said. 'Come along, Captain Robinson,' he shouted, with a sort of bullying deference under the
rim of the old man's hat; the Holy Terror gave a submissive little

jump. The ghost of a steamer was waiting for them, Fortune on that fair isle! They made a curious pair of Argonauts. Chester strode on leisurely, well set up, portly, and of conquering mien; the other, long, wasted, drooping, and hooked to his arm, shuffled his withered shanks with desperate haste."

CHAPTER XV

"I DID not start in search of Jim at once, only because I had really an appointment which I could not neglect. Then, as ill-luck would have it, in my agent's office I was fastened upon by a fellow fresh from Madagascar with a little scheme for a wonderful piece of business. It had something to do with cattle and cartridges and a Prince Ravonalo something; but the pivot of the whole affair was the stupidity of some admiral — Admiral Pierre, I think. Everything turned on that, and the chap couldn't find words strong enough to express his confidence. He had globular eyes starting out of his head with a fishy glitter, bumps on his forehead, and wore his long hair brushed back without a parting. He had a favourite phrase which he kept on repeating triumphantly, 'The minimum of risk with the maximum of profit is my motto. What?' He made my head ache, spoiled my tiffin, but got his own out of me all right; and as soon as I had shaken him off, I made straight for the water-side. I caught sight of Jim leaning over the parapet of the quay. Three native boatmen quarrelling over five annas were making an awful row at his elbow. He didn't hear me come up, but spun round as if the slight contact of my finger had released a catch. 'I was looking,' he stammered. I don't remember what I said, not much anyhow, but he made no difficulty in following me to the hotel.

"He followed me as manageable as a little child, with an obedient air, with no sort of manifestation, rather as though he had been waiting for me there to come along and carry him off. I need not have been so surprised as I was at his tractability. On all the round earth, which to some seems so big and that others

affect to consider as rather smaller than a mustard-seed, he had
no place where he could — what shall I say? — where he could
withdraw. That's it! Withdraw — be alone with his loneliness.
He walked by my side very calm, glancing here and there, and
once turned his head to look after a Sidiboy fireman in a cutaway
coat and yellowish trousers, whose black face had silky gleams
like a lump of anthracite coal. I doubt, however, whether he saw
anything, or even remained all the time aware of my companionship, because if I had not edged him to the left here, or pulled
him to the right there, I believe he would have gone straight before him in any direction till stopped by a wall or some other
obstacle. I steered him into my bedroom, and sat down at once
to write letters. This was the only place in the world (unless,
perhaps, the Walpole Reef — but that was not so handy) where
he could have it out with himself without being bothered by the
rest of the universe. The damned thing — as he had expressed it —
had not made him invisible, but I behaved exactly as though he
were. No sooner in my chair I bent over my writing-desk like
a medieval scribe, and, but for the moment of the hand holding the
pen, remained anxiously quiet. I can't say I was frightened; but I
certainly kept as still as if there had been something dangerous in
the room, that at the first hint of a movement on my part would
be provoked to pounce upon me. There was not much in the
room — you know how these bed-rooms are — a sort of four-
poster bedstead under a mosquito-net, two or three chairs, the
table I was writing at, a bare floor. A glass door opened on an
upstairs verandah, and he stood with his face to it, having a hard
time with all possible privacy. Dusk fell; I lit a candle with the
greatest economy of movement and as much prudence as though
it were an illegal proceeding. There is no doubt that he had a
very hard time of it, and so had I, even to the point, I must own,
of wishing him to the devil, or on Walpole Reef at least. It occurred to me once or twice that, after all, Chester was, perhaps,
the man to deal effectively with such a disaster. That strange
idealist had found a practical use for it at once — unerringly, as
it were. It was enough to make one suspect that, maybe, he really
could see the true aspect of things that appeared mysterious or
utterly hopeless to less imaginative persons. I wrote and wrote;
I liquidated all the arrears of my correspondence, and then went
on writing to people who had no reason whatever to expect from

me a gossipy letter about nothing at all. At times I stole a sidelong glance. He was rooted to the spot, but convulsive shudders
ran down his back; his shoulders would heave suddenly. He was
fighting, he was fighting — mostly for his breath, as it seemed.
The massive shadows, cast all one way from the straight flame
of the candle, seemed possessed of gloomy consciousness; the immobility of the furniture had to my furtive eye an air of attention. I was becoming fanciful in the midst of my industrious
scribbling; and though, when the scratching of my pen stopped
for a moment, there was complete silence and stillness in the
room, I suffered from that profound disturbance and confusion
of thought which is caused by a violent and menacing uproar —
of a heavy gale at sea, for instance. Some of you may know
what I mean, — that mingled anxiety, distress, and irritation with
a sort of craven feeling creeping in — not pleasant to acknowl-
edge, but which gives a quiet special merit to one's endurance.
I don't claim any merit for standing the stress of Jim's emotions;
I could take refuge in the letters; I could have written to strangers
if necessary. Suddenly, as I was taking up a fresh sheet of note-
paper, I heard a low sound, the first sound that, since we had been
shut up together, had come to my ears in the dim stillness of the
room. I remained with my head down, with my hand arrested.
Those who have kept vigil by a sick-bed have heard such faint
sounds in the stillness of the night watches, sounds wrung from a
racked body, from a weary soul. He pushed the glass door with
such force that all the panes rang: he stepped out, and I held my
breath, straining my ears without knowing what else I expected
to hear. He was really taking too much to heart an empty formality which to Chester's rigorous criticism seemed unworthy the
notice of a man who could see things as they were. An empty
formality; a piece of parchment. Well, well. As to the inaccessible guano deposit, that was another story altogether. One could
intelligibly break one's heart over that. A feeble burst of many
voices mingled with the tinkle of silver and glass floated up from
the dining-room below; through the open door the outer edge of
the light from my candle fell on his back faintly; beyond all was
black; he stood on the brink of a vast obscurity, like a lonely
figure by the shore of a sombre and hopeless ocean. There was
the Walpole Reef in it — to be sure — a speck in the dark void,
a straw for the drowning man. My compassion for him took the

shape of the thought that I wouldn't have liked his people to see him at that moment. I found it trying myself. His back was no longer shaken by his gasps; he stood straight as an arrow, faintly visible and still; and the meaning of this stillness sank to the bottom of my soul like lead into the water, and made it so heavy that for a second I wished heartily that the only course left open for me were to pay for his funeral. Even the law had done with him. To bury him would have been such an easy kindness! It would have been so much in accordance with the wisdom of life, which consists in putting out of sight all the reminders of our folly, of our weakness, of our mortality; all that makes against our efficiency — the memory of our failures, the hints of our undying fears, the bodies of our dead friends. Perhaps he did take it too much to heart. And if so then — Chester's offer. . . . At this point I took up a fresh sheet and began to write resolutely. There was nothing but myself between him and the dark ocean. I had a sense of responsibility. If I spoke, would that motionless and suffering youth leap into the obscurity — clutch at the straw? I found out how difficult it may be sometimes to make a sound. There is a weird power in a spoken word. And why the devil not? I was asking myself persistently while I drove on with my writing. All at once, on the blank page, under the very point of the pen, the two figures of Chester and his antique partner, very distinct and complete, would dodge into view with stride and gestures, as if reproduced in the field of some optical toy. I would watch them for a while. No! They were too phantasmal and extravagant to enter into any one's fate. And a word carries far — very far — deals destruction through time as the bullets go flying through space. I said nothing; and he, out there with his back to the light, as if bound and gagged by all the invisible foes of man, made no stir and made no sound."

CHAPTER XVI

"THE time was coming when I should see him loved, trusted, admired, with a legend of strength and prowess forming round his name as though he had been the stuff of a hero. It's true — I assure you; as true as I'm sitting here talking about him in vain. He, on his side, had that faculty of beholding at a hint the face of his desire and the shape of his dream, without which the earth would know no lover and no adventurer. He captured much honour and an Arcadian happiness (I won't say anything about innocence) in the bush, and it was as good to him as the honour and the Arcadian happiness of the streets to another man. Felicity, felicity — how shall I say it? — is quaffed out of a golden cup in every latitude: the flavour is with you — with you alone, and you can make it as intoxicating as you please. He was of the sort that would drink deep, as you may guess from what went before. I found him, if not exactly intoxicated, then at least flushed with the elixir at his lips. He had not obtained it at once. There had been, as you know, a period of probation amongst infernal ship-chandlers, during which he had suffered and I had worried about — about — my trust — you may call it. I don't know that I am completely reassured now, after beholding him in all his brilliance. That was my last view of him — in a strong light, dominating, and yet in complete accord with his surroundings — with the life of the forests and with the life of men. I own that I was impressed, but I must admit to myself that after all this is not the lasting impression. He was protected by his isolation, alone of his own superior kind, in close touch with Nature, that keeps faith on such easy terms with her lovers. But I cannot fix before my eye the image of his safety. I shall always remember him as seen through the open door of my room, taking, perhaps, too much to heart the mere consequences of his failure. I am pleased, of course, that some good — and even some splendour — came out of my endeavours; but at times it seems to me it would have been better for my peace of mind if I had not stood between him and Chester's confoundedly generous offer. I wonder what his exuberant imagination would have made of Walpole islet — that most hopelessly forsaken crumb of dry land on the face of the waters. It is not likely I would ever have heard, for I must tell you that Chester, after calling at some Australian port to patch up his brig-rigged sea-anachronism, steamed out into the Pacific with a crew of twenty-two hands all told, and the only news having a possible bearing upon the mystery of his fate was the news of a hurricane which is supposed to have swept in its course over the Walpole shoals, a month or so afterwards. Not a vestige of the Argonauts ever turned up; not a sound came out of the waste. Finis! The Pacific is the most discreet of live, hot-tempered oceans: the chilly Antarctic can keep a secret, too, but more in the manner of a grave.

"And there is a sense of blessed finality in such discretion, which is what we all more or less sincerely are ready to admit — for what else is it that makes the idea of death supportable? End! Finis! the potent word that exorcises from the house of life the haunting shadow of fate. This is what — notwithstanding the testimony of my eyes and his own earnest assurances — I miss when I look back upon Jim's success. While there's life there is hope, truly; but there is fear, too. I don't mean to say that I regret my action, nor will I pretend that I can't sleep o' nights in consequence; still the idea obtrudes itself that he made so much of his disgrace while it is the guilt alone that matters. He was not — if I may say so — clear to me. He was not clear. And there is a suspicion he was not clear to himself either. There were his fine sensibilities, his fine feelings, his fine longings — a sort of sublimated, idealised selfishness. He was — if you allow me to say so — very fine; very fine — and very unfortunate. A little coarser nature would not have borne the strain; it would have had to come to terms with itself — with a sigh, with a grunt, or even with a guffaw; a still coarser one would have remained invulnerably ignorant and completely uninteresting.

"But he was too interesting or too unfortunate to be thrown to the dogs, or even to Chester. I felt this while I sat with my face over the paper and he fought and gasped, struggling for his breath in that terribly stealthy way, in my room; I felt it when he rushed out on the verandah as if to fling himself over — and didn't; I felt it more and more all the time he remained outside, faintly lighted on the background of night, as if standing on the shore of a sombre and hopeless sea.

"An abrupt heavy rumble made me lift my head. The noise seemed to roll away, and suddenly a searching and violent glare fell on the blind face of the night. The sustained and dazzling flickers seemed to last for an unconscionable time. The growl of the thunder increased steadily while I looked at him, distinct and black, planted solidly upon the shores of a sea of light. At the moment of greatest brilliance the darkness leaped back with a culminating crash, and he vanished before my dazzled eyes as utterly as though he had been blown to atoms. A blustering sigh passed; furious hands seemed to tear at the shrubs, shake the tops of the trees below, slam doors, break window-panes, all along the front of the building. He stepped in, closing the door behind him, and found me bending over the table: my sudden anxiety as to what he would say was very great, and akin to a fright. 'May I have a cigarette?' he asked. I gave a push to the box without raising my head. 'I want — want — tobacco,' he muttered. I became extremely buoyant. 'Just a moment,' I grunted, pleasantly. He took a few steps here and there. 'That's over,' I heard him say. A single distant clap of thunder came from the sea like a gun of distress. 'The monsoon breaks up early this year,' he remarked, conversationally, somewhere behind me. This encouraged me to turn round, which I did as soon as I had finished addressing the last envelope. He was smoking greedily in the middle of the room, and though he heard the stir I made, he remained with his back to me for a time.

" 'Come — I carried it off pretty well,' he said, wheeling suddenly. 'Something's paid off — not much. I wonder what's to come.' His face did not show any emotion, only it appeared a little darkened and swollen, as though he had been holding his breath. He smiled reluctantly as it were, and went on while I gazed up at him mutely. . . . 'Thank you, though — your room — jolly convenient — for a chap — badly hipped.' . . . The rain pattered and swished in the garden; a water-pipe (it must have had a hole in it) performed just outside the window a parody of blubbering woe with funny sobs and gurgling lamentations, interrupted by jerky spasms of silence. . . . 'A bit of shelter,' he mumbled and ceased.

"A flash of faded lightning darted in through the black framework of the windows and ebbed out without any noise. I was thinking how I had best approach him (I did not want to be flung off again) when he gave a little laugh. 'No better than a vagabond now' . . . the end of the cigarette smouldered between his fingers . . . 'without a single — single,' he pronounced slowly; 'and yet . . .' He paused; the rain fell with redoubled violence. 'Some day one's bound to come upon some sort of chance to get it all back again. Must!' he whispered, distinctly, glaring at my boots.

"I did not even know what it was he wished so much to regain, what it was he had so terribly missed. It might have been so much that it was impossible to say. A piece of ass's skin, according to Chester. . . . He looked up at me inquisitively. 'Perhaps. If life's long enough,' I muttered through my teeth with unreasonable animosity. 'Don't reckon too much on it.'

" 'Jove! I feel as if nothing could ever touch me,' he said in a tone of sombre conviction. 'If this business couldn't knock me over, then there's no fear of there being not enough time to — climb out, and . . .' He looked upwards.

"It struck me that it is from such as he that the great army of waifs and strays is recruited, the army that marches down, down into all the gutters of the earth. As soon as he left my room, that 'bit of shelter,' he would take his place in the ranks, and begin the journey towards the bottomless pit. I at least had no illusions; but it was I, too, who a moment ago had been so sure of the power of words, and now was afraid to speak, in the same way one dares not move for fear of losing a slippery hold. It is when we try to grapple with another man's intimate need that we perceive how incomprehensible, wavering, and misty are the beings that share with us the sight of the stars and the warmth of the sun. It is as if loneliness were a hard and absolute condition of existence; the envelope of flesh and blood on which our eyes are fixed melts before the outstretched hand, and there remains only the capricious, unconsolable, and elusive spirit that no eye can follow, no hand can grasp. It was the fear of losing him that kept me silent, for it was borne upon me suddenly and with unaccountable force that should I let him slip away into the darkness I would never forgive myself.

" 'Well. Thanks — once more. You've been — er — uncommonly — really there's no word to . . . Uncommonly! I don't know why, I am sure. I am afraid I don't feel as grateful as I would if the whole thing hadn't been so brutally sprung on me. Because at bottom . . . you, yourself . . .' He stuttered.

" 'Possibly,' I struck in. He frowned.

" 'All the same, one is responsible.' He watched me like a hawk.

" 'And that's true, too,' I said.

" 'Well. I've gone with it to the end, and I don't intend to let any man cast it in my teeth without — without — resenting.' He clenched his fist.

" 'There's yourself,' I said with a smile — mirthless enough, God knows — but he looked at me menacingly. 'That's my business,' he said. An air of indomitable resolution came and went upon his face like a vain and passing shadow. Next moment he looked a dear good boy in trouble, as before. He flung away the cigarette. 'Good-bye,' he said, with the sudden haste of a man who had lingered too long in view of a pressing bit of work waiting for him; and then for a second or so he made not the slightest movement. The downpour fell with the heavy uninterrupted rush of a sweeping flood, with a sound of unchecked overwhelming fury that called to one's mind the images of collapsing bridges, of uprooted trees, of undermined mountains. No man could breast the colossal and headlong stream that seemed to break and swirl against the dim stillness in which we were precariously sheltered as if on an island. The perforated pipe gurgled, choked, spat, and splashed in odious ridicule of a swimmer fighting for his life. 'It is raining,' I remonstrated, 'and I . . .' 'Rain or shine,' he began, brusquely, checked himself, and walked to the window. 'Perfect deluge,' he muttered after a while: he leaned his forehead on the glass. 'It's dark, too.'

" 'Yes, it is very dark,' I said.

"He pivoted on his heels, crossed the room, and had actually opened the door leading into the corridor before I leaped up from my chair. 'Wait,' I cried, 'I want you to . . .' 'I can't dine with you again to-night,' he flung at me, with one leg out of the room already. 'I haven't the slightest intention to ask you,' I shouted. At this he drew back his foot, but remained mistrustfully in the very doorway. I lost no time in entreating him earnestly not to be absurd; to come in and shut the door."

CHAPTER XVII

"He came in at last; but I believe it was mostly the rain that did it; it was falling just then with a devastating violence which quieted down gradually while we talked. His manner was very sober and set; his bearing was that of a naturally taciturn man possessed by an idea. My talk was of the material aspect of his position; it had the sole aim of saving him from the degradation, ruin, and despair that out there close so swiftly upon a friendless, homeless man; I pleaded with him to accept my help; I argued reasonably: and every time I looked up at that absorbed smooth face, so grave and youthful, I had a disturbing sense of being no help but rather an obstacle to some mysterious, inexplicable, impalpable striving of his wounded spirit.

"'I suppose you intend to eat and drink and to sleep under shelter in the usual way,' I remember saying with irritation. 'You say you won't touch the money that is due to you.' . . . He came as near as his sort can to making a gesture of horror. (There were three weeks and five days' pay owing him as mate of the *Patna*.) 'Well, that's too little to matter anyhow; but what will you do to-morrow? Where will you turn? You must live . . .' 'That isn't the thing,' was the comment that escaped him under his breath. I ignored it, and went on combating what I assumed to be the scruples of an exaggerated delicacy. 'On every conceivable ground,' I concluded, 'you must let me help you.' 'You can't,' he said very simply and gently, and holding fast to some deep idea which I could detect shimmering like a pool of water in the dark, but which I despaired of ever approaching near enough to fathom. I surveyed his well-proportioned bulk. 'At any rate,' I said, 'I am able to help what I can see of you. I don't pretend to do more.' He shook his head sceptically without looking at me. I got very warm. 'But I can,' I insisted. 'I can do even more. I *am* doing more. I am trusting you . . .' 'The money . . .' he began. 'Upon my word you deserve being told to go to the devil,' I cried, forcing the note of indignation. He was startled, smiled, and I pressed my attack home. 'It isn't a

question of money at all. You are too superficial,' I said (and at
the same time I was thinking to myself: Well, here goes! And
perhaps he is after all). 'Look at the letter I want you to take.
I am writing to a man of whom I've never asked a favour, and I
am writing about you in terms that one only ventures to use when
speaking of an intimate friend. I make myself unreservedly responsible for you. That's what I am doing. And really if you will
only reflect a little what that means . . .'

"He lifted his head. The rain had passed away; only the water-
pipe went on shedding tears with an absurd drip, drip outside the
window. It was very quiet in the room, whose shadows huddled
together in corners, away from the still flame of the candle flar-
ing upright in the shape of a dagger; his face after a while seemed
suffused by a reflection of a soft light as if the dawn had broken
already.

" 'Jove!' he gasped out. It is noble of you!'

"Had he suddenly put out his tongue at me in derision, I could
not have felt more humiliated. I thought to myself — Serve me
right for a sneaking humbug. . . . His eyes shone straight into
my face, but I perceived it was not a mocking brightness. All at
once he sprang into jerky agitation, like one of those flat wooden
figures that are worked by a string. His arms went up, then came
down with a slap. He became another man altogether. 'And I
had never seen,' he shouted; then suddenly bit his lip and frowned.
'What a bally ass I've been,' he said very slow in an awed tone.
. . . 'You are a brick,' he cried next in a muffled voice. He
snatched my hand as though he had just then seen it for the first
time, and dropped it at once. 'Why! this is what I — you —
I . . .' he stammered, and then with a return of his old stolid,
I may say mulish, manner he began heavily, 'I would be a brute
now if I . . .' and then his voice seemed to break. 'That's all
right,' I said. I was almost alarmed by this display of feeling,
through which pierced a strange elation. I had pulled the string
accidentally, as it were; I did not fully understand the working of
the toy. 'I must go now,' he said. 'Jove! You *have* helped me.
Can't sit still. The very thing . . .' He looked at me with puzzled admiration. 'The very thing . . .'

"Of course it was the thing. It was ten to one that I had saved
him from starvation — of that peculiar sort that is almost invariably associated with drink. This was all. I had not a single illu-

sion on that score, but looking at him, I allowed myself to wonder at the nature of the one he had, within the last three minutes,
so evidently taken into his bosom. I had forced into his hand the
means to carry on decently the serious business of life, to get
food, drink, and shelter of the customary kind while his wounded
spirit, like a bird with a broken wing, might hop and flutter into
some hole to die quietly of inanition there. This is what I had
thrust upon him: a definitely small thing; and — behold! — by the
manner of its reception it loomed in the dim light of the candle
like a big, indistinct, perhaps a dangerous shadow. 'You don't
mind me not saying anything appropriate,' he burst out. 'There
isn't anything one could say. Last night already you had done
me no end of good. Listening to me — you know. I give you my
word I've thought more than once the top of my head would fly
off . . .' He darted — positively darted — here and there, rammed
his hands into his pockets, jerked them out again, flung his cap
on his head. I had no idea it was in him to be so airily brisk. I
thought of a dry leaf imprisoned in an eddy of wind, while a
mysterious apprehension, a load of indefinite doubt, weighed me
down in my chair. He stood stock-still, as if struck motionless
by a discovery. 'You have given me confidence,' he declared,
soberly. 'Oh! for God's sake, my dear fellow — don't!' I entreated, as though he had hurt me. 'All right. I'll shut up now
and henceforth. Can't prevent me thinking though. . . . Never
mind! . . . I'll show yet . . .' He went to the door in a hurry,
paused with his head down, and came back, stepping deliberately.
'I always thought that if a fellow could begin with a clean
slate . . . And now you . . . in a measure . . . yes . . . clean
slate.' I waved my hand, and he marched out without looking
back; the sound of his footfalls died out gradually behind the
closed door — the unhesitating tread of a man walking in broad
daylight.

"But as to me, left alone with the solitary candle, I remained
strangely unenlightened. I was no longer young enough to behold at every turn the magnificence that besets our insignificant
footsteps in good and in evil. I smiled to think that, after all, it
was yet he, of us two, who had the light. And I felt sad. A clean
slate, did he say? As if the initial word of each our destiny were
not graven in imperishable characters upon the face of a rock."

CHAPTER XVIII

"Six months afterwards my friend (he was a cynical, more than middle-aged bachelor, with a reputation for eccentricity, and owned a rice-mill) wrote to me, and judging, from the warmth of my recommendation, that I would like to hear, enlarged a little upon Jim's perfections. These were apparently of a quiet and effective sort. 'Not having been able so far to find more in my heart than a resigned toleration for any individual of my kind, I have lived till now alone in a house that even in this steaming climate could be considered as too big for one man. I have had him to live with me for some time past. It seems I haven't made a mistake.' It seemed to me on reading this letter that my friend had found in his heart more than tolerance for Jim, — that there were the beginnings of active liking. Of course he stated his grounds in a characteristic way. For one thing, Jim kept his freshness in the climate. Had he been a girl — my friend wrote — one could have said he was blooming — blooming modestly — like a violet, not like some of these blatant tropical flowers. He had been in the house for six weeks, and had not as yet attempted to slap him on the back, or address him as 'old boy,' or try to make him feel a superannuated fossil. He had nothing of the exasperating young man's chatter. He was good-tempered, had not much to say for himself, was not clever by any means, thank goodness — wrote my friend. It appeared, however, that Jim was clever enough to be quietly appreciative of his wit, while, on the other hand, he amused him by his naïveness. 'The dew is yet on him, and since I had the bright idea of giving him a room in the house and having him at meals I feel less withered myself. The other day he took it into his head to cross the room with no other purpose but to open a door for me; and I felt more in touch with mankind than I had been for years. Ridiculous, isn't it? Of course I guess there is something — some awful little scrape — which you know all about — but if I am sure that it is terribly heinous, I fancy one could manage to forgive it. For my part, I declare I am unable to imagine him guilty of anything much worse than robbing an orchard. Is *it* much worse? Perhaps you

ought to have told me; but it is such a long time since we both
turned saints that you may have forgotten we, too, had sinned in
our time? It may be that some day I shall have to ask you, and
then I shall expect to be told. I don't care to question him myself
till I have some idea what it is. Moreover, it's too soon as yet.
Let him open the door a few times more for me. . . .' Thus my
friend. I was trebly pleased — at Jim's shaping so well, at the tone
of the letter, at my own cleverness. Evidently I had known what
I was doing. I had read characters aright, and so on. And what
if something unexpected and wonderful were to come of it? That
evening, reposing in a deck-chair under the shade of my own poop
awning (it was in Hong-Kong harbour), I laid on Jim's behalf the
first stone of a castle in Spain.

"I made a trip to the northward, and when I returned I found
another letter from my friend waiting for me. It was the first
envelope I tore open. 'There are no spoons missing, as far as I
know,' ran the first line; 'I haven't been interested enough to inquire. He is gone, leaving on the breakfast-table a formal little
note of apology, which is either silly or heartless. Probably both
— and it's all one to me. Allow me to say, lest you should have
some more mysterious young men in reserve, that I have shut up
shop, definitely and for ever. This is the last eccentricity I shall
be guilty of. Do not imagine for a moment that I care a hang;
but he is very much regretted at tennis-parties, and for my own
sake I've told a plausible lie at the club. . . .' I flung the letter
aside and started looking through the batch on my table, till I
came upon Jim's handwriting. Would you believe it? One chance
in a hundred! But it is always that hundredth chance! That little second engineer of the *Patna* had turned up in a more or less
destitute state, and got a temporary job of looking after the ma-
chinery of the mill. 'I couldn't stand the familiarity of the little
beast,' Jim wrote from a seaport seven hundred miles south of the
place where he should have been in clover. 'I am now for the
time with Egström & Blake, ship-chandlers, as their — well — run-
ner, to call the thing by its right name. For reference I gave them
your name, which they know of course, and if you could write
a word in my favour it would be a permanent employment.' I was
utterly crushed under the ruins of my castle, but of course I wrote
as desired. Before the end of the year my new charter took me
that way, and I had an opportunity of seeing him.

"He was still with Egström & Blake, and we met in what they called 'our parlour' opening out of the store. He had that moment come in from boarding a ship, and confronted me head down, ready for a tussle. 'What have you got to say for yourself?' I began as soon as we had shaken hands. 'What I wrote you — nothing more,' he said stubbornly. 'Did the fellow blab — or what?' I asked. He looked up at me with a troubled smile. 'Oh, no! He didn't. He made it a kind of confidential business between us. He was most damnably mysterious whenever I came over to the mill; he would wink at me in a respectful manner — as much as to say, "We know what we know." Infernally fawning and familiar — and that sort of thing.' He threw himself into a chair and stared down his legs. 'One day we happened to be alone and the fellow had the cheek to say, "Well, Mr. James" — I was called Mr. James there as if I had been the son — "here we are together once more. This is better than the old ship — ain't it?" . . . Wasn't it appalling, eh? I looked at him, and he put on a knowing air. "Don't you be uneasy, sir," he says. "I know a gentleman when I see one, and I know how a gentleman feels. I hope, though, you will be keeping me on this job. I had a hard time of it, too, along of that rotten old *Patna* racket." Jove! It was awful. I don't know what I should have said or done if I had not just then heard Mr. Denver calling me in the passage. It was tiffin-time, and we walked together across the yard and through the garden to the bungalow. He began to chaff me in his kindly way . . . I believe he liked me . . .'

"Jim was silent for a while.

"'I know he liked me. That's what made it so hard. Such a splendid man! That morning he slipped his hand under my arm. . . . He, too, was familiar with me.' He burst into a short laugh, and dropped his chin on his breast. 'Pah! When I remembered how that mean little beast had been talking to me,' he began suddenly in a vibrating voice, 'I couldn't bear to think of myself . . . I suppose you know . . .' I nodded. . . . 'More like a father,' he cried; his voice sank. 'I would have had to tell him. I couldn't let it go on — could I?' 'Well?' I murmured, after waiting a while 'I preferred to go,' he said, slowly; 'this thing must be buried.'

"We could hear in the shop Blake upbraiding Egström in an abusive, strained voice. They had been associated for many years, and every day from the moment the doors were opened to the last minute before closing, Blake, a little man with sleek, jetty hair and unhappy, beady eyes, could be heard rowing his partner incessantly with a sort of scathing and plaintive fury. The sound of that everlasting scolding was part of the place like the other fixtures; even strangers would very soon come to disregard it completely unless it be perhaps to mutter 'Nuisance,' or to get up suddenly and shut the door of the 'parlour.' Egström himself, a raw-boned, heavy Scandinavian, with a busy manner and immense blonde whiskers, went on directing his people, checking parcels, making out bills or writing letters at a stand-up desk in the shop, and comported himself in that clatter exactly as though he had been stone-deaf. Now and again he would emit a bothered perfunctory 'Sssh,' which neither produced nor was expected to produce the slightest effect. 'They are very decent to me here,' said Jim. 'Blake's a little cad, but Egström's all right.' He stood up quickly, and walking with measured steps to a tripod telescope standing in the window and pointed at the roadstead, he applied his eye to it. 'There's that ship which had been becalmed outside all the morning has got a breeze now and is coming in,' he remarked, patiently; 'I must go and board.' We shook hands in silence, and he turned to go. 'Jim!' I cried. He looked round with his hand on the lock. 'You — you have thrown away something like a fortune.' He came back to me all the way from the door. 'Such a splendid old chap,' he said. 'How could I? How could I?' His lips twitched. '*Here* it does not matter.' 'Oh! you — you — ' I began, and had to cast about for a suitable word, but before I became aware that there was no name that would just do, he was gone. I heard outside Egström's deep gentle voice saying cheerily, 'That's the *Sarah W. Granger*, Jimmy. You must manage to be first aboard;' and directly Blake struck in, screaming after the manner of an outraged cockatoo, 'Tell the captain we've got some of his mail here. That'll fetch him. D'ye hear, Mister What's-your-name?' And there was Jim answering Egström with something boyish in his tone. 'All right. I'll make a race of it.' He seemed to take refuge in the boat-sailing part of that sorry business.

"I did not see him again that trip, but on my next (I had a six months' charter) I went up to the store. Ten yards away from the door Blake's scolding met my ears, and when I came in he gave me a glance of utter wretchedness; Egström, all smiles, ad-

vanced, extending a large bony hand. 'Glad to see you, captain.
. . . Sssh. . . . Been thinking you were about due back here.
What did you say, sir? . . . Sssh. . . . Oh! him! He has left us.
Come into the parlour.' . . . After the slam of the door Blake's
strained voice became faint, as the voice of one scolding desperately
in a wilderness. . . . 'Put us to a great inconvenience, too. Used
us badly — I must say . . .' 'Where's he gone to? Do you know?'
I asked. 'No. It's no use asking either,' said Egström, standing
bewhiskered and obliging before me with his arms hanging down
his sides clumsily and a thin silver watch-chain looped very low
on a rucked-up blue serge waistcoat. 'A man like that don't go
anywhere in particular.' I was too concerned at the news to ask
for the explanation of that pronouncement, and he went on. 'He
left — let's see — the very day a steamer with returning pilgrims
from the Red Sea put in here with two blades of her propeller
gone. Three weeks ago now.' 'Wasn't there something said about
the *Patna* case?' I asked, fearing the worst. He gave a start, and
looked at me as if I had been a sorcerer. 'Why, yes! How do you
know? Some of them were talking about it here. There was a
captain or two, the manager of Vanlo's engineering shop at the
harbour, two or three others, and myself. Jim was in here, too,
having a sandwich and a glass of beer; when we are busy — you
see, captain — there's no time for a proper tiffin. He was standing
by this table eating sandwiches, and the rest of us were round the
telescope watching that steamer come in; and by and by Vanlo's
manager began to talk about the chief of the *Patna*; he had done
some repairs for him once, and from that he went on to tell us
what an old ruin she was, and the money that had been made out
of her. He came to mention her last voyage, and then we all
struck in. Some said one thing and some another — not much —
what you or any other man might say; and there was some laughing. Captain O'Brien of the *Sarah W. Granger*, a large, noisy old
man with a stick — he was sitting listening to us in this arm-chair
here — he let drive suddenly with his stick at the floor, and roars
out, "Skunks!" . . . Made us all jump. Vanlo's manager winks
at us and asks, "What's the matter, Captain O'Brien?" "Matter!
matter!" the old man began to shout; "what are you Injuns laughing at? It's no laughing matter. It's a disgrace to human natur' —
that's what it is. I would despise being seen in the same room with
one of those men. Yes, sir!" He seemed to catch my eye like,

and I had to speak out of civility. "Skunks!" says I, "of course, Captain O'Brien, and I wouldn't care to have them here myself, so you're quite safe in this room, Captain O'Brien. Have a little something cool to drink." "Dam' your drink, Egström," says he, with a twinkle in his eye; "when I want a drink I will shout for it. I am going to quit. It stinks here now." At this all the others burst out laughing, and out they go after the old man. And then, sir, that blasted Jim he puts down the sandwich he had in his hand and walks round the table to me; there was his glass of beer poured out quite full. "I am off," he says — just like this. "It isn't half-past one yet," says I; "you might snatch a smoke first." I thought he meant it was time for him to go down to his work. When I understood what he was up to, my arms fell — so! Can't get a man like that every day, you know, sir; a regular devil for sailing a boat; ready to go out miles to sea to meet ships in any sort of weather. More than once a captain would come in here full of it, and the first thing he would say would be, "That's a reckless sort of a lunatic you've got for water-clerk, Egström. I was feeling my way in at daylight under short canvas when there comes flying out of the mist right under my forefoot a boat half under water, sprays going over the mast-head, two frightened niggers on the bottom boards, a yelling fiend at the tiller. Hey! hey! Ship ahoy! ahoy! Captain! Hey! hey! Egström & Blake's man first to speak to you! Hey! hey! Egström & Blake! Hallo! hey! whoop! Kick the niggers — out reefs — a squall on at the time — shoots ahead whooping and yelling to me to make sail and he would give me a lead in — more like a demon than a man. Never saw a boat handled like that in all my life. Couldn't have been drunk — was he? Such a quiet, soft-spoken chap, too — blush like a girl when he came on board. . . ." I tell you, Captain Marlow, nobody had a chance against us with a strange ship when Jim was out. The other shipchandlers just kept their old customers, and . . .'

"Egström appeared overcome with emotion.

" 'Why, sir — it seemed as though he wouldn't mind going a hundred miles out to sea in an old shoe to nab a ship for the firm. If the business had been his own and all to make yet, he couldn't have done more in that way. And now . . . all at once . . . like this! Thinks I to myself: "Oho! a rise in the screw — that's the trouble — is it? All right," says I, "no need of all that fuss with me, Jimmy. Just mention your figure. Anything in reason." He looks at me as if he wanted to swallow something that stuck in his throat. "I can't stop with you." "What's that blooming joke?" I asks. He shakes his head, and I could see in his eye he was as good as gone already, sir. So I turned to him and slanged him till all was blue. "What is it you're running away from?" I asks. "Who has been getting at you? What scared you? You haven't as much sense as a rat; they don't clear out from a good ship. Where do you expect to get a better berth? — you this and you that." I made him look sick, I can tell you. "This business ain't going to sink," says I. He gave a big jump. "Good-bye," he says, nodding at me like a lord; "you ain't half a bad chap, Egström. I give you my word that if you knew my reasons you wouldn't care to keep me." "That's the biggest lie you ever told in your life," says I; "I know my own mind." He made me so mad that I had to laugh. "Can't you really stop long enough to drink this glass of beer here, you funny beggar, you?" I don't know what came over him; he didn't seem able to find the door; something comical, I can tell you, captain. I drank the beer myself. "Well, if you're in such a hurry, here's luck to you in your own drink," says I; "only, you mark my words, if you keep up this game you'll very soon find that the earth ain't big enough to hold you — that's all." He gave me one black look, and out he rushed with a face fit to scare little children.'

Egström snorted bitterly, and combed one auburn whisker with knotty fingers. 'Haven't been able to get a man that was any good since. It's nothing but worry, worry, worry in business. And where might you have come across him, captain, if it's fair to ask?'

" 'He was the mate of the *Patna* that voyage,' I said, feeling that I owed some explanation. For a time Egström remained very still, with his fingers plunged in the hair at the side of his face, and then exploded. 'And who the devil cares about that?' 'I daresay no one,' I began . . . 'And what the devil is he — anyhow — for to go on like this?' He stuffed suddenly his left whisker into his mouth and stood amazed. 'Jee!' he exclaimed, 'I told him the earth wouldn't be big enough to hold his caper.' "

CHAPTER XIX

"I HAVE told you these two episodes at length to show his manner of dealing with himself under the new conditions of his life. There were many others of the sort, more than I could count on the fingers of my two hands.

"They were all equally tinged by a high-minded absurdity of intention which made their futility profound and touching. To fling away your daily bread so as to get your hands free for a grapple with a ghost may be an act of prosaic heroism. Men had done it before (though we who have lived know full well that it is not the haunted soul but the hungry body that makes an outcast), and men who had eaten and meant to eat every day had applauded the creditable folly. He was indeed unfortunate, for all his recklessness could not carry him out from under the shadow. There was always a doubt of his courage. The truth seems to be that it is impossible to lay the ghost of a fact. You can face it or shirk it — and I have come across a man or two who could wink at their familiar shades. Obviously Jim was not of the winking sort; but what I could never make up my mind about was whether his line of conduct amounted to shirking his ghost or to facing him out.

"I strained my mental eyesight only to discover that, as with the complexion of all our actions, the shade of difference was so delicate that it was impossible to say. It might have been flight and it might have been a mode of combat. To the common mind he became known as a rolling stone, because this was the funniest part; he did after a time become perfectly known, and even notorious, within the circle of his wanderings (which had a diameter of, say, three thousand miles), in the same way as an eccentric character is known to a whole countryside. For instance, in Bankok, where he found employment with Yucker Brothers, charterers and teak merchants, it was almost pathetic to see him go about in sunshine hugging his secret, which was known to the very up-country logs on the river. Schomberg, the keeper of the hotel where he boarded, a hirsute Alsatian of manly bearing and an irrepressible retailer of all the scandalous gossip of the place, would, with both elbows on the table, impart an adorned version of the story to any guest who cared to imbibe knowledge along with the more costly liquors. 'And, mind you, the nicest fellow you could meet,' would be his generous conclusion; 'quite superior.' It says a lot for the casual crowd that frequented Schomberg's establishment that Jim managed to hang out in Bankok for a whole six months. I remarked that people, perfect strangers, took to him as one takes to a nice child. His manner was reserved, but it was as though his personal appearance, his hair, his eyes, his smile, made friends for him wherever he went. And, of course, he was no fool. I heard Siegmund Yucker (native of Switzerland), a gentle creature ravaged by a cruel dyspepsia, and so frightfully lame that his head swung through a quarter of a circle at every step he took, declare appreciatively that for one so young he was 'of great gabasidy,' as though it had been a mere question of cubic contents. 'Why not send him up country?' I suggested anxiously. (Yucker Brothers had concessions and teak forests in the interior.) 'If he has capacity, as you say, he will soon get hold of the work. And physically he is very fit. His health is always excellent.' 'Ach! It's a great ting in dis goundry to be vree vrom tispep-shia,' sighed poor Yucker enviously, casting a stealthy glance at the pit of his ruined stomach. I left him drumming pensively on his desk and muttering, 'Es ist ein idee. Es ist ein idee.' Unfortunately, that very evening an unpleasant affair took place in the hotel.

"I don't know that I blame Jim very much, but it was a truly regrettable incident. It belonged to the lamentable species of bar-room scuffles, and the other party to it was a cross-eyed Dane of sorts whose visiting card recited under his misbegotten name: first lieutenant in the Royal Siamese Navy. The fellow, of course, was utterly hopeless at billiards, but did not like to be beaten, I suppose. He had had enough to drink to turn nasty after the sixth game, and make some scornful remark at Jim's expense. Most of the people there didn't hear what was said, and those who had heard seemed to have had all precise recollection scared out of them by the appalling nature of the consequences that immediately ensued. It was very lucky for the Dane that he could swim, because the room opened on a verandah and the Menam flowed below very wide and black. A boat-load of Chinamen.

bound, as likely as not, on some thieving expedition, fished out the officer of the King of Siam, and Jim turned up at about midnight on board my ship without a hat. 'Everybody in the room seemed to know,' he said, gasping yet from the contest, as it were. He was rather sorry, on general principles, for what had happened, though in this case there had been, he said, 'no option.' But what dismayed him was to find the nature of his burden as well known to everybody as though he had gone about all that time carrying it on his shoulders. Naturally after this he couldn't remain in the place. He was universally condemned for the brutal violence, so unbecoming a man in his delicate position; some maintained he had been disgracefully drunk at the time; others criticised his want of tact. Even Schomberg was very much annoyed. 'He is a very nice young man,' he said, argumentatively, to me, 'but the lieutenant is a first-rate fellow, too. He dines every night at my *table d'hôte*, you know. And there's a billiard-cue broken. I can't allow that. First thing this morning I went over with my apologies to the lieutenant, and I think I've made it all right for myself; but only think, captain, if everybody started such games! Why, the man might have been drowned! And here I can't run out into the next street and buy a new cue. I've got to write to Europe for them. No, no! A temper like that won't do!' . . . He was extremely sore on the subject.

"This was the worst incident of all in his — his retreat. Nobody could deplore it more than myself; for if, as somebody said hearing him mentioned, 'Oh, yes! I know. He has knocked about a good deal out here,' yet he had somehow avoided being battered and chipped in the process. This last affair, however, made me seriously uneasy, because if his exquisite sensibilities were to go the length of involving him in pot-house shindies, he would lose his name of an inoffensive, if aggravating, fool, and acquire that of a common loafer. For all my confidence in him I could not help reflecting that in such cases from the name to the thing itself is but a step. I suppose you will understand that by that time I could not think of washing my hands of him. I took him away from Bankok in my ship, and we had a longish passage. It was pitiful to see how he shrank within himself. A seaman, even if a mere passenger, takes an interest in a ship, and looks at the sea-life around him with the critical enjoyment of a painter, for

instance, looking at another man's work. In every sense of the
expression he is 'on deck'; but my Jim, for the most part, skulked
down below as though he had been a stowaway. He infected me
so that I avoided speaking on professional matters, such as would
suggest themselves naturally to two sailors during a passage. For
whole days we did not exchange a word; I felt extremely unwill-
ing to give orders to my officers in his presence. Often, when
alone with him on deck or in the cabin, we didn't know what
to do with our eyes.

"I placed him with De Jongh, as you know, glad enough to dispose of him in any way, yet persuaded that his position was now
growing intolerable. He had lost some of that elasticity which
had enabled him to rebound back into his uncompromising position after every overthrow. One day, coming ashore, I saw him
standing on the quay; the water of the roadstead and the sea in
the offing made one smooth ascending plane, and the outermost
ships at anchor seemed to ride motionless in the sky. He was
waiting for his boat, which was being loaded at our feet with
packages of small stores for some vessel ready to leave. After
exchanging greetings, we remained silent — side by side. 'Jove!'
he said, suddenly, 'this is killing work.'

"He smiled at me; I must say he generally could manage a
smile. I made no reply. I knew very well he was not alluding
to his duties; he had an easy time of it with De Jongh. Nevertheless, as soon as he had spoken I became completely convinced that
the work was killing. I did not even look at him. 'Would you
like,' said I, 'to leave this part of the world altogether; try Cali-
fornia or the West Coast? I'll see what I can do . . .' He interrupted me a little scornfully. 'What difference would it make?'
. . . I felt at once convinced that he was right. It would make no
difference; it was not relief he wanted; I seemed to perceive dimly
that what he wanted, what he was, as it were, waiting for, was
something not easy to define — something in the nature of an opportunity. I had given him many opportunities, but they had been
merely opportunities to earn his bread. Yet what more could any
man do?" The position struck me as hopeless, and poor Brierly's
saying recurred to me, 'Let him creep twenty feet underground
and stay there.' Better that, I thought, than this waiting above
ground for the impossible. Yet one could not be sure even of that.
There and then, before his boat was three oars' lengths away from

the quay, I had made up my mind to go and consult Stein in the evening.

"This Stein was a wealthy and respected merchant. His 'house' (because it was a house, Stein & Co., and there was some sort of partner who, as Stein said, 'looked after the Moluccas') had a large inter-island business, with a lot of trading posts established in the most out-of-the-way places for collecting the produce. His wealth and his respectability were not exactly the reasons why I was anxious to seek his advice. I desired to confide my difficulty to him because he was one of the most trustworthy men I had ever known. The gentle light of a simple unwearied, as it were, and intelligent good-nature illumined his long hairless face. It had deep downward folds, and was pale as of a man who had always led a sedentary life — which was indeed very far from being the case. His hair was thin, and brushed back from a massive and lofty forehead. One fancied that at twenty he must have looked very much like what he was now at threescore. It was a student's face; only the eyebrows nearly all white, thick and bushy, together with the resolute searching glance that came from under them, were not in accord with his, I may say, learned appearance. He was tall and loose-jointed; his slight stoop, together with an innocent smile, made him appear benevolently ready to lend you his ear; his long arms with pale big hands had rare deliberate gestures of a pointing out, demonstrating kind. I speak of him at length, because under this exterior, and in conjunction with an upright and indulgent nature, this man possessed an intrepidity of spirit and a physical courage that could have been called reckless had it not been like a natural function of the body — say good digestion, for instance — completely unconscious of itself. It is sometimes said of a man that he carries his life in his hand. Such a saying would have been inadequate if applied to him; during the early part of his existence in the East he had been playing ball with it. All this was in the past, but I knew the story of his life and the origin of his fortune. He was also a naturalist of some distinction, or perhaps I should say a learned collector. Entomology was his special study. His collection of *Buprestidœ* and *Longicorns* — beetles all — horrible miniature monsters, looking malevolent in death and immobility, and his cabinet of butterflies, beautiful and hovering under the glass of cases of lifeless wings, had spread his fame far over the earth. The name of this merchant, adventurer, sometime adviser of a Malay sultan (to whom he never alluded otherwise than as 'my poor Mohammed Bonso'), had, on account of a few bushels of dead insects, become known to learned persons in Europe, who could have had no conception, and certainly would not have cared to know anything, of his life or character. I, who knew, considered him an eminently suitable person to receive my confidences about Jim's difficulties as well as my own."

CHAPTER XX

"LATE in the evening I entered his study, after traversing an imposing but empty dining-room very dimly lit. The house was silent. I was preceded by an elderly grim Javanese servant in a sort of livery of white jacket and yellow sarong, who, after throwing the door open, exclaimed low, 'O master!' and stepping aside, vanished in a mysterious way as though he had been a ghost only momentarily embodied for that particular service. Stein turned round with the chair, and in the same movement his spectacles seemed to get pushed up on his forehead. He welcomed me in his quiet and humorous voice. Only one corner of the vast room, the corner in which stood his writing-desk, was strongly lighted by a shaded reading-lamp, and the rest of the spacious apartment melted into shapeless gloom like a cavern. Narrow shelves filled with dark boxes of uniform shape and colour ran round the walls, not from floor to ceiling, but in a sombre belt about four feet broad. Catacombs of beetles. Wooden tablets were hung above at irregular intervals. The light reached one of them, and the word *Coleoptera* written in gold letters glittered mysteriously upon a vast dimness. The glass cases containing the collection of butterflies were ranged in three long rows upon slender-legged little tables. One of these cases had been removed from its place and stood on the desk, which was bestrewn with oblong slips of paper blackened with minute handwriting.

" 'So you see me — so,' he said. His hand hovered over the case

where a butterfly in solitary grandeur spread out dark bronze
wings, seven inches or more across, with exquisite white veinings
and a gorgeous border of yellow spots. 'Only one specimen like
this they have in *your* London, and then — no more. To my small
native town this my collection I shall bequeath. Something of me.
The best.'

"He bent forward in the chair and gazed intently, his chin over
the front of the case. I stood at his back. 'Marvellous,' he whispered, and seemed to forget my presence. His history was curious. He had been born in Bavaria, and when a youth of twenty-
two had taken an active part in the revolutionary movement of
1848. Heavily compromised, he managed to make his escape,
and at first found a refuge with a poor republican watch-maker
in Trieste. From there he made his way to Tripoli with a stock
of cheap watches to hawk about, — not a very great opening
truly, but it turned out lucky enough, because it was there he
came upon a Dutch traveller — a rather famous man, I believe, but
I don't remember his name. It was that naturalist who, engaging
him as a sort of assistant, took him to the East. They travelled in
the Archipelago together and separately, collecting insects and
birds, for four years or more. Then the naturalist went home, and
Stein, having no home to go to, remained with an old trader he
had come across in his journeys in the interior of Celebes — if
Celebes may be said to have an interior. This old Scotsman, the
only white man allowed to reside in the country at the time, was
a privileged friend of the chief ruler of Wajo States, who was a
woman. I often heard Stein relate how that chap, who was slightly
paralysed on one side, had introduced him to the native court a
short time before another stroke carried him off. He was a heavy
man with a patriarchal white beard, and of imposing stature. He
came into the council-hall where all the rajahs, pangerans, and
head-men were assembled, with the queen, a fat wrinkled woman
(very free in her speech, Stein said), reclining on a high couch
under a canopy. He dragged his leg, thumping with his stick,
and grasped Stein's arm, leading him right up to the couch. 'Look,
queen, and you rajahs, this is my son,' he proclaimed in a stento-
rian voice. 'I have traded with your fathers, and when I die he
shall trade with you and your sons.'

"By means of this simple formality Stein inherited the Scotsman's privileged position and all his stock-in-trade, together with

a fortified house on the banks of the only navigable river in the country. Shortly afterwards the old queen, who was so free in her speech, died, and the country became disturbed by various pretenders to the throne. Stein joined the party of a younger son, the one of whom thirty years later he never spoke otherwise but as 'my poor Mohammed Bonso.' They both became the heroes of innumerable exploits; they had wonderful adventures, and once stood a siege in the Scotsman's house for a month, with only a score of followers against a whole army. I believe the natives talk of that war to this day. Meantime, it seems, Stein never failed to annex on his own account every butterfly or beetle he could lay hands on. After some eight years of war, negotiations, false truces, sudden outbreaks, reconciliation, treachery, and so on, and just as peace seemed at last permanently established, his 'poor Mohammed Bonso' was assassinated at the gate of his own royal residence while dismounting in the highest spirits on his return from a successful deer-hunt. This event rendered Stein's position extremely insecure, but he would have stayed perhaps had it not been that a short time afterwards he lost Mohammed's sister ('my dear wife the princess,' he used to say solemnly), by whom he had had a daughter — mother and child both dying within three days of each other from some infectious fever. He left the country, which this cruel loss had made unbearable to him. Thus ended the first and adventurous part of his existence. What followed was so different that, but for the reality of sorrow which remained with him, this strange part must have resembled a dream. He had a little money; he started life afresh, and in the course of years acquired a considerable fortune. At first he had travelled a good deal amongst the islands, but age had stolen upon him, and of late he seldom left his spacious house three miles out of town, with an extensive garden, and surrounded by stables, offices, and bamboo cottages for his servants and dependants, of whom he had many. He drove in his buggy every morning to town, where he had an office with white and Chinese clerks. He owned a small fleet of schooners and native craft, and dealt in island produce on a large scale. For the rest he lived solitary, but not misanthropic, with his books and his collection, classing and arranging specimens, corresponding with entomologists in Europe, writing up a descriptive catalogue of his treasures. Such was the history of the man whom I had come to consult upon Jim's case without any definite hope. Simply to hear what he would have to say would have been a relief. I was very anxious, but I respected the intense, almost passionate, absorption with which he looked at a butterfly, as though on the bronze sheen of these frail wings, in the white tracings, in the gorgeous markings, he could see other things, an image of something as perishable and defying destruction as these delicate and lifeless tissues displaying a splendour unmarred by death.

" 'Marvellous!' he repeated, looking up at me. 'Look! The beauty — but that is nothing — look at the accuracy, the harmony. And so fragile! And so strong! And so exact! This is Nature — the balance of colossal forces. Every star is so — and every blade of grass stands *so* — and the mighty Kosmos in perfect equilibrium produces — this. This wonder; this masterpiece of Nature — the great artist.'

" 'Never heard an entomologist go on like this,' I observed, cheerfully. 'Masterpiece! And what of man?'

" 'Man is amazing, but he is not a masterpiece,' he said, keeping his eyes fixed on the glass case. 'Perhaps the artist was a little mad. Eh? What do you think? Sometimes it seems to me that man is come where he is not wanted, where there is no place for him; for if not, why should he want all the place? Why should he run about here and there making a great noise about himself, talking about the stars, disturbing the blades of grass? . . .'

" 'Catching butterflies,' I chimed in.

"He smiled, threw himself back in his chair, and stretched his legs. 'Sit down,' he said. 'I captured this rare specimen myself one very fine morning. And I had a very big emotion. You don't know what it is for a collector to capture such a rare specimen. You can't know.'

"I smiled at my ease in a rocking-chair. His eyes seemed to look far beyond the wall at which they stared; and he narrated how, one night, a messenger arrived from his 'poor Mohammed,' requiring his presence at the 'residenz' — as he called it — which was distant some nine or ten miles by a bridle-path over a cultivated plain, with patches of forest here and there. Early in the morning he started from his fortified house, after embracing his little Emma, and leaving the 'princess,' his wife, in command. He described how she came with him as far as the gate, walking with one hand on the neck of his horse; she had on a white jacket, gold pins in her hair, and a brown leather belt over her left shoulder with a revolver in it. 'She talked as women will talk,' he said, 'telling me to be careful, and to try to get back before dark, and what a great wickedness it was for me to go alone. We were at war, and the country was not safe; my men were putting up bullet-proof shutters to the house and loading their rifles, and she begged me to have no fear for her. She could defend the house against anybody till I returned. And I laughed with pleasure a little. I liked to see her so brave and young and strong. I, too, was young then. At the gate she caught hold of my hand and gave it one squeeze and fell back. I made my horse stand still outside till I heard the bars of the gate put up behind me. There was a great enemy of mine, a great noble — a great rascal, too — roaming with a band in the neighbourhood. I cantered for four or five miles; there had been rain in the night, but the mists had gone up, up — and the face of the earth was clean; it lay smiling to me, so fresh and innocent — like a little child. Suddenly some-body fires a volley — twenty shots at least it seemed to me. I hear bullets sing in my ear, and my hat jumps to the back of my head. It was a little intrigue, you understand. They got my poor Mo-hammed to send for me and then laid that ambush. I see it all in a minute, and I think —— This wants a little management. My pony snort, jump, and stand, and I fall slowly forward with my head on his mane. He begins to walk, and with one eye I could see over his neck a faint cloud of smoke hanging in front of a clump of bamboos to my left. I think —— Aha! my friends, why you not wait long enough before you shoot? This is not yet *gelungen*. Oh, no! I get hold of my revolver with my right hand — quiet — quiet. After all, there were only seven of these rascals. They get up from the grass and start running with their sarongs tucked up, waving spears above their heads, and yelling to each other to look out and catch the horse, because I was dead. I let them come as close as the door here, and then bang, bang, bang — take aim each time, too. One more shot I fire at a man's back, but I miss. Too far already. And then I sit alone on my horse with the clean earth smiling at me, and there are the bodies of three men lying on the ground. One was curled up like a dog, another on his back had an arm over his eyes as if to keep off the sun, and the third man he draws up his leg very slowly and makes it with one kick straight again. I watch him very carefully from

my horse, but there is no more — *bleibt ganz ruhig* — keep still,
so. And as I looked at his face for some sign of life I observed
something like a faint shadow pass over his forehead. It was the
shadow of this butterfly. Look at the form of the wing. This
species fly high with a strong flight. I raised my eyes and I saw
him fluttering away. I think —— Can it be possible? And then I
lost him. I dismounted and went on very slow, leading my horse
and holding my revolver with one hand and my eyes darting up
and down and right and left, everywhere! At last I saw him sitting on a small heap of dirt ten feet away. At once my heart began to beat quick. I let go my horse, keep my revolver in one
hand, and with the other snatch my soft felt hat off my head.
One step. Steady. Another step. Flop! I got him! When I got
up I shook like a leaf with excitement, and when I opened these
beautiful wings and made sure what a rare and so extraordinary
perfect specimen I had, my head went round and my legs became
so weak with emotion that I had to sit on the ground. I had
greatly desired to possess myself of a specimen of that species
when collecting for the professor. I took long journeys and un-
derwent great privations; I had dreamed of him in my sleep, and
here suddenly I had him in my fingers — for myself! In the
words of the poet' (he pronounced it 'boet') —

> ' "So halt' ich's endlich denn in meinen Händen,
> Und nenn' es in gewissem Sinne mein." '

He gave to the last word the emphasis of a suddenly lowered
voice, and withdrew his eyes slowly from my face. He began
to charge a long-stemmed pipe busily and in silence, then, paus-
ing with his thumb on the orifice of the bowl, looked again at
me significantly.

" 'Yes, my good friend. On that day I had nothing to desire; I
had greatly annoyed my principal enemy; I was young, strong;
I had friendship; I had the love' (he said 'lof') 'of woman, a child
I had, to make my heart very full — and even what I had once
dreamed in my sleep had come into my hand, too!'

"He struck a match, which flared violently. His thoughtful
placid face twitched once.

" 'Friend, wife, child,' he said, slowly, gazing at the small flame
— 'phoo!' The match was blown out. He sighed and turned again
to the glass case. The frail and beautiful wings quivered faintly,

as if his breath had for an instant called back to life that gorgeous object of his dreams.

" 'The work,' he began, suddenly, pointing to the scattered slips, and in his usual gentle and cheery tone, 'is making great progress. I have been this rare specimen describing. . . . Na! And what is your good news?'

" 'To tell you the truth, Stein,' I said with an effort that surprised me, 'I came here to describe a specimen. . . .'

" 'Butterfly?' he asked, with an unbelieving and humorous eagerness.

" 'Nothing so perfect,' I answered, feeling suddenly dispirited with all sorts of doubts. 'A man!'

" 'Ach so!' he murmured, and his smiling countenance, turned to me, became grave. Then after looking at me for a while he said slowly, 'Well — I am a man, too.'

"Here you have him as he was; he knew how to be so generously encouraging as to make a scrupulous man hesitate on the brink of confidence; but if I did hesitate it was not for long.

"He heard me out, sitting with crossed legs. Sometimes his head would disappear completely in a great eruption of smoke, and a sympathetic growl would come out from the cloud. When I finished he uncrossed his legs, laid down his pipe, leaned forward towards me earnestly with his elbows on the arms of his chair, the tips of his fingers together.

" 'I understand very well. He is romantic.'

"He had diagnosed the case for me, and at first I was quite startled to find how simple it was; and indeed our conference resembled so much a medical consultation — Stein, of learned aspect, sitting in an arm-chair before his desk; I, anxious, in another, facing him, but a little to one side — that it seemed natural to ask —

" 'What's good for it?'

"He lifted up a long forefinger.

" 'There is only one remedy! One thing alone can us from being ourselves cure!' The finger came down on the desk with a smart rap. The case which he had made to look so simple before became if possible still simpler — and altogether hopeless. There was a pause. 'Yes,' said I, 'strictly speaking, the question is not how to get cured, but how to live.'

"He approved with his head, a little sadly as it seemed. '*Ja! ja!*

In general, adapting the words of your great poet: That is the question. . . .' He went on nodding sympathetically. . . . 'How to be! *Ach!* How to be.'

"He stood up with the tips of his fingers resting on the desk.

" 'We want in so many different ways to be,' he began again. 'This magnificent butterfly finds a little heap of dirt and sits still on it; but man he will never on his heap of mud keep still. He want to be so, and again he want to be so. . . .' He moved his hand up, then down. . . . 'He wants to be a saint, and he wants to be a devil — and every time he shuts his eyes he sees himself as a very fine fellow — so fine as he can never be. . . . In a dream. . . .'

"He lowered the glass lid, the automatic lock clicked sharply, and taking up the case in both hands he bore it religiously away to its place, passing out of the bright circle of the lamp into the ring of fainter light — into shapeless dusk at last. It had an odd effect — as if these few steps had carried him out of this concrete and perplexed world. His tall form, as though robbed of its substance, hovered noiselessly over invisible things with stooping and indefinite movements; his voice, heard in that remoteness where he could be glimpsed mysteriously busy with immaterial cares, was no longer incisive, seemed to roll voluminous and grave — mellowed by distance.

" 'And because you not always can keep your eyes shut there comes the real trouble — the heart pain — the world pain. I tell you, my friend, it is not good for you to find you cannot make your dream come true, for the reason that you not strong enough are, or not clever enough. *Ja!* . . . And all the time you are such a fine fellow, too! *Wie? Was? Gott in Himmel!* How can that be? Ha! ha! ha!'

"The shadow prowling amongst the graves of butterflies laughed boisterously.

" 'Yes! Very funny this terrible thing is. A man that is born falls into a dream like a man who falls into the sea. If he tries to climb out into the air as inexperienced people endeavour to do, he drowns — *nicht war?* . . . No! I tell you! The way is to the destructive element submit yourself, and with the exertions of your hands and feet in the water make the deep, deep sea keep you up. So if you ask me — how to be?'

"His voice leaped up extraordinarily strong, as though away

there in the dusk he had been inspired by some whisper of knowledge. 'I will tell you! For that, too, there is only one way.'

"With a hasty swish swish of his slippers he loomed up in the ring of faint light, and suddenly appeared in the bright circle of the lamp. His extended hand aimed at my breast like a pistol; his deep-set eyes seemed to pierce through me, but his twitching lips uttered no word, and the austere exaltation of a certitude seen in the dusk vanished from his face. The hand that had been pointing at my breast fell, and by-and-by, coming a step nearer, he laid it gently on my shoulder. There were things, he said mournfully, that perhaps could never be told, only he had lived so much alone that sometimes he forgot — he forgot. The light had destroyed the assurance which had inspired him in the distant shadows. He sat down and, with both elbows on the desk, rubbed his forehead. 'And yet it is true — it is true. In the destructive element immerse.' . . . He spoke in a subdued tone, without looking at me, one hand on each side of his face. 'That was the way. To follow the dream, and again to follow the dream — and so — *ewig — usque ad finem.* . . .' The whisper of his conviction seemed to open before me a vast and uncertain expanse, as of a crepuscular horizon on a plain at dawn — or was it, perchance, at the coming of the night? One had not the courage to decide; but it was a charming and deceptive light, throwing the impalpable poesy of its dimness over pitfalls — over graves. His life had begun in sacrifice, in enthusiasm for generous ideas; he had travelled very far, on various ways, on strange paths, and whatever he followed it had been without faltering, and therefore without shame and without regret. In so far he was right. That was the way, no doubt. Yet for all that the great plain on which men wander amongst graves and pitfalls remained very desolate under the impalpable poesy of its crepuscular light, overshadowed in the centre, circled with a bright edge as if surrounded by an abyss full of flames. When at last I broke the silence it was to express the opinion that no one could be more romantic than himself.

"He shook his head slowly, and afterwards looked at me with a patient and inquiring glance. It was a shame, he said. There we were sitting and talking like two boys, instead of putting our heads together to find something practical — a practical remedy — for the evil — for the great evil — he repeated, with a humorous and indulgent smile. For all that, our talk did not grow more practical. We avoided pronouncing Jim's name as though we had tried to keep flesh and blood out of our discussion, or he were nothing but an erring spirit, a suffering and nameless shade. 'Na!' said Stein, rising. 'To-night you sleep here, and in the morning we shall do something practical — practical. . . .' He lit a two-branched candlestick and led the way. We passed through empty dark rooms, escorted by gleams from the lights Stein carried. They glided along the waxed floors, sweeping here and there over the polished surface of the table, leaped upon a fragmentary curve of a piece of furniture, or flashed perpendicularly in and out of distant mirrors, while the forms of two men and the flicker of two flames could be seen for a moment stealing silently across the depths of a crystalline void. He walked slowly a pace in advance with stooping courtesy, there was a profound, as it were a listening, quietude on his face; the long flaxen locks mixed with white threads were scattered thinly upon his slightly bowed neck.

" 'He is romantic — romantic,' he repeated. 'And that is very bad — very bad. . . . Very good, too, he added. 'But *is he?*' I queried.

" '*Gewiss*,' he said, and stood still holding up the candelabrum, but without looking at me. 'Evident! What is it that by inward pain makes him know himself? What is it that for you and me makes him — exist?'

"At that moment it was difficult to believe in Jim's existence — starting from a country parsonage, blurred by crowds of men as by clouds of dust, silenced by the clashing claims of life and death in a material world — but his imperishable reality came to me with a convincing, with an irresistible force! I saw it vividly, as though in our progress through the lofty silent rooms amongst fleeting gleams of light and the sudden revelations of human figures steal-ing with flickering flames within unfathomable and pellucid depths, we had approached nearer to absolute Truth, which, like Beauty it-self, floats elusive, obscure, half submerged, in the silent still waters of mystery. 'Perhaps he is,' I admitted with a slight laugh, whose unexpectedly loud reverberation made me lower my voice di-rectly; 'but I am sure you are.' With his head dropping on his breast and the light held high he began to walk again. 'Well — I exist, too,' he said.

"He preceded me. My eyes followed his movements, but what I did see was not the head of the firm, the welcome guest at aft-

ernoon receptions, the correspondent of learned societies, the en-
tertainer of stray naturalists; I saw only the reality of his destiny,
which he had known how to follow with unfaltering footsteps,
that life begun in humble surroundings, rich in generous enthusi-
asms, in friendship, love, war — in all the exalted elements of romance. At the door of my room he faced me. 'Yes,' I said, as
though carrying on a discussion, 'and amongst other things you
dreamed foolishly of a certain butterfly; but when one fine morning your dream came in your way you did not let the splendid
opportunity escape. Did you? Whereas he . . .' Stein lifted his
hand. 'And do you know how many opportunities I let escape;
how many dreams I had lost that had come in my way?' He
shook his head regretfully. 'It seems to me that some would have
been very fine — if I had made them come true. Do you know
how many? Perhaps I myself don't know.' 'Whether his were
fine or not,' I said, 'he knows of one which he certainly did not
catch.' 'Everybody knows of one or two like that,' said Stein;
'and that is the trouble — the great trouble. . . .'

"He shook hands on the threshold, peered into my room under his raised arm. 'Sleep well. And to-morrow we must do
something practical — practical. . . .'

"Though his own room was beyond mine I saw him return the
way he came. He was going back to his butterflies."

CHAPTER XXI

"I DON'T suppose any of you had ever heard of Patusan?"
Marlow resumed, after a silence occupied in the careful lighting
of a cigar. "It does not matter; there's many a heavenly body in
the lot crowding upon us of a night that mankind had never heard
of, it being outside the sphere of its activities and of no earthly
importance to anybody but to the astronomers who are paid to
talk learnedly about its composition, weight, path — the irregularities of its conduct, the aberrations of its light — a sort of sci-
entific scandal-mongering. Thus with Patusan. It was referred

to knowingly in the inner government circles in Batavia, especially as to its irregularities and aberrations, and it was known by name to some few, very few, in the mercantile world. Nobody, however, had been there, and I suspect no one desired to go there in person, just as an astronomer, I should fancy, would strongly object to being transported into a distant heavenly body, where, parted from his earthly emoluments, he would be bewildered by the view of an unfamiliar heavens. However, neither heavenly bodies nor astronomers have anything to do with Patusan. It was Jim who went there. I only meant you to understand that had Stein arranged to send him into a star of the fifth magnitude the change could not have been greater. He left his earthly failings behind him and that sort of reputation he had, and there was a totally new set of conditions for his imaginative faculty to work upon. Entirely new, entirely remarkable. And he got hold of them in a remarkable way.

"Stein was the man who knew more about Patusan than anybody else. More than was known in the government circles I suspect. I have no doubt he had been there, either in his butterfly-hunting days or later on, when he tried in his incorrigible way to season with a pinch of romance the fattening dishes of his commercial kitchen. There were very few places in the Archipelago he had not seen in the original dusk of their being, before light (and even electric light) had been carried into them for the sake of better morality and — and — well — the greater profit, too. It was at breakfast of the morning following our talk about Jim that he mentioned the place, after I had quoted poor Brierly's remark: 'Let him creep twenty feet underground and stay there.' He looked up at me with interested attention, as though I had been a rare insect. 'This could be done, too,' he remarked, sipping his coffee. 'Bury him in some sort,' I explained. 'One doesn't like to do it of course, but it would be the best thing, seeing what he is.' 'Yes; he is young,' Stein mused. 'The youngest human being now in existence,' I affirmed. '*Schön*. There's Patusan,' he went on in the same tone. . . . 'And the woman is dead now,' he added incomprehensibly.

"Of course I don't know that story; I can only guess that once before Patusan had been used as a grave for some sin, transgression, or misfortune. It is impossible to suspect Stein. The only woman that had ever existed for him was the Malay girl he called

'My wife the princess,' or, more rarely in moments of expansion, 'the mother of my Emma.' Who was the woman he had mentioned in connection with Patusan I can't say; but from his allusions I understand she had been an educated and very good-looking Dutch-Malay girl, with a tragic or perhaps only a pitiful history, whose most painful part no doubt was her marriage with a Malacca Portuguese who had been clerk in some commercial house in the Dutch colonies. I gathered from Stein that this man was an unsatisfactory person in more ways than one, all being more or less indefinite and offensive. It was solely for his wife's sake that Stein had appointed him manager of Stein & Co.'s trading post in Patusan; but commercially the arrangement was not a success, at any rate for the firm, and now the woman had died, Stein was disposed to try another agent there. The Portuguese, whose name was Cornelius, considered himself a very deserving but ill-used person, entitled by his abilities to a better position. This man Jim would have to relieve. 'But I don't think he will go away from the place,' remarked Stein. 'That has nothing to do with me. It was only for the sake of the woman that I . . . But as I think there is a daughter left, I shall let him, if he likes to stay, keep the old house.

"Patusan is a remote district of a native-ruled State, and the chief settlement bears the same name. At a point on the river about forty miles from the sea, where the first houses come into view, there can be seen rising above the level of the forests the summits of two steep hills very close together, and separated by what looks like a deep fissure, the cleavage of some mighty stroke. As a matter of fact, the valley between is nothing but a narrow ravine; the appearance from the settlement is of one irregularly conical hill split in two, and with the two halves leaning slightly apart. On the third day after the full, the moon, as seen from the open space in front of Jim's house (he had a very fine house in the native style when I visited him), rose exactly behind these hills, its diffused light at first throwing the two masses into intensely black relief, and then the nearly perfect disc, glowing ruddily, appeared, gliding upwards between the sides of the chasm, till it floated away above the summits, as if escaping from a yawning grave in gentle triumph. 'Wonderful effect,' said Jim by my side. 'Worth seeing. Is it not?'

"And this question was put with a note of personal pride that made me smile, as though he had had a hand in regulating that unique spectacle. He had regulated so many things in Patusan! Things that would have appeared as much beyond his control as the motions of the moon and the stars.

"It was inconceivable. That was the distinctive quality of the part into which Stein and I had tumbled him unwittingly, with no other notion than to get him out of the way; out of his own way, be it understood. That was our main purpose, though, I own, I might have had another motive which had influenced me a little. I was about to go home for a time; and it may be I desired, more than I was aware of myself, to dispose of him — to dispose of him, you understand — before I left. I was going home, and he had come to me from there, with his miserable trouble and his shadowy claim, like a man panting under a burden in a mist. I cannot say I had ever seen him distinctly — not even to this day, after I had my last view of him; but it seemed to me that the less I understood the more I was bound to him in the name of that doubt which is the inseparable part of our knowledge. I did not know so much more about myself. And then, I repeat, I was going home — to that home distant enough for all its hearthstones to be like one hearthstone, by which the humblest of us has the right to sit. We wander in our thousands over the face of the earth, the illustrious and the obscure, earning beyond the seas our fame, our money, or only a crust of bread; but it seems to me that for each of us going home must be like going to render an account. We return to face our superiors, our kindred, our friends — those whom we obey, and those whom we love; but even they who have neither, the most free, lonely, irresponsible and bereft of ties, — even those for whom home holds no dear face, no familiar voice, — even they have to meet the spirit that dwells within the land, under its sky, in its air, in its valleys, and on its rises, in its fields, in its waters and its trees — a mute friend, judge, and inspirer. Say what you like, to get its joy, to breathe its peace, to face its truth, one must return with a clear consciousness. All this may seem to you sheer sentimentalism; and indeed very few of us have the will or the capacity to look consciously under the surface of familiar emotions. There are the girls we love, the men we look up to, the tenderness, the friendships, the opportunities, the pleasures! But the fact remains that you must touch your reward with clean hands, lest it turn to dead leaves, to thorns, in your grasp. I think it is the lonely, without a fireside or an affection they may call their own, those who return not to a dwelling but to the land itself, to meet its disembodied, eternal, and unchangeable spirit — it is those who understand best its severity, its saving power, the grace of its secular right to our fidelity, to our obedience. Yes! few of us understand, but we all feel it though, and I say *all* without exception, because those who do not feel do not count. Each blade of grass has its spot on earth whence it draws its life, its strength; and so is man rooted to the land from which he draws his faith together with his life. I don't know how much Jim understood; but I know he felt, he felt confusedly but powerfully, the demand of some such truth or some such illusion — I don't care how you call it, there is so little difference, and the difference means so little. The thing is that in virtue of his feeling he mattered. He would never go home now. Not he. Never. Had he been capable of picturesque manifestations he would have shuddered at the thought and made you shudder, too. But he was not of that sort, though he was expressive enough in his way. Before the idea of going home he would grow desperately stiff and immovable, with lowered chin and pouted lips, and with those candid blue eyes of his glowering darkly under a frown, as if before something unbearable, as if before something revolting. There was imagination in that hard skull of his, over which the thick clustering hair fitted like a cap. As to me, I have no imagination (I would be more certain about him to-day, if I had), and I do not mean to imply that I figured to myself the spirit of the land uprising above the white cliffs of Dover, to ask me what I — returning with no bones broken, so to speak — had done with my very young brother. I could not make such a mistake. I knew very well he was of those about whom there is no inquiry; I had seen better men go out, disappear, vanish utterly, without provoking a sound of curiosity or sorrow. The spirit of the land, as becomes the ruler of great enterprises, is careless of innumerable lives. Woe to the stragglers! We exist only in so far as we hang together. He had straggled in a way; he had not hung on; but he was aware of it with an intensity that made him touching, just as a man's more intense life makes his death more touching than the death of a tree. I happened to be handy, and I happened to be touched. That's all there is to it. I was concerned as to the way he would go out. It would have hurt me if, for instance, he had taken to drink. The earth is so small that I was afraid of, some day, being waylaid by a blear-eyed, swollen-faced, besmirched loafer, with no soles to his canvas shoes, and with a flutter of rags about the elbows, who, on the strength of old acquaintance, would ask for a loan of five dollars. You know the awful jaunty bearing of these scarecrows coming to you from a decent past, the rasping careless voice, the half-averted impudent glances — those meetings more trying to a man who believes in the solidarity of our lives than the sight of an impenitent deathbed to a priest. That, to tell you the truth, was the only danger I could see for him and for me; but I also mistrusted my want of imagination. It might even come to something worse, in some way it was beyond my powers of fancy to foresee. He wouldn't let me forget how imaginative he was, and your imaginative people swing farther in any direction, as if given a longer scope of cable in the uneasy anchorage of life. They do. They take to drink, too. It may be I was belittling him by such a fear. How could I tell? Even Stein could say no more than that he was romantic. I only knew he was one of us. And what business had he to be romantic? I am telling you so much about my own instinctive feelings and bemused reflections because there remains so little to be told of him. He existed for me, and after all it is only through me that he exists for you. I've led him out by the hand; I have paraded him before you. Were my commonplace fears unjust? I won't say — not even now. You may be able to tell better, since the proverb has it that the onlookers see most of the game. At any rate, they were superfluous. He did not go out, not at all; on the contrary, he came on wonderfully, came on straight as a die and in excellent form, which showed that he could stay as well as spurt. I ought to be delighted, for it is a victory in which I had taken my part; but I am not so pleased as I would have expected to be. I ask myself whether his rush had really carried him out of that mist in which he loomed interesting if not very big, with floating outlines — a straggler yearning inconsolably for his humble place in the ranks. And besides, the last word is not said, — probably shall never be said. Are not our lives too short for that full utterance which through all our stammerings is of course our only and abiding intention? I have given up expecting those last words, whose ring, if they could only be pronounced, would shake both heaven and earth. There is never time to say our last word — the last word of our love, of our desire, faith, remorse, submission, revolt. The heaven and the earth must not be shaken. I suppose — at least, not by us who know so many truths about either. My last words about Jim shall be few. I affirm he had achieved greatness; but the thing would be dwarfed in the telling, or rather in the hearing. Frankly, it is not my words that I mistrust but your minds. I could be eloquent were I not afraid you fellows had starved your imaginations to feed your bodies. I do not mean to be offensive; it is respectable to have no illusions — and safe — and profitable — and dull. Yet you, too, in your time must have known the intensity of life, that light of glamour created in the shock of trifles, as amazing as the glow of sparks struck from a cold stone — and as short-lived, alas!"

CHAPTER XXII

"THE conquest of love, honour, men's confidence — the pride of it, the power of it, are fit materials for a heroic tale; only our minds are struck by the externals of such a success, and to Jim's successes there were no externals. Thirty miles of forest shut it off from the sight of an indifferent world, and the noise of the white surf along the coast overpowered the voice of fame. The stream of civilisation, as if divided on a headland a hundred miles north of Patusan, branches east and south-east, leaving its plains and valleys, its old trees and its old mankind, neglected and isolated, such as an insignificant and crumbling islet between the two branches of a mighty, devouring stream. You find the name of the country pretty often in collections of old voyages. The seventeenth-century traders went there for pepper, because the passion for pepper seemed to burn like a flame of love in the breast of Dutch and English adventurers about the time of James the First. Where wouldn't they go for pepper! For a bag of pepper they would cut each other's throats without hesitation, and would forswear their souls, of which they were so careful otherwise:

the bizarre obstinacy of that desire made them defy death in a thousand shapes; the unknown seas, the loathsome and strange diseases; wounds, captivity, hunger, pestilence, and despair. It made them great! By heavens! it made them heroic; and it made them pathetic, too, in their craving for trade with the inflexible death levying its toll on young and old. It seems impossible to believe that mere greed could hold men to such a steadfastness of purpose, to such a blind persistence in endeavour and sacrifice. And indeed those who adventured their persons and lives risked all they had for a slender reward. They left their bones to lie bleaching on distant shores, so that wealth might flow to the living at home. To us, their less tried successors, they appear magnified, not as agents of trade but as instruments of a recorded destiny, pushing out into the unknown in obedience to an inward voice, to an impulse beating in the blood, to a dream of the future. They were wonderful; and it must be owned they were ready for the wonderful. They recorded it complacently in their sufferings, in the aspect of the seas, in the customs of strange nations, in the glory of splendid rulers.

"In Patusan they had found lots of pepper, and had been impressed by the magnificence and the wisdom of the Sultan; but somehow, after a century of checkered intercourse, the country seems to drop gradually out of the trade. Perhaps the pepper had given out. Be it as it may, nobody cares for it now; the glory has departed, the Sultan is an imbecile youth with two thumbs on his left hand and an uncertain and beggarly revenue extorted from a miserable population and stolen from him by his many uncles.

"This of course I have from Stein. He gave me their names and a short sketch of the life and character of each. He was as full of information about native States as an official report, but infinitely more amusing. He *had* to know. He traded in so many, and in some districts — as in Patusan, for instance — his firm was the only one to have an agency by special permit from the Dutch authorities. The Government trusted his discretion, and it was understood that he took all the risks. The men he employed understood that, too, but he made it worth their while apparently. He was perfectly frank with me over the breakfast-table in the morning. As far as he was aware (the last news was thirteen months old, he stated precisely), utter insecurity for life and

property was the normal condition. There were in Patusan antagonistic forces, and one of them was Rajah Allang, the worst
of the Sultan's uncles, the governor of the river, who did the
extorting and the stealing, and ground down to the point of extinction the country-born Malays, who, utterly defenceless, had
not even the resource of emigrating, — 'for indeed,' as Stein remarked, 'where could they go, and how could they get away?'
No doubt they did not even desire to get away. The world
(which is circumscribed by lofty impassable mountains) has been
given into the hand of the high-born, and *this* Rajah they knew:
he was of their own royal house. I had the pleasure of meeting
the gentleman later on. He was a dirty, little, used-up old man
with evil eyes and a weak mouth, who swallowed an opium pill
every two hours, and in defiance of common decency wore his
hair uncovered and falling in wild stringy locks about his wizened grimy face. When giving audience he would clamber upon
a sort of narrow stage erected in a hall like a ruinous barn with
a rotten bamboo floor, through the cracks of which you could see
twelve or fifteen feet below the heaps of refuse and garbage of
all kinds lying under the house. That is where and how he received us when, accompanied by Jim, I paid him a visit of ceremony. There were about forty people in the room, and perhaps
three times as many in the great courtyard below. There was
constant movement, coming and going, pushing and murmuring,
at our backs. A few youths in gay silks glared from the distance;
the majority, slaves and humble dependants, were half naked, in
ragged sarongs, dirty with ashes and mud-stains. I had never
seen Jim look so grave, so self-possessed, in an impenetrable, im-
pressive way. In the midst of these dark-faced men, his stalwart
figure in white apparel, the gleaming clusters of his fair hair,
seemed to catch all the sunshine that trickled through the cracks
in the closed shutters of that dim hall, with its walls of mats and
a roof of thatch. He appeared like a creature not only of another
kind but of another essence. Had they not seen him come up in
a canoe they might have thought he had descended upon them
from the clouds. He did, however, come in a crazy dug-out,
sitting (very still and with his knees together, for fear of over-
turning the thing) — sitting on a tin box — which I had lent him
— nursing on his lap a revolver of the Navy pattern — presented
by me on parting — which, through an interposition of Provi-

dence, or through some wrong-headed notion, that was just like him, or else from sheer instinctive sagacity, he had decided to carry unloaded. That's how he ascended the Patusan river. Nothing could have been more prosaic and more unsafe, more extravagantly casual, more lonely. Strange, this fatality that would cast the complexion of a flight upon all his acts, of impulsive unreflecting desertion — of a jump into the unknown.

"It is precisely the casualness of it that strikes me most. Neither Stein nor I had a clear conception of what might be on the other side when we, metaphorically speaking, took him up and hove him over the wall with scant ceremony. At the moment I merely wished to achieve his disappearance. Stein characteristically enough had a sentimental motive. He had a notion of paying off (in kind, I suppose) the old debt he had never forgotten. Indeed he had been all his life especially friendly to anybody from the British Isles. His late benefactor, it is true, was a Scot — even to the length of being called Alexander M'Neil — and Jim came from a long way south of the Tweed; but at the distance of six or seven thousand miles Great Britain, though never diminished, looks foreshortened enough even to its own children to rob such details of their importance. Stein was excusable, and his hinted intentions were so generous that I begged him 'most earnestly to keep them secret for a time. I felt that no consideration of personal advantage should be allowed to influence Jim; that not even the risk of such influence should be run. We had to deal with another sort of reality. He wanted a refuge, and a refuge at the cost of danger should be offered him — nothing more.

"Upon every other point I was perfectly frank with him, and I even (as I believed at the time) exaggerated the danger of the undertaking. As a matter of fact I did not do it justice; his first day in Patusan was nearly his last — would have been his last if he had not been so reckless or so hard on himself and had condescended to load that revolver. I remember, as I unfolded our precious scheme for his retreat, how his stubborn but weary resignation was gradually replaced by surprise, interest, wonder, and by boyish eagerness. This was a chance he had been dreaming of. He couldn't think how he merited that I . . . He would be shot if he could see to what he owed. . . . And it was Stein, Stein the merchant, who . . . but of course it was me he had to . . . I cut him short. He was not articulate, and his gratitude caused me inexplicable pain. I told him that if he owed this chance to any one especially, it was to an old Scot of whom he had never heard, who had died many years ago, of whom little was remembered besides a roaring voice and a rough sort of honesty. There was really no one to receive his thanks. Stein was passing on to a young man the help he had received in his own young days, and I had done no more than to mention his name. Upon this he coloured, and, twisting a bit of paper in his fingers, he remarked bashfully that I had always trusted him.

"I admitted that such was the case, and added after a pause that I wished he had been able to follow my example. 'You think I don't?' he asked uneasily, and remarked in a mutter that one had to get some sort of show first; then brightening up, and in a loud voice he protested he would give me no occasion to regret my confidence, which — which . . .

" 'Do not misapprehend,' I interrupted. 'It is not in your power to make me regret anything.' There would be no regrets; but if there were, it would be altogether my own affair: on the other hand, I wished him to understand clearly that this arrangement, this — this — experiment, was his own doing; he was responsible for it and no one else. 'Why? Why,' he stammered, 'this is the very thing that I . . .' I begged him not to be dense, and he looked more puzzled than ever. He was in a fair way to make life intolerable to himself. . . . 'Do you think so?' he asked, disturbed; but in a moment added confidently, 'I was going on though. Was I not?' It was impossible to be angry with him: I could not help a smile, and told him that in the old days people who went on like this were on the way of becoming hermits in a wilderness. 'Hermits be hanged!' he commented with engaging impulsiveness. Of course he didn't mind a wilderness. . . . 'I was glad of it,' I said. That was where he would be going to. He would find it lively enough, I ventured to promise. 'Yes, yes,' he said, keenly. He had shown a desire, I continued inflexibly, to go out and shut the door after him. . . . 'Did I?' he interrupted in a strange access of gloom that seemed to envelop him from head to foot like the shadow of a passing cloud. He was wonderfully expressive after all. Wonderfully! 'Did I?' he repeated, bitterly. 'You can't say I made much noise about it. And I can keep it up, too — only, confound it! you show me a door.' . . . 'Very well. Pass on,' I struck in. I could make him a solemn promise that it would be shut behind him with a vengeance. His fate, whatever it was, would be ignored, because the country, for all its rotten state, was not judged ripe for interference. Once he got in, it would be for the outside world as though he had never existed. He would have nothing but the soles of his two feet to stand upon, and he would have first to find his ground at that. 'Never existed — that's it, by Jove!' he murmured to himself. His eyes, fastened upon my lips, sparkled. If he had thoroughly understood the conditions, I concluded, he had better jump into the first gharry he could see and drive on to Stein's house for his final instructions. He flung out of the room before I had fairly finished speaking."

CHAPTER XXIII

"HE DID not return till next morning. He had been kept to dinner and for the night. There never had been such a wonderful man as Mr. Stein. He had in his pocket a letter for Cornelius ('the Johnnie who's going to get the sack,' he explained with a momentary drop in his elation), and he exhibited with glee a silver ring, such as natives use, worn down very thin and showing faint traces of chasing.

"This was his introduction to an old chap called Doramin — one of the principal men out there — a big pot — who had been Mr. Stein's friend in that country where he had all these adventures. Mr. Stein called him 'war-comrade.' War-comrade was good. Wasn't it? And didn't Mr. Stein speak English wonderfully well? Said he had learned it in Celebes — of all places! That was awfully funny. Was it not? He did speak with an accent — a twang — did I notice? That chap Doramin had given him the ring. They had exchanged presents when they parted for the last time. Sort of promising eternal friendship. He called it fine — did I not? They had to make a dash for dear life out of the country when that Mohammed — Mohammed — What's-his-name had been killed. I knew the story, of course. Seemed a beastly shame, didn't it? . . .

"He ran on like this, forgetting his plate, with a knife and fork

in hand (he had found me at tiffin), slightly flushed, and with his
eyes darkened many shades, which was with him a sign of excitement. The ring was a sort of credential — ('It's like something you read of in books,' he threw in appreciatively) and
Doramin would do his best for him. Mr. Stein had been the means
of saving that chap's life on some occasion; purely by accident,
Mr. Stein had said, but he — Jim — had his own opinion about that.
Mr. Stein was just the man to look out for such accidents. No
matter. Accident or purpose, this would serve his turn immensely.
Hoped to goodness the jolly old beggar had not gone off the
hooks meantime. Mr. Stein could not tell. There had been no
news for more than a year; they were kicking up no end of an
all-fired row amongst themselves, and the river was closed. Jolly
awkward, this; but, no fear; he would manage to find a crack to
get in.

"He impressed, almost frightened, me with his elated rattle. He
was voluble like a youngster on the eve of a long holiday with a
prospect of delightful scrapes, and such an attitude of mind in a
grown man and in this connection had in it something phenome-
nal, a little mad, dangerous, unsafe. I was on the point of entreating him to take things seriously when he dropped his knife and
fork (he had begun eating, or rather swallowing food, as it were,
unconsciously), and began a search all round his plate. The ring!
The ring! Where the devil . . . Ah! Here it was. . . . He closed
his big hand on it, and tried all his pockets one after another. Jove!
wouldn't do to lose the thing. He meditated gravely over his fist.
Had it? Would hang the bally affair round his neck! And he pro-
ceeded to do this immediately, producing a string (which looked
like a bit of a cotton shoe-lace) for the purpose. There! That
would do the trick! It would be the deuce if . . . He seemed to
catch sight of my face for the first time, and it steadied him a
little. I probably didn't realise, he said with a naïve gravity, how
much importance he attached to that token. It meant a friend;
and it is a good thing to have a friend. He knew something about
that. He nodded at me expressively, but before my disclaiming
gesture he leaned his head on his hand and for a while sat silent,
playing thoughtfully with the bread-crumbs on the cloth. . . .
'Slam the door — that was jolly well put,' he cried, and jumping
up, began to pace the room, reminding me by the set of the shoulders, the turn of his head, the headlong and uneven stride, of that
night when he had paced thus, confessing, explaining — what you

will — but, in the last instance, living — living before me, under his own little cloud, with all his unconscious subtlety which could draw consolation from the very source of sorrow. It was the same mood, the same and different, like a fickle companion that to-day guiding you on the true path, with the same eyes, the same step, the same impulse, to-morrow will lead you hopelessly astray. His tread was assured, his straying, darkened eyes seemed to search the room for something. One of his footfalls somehow sounded louder than the other — the fault of his boots probably — and gave a curious impression of an invisible halt in his gait. One of his hands was rammed deep into his trousers-pocket, the other waved suddenly above his head. 'Slam the door!' he shouted. 'I've been waiting for that. I'll show yet . . . I'll . . . I'm ready for any confounded thing. . . . I've been dreaming of it . . . Jove! Get out of this. Jove! This is luck at last. . . . You wait. I'll . . .'

"He tossed his head fearlessly, and I confess that for the first and last time in our acquaintance I perceived myself unexpectedly to be thoroughly sick of him. Why these vapourings? He was stumping about the room flourishing his arm absurdly, and now and then feeling on his breast for the ring under his clothes. Where was the sense of such exaltation in a man appointed to be a trading-clerk, and in a place where there was no trade — at that? Why hurl defiance at the universe? This was not a proper frame of mind to approach any undertaking; an improper frame of mind not only for him, I said, but for any man. He stood still over me. Did I think so? he asked, by no means subdued, and with a smile in which I seemed to detect suddenly something insolent. But then I am twenty years his senior. Youth *is* insolent; it is its right — its necessity; it has got to assert itself, and all assertion in this world of doubts is a defiance, is an insolence. He went off into a far corner, and coming back, he, figuratively speaking, turned to rend me. I spoke like that because I — even I, who had been no end kind to him — even I remembered — remembered — against him — what — what had happened. And what about others — the — the — world? Where's the wonder he wanted to get out, meant to get out, meant to stay out — by heavens! And I talked about proper frames of mind!

" 'It is not I or the world who remember,' I shouted. 'It is you — you, who remember.'

"He did not flinch, and went on with heat, 'Forget everything, everybody, everybody.' . . . His voice fell. . . . 'But you,' he added.

" 'Yes — me, too — if it would help,' I said, also in a low tone. After this we remained silent and languid for a time as if exhausted. Then he began again, composedly, and told me that Mr. Stein had instructed him to wait for a month or so, to see whether it was possible for him to remain, before he began building a new house for himself, so as to avoid 'vain expense.' He did make use of funny expressions — Stein did. 'Vain expense' was good. . . . Remain? Why! of course. He would hang on. Let him only get in — that's all; he would answer for it he would remain. Never get out. It was easy enough to remain.

" 'Don't be foolhardy,' I said, rendered uneasy by his threatening tone. 'If you only live long enough you will want to come back.'

" 'Come back to what?' he asked, absently, with his eyes fixed upon the face of a clock on the wall.

"I was silent for a while. 'Is it to be never, then?' I said. 'Never,' he repeated, dreamily, without looking at me, and then flew into sudden activity. 'Jove! Two o'clock, and I sail at four?'

"It was true. A brigantine of Stein's was leaving for the westward that afternoon, and he had been instructed to take his passage in her, only no orders to delay the sailing had been given. I suppose Stein forgot. He made a rush to get his things while I went aboard my ship, where he promised to call on his way to the outer roadster. He turned up accordingly in a great hurry and with a small leather valise in his hand. This wouldn't do, and I offered him an old tin trunk of mine supposed to be water-tight, or at least damp-tight. He effected the transfer by the simple process of shooting out the contents of his valise as you would empty a sack of wheat. I saw three books in the tumble; two small, in dark covers, and a thick green-and-gold volume — a half-crown complete Shakespeare. 'You read this?' I asked. 'Yes. Best thing to cheer up a fellow,' he said, hastily. I was struck by this appreciation, but there was no time for Shakespearian talk. A heavy revolver and two small boxes of cartridges were lying on the cuddy-table. 'Pray take this,' I said. 'It may help you to remain.' No sooner were these words out of my mouth than I perceived what grim meaning they could bear. 'May help you to get in,' I corrected myself, remorsefully. He, however, was not troubled by obscure meanings; he thanked me effusively and bolted out, calling Good-bye over his shoulder. I heard his voice through the ship's side urging his boatmen to give way, and looking out of the stern-port I saw the boat rounding under the counter. He sat in her leaning forward, exciting his men with voice and gestures; and as he had kept the revolver in his hand and seemed to be presenting it at their heads, I shall never forget the scared faces of the four Javanese, and the frantic swing of their stroke which snatched that vision from under my eyes. Then turning away, the first thing I saw were the two boxes of cartridges on the cuddy-table. He had forgotten to take them.

"I ordered my gig manned at once; but Jim's rowers, under the impression that their lives hung on a thread while they had that madman in the boat, made such excellent time that before I had traversed half the distance between the two vessels I caught sight of him clambering over the rail, and of his box being passed up. All the brigantine's canvas was loose, her mainsail was set, and the windlass was just beginning to clink as I stepped upon her deck: her master, a dapper little half-caste of forty or so, in a blue flannel suit, with lively eyes, his round face the colour of lemon-peel, and with a thin little black moustache drooping on each side of his thick, dark lips, came forward smirking. He turned out, notwithstanding his self-satisfied and cheery exterior, to be of a careworn temperament. In answer to a remark of mine (while Jim had gone below for a moment) he said, 'Oh, yes. Patusan.' He was going to carry the gentleman to the mouth of the river, but would 'never ascend.' His flowing English seemed to be derived from a dictionary compiled by a lunatic. Had Mr. Stein desired him to 'ascend,' he would have 'reverentially' — (I think he wanted to say respectfully — but devil only knows) — 'reverentially made objects for the safety of properties.' If disregarded, he would have presented 'resignation to quit.' Twelve months ago he had made his last voyage there, and though Mr. Cornelius 'propitiated many offertories' to Mr. Rajah Allang and the 'principal populations,' on conditions which made the trade 'a snare and ashes in the mouth,' yet his ship had been fired upon from the woods by 'irresponsive parties' all the way down the river; which causing his crew 'from exposure to limb to remain silent in hidings,' the brigantine was nearly stranded on a sandbank at the bar, where she 'would have been perishable beyond

the act of man.' The angry disgust at the recollection, the pride
of his fluency, to which he turned an attentive ear, struggled for
the possession of his broad simple face. He scowled and beamed
at me, and watched with satisfaction the undeniable effect of his
phraseology. Dark frowns ran swiftly over the placid sea, and
the brigantine, with her fore-topsail to the mast and her main-
boom amidships, seemed bewildered amongst the cat's-paws. He
told me further, gnashing his teeth, that the Rajah was a 'laugh-
able hyæna' (can't imagine how he got hold of hyænas); while
somebody else was many times falser than the 'weapons of a
crocodile.' Keeping one eye on the movements of his crew forward, he let loose his volubility — comparing the place to a 'cage
of beasts made ravenous by long impenitence.' I fancy he meant
impunity. He had no intention, he cried, to 'exhibit himself to
be made attached purposefully to robbery.' The long-drawn
wails, giving the time for the pull of the men catting the anchor,
came to an end, and he lowered his voice. 'Plenty too much
enough of Patusan,' he concluded, with energy.

"I heard afterwards he had been so indiscreet as to get himself tied up by the neck with a rattan halter to a post planted in
the middle of a mud-hole before the Rajah's house. He spent the
best part of a day and a whole night in that unwholesome situation, but there is every reason to believe the thing had been meant
as a sort of joke. He brooded for a while over that horrid memory, I suppose, and then addressed in a quarrelsome tone the man
coming aft to the helm. When he turned to me again it was to
speak judicially, without passion. He would take the gentleman
to the mouth of the river at Batu Kring (Patusan town 'being
situated internally,' he remarked, 'thirty miles'). But in his eyes,
he continued — a tone of bored, weary conviction replacing his
previous voluble delivery — the gentleman was already 'in the
similitude of a corpse.' 'What? What do you say?' I asked. He
assumed a startlingly ferocious demeanour, and imitated to per-
fection the act of stabbing from behind. 'Already like the body
of one deported,' he explained, with the insufferably conceited
air of his kind after what they imagine a display of cleverness.
Behind him I perceived Jim smiling silently at me, and with a
raised hand checking the exclamation on my lips.

"Then, while the half-caste, bursting with importance, shouted
his orders, while the yards swung creaking and the heavy boom

came surging over, Jim and I, alone as it were, to leeward of the
mainsail, clasped each other's hands and exchanged the last hurried words. My heart was freed from that dull resentment which
had existed side by side with interest in his fate. The absurd
chatter of the half-caste had given more reality to the miserable
dangers of his path than Stein's careful statements. On that occasion the sort of formality that had been always present in our intercourse vanished from our speech; I believe I called him 'dear
boy,' and he tacked on the words 'old man' to some half-uttered
expression of gratitude, as though his risk set off against my years
had made us more equal in age and in feeling. There was a moment of real and profound intimacy, unexpected and short-lived
like a glimpse of some everlasting, of some saving truth. He ex-
erted himself to soothe me as though he had been the more mature of the two. 'All right, all right,' he said, rapidly, and with
feeling. 'I promise to take care of myself. Yes; I won't take any
risks. Not a single blessed risk. Of course not. I mean to hang
out. Don't you worry. Jove! I feel as if nothing could touch
me. Why! this is luck from the word Go. I wouldn't spoil such
a magnificent chance!' . . . A magnificent chance! Well, it *was*
magnificent, but chances are what men make them, and how was
I to know? As he had said, even I — even I remembered — his —
his misfortunes against him. It was true. And the best thing for
him was to go.

"My gig had dropped in the wake of the brigantine, and I saw
him aft detached upon the light of the westering sun, raising
his cap high above his head. I heard an indistinct shout, 'You —
shall — hear — of — me.' Of me, or from me, I don't know which.
I think it must have been *of* me. My eyes were too dazzled by
the glitter of the sea below his feet to see him clearly; I am
fated never to see him clearly; but I can assure you no man could
have appeared less 'in the similitude of a corpse,' as that half-caste
croaker had put it. I could see the little wretch's face, the shape
and colour of a ripe pumpkin, poked out somewhere under Jim's
elbow. He, too, raised his arm as if for a downward thrust. *Absit
omen!*"

CHAPTER XXIV

"The coast of Patusan (I saw it nearly two years afterwards) is straight and sombre, and faces a misty ocean. Red trails are seen like cataracts of rust streaming under the dark-green foliage of bushes and creepers clothing the low cliffs. Swampy plains open out at the mouth of rivers, with a view of jagged blue peaks beyond the vast forests. In the offing a chain of islands, dark, crumbling shapes, stand out in the everlasting sunlit haze like the remnants of a wall breached by the sea.

"There is a village of fisher-folk at the mouth of the Batu Kring branch of the estuary. The river, which had been closed so long, was open then, and Stein's little schooner, in which I had my passage, worked her way up in three tides without being exposed to a fusillade from 'irresponsive parties.' Such a state of affairs belonged already to ancient history, if I could believe the elderly headman of the fishing village, who came on board to act as a sort of pilot. He talked to me (the second white man he had ever seen) with confidence, and most of his talk was about the first white man he had ever seen. He called him Tuan Jim, and the tone of his references was made remarkable by a strange mixture of familiarity and awe. They, in the village, were under that lord's special protection, which showed that Jim bore no grudge. If he had warned me that I would hear of him it was perfectly true. I was hearing of him. There was already a story that the tide had turned two hours before its time to help him on his journey up the river. The talkative old man himself had steered the canoe and had marvelled at the phenomenon. Moreover, all the glory was in his family. His son and his son-in-law had paddled; but they were only youths without experience, who did not notice the speed of the canoe till he pointed out to them the amazing fact.

"Jim's coming to that fishing village was a blessing; but to them, as to many of us, the blessing came heralded by terrors. So many generations had been released since the last white man had visited the river that the very tradition had been lost. The appear-

ance of the being that descended upon them and demanded inflexibly to be taken up to Patusan was discomposing; his insistence
was alarming; his generosity more than suspicious. It was an
unheard-of request. There was no precedent. What would the
Rajah say to this? What would he do to them? The best part of
the night was spent in consultation; but the immediate risk from
the anger of that strange man seemed so great that at last a cranky
dug-out was got ready. The women shrieked with grief as it put
off. A fearless old hag cursed the stranger.

"He sat in it, as I've told you, on his tin box, nursing the unloaded revolver on his lap. He sat with precaution — than which
there is nothing more fatiguing — and thus entered the land he was
destined to fill with the fame of his virtues, from the blue peaks
inland to the white ribbon of surf on the coast. At the first bend
he lost sight of the sea with its labouring waves for ever rising,
sinking, and vanishing to rise again — the very image of struggling
mankind — and faced the immovable forests rooted deep in the
soil, soaring towards the sunshine, everlasting in the shadowy
might of their tradition, like life itself. And his opportunity sat
veiled by his side like an Eastern bride waiting to be uncovered
by the hand of the master. He, too, was the heir of a shadowy
and mighty tradition! He told me, however, that he had never in
his life felt so depressed and tired as in that canoe. All the movement he dared to allow himself was to reach, as it were by stealth,
after the shell of half a cocoa-nut floating between his shoes, and
bale some of the water out with a carefully restrained action. He
discovered how hard the lid of a block-tin case was to sit upon.
He had heroic health; but several times during that journey he
experienced fits of giddiness, and between whiles he speculated
hazily as to the size of the blister the sun was raising on his back.
For amusement he tried by looking ahead to decide whether the
muddy object he saw lying on the water's edge was a log of wood
or an alligator. Only very soon he had to give that up. No fun
in it. Always alligator. One of them flopped into the river and
all but capsized the canoe. But this excitement was over directly.
Then in a long empty reach he was very grateful to a troop of
monkeys who came right down on the bank and made an insulting hullabaloo on his passage. Such was the way in which he was
approaching greatness as genuine as any man ever achieved.
Principally, he longed for sunset; and meantime his three pad-

dlers were preparing to put into execution their plan of delivering him up to the Rajah.

" 'I suppose I must have been stupid with fatigue, or perhaps I did doze off for a time,' he said. The first thing he knew was his canoe coming to the bank. He became instantaneously aware of the forest having been left behind, of the first houses being visible higher up, of a stockade on his left, and of his boatmen leaping out together upon a low point of land and taking to their heels. Instinctively he leaped out after them. At first he thought himself deserted for some inconceivable reason, but he heard excited shouts, a gate swung open, and a lot of people poured out, making towards him. At the same time a boat full of armed men appeared on the river and came alongside his empty canoe, thus shutting off his retreat.

" 'I was too startled to be quite cool — don't you know? and if that revolver had been loaded I would have shot somebody — perhaps two, three bodies, and that would have been the end of me. But it wasn't. . . .' 'Why not?' I asked. 'Well, I couldn't fight the whole population, and I wasn't coming to them as if I were afraid of my life,' he said, with just a faint hint of his stubborn sulkiness in the glance he gave me. I refrained from pointing out to him that they could not have known the chambers were actually empty. He had to satisfy himself in his own way. . . . 'Anyhow it wasn't,' he repeated, good-humouredly, 'and so I just stood still and asked them what was the matter. That seemed to strike them dumb. I saw some of these thieves going off with my box. That long-legged old scoundrel Kassim (I'll show him to you to-morrow) ran out fussing to me about the Rajah wanting to see me. I said, "All right"; I, too, wanted to see the Rajah, and I simply walked in through the gate and — and — here I am.' He laughed, and then with unexpected emphasis, 'And do you know what's the best in it?' he asked. 'I'll tell you. It's the knowledge that had I been wiped out it is this place that would have been the loser.'

"He spoke thus to me before his house on that evening I've mentioned — after we had watched the moon float away above the chasm between the hills like an ascending spirit out of a grave; its sheen descended, cold and pale, like the ghost of dead sunlight. There is something haunting in the light of the moon; it has all the dispassionateness of a disembodied soul, and some-

thing of its inconceivable mystery. It is to our sunshine, which —
say what you like — is all we have to live by, what the echo is to
the sound: misleading and confusing whether the note be mocking
or sad. It robs all forms of matter — which, after all, is our do-
main — of their substance, and gives a sinister reality to shadows
alone. And the shadows were very real around us, but Jim by
my side looked very stalwart, as though nothing — not even the
occult power of moonlight — could rob him of his reality in my
eyes. Perhaps, indeed, nothing could touch him since he had
survived the assault of the dark powers. All was silent, all was
still; even on the river the moonbeams slept as on a pool. It was
the moment of high water, a moment of immobility that accentu-
ated the utter isolation of this lost corner of the earth. The houses
crowding along the wide shining sweep without ripple or glitter,
stepping into the water in a line of jostling, vague, grey, silvery
forms mingled with black masses of shadow, were like a spectral
herd of shapeless creatures pressing forward to drink in a spectral
and lifeless stream. Here and there a red gleam twinkled within
the bamboo walls, warm, like a living spark, significant of human
affections, of shelter, of repose.

"He confessed to me that he often watched these tiny warm
gleams go out one by one, that he loved to see people go to sleep
under his eyes, confident in the security of to-morrow. 'Peaceful
here, eh?' he asked. He was not eloquent, but there was a deep
meaning in the words that followed. 'Look at these houses; there's
not one where I am not trusted. Jove! I told you I would hang
on. Ask any man, woman, or child . . .' He paused. 'Well, I
am all right anyhow.'

"I observed quickly that he had found that out in the end. I had
been sure of it, I added. He shook his head. 'Were you?' He
pressed my arm lightly above the elbow. 'Well, then — you were
right.'

"There was elation and pride, there was awe almost, in that
low exclamation. 'Jove!' he cried, 'only think what it is to me.'
Again he pressed my arm. 'And you asked me whether I thought
of leaving. Good God! I! want to leave! Especially now after
what you told me of Mr. Stein's . . . Leave! Why! That's what
I was afraid of. It would have been — it would have been harder
than dying. No — on my word. Don't laugh. I must feel —
every day, every time I open my eyes — that I am trusted — that

nobody has a right — don't you know? Leave! For where? What for? To get what?'

"I had told him (indeed it was the main object of my visit) that it was Stein's intention to present him at once with the house and the stock of trading goods, on certain easy conditions which would make the transaction perfectly regular and valid. He began to snort and plunge at first. 'Confound your delicacy!' I shouted. 'It isn't Stein at all. It's giving you what you had made for yourself. And in any case keep your remarks for M'Neil — when you meet him in the other world. I hope it won't happen soon. . . .' He had to give in to my arguments, because all his conquests, the trust, the fame, the friendships, the love — all these things that made him master had made him a captive, too. He looked with an owner's eye at the peace of the evening, at the river, at the houses, at the everlasting life of the forests, at the life of the old mankind, at the secrets of the land, at the pride of his own heart: but it was they that possessed him and made him their own to the innermost thought, to the slightest stir of blood, to his last breath.

"It was something to be proud of. I, too, was proud — for him, if not so certain of the fabulous value of the bargain. It was wonderful. It was not so much of his fearlessness that I thought. It is strange how little account I took of it: as if it had been something too conventional to be at the root of the matter. No. I was more struck by the other gifts he had displayed. He had proved his grasp of the unfamiliar situation, his intellectual alertness in that field of thought. There was his readiness, too! Amazing. And all this had come to him in a manner like keen scent to a well-bred hound. He was not eloquent, but there was a dignity in this constitutional reticence, there was a high seriousness in his stammerings. He had still his old trick of stubborn blushing. Now and then, though, a word, a sentence, would escape him that showed how deeply, how solemnly, he felt about that work which had given him the certitude of rehabilitation. That is why he seemed to love the land and the people with a sort of fierce egoism, with a contemptuous tenderness."

CHAPTER XXV

" 'THIS is where I was prisoner for three days,' he murmured
to me (it was on the occasion of our visit to the Rajah), while
we were making our way slowly through a kind of awestruck
riot of dependants across Tunku Allang's courtyard. 'Filthy
place, isn't it? And I couldn't get anything to eat either, unless
I made a row about it, and then it was only a small plate of rice
and a fried fish not much bigger than a stickle-back — confound
them! Jove! *I've* been hungry prowling inside this stinking enclosure with some of these vagabonds shoving their mugs right
under my nose. I had given up that famous revolver of yours at
the first demand. Glad to get rid of the bally thing. Look like
a fool walking about with an empty shooting-iron in my hand.'
At that moment we came into the presence, and he became un-
flinchingly grave and complimentary with his late captor. Oh!
magnificent! I want to laugh when I think of it. But I was impressed, too. The old disreputable Tunku Allang could not help
showing his fear (he was no hero, for all the tales of his hot youth
he was fond of telling); and at the same time there was a wistful
confidence in his manner towards his late prisoner. Note! Even
where he would be most hated he was still trusted. Jim — as
far as I could follow the conversation — was improving the occasion by the delivery of a lecture. Some poor villagers had been
waylaid and robbed while on their way to Doramin's house with a
few pieces of gum or beeswax which they wished to exchange for
rice. 'It was Doramin who was a thief,' burst out the Rajah.
A shaking fury seemed to enter that old frail body. He writhed
weirdly on his mat, gesticulating with his hands and feet, tossing
the tangled strings of his mop — an important incarnation of rage.
There were staring eyes and dropping jaws all around us. Jim
began to speak. Resolutely, coolly, and for some time he enlarged upon the text that no man should be prevented from getting his food and his children's food honestly. The other sat like
a tailor at his board, one palm on each knee, his head low, and fix-
ing Jim through the grey hair that fell over his very eyes. When

Jim had done there was a great stillness. Nobody seemed to breathe even; no one made a sound till the old Rajah sighed faintly, and looking up, with a toss of his head, said quickly, 'You hear, my people! No more of these little games.' This decree was received in profound silence. A rather heavy man, evidently in a position of confidence, with intelligent eyes, a bony, broad, very dark face, and a cheerily officious manner (I learned later on he was the executioner), presented to us two cups of coffee on a brass tray, which he took from the hands of an inferior attendant. 'You needn't drink,' muttered Jim very rapidly. I didn't perceive the meaning at first, and only looked at him. He took a good sip and sat composedly, holding the saucer in his left hand. In a moment I felt excessively annoyed. 'Why the devil,' I whispered, smiling at him amiably, 'do you expose me to such a stupid risk?' I drank, of course, there was nothing for it, while he gave no sign, and almost immediately afterwards we took our leave. While we were going down the courtyard to our boat, escorted by the intelligent and cheery executioner, Jim said he was very sorry. It was the barest chance, of course. Personally he thought nothing of poison. The remotest chance. He was — he assured me — considered to be infinitely more useful than dangerous, and so . . . 'But the Rajah is afraid of you abominably. Anybody can see that,' I argued, with, I own, a certain peevishness, and all the time watching anxiously for the first twist of some sort of ghastly colic. I was awfully disgusted. 'If I am to do any good here and preserve my position,' he said, taking his seat by my side in the boat, 'I must stand the risk: I take it once every month, at least. Many people trust me to do that — for them. Afraid of me! That's just it. Most likely he is afraid of me because I am not afraid of his coffee.' Then showing me a place on the north front of the stockade where the pointed tops of several stakes were broken, 'This is where I leaped over on my third day at Patusan. They haven't put new stakes there yet. Good leap, eh?' A moment later we passed the mouth of a muddy creek. 'This is my second leap. I had a bit of a run and took this one flying, but fell short. Thought I would leave my skin there. Lost my shoes struggling. And all the time I was thinking to myself how beastly it would be to get a jab with a bally long spear while sticking in the mud like this. I remember how sick I felt wriggling in that slime. I mean really sick — as if I had bitten something rotten.'

"That's how it was — and the opportunity ran by his side, leaped over the gap, floundered in the mud . . . still veiled. The unexpectedness of his coming was the only thing, you understand, that saved him from being at once despatched with krises and flung into the river. They had him, but it was like getting hold of an apparition, a wraith, a portent. What did it mean? What to do with it? Was it too late to conciliate him? Hadn't he better be killed without more delay? But what would happen then? Wretched old Allang went nearly mad with apprehension and through the difficulty of making up his mind. Several times the council was broken up, and the advisers made a break helter-skelter for the door and out on to the verandah. One — it is said — even jumped down to the ground — fifteen feet, I should judge — and broke his leg. The royal governor of Patusan had bizarre mannerisms, and one of them was to introduce boastful rhapsodies into every arduous discussion, when, getting gradually excited, he would end by flying off his perch with a kris in his hand. But, barring such interruptions, the deliberations upon Jim's fate went on night and day.

"Meanwhile he wandered about the courtyard, shunned by some, glared at by others, but watched by all, and practically at the mercy of the first casual ragamuffin with a chopper, in there. He took possession of a small tumble-down shed to sleep in; the effluvia of filth and rotten matter incommoded him greatly: it seems he had not lost his appetite though, because — he told me — he had been hungry all the blessed time. Now and again 'some fussy ass' deputed from the council-room would come out running to him, and in honeyed tones would administer amazing interrogatories: 'Were the Dutch coming to take the country? Would the white man like to go back down the river? What was the object of coming to such a miserable country? The Rajah wanted to know whether the white man could repair a watch? They did actually bring out to him a nickel clock of New England make, and out of sheer unbearable boredom he busied himself in trying to get the alarum to work. It was apparently when thus occupied in his shed that the true perception of his extreme peril dawned upon him. He dropped the thing — he says — 'like a hot potato,' and walked out hastily, without the slightest idea of what he would, or indeed could, do. He only knew that the position was intolerable. He strolled aimlessly beyond a sort of ramshackle little granary on posts, and his eyes

fell on the broken stakes of the palisade; and then — he says — at
once, without any mental process as it were, without any stir of
emotion, he set about his escape as if executing a plan matured
for a month. He walked off carelessly to give himself a good run,
and when he faced about there was some dignitary, with two
spearmen in attendance, close at his elbow ready with a question. He started off 'from under his very nose,' went over 'like a
bird,' and landed on the other side with a fall that jarred all his
bones and seemed to split his head. He picked himself up instantly. He never thought of anything at the time; all he could
remember — he said — was a great yell; the first houses of Patusan
were before him four hundred yards away; he saw the creek, and
as it were mechanically put on more pace. The earth seemed
fairly to fly backwards under his feet. He took off from the last
dry spot, felt himself flying through the air, felt himself, without
any shock, planted upright in an extremely soft and sticky mud-
bank. It was only when he tried to move his legs and found he
couldn't that, in his own words, 'he came to himself.' He began
to think of the 'bally long spears.' As a matter of fact, considering that the people inside the stockade had to run to the gate,
then get down to the landing-place, get into boats, and pull round
a point of land, he had more advance than he imagined. Besides,
it being low water, the creek was without water — you couldn't
call it dry — and practically he was safe for a time from everything but a very long shot perhaps. The higher firm ground was
about six feet in front of him. 'I thought I would have to die
there all the same,' he said. He reached and grabbed desperately
with his hands, and only succeeded in gathering a horrible cold
shiny heap of slime against his breast — up to his very chin. It
seemed to him he was burying himself alive, and then he struck
out madly, scattering the mud with his fists. It fell on his head,
on his face, over his eyes, into his mouth. He told me that he
remembered suddenly the courtyard, as you remember a place
where you had been very happy years ago. He longed — so he
said — to be back there again, mending the clock. Mending the
clock — that was the idea. He made efforts, tremendous sobbing,
gasping efforts, efforts that seemed to burst his eyeballs in their
sockets and make him blind, and culminating into one mighty
supreme effort in the darkness to crack the earth asunder, to
throw it off his limbs — and he felt himself creeping feebly up the

bank. He lay full length on the firm ground and saw the light, the sky. Then as a sort of happy thought the notion came to him that he would go to sleep. He will have it that he *did* actually go to sleep; that he slept — perhaps for a minute, perhaps for twenty seconds, or only for one second, but he recollects distinctly the violent convulsive start of awakening. He remained lying still for a while, and then he arose muddy from head to foot and stood there, thinking he was alone of his kind for hundreds of miles, alone, with no help, no sympathy, no pity to expect from any one, like a hunted animal. The first houses were not more than twenty yards from him; and it was the desperate screaming of a frightened woman trying to carry off a child that started him again. He pelted straight on in his socks, beplastered with filth out of all semblance to a human being. He traversed more than half the length of the settlement. The nimbler women fled right and left, the slower men just dropped whatever they had in their hands, and remained petrified with dropping jaws. He was a flying terror. He says he noticed the little children trying to run for life, falling on their little stomachs and kicking. He swerved between two houses up a slope, clambered in desperation over a barricade of felled trees (there wasn't a week without some fight in Patusan at that time), burst through a fence into a maize-patch, where a scared boy flung a stick at him, blundered upon a path, and ran all at once into the arms of several startled men. He just had breath enough to gasp out, 'Doramin! Doramin!' He remembers being half-carried, half-rushed to the top of the slope, and in a vast enclosure with palms and fruit-trees being run up to a large man sitting massively in a chair in the midst of the greatest possible commotion and excitement. He fumbled in mud and clothes to produce the ring, and, finding himself suddenly on his back, wondered who had knocked him down. They had simply let him go — don't you know? — but he couldn't stand. At the foot of the slope random shots were fired, and above the roofs of the settlement there rose a dull roar of amazement. But he was safe. Doramin's people were barricading the gate and pouring water down his throat; Doramin's old wife, full of business and commiseration, was issuing shrill orders to her girls. 'The old woman,' he said, softly, 'made a to-do over me as if I had been her own son. They put me into an immense bed — her state bed — and she ran in and out wiping her eyes to give me pats on the

back. I must have been a pitiful object. I just lay there like a log
for I don't know how long.'

"He seemed to have a great liking for Doramin's old wife.
She on her side had taken a motherly fancy to him. She had a
round, nut-brown, soft face, all fine wrinkles, large, bright red
lips (she chewed betel assiduously), and screwed-up, winking,
benevolent eyes. She was constantly in movement, scolding busily
and ordering unceasingly a troop of young women with clear
brown faces and big grave eyes, her daughters, her servants, her
slave-girls. You know how it is in these households: it's generally
impossible to tell the difference. She was very spare, and even her
ample outer garment, fastened in front with jewelled clasps, had
somehow a skimpy effect. Her dark bare feet were thrust into yellow straw slippers of Chinese make. I have seen her myself flitting
about with her extremely thick, long, grey hair falling about her
shoulders. She uttered homely shrewd sayings, was of noble birth,
and was eccentric and arbitrary. In the afternoon she would sit in
a very roomy arm-chair, opposite her husband, gazing steadily
through a wide opening in the wall which gave an extensive view
of the settlement and the river.

"She invariably tucked up her feet under her, but old Doramin
sat squarely, sat imposingly as a mountain sits on a plain. He was
only of the *nakhoda* or merchant class, but the respect shown to
him and the dignity of his bearing were very striking. He was
the chief of the second power in Patusan. The immigrants from
Celebes (about sixty families that, with dependants and so on,
could muster some two hundred men 'wearing the kris') had
elected him years ago for their head. The men of that race are
intelligent, enterprising, revengeful, but with a more frank courage than the other Malays, and restless under oppression. They
formed the party opposed to the Rajah. Of course the quarrels
were for trade. This was the primary cause of faction fights,
of the sudden outbreaks that would fill this or that part of the
settlement with smoke, flame, the noise of shots and shrieks.
Villages were burnt, men were dragged into the Rajah's stockade to be killed or tortured for the crime of trading with anybody else but himself. Only a day or two before Jim's arrival
several heads of households in the very fishing village that was
afterwards taken under his especial protection had been driven
over the cliffs by a party of the Rajah's spearmen, on suspicion

of having been collecting edible birds' nests for a Celebes trader.
Rajah Allang pretended to be the only trader in his country, and
the penalty for the breach of the monopoly was death; but his
idea of trading was indistinguishable from the commonest forms
of robbery. His cruelty and rapacity had no other bounds than
his cowardice, and he was afraid of the organised power of the
Celebes men, only — till Jim came — he was not afraid enough to
keep quiet. He struck at them through his subjects, and thought
himself pathetically in the right. The situation was complicated
by a wandering stranger, an Arab halfbreed, who, I believe, on
purely religious grounds, had incited the tribes in the interior (the
bush-folk, as Jim himself called them) to rise, and had established
himself in a fortified camp on the summit of one of the twin hills.
He hung over the town of Patusan like a hawk over a poultry-
yard, but he devastated the open country. Whole villages, deserted, rotted on their blackened posts over the banks of clear
streams, dropping piecemeal into the water the grass of their walls,
the leaves of their roofs, with a curious effect of natural decay as
if they had been a form of vegetation stricken by a blight at its
very root. The two parties in Patusan were not sure which one
this partisan most desired to plunder. The Rajah intrigued with
him feebly. Some of the Bugis settlers, weary with endless insecurity, were half inclined to call him in. The younger spirits
amongst them, chaffing, advised to 'get Sherif Ali with his wild
men and drive the Rajah Allang out of the country.' Doramin restrained them with difficulty. He was growing old, and, though
his influence had not diminished, the situation was getting beyond
him. This was the state of affairs when Jim, bolting from the
Rajah's stockade, appeared before the chief of the Bugis, produced
the ring, and was received, in a manner of speaking, into the heart
of the community."

CHAPTER XXVI

"DORAMIN was one of the most remarkable men of his race I had ever seen. His bulk for a Malay was immense, but he did not look merely fat; he looked imposing, monumental. This motionless body, clad in rich stuffs, coloured silks, gold embroideries; this huge head, enfolded in a red-and-gold head-kerchief; the flat, big, round face, wrinkled, furrowed, with two semicircular heavy folds starting on each side of wide, fierce nostrils, and enclosing a thick-lipped mouth; the throat like a bull; the vast corrugated brow overhanging the staring proud eyes — made a whole that, once seen, can never be forgotten. His impassive repose (he seldom stirred a limb when once he sat down) was like a display of dignity. He was never known to raise his voice. It was a hoarse and powerful murmur, slightly veiled as if heard from a distance. When he walked, two short, sturdy young fellows, naked to the waist, in white sarongs and with black skull-caps on the backs of their heads, sustained his elbows; they would ease him down and stand behind his chair till he wanted to rise, when he would turn his head slowly, as if with difficulty, to the right and to the left, and then they would catch him under his armpits and help him up. For all that, there was nothing of a cripple about him: on the contrary, all his ponderous movements were like manifestations of a mighty deliberate force. It was generally believed he consulted his wife as to public affairs; but nobody, as far as I know, had ever heard them exchange a single word. When they sat in state by the wide opening it was in silence. They could see below them in the declining light the vast expanse of the forest country, a dark sleeping sea of sombre green undulating as far as the violet and purple range of mountains; the shining sinuosity of the river like an immense letter S of beaten silver; the brown ribbon of houses following the sweep of both banks, overtopped by the twin hills uprising above the nearer tree-tops. They were wonderfully contrasted: she, light, delicate, spare, quick, a little witch-like, with a touch of motherly fussiness in her repose; he, facing her, immense and heavy, like a figure of a man roughly fashioned of stone, with something magnanimous and ruthless in his immobility. The son of these old people was a most distinguished youth.

"They had him late in life. Perhaps he was not really so young as he looked. Four- or five-and-twenty is not so young when a man is already father of a family at eighteen. When he entered the large room, lined and carpeted with fine mats, and with a high ceiling of white sheeting, where the couple sat in state surrounded by a most deferential retinue, he would make his way straight to Doramin, to kiss his hand — which the other abandoned to him majestically — and then would step across to stand by his mother's chair. I suppose I may say they idolised him, but I never caught them giving him an overt glance. Those, it is true, were public functions. The room was generally thronged. The solemn formality of greetings and leave-takings, the profound respect expressed in gestures, on the faces, in the low whispers, is simply indescribable. 'It's well worth seeing,' Jim had assured me while we were crossing the river, on our way back. 'They are like people in a book, aren't they?' he said triumphantly. 'And Dain Waris — their son — is the best friend (barring you) I ever had. What Mr. Stein would call a good "war-comrade." I was in luck. Jove! I was in luck when I tumbled amongst them at my last gasp.' He meditated with bowed head, then rousing himself he added:

" 'Of course I didn't go to sleep over it, but . . .' He paused again. 'It seemed to come to me,' he murmured. 'All at once I saw what I had to do . . .'

"There was no doubt that it had come to him; and it had come through the war, too, as is natural, since this power that came to him was the power to make peace. It is in this sense alone that might so often *is* right. You must not think he had seen his way at once. When he arrived the Bugis community was in a most critical position. 'They were all afraid,' he said to me — 'each man afraid for himself; while I could see as plain as possible that they must do something at once, if they did not want to go under one after another, what between the Rajah and that vagabond Sherif.' But to see that was nothing. When he got his idea he had to drive it into reluctant minds, through the bulwarks of fear, of selfishness. He drove it in at last. And that was nothing. He had to devise the means. He devised them — an audacious plan; and his task was only half done. He had to inspire with his own confidence a lot of people who had hidden and absurd reasons to hang back; he had to conciliate imbecile jealousies, and argue away all sorts of senseless mistrusts. Without the weight of Doramin's authority, and his son's fiery enthusiasm, he would have failed. Dain Waris, the distinguished youth, was the first to believe in him; theirs was one of those strange, profound, rare friendships between brown and white, in which the very difference of race seems to draw two human beings closer by some mystic element of sympathy. Of Dain Waris, his own people said with pride that he knew how to fight like a white man. This was true; he had that sort of courage — the courage in the open, I may say — but he had also a European mind. You meet them sometimes like that, and are surprised to discover unexpectedly a familiar turn of thought, an unobscured vision, a tenacity of purpose, a touch of altruism. Of small stature, but admirably well proportioned, Dain Waris had a proud carriage, a polished, easy bearing, a temperament like a clear flame. His dusky face, with big black eyes, was in action expressive, and in repose thoughtful. He was of a silent disposition; a firm glance, an ironic smile, a courteous deliberation of manner seemed to hint at great reserves of intelligence and power. Such beings open to the Western eye, so often concerned with mere surfaces, the hidden possibilities of races and lands over which hangs the mystery of unrecorded ages. He not only trusted Jim, he understood him, I firmly believe. I speak of him because he had captivated me. His — if I may say so — his caustic placidity, and, at the same time, his intelligent sympathy with Jim's aspirations, appealed to me. I seemed to behold the very origin of friendship. If Jim took the lead, the other had captivated his leader. In fact, Jim the leader was a captive in every sense. The land, the people, the friendship, the love, were like the jealous guardians of his body. Every day added a link to the fetters of that strange freedom. I felt convinced of it, as from day to day I learned more of the story.

"The story! Haven't I heard the story? I've heard it on the march, in camp (he made me scour the country after invisible game); I've listened to a good part of it on one of the twin summits, after climbing the last hundred feet or so on my hands and knees. Our escort (we had volunteer followers from village to village) had camped meantime on a bit of level ground half-way up the slope, and in the still breathless evening the smell of wood-smoke reached our nostrils from below with the penetrating delicacy of some choice scent. Voices also ascended, wonderful in their distinct and immaterial clearness. Jim sat on the trunk of a felled tree, and pulling out his pipe began to smoke. A new growth of grass and bushes was springing up; there were traces of an earthwork under a mass of thorny twigs. 'It all started from here,' he said, after a long and meditative silence. On the other hill, two hundred yards across a sombre precipice, I saw a line of high blackened stakes, showing here and there ruinously — the remnants of Sherif Ali's impregnable camp.

"But it had been taken though. That had been his idea. He had mounted Doramin's old ordnance on the top of that hill; two rusty iron 7-pounders, a lot of small brass cannon — currency cannon. But if the brass guns represent wealth, they can also, when crammed recklessly to the muzzle, send a solid shot to some little distance. The thing was to get them up there. He showed me where he had fastened the cables, explained how he had improvised a rude capstan out of a hollowed log turning upon a pointed stake, indicated with the bowl of his pipe the outline of the earthwork. The last hundred feet of the ascent had been the most difficult. He had made himself responsible for success on his own head. He had induced the war party to work hard all night. Big fires lighted at intervals blazed all down the slope, 'but up here,' he explained, 'the hoisting gang had to fly around in the dark.' From the top he saw men moving on the hillside like ants at work. He himself on that night had kept on rushing down and climbing up like a squirrel, directing, encouraging, watching all along the line. Old Doramin had himself carried up the hill in his armchair. They put him down on the level place upon the slope, and he sat there in the light of one of the big fires — 'amazing old chap — real old chieftain,' said Jim, 'with his little fierce eyes — a pair of immense flintlock pistols on his knees. Magnificent things, ebony, silver-mounted, with beautiful locks and a calibre like an old blunderbuss. A present from Stein, it seems — in exchange for that ring, you know. Used to belong to good old M'Neil. God only knows how *he* came by them. There he sat, moving neither hand nor foot, a flame of dry brushwood behind him, and lots of people rushing about, shouting and pulling round him — the most solemn, imposing old chap you can imagine. *He* wouldn't have had much chance if Sherif Ali had let his infernal crew loose at us and stampeded my lot. Eh? Anyhow, he had come up there to die if anything went wrong. No mistake! Jove! It thrilled me to see him there — like a rock. But the Sherif must have thought us mad, and never troubled to come and see how we got on. Nobody believed it could be done. Why! I think the very chaps who pulled and shoved and sweated over it did not believe it could be done! Upon my word I don't think they did. . . .'

"He stood erect, the smouldering brier-wood in his clutch, with a smile on his lips and a sparkle in his boyish eyes. I sat on the stump of a tree at his feet, and below us stretched the land, the great expanse of the forests, sombre under the sunshine, rolling like a sea, with glints of winding rivers, the grey spots of villages, and here and there a clearing, like an islet of light amongst the dark waves of continuous tree-tops. A brooding gloom lay over this vast and monotonous landscape; the light fell on it as if into an abyss. The land devoured the sunshine; only far off, along the coast, the empty ocean, smooth and polished within the faint haze, seemed to rise up to the sky in a wall of steel.

"And there I was with him, high in the sunshine on the top of that historic hill of his. He dominated the forest, the secular gloom, the old mankind. He was like a figure set up on a pedestal, to represent in his persistent youth the power, and perhaps the virtues, of races that never grow old, that have emerged from the gloom. I don't know why he should always have appeared to me symbolic. Perhaps this is the real cause of my interest in his fate. I don't know whether it was exactly fair to him to re- member the incident which had given a new direction to his life, but at that very moment I remembered very distinctly. It was like a shadow in the light."

CHAPTER XXVII

"ALREADY the legend had gifted him with supernatural powers. Yes, it was said, there had been many ropes cunningly disposed, and a strange contrivance that turned by the efforts of many men, and each gun went up tearing slowly through the bushes, like a wild pig rooting its way in the undergrowth, but . . . and the wisest shook their heads. There was something occult in all this, no doubt; for what is the strength of ropes and of men's arms? There is a rebellious soul in things which must be overcome by powerful charms and incantations. Thus old Sura — a very respectable householder of Patusan — with whom I had a quiet chat one evening. However, Sura was a professional sorcerer also, who attended all the rice sowings and reapings for miles around for the purpose of subduing the stubborn soul of things. This occupation he seemed to think a most arduous one, and perhaps the souls of things are more stubborn than the souls of men. As to the simple folk of outlying villages, they believed and said (as the most natural thing in the world) that Jim had carried the guns up the hill on his back — two at a time.

"This would make Jim stamp his foot in vexation and exclaim with an exasperated little laugh, 'What can you do with such silly beggars? They will sit up half the night talking bally rot, and the greater the lie the more they seem to like it.' You could trace the subtle influence of his surroundings in this irritation. It was part of his captivity. The earnestness of his denials was amusing, and at last I said, 'My dear fellow, you don't suppose *I* believe this.' He looked at me quite startled. 'Well, no! I suppose not,' he said, and burst into a Homeric peal of laughter. 'Well, anyhow the guns were there, and went off together at sunrise. Jove! You should have seen the splinters fly,' he cried. By his side Dain Waris, listening with a quiet smile, dropped his eyelids and shuffled his feet a little. It appears that the success in mounting the guns had given Jim's people such a feeling of confidence that he ventured to leave the battery under charge of two elderly Bugis who had seen some fighting in their day, and went to join Dain

Waris and the storming party who were concealed in the ravine.
In the small hours they began creeping up, and when two-thirds
of the way up, lay in the wet grass waiting for the appearance of
the sun, which was the agreed signal. He told me with what impatient anguishing emotion he watched the swift coming of the
dawn; how, heated with the work and the climbing, he felt the
cold dew chilling his very bones; how afraid he was he would
begin to shiver and shake like a leaf before the time came for the
advance. 'It was the slowest half-hour in my life,' he declared.
Gradually the silent stockade came out on the sky above him.
Men scattered all down the slope were crouching amongst the
dark stones and dripping bushes. Dain Waris was lying flattened
by his side. 'We looked at each other,' Jim said, resting a gentle
hand on his friend's shoulder. 'He smiled at me as cheery as you
please, and I dared not stir my lips for fear I would break out into
a shivering fit. 'Pon my word, it's true! I had been streaming
with perspiration when we took cover — so you may imagine . . .'
He declared, and I believe him that he had no fears as to the result. He was only anxious as to his ability to repress these shiv-
ers. He didn't bother about the result. He was bound to get to
the top of that hill and stay there, whatever might happen. There
could be no going back for him. Those people had trusted him
implicitly. Him alone! His bare word. . . .

"I remember how, at this point, he paused with his eyes fixed
upon me. 'As far as he knew, they never had an occasion to regret
it yet,' he said. 'Never. He hoped to God they never would.
Meantime — worse luck! — they had got into the habit of taking
his word for anything and everything. I could have no idea!
Why? Only the other day an old fool he had never seen in his
life came from some village miles away to find out if he should
divorce his wife. Fact. Solemn word. That's the sort of thing.
. . . He wouldn't have believed it. Would I? Squatted on the
verandah chewing betel-nut, sighing and spitting all over the
place for more than an hour, and as glum as an undertaker before
he came out with that dashed conundrum. That's the kind of
thing that isn't so funny as it looks. What was a fellow to say?
— Good wife? — Yes. Good wife — old though; started a confounded long story about some brass pots. Been living together
for fifteen years — twenty years — could not tell. A long, long
time. Good wife. Beat her a little — not much — just a little,

when she was young. Had to — for the sake of his honour. Suddenly in her old age she goes and lends three brass pots to her sister's son's wife, and begins to abuse him every day in a loud voice. His enemies jeered at him; his face was utterly blackened. Pots totally lost. Awfully cut up about it. Impossible to fathom a story like that; told him to go home, and promised to come along myself and settle it all. It's all very well to grin, but it was the dashedest nuisance! A day's journey through the forest, another day lost in coaxing a lot of silly villagers to get at the rights of the affair. There was the making of a sanguinary shindy in the thing. Every bally idiot took sides with one family or the other, and one half of the village was ready to go for the other half with anything that came handy. Honour bright! No joke! . . . Instead of attending to their bally crops. Got him the infernal pots back of course — and pacified all hands. No trouble to settle it. Of course not. Could settle the deadliest quarrel in the country by crooking his little finger. The trouble was to get at the truth of anything. Was not sure to this day whether he had been fair to all parties. It worried him. And the talk! Jove! There didn't seem to be any head or tail to it. Rather storm a twenty-foot-high old stockade any day. Much! Child's play to that other job. Wouldn't take so long either. Well, yes; a funny set out, upon the whole — the fool looked old enough to be his grandfather. But from another point of view it was no joke. His word decided everything — ever since the smashing of Sherif Ali. An awful responsibility,' he repeated. 'No, really — joking apart, had it been three lives instead of three rotten brass pots it would have been the same. . . .'

"Thus he illustrated the moral effect of his victory in war. It was in truth immense. It had led him from strife to peace, and through death into the innermost life of the people; but the gloom of the land spread out under the sunshine preserved its appearance of inscrutable, of secular repose. The sound of his fresh young voice — it's extraordinary how very few signs of wear he showed — floated lightly, and passed away over the unchanged face of the forests like the sound of the big guns on that cold dewy morning when he had no other concern on earth but the proper control of the chills in his body. With the first slant of sun-rays along these immovable tree-tops the summit of one hill wreathed itself, with heavy reports, in white clouds of smoke, and

the other burst into an amazing noise of yells, war-cries, shouts
of anger, of surprise, of dismay. Jim and Dain Waris were the
first to lay their hands on the stakes. The popular story has it that
Jim with a touch of one finger had thrown down the gate. He
was, of course, anxious to disclaim this achievement. The whole
stockade — he would insist on explaining to you — was a poor affair (Sherif Ali trusted mainly to the inaccessible position); and,
anyway, the thing had been already knocked to pieces and only
hung together by a miracle. He put his shoulder to it like a little
fool and went in head over heels. Jove! If it hadn't been for
Dain Waris, a pock-marked tattooed vagabond would have pinned
him with his spear to a baulk of timber like one of Stein's beetles.
The third man in, it seems, had been Tamb' Itam, Jim's own servant. This was a Malay from the north, a stranger who had wandered into Patusan, and had been forcibly detained by Rajah
Allang as paddler of one of the state boats. He had made a bolt
of it at the first opportunity, and finding a precarious refuge (but
very little to eat) amongst the Bugis settlers, had attached himself to Jim's person. His complexion was very dark, his face flat,
his eyes prominent and injected with bile. There was something
excessive, almost fanatical, in his devotion to his 'white lord.'
He was inseparable from Jim like a morose shadow. On state
occasions he would tread on his master's heels, one hand on the
haft of his kris, keeping the common people at a distance by his
truculent brooding glances. Jim had made him the headman of
his establishment, and all Patusan respected and courted him as a
person of much influence. At the taking of the stockade he had
distinguished himself greatly by the methodical ferocity of his
fighting. The storming-party had come on so quick — Jim said —
that notwithstanding the panic of the garrison, there was a 'hot
five minutes hand-to-hand inside that stockade, till some bally ass
set fire to the shelters of boughs and dry grass, and we all had
to clear out for dear life.'

"The rout, it seems, had been complete. Doramin waiting immovably in his chair on the hillside, with the smoke of the guns
spreading slowly above his big head, received the news with a
deep grunt. When informed that his son was safe and leading the
pursuit, he, without another sound, made a mighty effort to rise;
his attendants hurried to his help, and, held up reverently, he

shuffled with great dignity into a bit of shade where he laid himself down to sleep covered entirely with a piece of white sheeting. In Patusan the excitement was intense. Jim told me that from the hill, turning his back on the stockade with its embers, black ashes, and half-consumed corpses, he could see time after time the open spaces between the houses on both sides of the stream fill suddenly with a seething rush of people and get empty in a moment. His ears caught feebly from below the tremendous din of gongs and drums; the wild shouts of the crowd reached him in bursts of faint roaring. A lot of streamers made a flutter as of little white, red, yellow birds amongst the brown ridges of roofs. 'You must have enjoyed it,' I murmured, feeling the stir of sympathetic emotion.

" 'It was . . . it was immense! Immense!' he cried aloud, flinging his arms open. The sudden movement startled me as though I had seen him bare the secrets of his breast to the sunshine, to the brooding forests, to the steely sea. Below us the town reposed in easy curves upon the banks of a stream whose current seemed to sleep. 'Immense!' he repeated for a third time, speaking in a whisper, for himself alone.

"Immense! No doubt it was immense; the seal of success upon his words, the conquered ground for the soles of his feet, the blind trust of men, the belief in himself snatched from the fire, the solitude of his achievement. All this, as I've warned you, gets dwarfed in the telling. I can't with mere words convey to you the impression of his total and utter isolation. I know, of course, he was in every sense alone of his kind there, but the unsuspected qualities of his nature had brought him in such close touch with his surroundings that this isolation seemed only the effect of his power. His loneliness added to his stature. There was nothing within sight to compare him with, as though he had been one of those exceptional men who can be only measured by the greatness of their fame; and his fame, remember, was the greatest thing around for many a day's journey. You would have to paddle, pole, or track a long weary way through the jungle before you passed beyond the reach of its voice. Its voice was not the trumpeting of the disreputable goddess we all know — not blatant — not brazen. It took its tone from the stillness and gloom of the land without a past, where his word was the one truth of every

passing day. It shared something of the nature of that silence
through which it accompanied you into unexplored depths, heard
continuously by your side, penetrating, far-reaching — tinged with
wonder and mystery on the lips of whispering men."

CHAPTER XXVIII

"THE defeated Sherif Ali fled the country without making another stand, and when the miserable hunted villagers began to
crawl out of the jungle back to their rotting houses, it was Jim
who, in consultation with Dain Waris, appointed the headmen.
Thus he became the virtual ruler of the land. As to old Tunku
Allang, his fears at first had known no bounds. It is said that at
the intelligence of the successful storming of the hill he flung
himself, face down, on the bamboo floor of his audience-hall, and
lay motionless for a whole night and a whole day, uttering stifled
sounds of such an appalling nature that no man dared approach
his prostrate form nearer than a spear's length. Already he could
see himself driven ignominiously out of Patusan, wandering abandoned, stripped, without opium, without his women, without followers, a fair game for the first comer to kill. After Sherif Ali
his turn would come, and who could resist an attack led by such
a devil? And indeed he owed his life and such authority as he still
possessed at the time of my visit to Jim's idea of what was fair
alone. The Bugis had been extremely anxious to pay off old
scores, and the impassive old Doramin cherished the hope of yet
seeing his son ruler of Patusan. During one of our interviews he
deliberately allowed me to get a glimpse of this secret ambition.
Nothing could be finer in its way than the dignified wariness of
his approaches. He himself — he began by declaring — had used
his strength in his young days, but now he had grown old and
tired. . . . With his imposing bulk and haughty little eyes darting sagacious, inquisitive glances, he reminded one irresistibly of
a cunning old elephant; the slow rise and fall of his vast breast
went on powerful and regular, like the heave of a calm sea. He,
too, as he protested, had an unbounded confidence in Tuan Jim's

wisdom. If he could only obtain a promise! One word would be enough! . . . His breathing silences, the low rumblings of his voice, recalled the last efforts of a spent thunderstorm.

"I tried to put the subject aside. It was difficult, for there could be no question that Jim had the power; in his new sphere there did not seem to be anything that was not his to hold or to give. But that, I repeat, was nothing in comparison with the notion, which occurred to me, while I listened with a show of attention, that he seemed to have come very near at last to mastering his fate. Doramin was anxious about the future of the country, and I was struck by the turn he gave to the argument. The land remains where God had put it; but white men — he said — they come to us and in a little while they go. They go away. Those they leave behind do not know when to look for their return. They go to their own land, to their people, and so this white man, too, would. . . . I don't know what induced me to commit myself at this point by a vigorous 'No, no.' The whole extent of this indiscretion became apparent when Doramin, turning full upon me his face, whose expression, fixed in rugged deep folds, remained unalterable, like a huge brown mask, said that this was good news indeed, reflectively; and then wanted to know why.

"His little, motherly witch of a wife sat on my other hand, with her head covered and her feet tucked up, gazing through the great shutter-hole. I could only see a straying lock of grey hair, a high cheek-bone, the slight masticating motion of the sharp chin. Without removing her eyes from the vast prospect of forests stretching as far as the hills, she asked me in a pitying voice why was it that he so young had wandered from his home, coming so far, through so many dangers? Had he no household there, no kinsmen in his own country? Had he no old mother, who would always remember his face?

"I was completely unprepared for this. I could only mutter and shake my head vaguely. Afterwards I am perfectly aware I cut a very poor figure trying to extricate myself out of this difficulty. From that moment, however, the old *nakhoda* became taciturn. He was not very pleased, I fear, and evidently I had given him food for thought. Strangely enough, on the evening of that very day (which was my last in Patusan) I was once more confronted with the same question, with the unanswerable why of Jim's fate. And this brings me to the story of his love.

"I suppose you think it is a story that you can imagine for

yourselves. We have heard so many such stories, and the majority of us don't believe them to be stories of love at all. For the most part we look upon them as stories of opportunities: episodes of passion at best, or perhaps only of youth and temptation, doomed to forgetfulness in the end, even if they pass through the reality of tenderness and regret. This view mostly is right, and perhaps in this case, too. . . . Yet I don't know. To tell this story is by no means so easy as it should be — were the ordinary standpoint adequate. Apparently it is a story very much like the others: for me, however, there is visible in its background the melancholy figure of a woman, the shadow of a cruel wisdom buried in a lonely grave, looking on wistfully, helplessly, with sealed lips. The grave itself, as I came upon it during an early morning stroll, was a rather shapeless brown mound, with an inlaid neat border of white lumps of coral at the base, and enclosed within a circular fence made of split saplings, with the bark left on. A garland of leaves and flowers was woven about the heads of the slender posts — and the flowers were fresh.

"Thus, whether the shadow is of my imagination or not, I can at all events point out the significant fact of an unforgotten grave. When I tell you besides that Jim with his own hands had worked at the rustic fence, you will perceive directly the difference, the individual side of the story. There is in his espousal of memory and affection belonging to another human being something characteristic of his seriousness. He had a conscience, and it was a romantic conscience. Through her whole life the wife of the unspeakable Cornelius had no other companion, confidant, and friend but her daughter. How the poor woman had come to marry the awful Malacca Portuguese — after the separation from the father of her girl — and how that separation had been brought about, whether by death, which can be sometimes merciful, or by the merciless pressure of conventions, is a mystery to me. From the little which Stein (who knew so many stories) had let drop in my hearing, I am convinced that she was no ordinary woman. Her own father had been a white; a high official; one of the brilliantly endowed men who are not dull enough to nurse a success, and whose careers so often end under a cloud. I suppose she, too, must have lacked the saving dullness — and her career ended in Patusan. Our common fate . . . for where is the man — I mean a real sentient man — who does not remember

vaguely having been deserted in the fullness of possession by
some one or something more precious than life? . . . our common fate fastens upon the women with a peculiar cruelty. It does
not punish like a master, but inflicts lingering torment, as if to
gratify a secret, unappeasable spite. One would think that, appointed to rule on earth, it seeks to revenge itself upon the beings
that come nearest to rising above the trammels of earthly caution; for it is only women who manage to put at times into their
love an element just palpable enough to give one a fright — an
extra-terrestrial touch. I ask myself with wonder — how the world
can look to them — whether it has the shape and substance *we*
know, the air *we* breathe! Sometimes I fancy it must be a region
of unreasonable sublimities seething with the excitement of their
adventurous souls, lighted by the glory of all possible risks and
renunciations. However, I suspect there are very few women in
the world, though of course I am aware of the multitudes of
mankind and of the equality of sexes in point of numbers — that
is. But I am sure that the mother was as much of a woman as
the daughter seemed to be. I cannot help picturing to myself
these two, at first the young woman and the child, then the old
woman and the young girl, the awful sameness and the swift
passage of time, the barrier of forest, the solitude and the turmoil
round these two lonely lives, and every word spoken between
them penetrated with sad meaning. There must have been confidences, not so much of fact, I suppose, as of innermost feelings —
regrets — fears — warnings, no doubt: warnings that the younger
did not fully understand till the elder was dead — and Jim came
along. Then I am sure she understood much — not everything —
the fear mostly it seems. Jim called her by a word that means
precious, in the sense of a precious gem — jewel. Pretty, isn't it?
But he was capable of anything. He was equal to his fortune,
as he — after all — must have been equal to his misfortune. Jewel
he called her; and he would say this as he might have said 'Jane,'
don't you know — with a marital, homelike, peaceful effect. I
heard the name for the first time ten minutes after I had landed
in his courtyard, when, after nearly shaking my arm off, he
darted up the steps and began to make a joyous, boyish disturbance at the door under the heavy eaves. 'Jewel! O Jewel! Quick!
Here's a friend come,' . . . and suddenly peering at me in the
dim verandah, he mumbled earnestly, 'You know — this — no con-

founded nonsense about it — can't tell you how much I **owe to** her — and so — you understand — I — exactly as if . . .' His hurried, anxious whispers were cut short by the flitting **of a white** form within the house, a faint exclamation, and a childlike but energetic little face with delicate features and a profound, attentive glance peeped out of the inner gloom, like a bird **out of** the recess of a nest. I was struck by the name, of course; **but it** was not till later on that I connected it with an astonishing rumour that had met me on my journey, at a little place on **the coast** about 230 miles south of Patusan river. Stein's schooner, **in which** I had my passage, put in there, to collect some produce, **and** going ashore, I found to my great surprise that the wretched locality could boast of a third-class deputy-assistant resident, **a big,** fat, greasy, blinking fellow of mixed descent, with turned-out, shiny lips. I found him lying extended on his back in **a cane** chair, odiously unbuttoned, with a large green leaf of some sort on the top of his steaming head, and another in his hand which he used lazily as a fan. . . . Going to Patusan? Oh, yes. Stein's Trading Company. He knew. Had a permission. No business of his. It was not so bad there now, he remarked negligently, and, he went on drawling, 'There's some sort of white vagabond had got in there, I hear. . . . Eh? What you say? Friends of yours? So! . . . Then it was true there was one of these *verdammte* — What was he up to? Found his way in, the rascal. Eh? I had not been sure. Patusan — they cut throats there — no business of ours.' He interrupted himself to groan. 'Phoo! Almighty! The heat! The heat! Well, then, there might be something in the story, too, after all, and . . .' He shut one of his beastly glassy eyes (the eyelid went on quivering), while he leered at me atrociously with the other. 'Look here,' says he, mysteriously, 'if — do you understand? — if he has really got hold of something fairly good — none of your bits of green glass — understand? — I am a government official — you tell the rascal . . . Eh? What? Friend of yours?' . . . He continued wallowing calmly in the chair. . . . 'You said so; that's just it; and I am pleased to give you the hint. I suppose you, too, would like to get something out of it? Don't interrupt. You just tell him I've heard the tale, but to my government I have made no report. Not yet. See? Why make a report? Eh? Tell him to come to me if they let him get alive out of the country. He had better look

out for himself. Eh? I promise to ask no questions. On the quiet
— you understand? You, too — you shall get something from me.
Small commission for the trouble. Don't interrupt. I am a government official, and make no report. That's business. Understand? I know some good people that will buy anything worth
having, and can give him more money than the scoundrel ever
saw in his life. I know his sort.' He fixed me steadfastly with
both his eyes open, while I stood over him utterly amazed, and
asking myself whether he was mad or drunk. He perspired,
puffed, moaning feebly, and scratching himself with such horrible composure that I could not bear the sight long enough to
find out. Next day, talking casually with the people of the little
native court of the place, I discovered that a story was travel-
ling slowly down the coast about a mysterious white man in
Patusan who had got hold of an extraordinary gem — namely, an
emerald of an enormous size, and altogether priceless. The emerald seems to appeal more to the Eastern imagination than any
other precious stone. The white man had obtained it, I was told,
partly by the exercise of his wonderful strength and partly by
cunning, from the ruler of a distant country, whence he had fled
instantly arriving in Patusan in utmost distress, but frightening
the people by his extreme ferocity, which nothing seemed able
to subdue. Most of my informants were of the opinion that the
stone was probably unlucky, — like the famous stone of the Sultan of Succadana, which in the old times had brought wars and
untold calamities upon that country. Perhaps it was the same
stone — one couldn't say. Indeed the story of a fabulously large
emerald is as old as the arrival of the first white men in the Archipelago; and the belief in it is so persistent that less than forty
years ago there had been an official Dutch inquiry into the truth
of it. Such a jewel — it was explained to me by the old fellow
from whom I heard most of this amazing Jim-myth — a sort of
scribe to the wretched little Rajah of the place; — such a jewel,
he said, cocking his poor purblind eyes up at me (he was sitting
on the cabin floor out of respect), is best preserved by being concealed about the person of a woman. Yet it is not every woman
that would do. She must be young — he sighed deeply — and
insensible to the seductions of love. He shook his head sceptically. But such a woman seemed to be actually in existence. He
had been told of a tall girl, whom the white man treated with

great respect and care, and who never went forth from the house unattended. People said the white man could be seen with her almost any day; they walked side by side, openly, he holding her arm under his — pressed to his side — thus — in a most extraordinary way. This might be a lie, he conceded, for it was indeed a strange thing for any one to do: on the other hand, there could be no doubt she wore the white man's jewel concealed upon her bosom."

CHAPTER XXIX

"This was the theory of Jim's marital evening walks. I made a third on more than one occasion, unpleasantly aware every time of Cornelius, who nursed the aggrieved sense of his legal paternity, slinking in the neighbourhood with that peculiar twist of his mouth as if he were perpetually on the point of gnashing his teeth. But do you notice how, three hundred miles beyond the end of telegraph cables and mail-boat lines, the haggard utilitarian lies of our civilisation wither and die, to be replaced by pure exercises of imagination, that have the futility, often the charm, and sometimes the deep hidden truthfulness, of works of art? Romance had singled Jim for its own — and that was the true part of the story, which otherwise was all wrong. He did not hide his jewel. In fact, he was extremely proud of it.

"It comes to me now that I had, on the whole, seen very little of her. What I remember best is the even, olive pallor of her complexion, and the intense blue-black gleams of her hair, flowing abundantly from under a small crimson cap she wore far back on her shapely head. Her movements were free, assured, and she blushed a dusky red. While Jim and I were talking, she would come and go with rapid glances at us, leaving on her passage an impression of grace and charm and a distinct suggestion of watchfulness. Her manner presented a curious combination of shyness and audacity. Every pretty smile was succeeded swiftly by a look of silent, repressed anxiety, as if put to flight by the recol-

lection of some abiding danger. At times she would sit down
with us and, with her soft cheek dimpled by the knuckles of her
little hand, she would listen to our talk; her big clear eyes would
remain fastened on our lips, as though each pronounced word
had a visible shape. Her mother had taught her to read and
write; she had learned a good bit of English from Jim, and she
spoke it most amusingly, with his own clipping, boyish intonation. Her tenderness hovered over him like a flutter of wings.
She lived so completely in his contemplation that she had acquired something of his outward aspect, something that recalled
him in her movements, in the way she stretched her arm, turned
her head, directed her glances. Her vigilant affection had an intensity that made it almost perceptible to the senses; it seemed
actually to exist in the ambient matter of space, to envelop him
like a peculiar fragrance, to dwell in the sunshine like a tremu-
lous, subdued, and impassioned note. I suppose you think that I,
too, am romantic, but it is a mistake. I am relating to you the
sober impressions of a bit of youth, of a strange uneasy romance
that had come in my way. I observed with interest the work of
his — well — good fortune. He was jealously loved, but why she
should be jealous, and of what, I could not tell. The land, the
people, the forests were her accomplices, guarding him with vigilant accord, with an air of seclusion, of mystery, of invincible
possession. There was no appeal, as it were; he was imprisoned
within the very freedom of his power, and she, though ready to
make a footstool of her head for his feet, guarded her conquest inflexibly — as though he were hard to keep. The very Tamb' Itam,
marching on our journeys upon the heels of his white lord, with
his head thrown back, truculent and be-weaponed like a janis-
sary, with kris, chopper, and lance (besides carrying Jim's gun);
even Tamb' Itam allowed himself to put on the airs of uncompromising guardianship, like a surly devoted jailer ready to lay
down his life for his captive. On the evenings when we sat up
late his silent, indistinct form would pass and repass under the
verandah, with noiseless footsteps, or lifting my head I would
unexpectedly make him out standing rigidly erect in the shadow.
As a general rule he would vanish after a time, without a sound;
but when we rose he would spring up close to us as if from the
ground, ready for any orders Jim might wish to give. The girl,
too, I believe, never went to sleep till we had separated for the

night. More than once I saw her and Jim through the window
of my room come out together quietly and lean on the rough
balustrade — two white forms very close, his arm about her waist,
her head on his shoulder. Their soft murmurs reached me, penetrating, tender, with a calm sad note in the stillness of the night,
like a self-communion of one being carried on in two tones.
Later on, tossing on my bed under the mosquito-net, I was sure
to hear slight creakings, faint breathing, a throat cleared cautiously — and I would know that Tamb' Itam was still on the
prowl. Though he had (by the favour of the white lord) a
house in the compound, had 'taken wife,' and had lately been
blessed with a child, I believe that, during my stay at all events,
he slept on the verandah every night. It was very difficult to
make this faithful and grim retainer talk. Even Jim himself was
answered in jerky short sentences, under protest as it were. Talking, he seemed to imply, was no business of his. The longest
speech I heard him volunteer was one morning when, suddenly
extending his hand towards the courtyard, he pointed at Cornelius and said, 'Here comes the Nazarene.' I don't think he was
addressing me, though I stood at his side; his object seemed rather
to awaken the indignant attention of the universe. Some muttered allusions, which followed, to dogs and the smell of roast-
meat, struck me as singularly felicitous. The courtyard, a large
square space, was one torrid blaze of sunshine, and, bathed in
intense light, Cornelius was creeping across in full view with an
inexpressible effect of stealthiness, of dark and secret slinking.
He reminded one of everything that is unsavoury. His slow la-
borious walk resembled the creeping of a repulsive beetle, the
legs alone moving with horrid industry while the body glided
evenly. I suppose he made straight enough for the place where
he wanted to get to, but his progress with one shoulder carried
forward seemed oblique. He was often seen circling slowly
amongst the sheds, as if following a scent; passing before the verandah with upward stealthy glances; disappearing without haste
round the corner of some hut. That he seemed free of the place
demonstrated Jim's absurd carelessness or else his infinite disdain,
for Cornelius had played a very dubious part (to say the least of
it) in a certain episode which might have ended fatally for Jim.
As a matter of fact, it had redounded to his glory. But everything redounded to his glory; and it was the irony of his good

fortune that he, who had been too careful of it once, seemed to bear a charmed life.

"You must know he had left Doramin's place very soon after his arrival — much too soon, in fact, for his safety, and of course a long time before the war. In this he was actuated by a sense of duty; he had to look after Stein's business, he said. Hadn't he? To that end, with an utter disregard of his personal safety, he crossed the river and took up his quarters with Cornelius. How the latter had managed to exist through the troubled times I can't say. As Stein's agent, after all, he must have had Doramin's protection in a measure; and in one way or another he had managed to wriggle through all the deadly complications, while I have no doubt that his conduct, whatever line he was forced to take, was marked by that abjectness which was like the stamp of the man. That was his characteristic; he was fundamentally and outwardly abject, as other men are markedly of a generous, distinguished, or venerable appearance. It was the element of his nature which permeated all his acts and passions and emotions; he raged abjectly, smiled abjectly, was abjectly sad; his civilities and his indignations were alike abject. I am sure his love would have been the most abject of sentiments — but can one imagine a loathsome insect in love? And his loathsomeness, too, was abject, so that a simply disgusting person would have appeared noble by his side. He has his place neither in the background nor in the foreground of the story; he is simply seen skulking on its outskirts, enigmatical and unclean, tainting the fragrance of its youth and of its naïveness.

"His position in any case could not have been other than extremely miserable, yet it may very well be that he found some advantages in it. Jim told me he had been received at first with an abject display of the most amicable sentiments. 'The fellow apparently couldn't contain himself for joy,' said Jim with disgust. 'He flew at me every morning to shake both my hands — confound him! but I could never tell whether there would be any breakfast. If I got three meals in two days I considered myself jolly lucky, and he made me sign a chit for ten dollars every week. Said he was sure Mr. Stein did not mean him to keep me for nothing. Well — he kept me on nothing as near as possible. Put it down to the unsettled state of the country, and made as if to tear his hair out, begging my pardon twenty times a day, so that I had at last to entreat him not to worry. It made me sick. Half the roof of his house had fallen in, and the whole place had a mangy look, with wisps of dry grass sticking out and the corners of broken mats flapping on every wall. He did his best to make out that Mr. Stein owed him money on the last three years' trading, but his books were all torn, and some were missing. He tried to hint it was his late wife's fault. Disgusting scoundrel! At last I had to forbid him to mention his late wife at all. It made Jewel cry. I couldn't discover what became of all the trade-goods; there was nothing in the store but rats, having a high old time amongst a little of brown paper and old sacking. I was assured on every hand that he had a lot of money buried somewhere, but of course could get nothing out of him. It was the most miserable existence I led there in that wretched house. I tried to do my duty by Stein, but I had also other matters to think of. When I escaped to Doramin old Tunku Allang got frightened and returned all my things. It was done in a roundabout way, and with no end of mystery, through a Chinaman who keeps a small shop here; but as soon as I left the Bugis quarter and went to live with Cornelius it began to be said openly that the Rajah had made up his mind to have me killed before long. Pleasant, wasn't it? And I couldn't see what there was to prevent him if he really *had* made up his mind. The worst of it was, I couldn't help feeling I wasn't doing any good either for Stein or for myself. Oh! it was beastly — the whole six weeks of it.' "

CHAPTER XXX

"He told me further that he didn't know what made him hang on — but of course we may guess. He sympathised deeply with the defenceless girl, at the mercy of that 'mean, cowardly scoundrel.' It appears Cornelius led her an awful life, stopping only short of actual ill-usage, for which he had not the pluck, I suppose. He insisted upon her calling him father — 'and with respect, too — with respect,' he would scream, shaking a little yellow fist

in her face. 'I am a respectable man, and what are you? Tell me
— what are you? You think I am going to bring up somebody
else's child and not be treated with respect? You ought to be glad
I let you. Come — say Yes, father. . . . No? . . . You wait a
bit.' Thereupon he would begin to abuse the dead woman, till
the girl would run off with her hands to her head. He pursued
her, dashing in and out and round the house and amongst the
sheds, would drive her into some corner, where she would fall
on her knees stopping her ears, and then he would stand at a distance and declaim filthy denunciations at her back for half an
hour at a stretch. 'Your mother was a devil, a deceitful devil —
and you, too, are a devil,' he would shriek in a final outburst, pick
up a bit of dry earth or a handful of mud (there was plenty of
mud around the house), and fling it into her hair. Sometimes,
though, she would hold out full of scorn, confronting him in
silence, her face sombre and contracted, and only now and then
uttering a word or two that would make the other jump and
writhe with the sting. Jim told me these scenes were terrible.
It was indeed a strange thing to come upon in a wilderness. The
endlessness of such a subtly cruel situation was appalling — if you
think of it. The respectable Cornelius (Inchi 'Nelyus the Malays
called him, with a grimace that meant many things) was a much-
disappointed man. I don't know what he had expected would be
done for him in consideration of his marriage; but evidently the
liberty to steal, and embezzle, and appropriate to himself for
many years and in any way that suited him best, the goods of
Stein's Trading Company (Stein kept the supply up unfalteringly
as long as he could get his skippers to take it there) did not seem
to him a fair equivalent for the sacrifice of his honourable name.
Jim would have enjoyed exceedingly thrashing Cornelius within
an inch of his life; on the other hand, the scenes were of so pain-
full a character, so abominable, that his impulse would be to get
out of earshot, in order to spare the girl's feelings. They left her
agitated, speechless, clutching her bosom now and then with a
stony, desperate face, and then Jim would lounge up and say
unhappily, 'Now — come — really — what's the use — you must
try to eat a bit,' or give some such mark of sympathy. Cornelius
would keep on slinking through the doorways, across the verandah and back again, as mute as a fish, and with malevolent, mistrustful, underhand glances. 'I can stop his game,' Jim said to her

once. 'Just say the word.' And do you know what she answered?
She said — Jim told me impressively — that if she had not been
sure he was intensely wretched himself, she would have found
the courage to kill him with her own hands. 'Just fancy that!
The poor devil of a girl, almost a child, being driven to talk like
that,' he exclaimed in horror. It seemed impossible to save her
not only from that mean rascal but even from herself! It wasn't
that he pitied her so much, he affirmed; it was more than pity;
it was as if he had something on his conscience, while that life
went on. To leave the house would have appeared a base desertion. He had understood at last that there was nothing to expect from a longer stay, neither accounts nor money, nor truth
of any sort, but he stayed on, exasperating Cornelius to the verge,
I won't say of insanity, but almost of courage. Meantime he felt
all sorts of dangers gathering obscurely about him. Doramin had
sent over twice a trusty servant to tell him seriously that he could
do nothing for his safety unless he would recross the river again
and live amongst the Bugis as at first. People of every condition
used to call, often in the dead of night, in order to disclose to
him plots for his assassination. He was to be poisoned. He was
to be stabbed in the bath-house. Arrangements were being made
to have him shot from a boat on the river. Each of these informants professed himself to be his very good friend. It was
enough — he told me — to spoil a fellow's rest for ever. Something of the kind was extremely possible — nay, probable — but
the lying warnings gave him only the sense of deadly scheming
going on all around him, on all sides, in the dark. Nothing more
calculated to shake the best of nerve. Finally, one night, Cornelius himself, with a great apparatus of alarm and secrecy, unfolded in solemn wheedling tones a little plan wherein for one
hundred dollars — or even for eighty; let's say eighty — he, Cornelius, would procure a trustworthy man to smuggle Jim out of
the river, all safe. There was nothing else for it now — if Jim
cared a pin for his life. What's eighty dollars? A trifle. An insignificant sum. While he, Cornelius, who had to remain behind,
was absolutely courting death by his proof of devotion to Mr.
Stein's young friend. The sight of his abject grimacing was —
Jim told me — very hard to bear: he clutched at his hair, beat his
breast, rocked himself to and fro with his hands pressed to his
stomach, and actually pretended to shed tears. 'Your blood be

on your own head,' he squeaked at last, and rushed out. It is a curious question how far Cornelius was sincere in that performance. Jim confessed to me that he did not sleep a wink after the fellow had gone. He lay on his back on a thin mat spread over the bamboo flooring, trying idly to make out the bare rafters, and listening to the rustlings in the torn thatch. A star suddenly twinkled through a hole in the roof. His brain was in a whirl; but, nevertheless, it was on that very night that he matured his plan for overcoming Sherif Ali. It had been the thought of all the moments he could spare from the hopeless investigation into Stein's affairs, but the notion — he says — came to him then all at once. He could see, as it were, the guns mounted on the top of the hill. He got very hot and excited lying there; sleep was out of the question more than ever. He jumped up, and went out barefooted on the verandah. Walking silently, he came upon the girl, motionless against the wall, as if on the watch. In his then state of mind it did not surprise him to see her up, nor yet to hear her ask in an anxious whisper where Cornelius could be. He simply said he did not know. She moaned a little, and peered into the *campong*. Everything was very quiet. He was possessed by his new idea, and so full of it that he could not help telling the girl all about it at once. She listened, clapped her hands lightly, whispered softly her admiration, but was evidently on the alert all the time. It seems he had been used to make a confidant of her all along — and that she on her part could and did give him a lot of useful hints as to Patusan affairs there is no doubt. He assured me more than once that he had never found himself the worse for her advice. At any rate, he was proceeding to explain his plan fully to her there and then, when she pressed his arm once, and vanished from his side. Then Cornelius appeared from somewhere, and, perceiving Jim, ducked sideways, as though he had been shot at, and afterwards stood very still in the dusk. At last he came forward prudently, like a suspicious cat. 'There were some fishermen there — with fish,' he said in a shaky voice. 'To sell fish — you understand.' . . . It must have been then two o'clock in the morning — a likely time for anybody to hawk fish about!

"Jim, however, let the statement pass, and did not give it a single thought. Other matters occupied his mind, and besides he had neither seen nor heard anything. He contented himself by

saying, 'Oh!' absently, got a drink of water out of a pitcher standing there, and leaving Cornelius a prey to some inexplicable emotion — that made him embrace with both arms the worm-eaten
rail of the verandah as if his legs had failed — went in again and
lay down on his mat to think. By-and-by he heard stealthy footsteps. They stopped. A voice whispered tremulously through the
wall, 'Are you asleep?' 'No! What is it?' he answered, briskly,
and there was an abrupt movement outside, and then all was still,
as if the whisperer had been startled. Extremely annoyed at this,
Jim came out impetuously, and Cornelius with a faint shriek fled
along the verandah as far as the steps, where he hung on to the
broken banister. Very puzzled, Jim called out to him from the
distance to know what the devil he meant. 'Have you given your
consideration to what I spoke to you about?' asked Cornelius,
pronouncing the words with difficulty, like a man in the cold
fit of a fever. 'No!' shouted Jim in a passion. 'I did not, and I
don't intend to. I am going to live here, in Patusan.' 'You shall
d-d-die h-h-here,' answered Cornelius, still shaking violently, and
in a sort of expiring voice. The whole performance was so absurd and provoking that Jim didn't know whether he ought to
be amused or angry. 'Not till I have seen you tucked away, you
bet,' he called out, exasperated yet ready to laugh. Half seriously (being excited with his own thoughts, you know) he went
on shouting, 'Nothing can touch me! You can do your damned-
est.' Somehow the shadowy Cornelius far off there seemed to
be the hateful embodiment of all the annoyances and difficulties
he had found in his path. He let himself go — his nerves had been
over-wrought for days — and called him many pretty names, —
swindler, liar, sorry rascal: in fact, carried on in an extraordinary
way. He admits he passed all bounds, that he was quite beside
himself — defied all Patusan to scare him away — declared he
would make them all dance to his own tune yet, and so on, in
a menacing, boasting strain. Perfectly bombastic and ridiculous,
he said. His ears burned at the bare recollection. Must have been
off his chump in some way. . . . The girl, who was sitting with
us, nodded her little head at me quickly, frowned faintly, and
said, 'I heard him,' with childlike solemnity. He laughed and
blushed. What stopped him at last, he said, was the silence, the
complete deathlike silence, of the indistinct figure far over there,
that seemed to hang collapsed, doubled over the rail in a weird

immobility. He came to his senses, and ceasing suddenly, wondered greatly at himself. He watched for a while. Not a stir, not a sound. 'Exactly as if the chap had died while I had been making all that noise,' he said. He was so ashamed of himself that he went indoors in a hurry without another word, and flung himself down again. The row seemed to have done him good though, because he went to sleep for the rest of the night like a baby. Hadn't slept like that for weeks. 'But *I* didn't sleep,' struck in the girl, one elbow on the table and nursing her cheek. 'I watched.' Her big eyes flashed, rolling a little, and then she fixed them on my face intently."

CHAPTER XXXI

"You may imagine with what interest I listened. All these details were perceived to have some significance twenty-four hours later. In the morning Cornelius made no allusion to the events of the night. 'I suppose you will come back to my poor house,' he muttered, surlily, slinking up just as Jim was entering the canoe to go over to Doramin's *campong*. Jim only nodded, without looking at him. 'You find it good fun, no doubt,' muttered the other in a sour tone. Jim spent the day with the old *nakhoda*, preaching the necessity of vigorous action to the principal men of the Bugis community, who had been summoned for a big talk. He remembered with pleasure how very eloquent and persuasive he had been. 'I managed to put some backbone into them that time, and no mistake,' he said. Sherif Ali's last raid had swept the outskirts of the settlement, and some women belonging to the town had been carried off to the stockade. Sherif Ali's emissaries had been seen in the market-place the day before, strutting about haughtily in white cloaks, and boasting of the Rajah's friendship for their master. One of them stood forward in the shade of a tree, and, leaning on the long barrel of a rifle, exhorted the people to prayer and repentance, advising them to kill all the strangers in their midst, some of whom, he said, were

infidels and others even worse — children of Satan in the guise
of Moslems. It was reported that several of the Rajah's people
amongst the listeners had loudly expressed their approbation.
The terror amongst the common people was intense. Jim, immensely pleased with his day's work, crossed the river again before sunset.

"As he had got the Bugis irretrievably committed to action,
and had made himself responsible for success on his own head,
he was so elated that in the lightness of his heart he absolutely
tried to be civil with Cornelius. But Cornelius became wildly
jovial in response, and it was almost more than he could stand,
he says, to hear his little squeaks of false laughter, to see him
wriggle and blink, and suddenly catch hold of his chin and
crouch low over the table with a distracted stare. The girl did
not show herself, and Jim retired early. When he rose to say
good-night, Cornelius jumped up, knocking his chair over, and
ducked out of sight as if to pick up something he had dropped.
His good-night came huskily from under the table. Jim was
amazed to see him emerge out with a dropping jaw, and staring, stupidly frightened eyes. He clutched the edge of the table.
'What's the matter? Are you unwell?' asked Jim. 'Yes, yes, yes.
A great colic in my stomach,' says the other; and it is Jim's opinion that it was perfectly true. If so, it was, in view of his contemplated action, an abject sign of a still imperfect callousness
for which he must be given all due credit.

"Be it as it may, Jim's slumbers were disturbed by a dream of
heavens like brass resounding with a great voice, which called
upon him to Awake! Awake! so loud that, notwithstanding his
desperate determination to sleep on, he did wake up in reality.
The glare of a red spluttering conflagration going on in mid-air
fell on his eyes. Coils of black thick smoke curved round the
head of some apparition, some unearthly being, all in white, with
a severe, drawn, anxious face. After a second or so he recognised the girl. She was holding a dammar torch at arm's-length
aloft, and in a persistent, urgent monotone she was repeating,
'Get up! Get up! Get up!'

"Suddenly he leaped to his feet; at once she put into his hand
a revolver, his own revolver, which had been hanging on a nail,
but loaded this time. He gripped it in silence, bewildered, blinking in the light. He wondered what he could do for her.

"She asked rapidly and very low, 'Can you face four men with this?' He laughed while narrating this part at the recollection of his polite alacrity. It seems he made a great display of it. 'Certainly — of course — certainly — command me.' He was not properly awake, and had a notion of being very civil in these extraordinary circumstances, of showing his unquestioning, devoted readiness. She left the room, and he followed her; in the passage they disturbed an old hag who did the casual cooking of the household, though she was so decrepit as to be hardly able to understand human speech. She got up and hobbled behind them, mumbling toothlessly. On the verandah a hammock of sailcloth, belonging to Cornelius, swayed lightly to the touch of Jim's elbow. It was empty.

"The Patusan establishment, like all the posts of Stein's Trading Company, had originally consisted of four buildings. Two of them were represented by two heaps of sticks, broken bamboos, rotten thatch, over which the four corner-posts of hardwood leaned sadly at different angles: the principal storeroom, however, stood yet, facing the agent's house. It was an oblong hut, built of mud and clay: it had at one end a wide door of stout planking, which so far had not come off the hinges, and in one of the side walls there was a square aperture, a sort of window, with three wooden bars. Before descending the few steps the girl turned her face over her shoulder and said quickly, 'You were to be set upon while you slept.' Jim tells me he experienced a sense of deception. It was the old story. He was weary of these attempts upon his life. He had had his fill of these alarms. He was sick of them. He assured me he was angry with the girl for deceiving him. He had followed her under the impression that it was she who wanted his help, and now he had half a mind to turn on his heel and go back in disgust. 'Do you know,' he commented, profoundly, 'I rather think I was not quite myself for whole weeks on end about that time.' 'Oh, yes. You were though,' I couldn't help contradicting.

"But she moved on swiftly, and he followed her into the courtyard. All its fences had fallen in a long time ago; the neighbours' buffaloes would pace in the morning across the open space, snorting profoundly, without haste; the very jungle was invading it already. Jim and the girl stopped in the rank grass. The light in which they stood made a dense blackness all round, and

only above their heads there was an opulent glitter of stars. He
told me it was a beautiful night — quite cool, with a little stir of
breeze from the river. It seems he noticed its friendly beauty.
Remember this is a love-story I am telling you now. A lovely
night that seemed to breathe on them a soft caress. The flame
of the torch streamed now and then with a fluttering noise like
a flag, and for a time this was the only sound. 'They are in the
storeroom waiting,' whispered the girl; 'they are waiting for the
signal.' 'Who's to give it?' he asked. She shook the torch, which
blazed up after a shower of sparks. 'Only you have been sleeping so restlessly,' she continued in a murmur. 'I watched your
sleep, too.' 'You!' he exclaimed, craning his neck to look about
him. 'You think I watched on this night only!' she said, with a
sort of despairing indignation.

"He says it was as if he had received a blow on the chest. He
gasped. He thought he had been an awful brute somehow, and
he felt remorseful, touched, happy, elated. This, let me remind
you again, is a love story; you can see it by the imbecility, not
a repulsive imbecility, the exalted imbecility of these proceedings, this station in torchlight, as if they had come there on purpose to have it out for the edification of concealed murderers.
If Sherif Ali's emissaries had been possessed — as Jim remarked —
of a pennyworth of spunk, this was the time to make a rush.
His heart was thumping — not with fear — but he seemed to hear
the grass rustle, and he stepped smartly out of the light. Something dark, imperfectly seen, flitted rapidly out of sight. He
called out in a strong voice, 'Cornelius! O Cornelius!' A profound silence succeeded: his voice did not seem to have carried
twenty feet. Again the girl was by his side. 'Fly!' she said. The
old woman was coming up; her broken figure hovered in crip-
pled little jumps on the edge of the light; they heard her mumbling, and a light, moaning sigh. 'Fly!' repeated the girl, excitedly. 'They are frightened now — this light — the voices. They
know you are awake now — they know you are big, strong, fearless . . .' 'If I am all that,' he began, but she interrupted him.
'Yes — to-night! But what of to-morrow night? Of the next
night? Of the night after — of all the many, many nights? Can
I be always watching?' A sobbing catch of her breath affected
him beyond the power of words.

"He told me that he had never felt so small, so powerless —

and as to courage, what was the good of it? he thought. He was so helpless that even flight seemed of no use; and though she kept on whispering, 'Go to Doramin, go to Doramin,' with feverish insistence, he realised that for him there was no refuge from that loneliness which centupled all his dangers except — in her. 'I thought,' he said to me, 'that if I went away from her it would be the end of everything somehow.' Only as they couldn't stop there for ever in the middle of that courtyard, he made up his mind to go and look into the storehouse. He let her follow him without thinking of any protest, as if they had been indissolubly united. 'I am fearless — am I?' he muttered through his teeth. She restrained his arm. 'Wait till you hear my voice,' she said, and, torch in hand, ran lightly round the corner. He remained alone in the darkness, his face to the door: not a sound, not a breath came from the other side. The old hag let out a dreary groan somewhere behind his back. He heard a high-pitched almost screaming call from the girl. 'Now! Push!' He pushed violently; the door swung with a creak and a clatter, disclosing to his intense astonishment the low dungeon-like interior illuminated by a lurid, wavering glare. A turmoil of smoke eddied down upon an empty wooden crate in the middle of the floor, a litter of rags and straw tried to soar, but only stirred feebly in the draught. She had thrust the light through the bars of the window. He saw her bare round arm extended and rigid, holding up the torch with the steadiness of an iron bracket. A conical ragged heap of old mats cumbered a distant corner almost to the ceiling, and that was all.

"He explained to me that he was bitterly disappointed at this. His fortitude had been tried by so many warnings, he had been for weeks surrounded by so many hints of danger, that he wanted the relief of some reality, of something tangible that he could meet. 'It would have cleared the air for a couple of hours at least, if you know what I mean,' he said to me. 'Jove! I had been living for days with a stone on my chest.' Now at last he had thought he would get hold of something, and — nothing! Not a trace, not a sign of anybody. He had raised his weapon as the door flew open, but now his arm fell. 'Fire! Defend yourself,' the girl outside cried in an agonising voice. She, being in the dark and with her arm thrust in to the shoulder through the small hole, couldn't see what was going on, and she dared not withdraw the torch now to run round. 'There's nobody here!' yelled Jim, contemptuously, but his impulse to burst into a resentful exasperated laugh died without a sound: he had perceived in the very act of turning away that he was exchanging glances with a pair of eyes in the heap of mats. He saw a shifting gleam of whites. 'Come out!' he cried in a fury, a little doubtful, and a dark-faced head, a head without a body, shaped itself in the rubbish, a strangely detached head, that looked at him with a steady scowl. Next moment the whole mound stirred, and with a low grunt a man emerged swiftly, and bounded towards Jim. Behind him the mats as it were jumped and flew, his right arm was raised with a crooked elbow, and the dull blade of a kris protruded from his fist held off, a little above his head. A cloth wound tight round his loins seemed dazzlingly white on his bronze skin; his naked body glistened as if wet.

"Jim noted all this. He told me he was experiencing a feeling of unutterable relief, of vengeful elation. He held his shot, he says, deliberately. He held it for the tenth part of a second, for three strides of the man – an unconscionable time. He held it for the pleasure of saying to himself, That's a dead man! He was absolutely positive and certain. He let him come on because it did not matter. A dead man, anyhow. He noticed the dilated nostrils, the wide eyes, the intent, eager stillness of the face, and then he fired.

"The explosion in that confined space was stunning. He stepped back a pace. He saw the man jerk his head up, fling his arms forward, and drop the kris. He ascertained afterwards that he had shot him through the mouth, a little upwards, the bullet coming out high at the back of the skull. With the impetus of his rush the man drove straight on, his face suddenly gaping disfigured, with his hands open before him gropingly, as though blinded, and landed with terrific violence on his forehead, just short of Jim's bare toes. Jim says he didn't lose the smallest detail of all this. He found himself calm, appeased, without rancour, without uneasiness, as if the death of that man had atoned for everything. The place was getting very full of sooty smoke from the torch, in which the unswaying flame burned blood-red without a flicker. He walked in resolutely, striding over the dead body, and covered with his revolver another naked figure outlined vaguely at the other end. As he was about to pull the trigger, the man threw away with force a short heavy spear, and squatted submissively on his hams, his back to the wall and his clasped hands between his legs. 'You want your life?' Jim said. The other made no sound. 'How many more of you?' asked Jim again. 'Two more, Tuan,' said the man very softly, looking with big fascinated eyes into the muzzle of the revolver. Accordingly two more crawled from under the mats, holding out ostentatiously their empty hands."

CHAPTER XXXII

"Jim took up an advantageous position and shepherded them out in a bunch through the doorway: all that time the torch had remained vertical in the grip of a little hand, without so much as a tremble. The three men obeyed him, perfectly mute, moving automatically. He ranged them in a row. 'Link arms!' he ordered. They did so. 'The first who withdraws his arm or turns his head is a dead man,' he said. 'March!' They stepped out together, rigidly; he followed, and at the side the girl, in a trailing white gown, her black hair falling as low as her waist, bore the light. Erect and swaying, she seemed to glide without touching the earth; the only sound was the silky swish and rustle of the long grass. 'Stop!' cried Jim.

"The river-bank was steep; a great freshness ascended, the light fell on the edge of smooth dark water frothing without a ripple; right and left the shapes of the houses ran together below the sharp outlines of the roofs. 'Take my greetings to Sherif Ali — till I come myself,' said Jim. Not one head of the three budged. 'Jump!' he thundered. The three splashes made one splash, a shower flew up, black heads bobbed convulsively, and disappeared; but a great blowing and spluttering went on, growing faint, for they were diving industriously, in great fear of a parting shot. Jim turned to the girl, who had been a silent and attentive observer. His heart seemed suddenly to grow too big for his breast and choke him in the hollow of his throat. This probably made him speechless for so long, and after returning his gaze she flung the burning torch with a wide sweep of the arm into the river. The ruddy fiery glare, taking a long flight through the night, sank with a vicious hiss, and the calm soft starlight descended upon them, unchecked.

"He did not tell me what it was he said when at last he recovered his voice. I don't suppose he could be very eloquent. The world was still, the night breathed on them, one of those nights that seem created for the sheltering of tenderness, and there are moments when our souls, as if freed from their dark envelope, glow with an exquisite sensibility that makes certain silences more lucid than speeches. As to the girl, he told me, 'She broke down a bit. Excitement — don't you know. Reaction. Deucedly tired she must have been — and all that kind of thing. And — and — hang it all — she was fond of me, don't you see. . . . I, too . . . didn't know, of course . . . never entered my head. . . .'

"There he got up and began to walk about in some agitation. 'I — I love her dearly. More than I could tell. Of course one cannot tell. You take a different view of your actions when you come to understand, when you are *made* to understand every day that your existence is necessary — you see, absolutely necessary — to another person. I am made to feel that. Wonderful. But only try to think what her life has been. It is too extravagantly awful! Isn't it? And me finding her here like this — as you may go out for a stroll and come suddenly upon somebody drowning in a lonely dark place. Jove! No time to lose. Well, it is a trust, too . . . I believe I am equal to it. . . .'

"I must tell you the girl had left us to ourselves some time before. He slapped his chest. 'Yes! I feel that, but I believe I am equal to all my luck!' He had the gift of finding a special meaning in everything that happened to him. This was the view he took of his love-affair; it was idyllic, a little solemn, and also true, since his belief had all the unshakable seriousness of youth. Some time after, on another occasion, he said to me, 'I've been only two years here, and now, upon my word, I can't conceive being able to live anywhere else. The very thought of the world outside is enough to give me a fright; because, don't you see,' he continued, with downcast eyes watching the action of his boot busied in squashing thoroughly a tiny bit of dried mud (we were strolling on the river-bank) — 'because I have not forgotten why I came here. Not yet!'

"I refrained from looking at him, but I think I heard a short sigh; we took a turn or two in silence. 'Upon my soul and conscience,' he began again, 'if such a thing can be forgotten, then I think I have a right to dismiss it from my mind. Ask any man here' . . . his voice changed. 'Is it not strange,' he went on in a gentle, almost yearning tone, 'that all these people, all these people who would do anything for me, can never be made to understand? Never! If you disbelieve me I could not call them up. It seems hard, somehow. I am stupid, am I not? What more can I want? If you ask them who is brave — who is true — who is just — who is it they would trust with their lives? — they would say, Tuan Jim. And yet they can never know the real, real truth. . . .'

"That's what he said to me on my last day with him. I did not let a murmur escape me: I felt he was going to say more, and come no nearer to the root of the matter. The sun, whose concentrated glare dwarfs the earth into a restless mote of dust, had sunk behind the forest, and the diffused light from an opal sky seemed to cast upon a world without shadows and without brilliance the illusion of a calm and pensive greatness. I don't know why, listening to him, I should have noted so distinctly the gradual darkening of the river, of the air; the irresistible slow work of the night settling silently on all the visible forms, effacing the outlines, burying the shapes deeper and deeper, like a steady fall of impalpable black dust.

" 'Jove!' he began, abruptly, 'there are days when a fellow is too absurd for anything; only I know I can tell you what I like. I talk about being done with it — with the bally thing at the back of my head. . . . Forgetting. . . . Hang me if I know! I can think of it quietly. After all, what has it proved? Nothing. I suppose you don't think so. . . .'

"I made a protesting murmur.

" 'No matter,' he said. 'I am satisfied . . . nearly. I've got to look only at the face of the first man that comes along, to regain my confidence. They can't be made to understand what is going on in me. What of that? Come! I haven't done so badly.'

" 'Not so badly,' I said.

" 'But all the same, you wouldn't like to have me aboard your own ship — hey?'

" 'Confound you!' I cried. 'Stop this.'

" 'Aha! You see,' he cried, crowing, as it were, over me placidly. 'Only,' he went on, 'you just try to tell this to any of them here. They would think you a fool, a liar, or worse. And so I can stand it. I've done a thing or two for them, but this is what they have done for me.'

" 'My dear chap,' I cried, 'you shall always remain for them an insoluble mystery.' Thereupon we were silent.

" 'Mystery,' he repeated, before looking up. 'Well, then let me always remain here.'

"After the sun had set, the darkness seemed to drive upon us, borne in every faint puff of the breeze. In the middle of a hedged path I saw the arrested, gaunt, watchful, and apparently one-legged silhouette of Tamb' Itam; and across the dusky space my eye detected something white moving to and fro behind the supports of the roof. As soon as Jim, with Tamb' Itam at his heels, had started upon his evening rounds, I went up to the house alone, and, unexpectedly, found myself waylaid by the girl, who had been clearly waiting for this opportunity.

"It is hard to tell you what it was precisely she wanted to wrest from me. Obviously it would be something very simple — the simplest impossibility in the world; as, for instance, the exact de-scription of the form of a cloud. She wanted an assurance, a statement, a promise, an explanation — I don't know how to call it: the thing has no name. It was dark under the projecting roof, and all I could see were the flowing lines of her gown, the pale small oval of her face, with the white flash of her teeth, and, turned towards me, the big sombre orbits of her eyes, where there seemed to be a faint stir, such as you may fancy you can detect when you plunge your gaze to the bottom of an immensely deep well. What is it that moves there? you ask yourself. Is it a blind monster or only a lost gleam from the universe? It occurred to me — don't laugh — that all things being dissimilar, she was more inscrutable in her childish ignorance than the Sphinx propound-ing childish riddles to wayfarers. She had been carried off to Patusan before her eyes were open. She had grown up there; she had seen nothing, she had known nothing, she had no con-ception of anything. I ask myself whether she were sure that anything else existed. What notions she may have formed of the outside world is to me inconceivable: all that she knew of its inhabitants were a betrayed woman and a sinister pantaloon. Her lover also came to her from there, gifted with irresistible seduc-tions; but what would become of her if he should return to these inconceivable regions that seemed always to claim back their own? Her mother had warned her of this with tears, before she died. . . .

"She had caught hold of my arm firmly, and as soon as I had stopped she had withdrawn her hand in haste. She was audacious and shrinking. She feared nothing, but she was checked by the profound incertitude and the extreme strangeness — a brave person groping in the dark. I belonged to this Unknown that might claim Jim for its own at any moment. I was, as it were, in the secret of its nature and of its intentions; — the confidant of a threatening mystery; — armed with its power perhaps! I believe she supposed I could with a word whisk Jim away out of her very arms; it is my sober conviction she went through agonies of apprehension during my long talks with Jim; through a real and intolerable anguish that might have conceivably driven her into plotting my murder, had the fierceness of her soul been equal to the tremendous situation it had created. This is my impression, and it is all I can give you: the whole thing dawned gradually upon me, and as it got clearer and clearer I was overwhelmed by a slow incredulous amazement. She made me believe her, but there is no word that on my lips could render the effect of the headlong and vehement whisper, of the soft, passionate tones, of the sudden breathless pause and the appealing movement of the white arms extended swiftly. They fell; the ghostly figure swayed like a slender tree in the wind, the pale oval of the face drooped; it was impossible to distinguish her features, the darkness of the eyes was unfathomable; two wide sleeves uprose in the dark like unfolding wings, and she stood silent, holding her head in her hands."

CHAPTER XXXIII

"I was immensely touched: her youth, her ignorance, her pretty beauty, which had the simple charm and the delicate vigour of a wild-flower, her pathetic pleading, her helplessness, appealed to me with almost the strength of her own unreasonable and natural fear. She feared the unknown as we all do, and her ignorance made the unknown infinitely vast. I stood for it, for myself, for you fellows, for all the world that neither cared for Jim nor needed him in the least. I would have been ready enough to answer for the indifference of the teeming earth but for the reflection that he, too, belonged to this mysterious unknown of her fears, and that, however much I stood for, I did not stand for him. This made me hesitate. A murmur of hopeless pain unsealed my lips. I began by protesting that I at least had come with no intention to take Jim away.

"Why did I come, then? After a slight movement she was as still as a marble statue in the night. I tried to explain briefly: friendship, business; if I had any wish in the matter it was rather to see him stay. . . . 'They always leave us,' she murmured. The breath of sad wisdom from the grave which her piety wreathed with flowers seemed to pass in a faint sigh. . . . Nothing, I said, could separate Jim from her.

"It is my firm conviction now; it was my conviction at the time; it was the only possible conclusion from the facts of the case. It was not made more certain by her whispering in a tone in which one speaks to oneself, 'He swore this to me.' 'Did you ask him?' I said.

"She made a step nearer. 'No. Never!' She had asked him only to go away. It was that night on the river-bank, after he had killed the man — after she had flung the torch in the water because he was looking at her so. There was too much light, and the danger was over then — for a little time — for a little time. He said then he would not abandon her to Cornelius. She had insisted. She wanted him to leave her. He said that he could not — that it was impossible. He trembled while he said this. She

222

had felt him tremble. . . . One does not require much imagination to see the scene, almost to hear their whispers. She was afraid for him, too. I believe that then she saw in him only a predestined victim of dangers which she understood better than himself. Though by nothing but his mere presence he had mastered her heart, had filled all her thoughts, and had possessed himself of all her affections, she under-estimated his chances of success. It is obvious that at about that time everybody was inclined to under-estimate his chances. Strictly speaking he didn't seem to have any. I know this was Cornelius's view. He confessed that much to me in extenuation of the shady part he had played in Sherif Ali's plot to do away with the infidel. Even Sherif Ali himself, as it seems certain now, had nothing but contempt for the white man. Jim was to be murdered mainly on religious grounds, I believe. A simple act of piety (and so far infinitely meritorious), but otherwise without much importance. In the last part of this opinion Cornelius concurred. 'Honourable sir,' he argued abjectly on the only occasion he managed to have me to himself — 'Honourable sir, how was I to know? Who was he? What could he do to make people believe him? What did Mr. Stein mean sending a boy like that to talk big to an old servant? I was ready to save him for eighty dollars. Only eighty dollars. Why didn't the fool go? Was I to get stabbed myself for the sake of a stranger?' He grovelled in spirit before me, with his body doubled up insinuatingly and his hands hovering about my knees, as though he were ready to embrace my legs. 'What's eighty dollars? An insignificant sum to give to a defenceless old man ruined for life by a deceased she-devil.' Here he wept. But I anticipate. I didn't that night chance upon Cornelius till I had had it out with the girl.

"She was unselfish when she urged Jim to leave her, and even to leave the country. It was his danger that was foremost in her thoughts — even if she wanted to save herself, too — perhaps unconsciously: but then look at the warning she had, look at the lesson that could be drawn from every moment of the recently ended life in which all her memories were centred. She fell at his feet — she told me so — there by the river, in the discreet light of stars which showed nothing except great masses of silent shadows, indefinite open spaces, and trembling faintly upon the broad stream made it appear as wide as the sea. He had lifted her up.

He lifted her up, and then she would struggle no more. Of course not. Strong arms, a tender voice, a stalwart shoulder to rest her poor lonely little head upon. The need — the infinite need — of all this for the aching heart, for the bewildered mind; — the promptings of youth — the necessity of the moment. What would you have? One understands — unless one is incapable of understanding anything under the sun. And so she was content to be lifted up — and held. 'You know — Jove! this is serious — no nonsense in it!' as Jim had whispered hurriedly with a troubled concerned face on the threshold of his house. I don't know so much about nonsense, but there was nothing lighthearted in their romance: they came together under the shadow of a life's disaster, like knight and maiden meeting to exchange vows amongst haunted ruins. The starlight was good enough for that story, a light so faint and remote that it cannot resolve shadows into shapes, and show the other shore of a stream. I did look upon the stream that night and from the very place; it rolled silent and as black as Styx: the next day I went away, but I am not likely to forget what it was she wanted to be saved from when she entreated him to leave her while there was time. She told me what it was, calmed — she was now too passionately interested for mere excitement — in a voice as quiet in the obscurity as her white half-lost figure. She told me, 'I didn't want to die weeping.' I thought I had not heard aright.

" 'You did not want to die weeping?' I repeated after her. 'Like my mother,' she added readily. The outlines of her white shape did not stir in the least. 'My mother had wept bitterly before she died,' she explained. An inconceivable calmness seemed to have risen from the ground around us, imperceptibly, like the still rise of a flood in the night, obliterating the familiar landmarks of emotions. There came upon me, as though I had felt myself losing my footing in the midst of waters, a sudden dread, the dread of the unknown depths. She went on explaining that, during the last moments, being alone with her mother, she had to leave the side of the couch to go and set her back against the door, in order to keep Cornelius out. He desired to get in, and kept on drumming with both fists, only desisting now and again to shout huskily, 'Let me in! Let me in! Let me in!' In a far corner upon a few mats the moribund woman, already speechless and unable to lift her arm, rolled her head over, and with a feeble movement of her hand seemed to command — 'No! No!' and the obedient daughter, setting her shoulders with all her strength against the door, was looking on. 'The tears fell from her eyes — and then she died,' concluded the girl in an imperturbable monotone, which more than anything else, more than the white statu-esque immobility of her person, more than mere words could do, troubled my mind profoundly with the passive, irremediable hor-ror of the scene. It had the power to drive me out of my con-ception of existence, out of that shelter each of us makes for him-self to creep under in moments of danger, as a tortoise withdraws within its shell. For a moment I had a view of a world that seemed to wear a vast and dismal aspect of disorder, while, in truth, thanks to our unwearied efforts, it is as sunny an arrange-ment of small conveniences as the mind of man can conceive. But still — it was only a moment: I went back into my shell di-rectly. One *must* — don't you know? — though I seemed to have lost all my words in the chaos of dark thoughts I had contem-plated for a second or two beyond the pale. These came back, too, very soon, for words also belong to the sheltering concep-tion of light and order which is our refuge. I had them ready at my disposal before she whispered softly, 'He swore he would never leave me, when we stood there alone! He swore to me!' . . . 'And is it possible that you — you! do not believe him?' I asked, sincerely reproachful, genuinely shocked. Why couldn't she believe? Wherefore this craving for incertitude, this cling-ing to fear, as if incertitude and fear had been the safeguards of her love. It was monstrous. She should have made for herself a shelter of inexpugnable peace out of that honest affection. She had not the knowledge — not the skill perhaps. The night had come on apace; it had grown pitch-dark where we were, so that without stirring she had faded like the intangible form of a wist-ful and perverse spirit. And suddenly I heard her quiet whis-per again, 'Other men had sworn the same thing.' It was like a meditative comment on some thoughts full of sadness, of awe. And she added, still lower if possible, 'My father did.' She paused the time to draw an inaudible breath. 'Her father, too.' . . . These were the things she knew! At once I said, 'Ah! but he is not like that.' This, it seemed, she did not intend to dispute; but after a time the strange still whisper wandering dreamily in the air stole into my ears. 'Why is he different? Is he better? Is

he . . .' 'Upon my word of honour,' I broke in, 'I believe he is.'
We subdued our tones to a mysterious pitch. Amongst the huts
of Jim's workmen (they were mostly liberated slaves from the
Sherif's stockade) somebody started a shrill, drawling song.
Across the river a big fire (at Doramin's, I think) made a glowing ball, completely isolated in the night. 'Is he more true?' she
murmured. 'Yes,' I said. 'More true than any other man,' she
repeated in lingering accents. 'Nobody here,' I said, 'would
dream of doubting his word — nobody would dare — except you.'

"I think she made a movement at this. 'More brave,' she went
on in a changed tone. 'Fear shall never drive him away from
you,' I said a little nervously. The song stopped short on a shrill
note, and was succeeded by several voices talking in the distance.
Jim's voice, too. I was struck by her silence. 'What has he been
telling you? He has been telling you something?' I asked. There
was no answer. 'What is it he told you?' I insisted.

" 'Do you think I can tell you? How am I to know? How am
I to understand?' she cried at last. There was a stir. I believe she
was wringing her hands. 'There is something he can never forget.'

" 'So much the better for you,' I said, gloomily.

" 'What is it? What is it?' She put an extraordinary force of
appeal into her supplicating tone. 'He says he had been afraid.
How can I believe this? Am I a mad woman to believe this?
You all remember something! You all go back to it. What is it?
You tell me! What is this thing? Is it alive? — is it dead? I hate
it. It is cruel. Has it got a face and a voice — this calamity? Will
he see it — will be hear it? In his sleep perhaps when he cannot
see me — and then arise and go. Ah! I shall never forgive him.
My mother had forgiven — but I, never! Will it be a sign — a
call?'

"It was a wonderful experience. She mistrusted his very slumbers — and she seemed to think I could tell her why! Thus a poor
mortal seduced by the charm of an apparition might have tried to
wring from another ghost the tremendous secret of the claim the
other world holds over a disembodied soul astray amongst the
passions of this earth. The very ground on which I stood seemed
to melt under my feet. And it was so simple, too; but if the
spirits evoked by our fears and our unrest have ever to vouch
for each other's constancy before the forlorn magicians that we

are, then I — I alone of us dwellers in the flesh — have shuddered
in the hopeless chill of such a task. A sign, a call! How telling
in its expression was her ignorance. A few words! How she
came to know them, how she came to pronounce them, I can't
imagine. Women find their inspiration in the stress of moments
that for us are merely awful, absurd, or futile. To discover that
she had a voice at all was enough to strike awe into the heart.
Had a spurned stone cried out in pain it could not have appeared
a greater and more pitiful miracle. These few sounds wandering
in the dark had made their two benighted lives tragic to my mind.
It was impossible to make her understand. I chafed silently at
my impotence. And Jim, too — poor devil! Who would need
him? Who would remember him? He had what he wanted.
His very existence probably had been forgotten by this time.
They had mastered their fates. They were tragic.

"Her immobility before me was clearly expectant, and my part
was to speak for my brother from the realm of forgetful shades.
I was deeply moved at my responsibility and at her distress. I
would have given anything for the power to soothe her frail
soul, tormenting itself in its invincible ignorance like a small bird
beating about the cruel wires of a cage. Nothing easier than to
say, Have no fear! Nothing more difficult. How does one kill
fear, I wonder? How do you shoot a spectre through the heart,
slash off its spectral head, take it by its spectral throat? It is an
enterprise you rush into while you dream, and are glad to make
your escape with wet hair and every limb shaking. The bullet
is not run, the blade not forged, the man not born; even the
winged words of truth drop at your feet like lumps of lead. You
require for such a desperate encounter an enchanted and poisoned shaft dipped in a lie too subtle to be found on earth. An
enterprise for a dream, my masters!

"I began my exorcism with a heavy heart, with a sort of sullen
anger in it, too. Jim's voice, suddenly raised with a stern intonation, carried across the courtyard, reproving the carelessness of
some dumb sinner by the river-side. Nothing — I said, speaking
in a distinct murmur — there could be nothing, in that unknown
world she fancied so eager to rob her of her happiness, there was
nothing neither living nor dead, there was no face, no voice, no
power, that could tear Jim from her side. I drew breath and she
whispered softly, 'He told me so.' 'He told you the truth,' I said.

'Nothing,' she sighed out, and abruptly turned upon me with a barely audible intensity of tone: 'Why did you come to us from out there? He speaks of you too often. You make me afraid. Do you — do you want him?' A sort of stealthy fierceness had crept into our hurried mutters. 'I shall never come again,' I said, bitterly. 'And I don't want him. No one wants him.' 'No one,' she repeated in a tone of doubt. 'No one,' I affirmed, feeling myself swayed by some strange excitement. 'You think him strong, wise, courageous, great — why not believe him to be true, too? I shall go to-morrow — and that is the end. You shall never be troubled by a voice from there again. This world you don't know is too big to miss him. You understand? Too big. You've got his heart in your hand. You must feel that. You must know that.' 'Yes, I know that,' she breathed out, hard and still, as a statue might whisper.

"I felt I had done nothing. And what is it that I had wished to do? I am not sure now. At the time I was animated by an inexplicable ardour, as if before some great and necessary task — the influence of the moment upon my mental and emotional state. There are in all our lives such moments, such influences, coming from the outside, as it were, irresistible, incomprehensible — as if brought about by the mysterious conjunctions of the planets. She owned, as I had put it to her, his heart. She had that and everything else — if she could only believe it. What I had to tell her was that in the whole world there was no one who ever would need his heart, his mind, his hand. It was a common fate, and yet it seemed an awful thing to say of any man. She listened without a word, and her stillness now was like the protest of an invincible unbelief. What need she care for the world beyond the forests? I asked. From all the multitudes that peopled the vastness of that unknown there would come, I assured her, as long as he lived, neither a call nor a sign for him. Never. I was carried away. Never! Never! I remember with wonder the sort of dogged fierceness I displayed. I had the illusion of having got the spectre by the throat at last. Indeed the whole real thing has left behind the detailed and amazing impression of a dream. Why should she fear? She knew him to be strong, true, wise, brave. He was all that. Certainly. He was more. He was great — invincible — and the world did not want him, it had forgotten him, it would not even know him.

"I stopped; the silence over Patusan was profound, and the feeble dry sound of a paddle striking the side of a canoe some-where in the middle of the river seemed to make it infinite. 'Why?' she murmured. I felt that sort of rage one feels during a hard tussle. The spectre was trying to slip out of my grasp. 'Why?' she repeated louder; 'tell me!' And as I remained con-founded, she stamped with her foot like a spoilt child. 'Why? Speak.' 'You want to know?' I asked in a fury. 'Yes!' she cried. 'Because he is not good enough,' I said, brutally. During the moment's pause I noticed the fire on the other shore blaze up, dilating the circle of its glow like an amazed stare, and contract suddenly to a red pin-point. I only knew how close to me she had been when I felt the clutch of her fingers on my forearm. Without raising her voice, she threw into it an infinity of scath-ing contempt, bitterness, and despair.

" 'This is the very thing he said. . . . You lie!'

"The last two words she cried at me in the native dialect. 'Hear me out!' I entreated; she caught her breath tremulously, flung my arm away. 'Nobody, nobody is good enough,' I began with the greatest earnestness. I could hear the sobbing labour of her breath frightfully quickened. I hung my head. What was the use? Footsteps were approaching; I slipped away without another word. . . ."

CHAPTER XXXIV

MARLOW swung his legs out, got up quickly, and staggered a little, as though he had been set down after a rush through space. He leaned his back against the balustrade and faced a disordered array of long cane-chairs. The bodies prone in them seemed startled out of their torpor by his movement. One or two sat up as if alarmed; here and there a cigar glowed yet; Marlow looked at them all with the eyes of a man returning from the excessive remoteness of a dream. A throat was cleared; a calm voice encouraged negligently, "Well."

"Nothing," said Marlow with a slight start. "He had told her — that's all. She did not believe him — nothing more. As to myself, I do not know whether it be just, proper, decent for me to rejoice or to be sorry. For my part, I cannot say what I believed — indeed I don't know to this day, and never shall probably. But what did the poor devil believe himself? Truth shall prevail — don't you know *Magna est veritas et* . . . Yes, when it gets a chance. There is a law, no doubt — and likewise a law regulates your luck in the throwing of dice. It is not Justice the servant of men, but accident, hazard, Fortune — the ally of patient Time — that holds an even and scrupulous balance. Both of us had said the very same thing. Did we both speak the truth — or one of us did — or neither? . . ."

Marlow paused, crossed his arms on his breast, and in a changed tone —

"She said we lied. Poor soul. Well — let's leave it to chance, whose ally is Time, that cannot be hurried, and whose enemy is Death, that will not wait. I had retreated — a little cowed, I must own. I had tried a fall with fear itself and got thrown — of course. I had only succeeded in adding to her anguish the hint of some mysterious collusion, of an inexplicable and incomprehensible conspiracy to keep her for ever in the dark. And it had come easily, naturally, unavoidably, by his act, by her own act! It was as though I had been shown the working of the implacable destiny of which we are the victims — and the tools. It was appalling to think of the girl whom I had left standing there motionless; Jim's footsteps had a fateful sound as he tramped by, without seeing me, in his heavy laced boots. 'What? No lights!' he said in a loud, surprised voice. 'What are you doing in the dark — you two?' Next moment he caught sight of her, I suppose. 'Hallo, girl!' he cried, cheerily. 'Hallo, boy!' she answered at once, with amazing pluck.

"This was their usual greeting to each other, and the bit of swagger she would put into her rather high but sweet voice was very droll, pretty, and childlike. It delighted Jim greatly. This was the last occasion on which I heard them exchange this familiar hail, and it struck a chill into my heart. There was the high sweet voice, the pretty effort, the swagger; but it all seemed to die out prematurely, and the playful call sounded like a moan. It was too confoundedly awful. 'What have you done with Marlow?' Jim was asking; and then, 'Gone down — has he? Funny I didn't meet him. . . . You there, Marlow?'

"I didn't answer. I wasn't going in — not yet at any rate. I really couldn't. While he was calling me I was engaged in making my escape through a little gate leading out upon a stretch of newly cleared ground. No; I couldn't face them yet. I walked hastily with lowered head along a trodden path. The ground rose gently, the few big trees had been felled, the undergrowth had been cut down and the grass fired. He had a mind to try a coffee-plantation there. The big hill, rearing its double summit coal-black in the clear yellow glow of the rising moon, seemed to cast its shadow upon the ground prepared for that experiment. He was going to try ever so many experiments; I had admired his energy, his enterprise, and his shrewdness. Nothing on earth seemed less real now than his plans, his energy, and his enthusiasm; and raising my eyes, I saw part of the moon glittering through the bushes at the bottom of the chasm. For a moment it looked as though the smooth disc, falling from its place in the sky upon the earth, had rolled to the bottom of that precipice: its ascending movement was like a leisurely rebound; it disengaged itself from the tangle of twigs; the bare contorted limb of some tree, growing on the slope, made a black crack right across its face. It threw its level rays afar as if from a cavern, and in this mournful eclipse-like light the stumps of felled trees uprose very dark, the heavy shadows fell at my feet on all sides, my own moving shadow, and across my path the shadow of the solitary grave perpetually garlanded with flowers. In the darkened moonlight the interlaced blossoms took on shapes foreign to one's memory and colours indefinable to the eye, as though they had been special flowers gathered by no man, grown not in this world, and destined for the use of the dead alone. Their powerful scent hung in the warm air, making it thick and heavy like the fumes of incense. The lumps of white coral shone round the dark mound like a chaplet of bleached skulls, and everything around was so quiet that when I stood still all sound and all movements in the world seemed to come to an end.

"It was a great peace, as if the earth had been one grave, and for a time I stood there thinking mostly of the living who, buried in remote places out of the knowledge of mankind, still are fated to share in its tragic or grotesque miseries. In its noble struggles, too — who knows? The human heart is vast enough to contain all the world. It is valiant enough to bear the burden, but where is the courage that would cast it off?

"I suppose I must have fallen into a sentimental mood; I only know that I stood there long enough for the sense of utter solitude to get hold of me so completely that all I had lately seen, all I had heard, and the very human speech itself, seemed to have passed away out of existence, living only for a while longer in my memory, as though I had been the last of mankind. It was a strange and melancholy illusion, evolved half-consciously like all our illusions, which I suspect only to be visions of remote unattainable truth, seen dimly. This was, indeed, one of the lost, forgotten, unknown places of the earth; I had looked under its obscure surface; and I felt that when to-morrow I had left it for ever, it would slip out of existence, to live only in my memory till I myself passed into oblivion. I have that feeling about me now; perhaps it is that feeling which had incited me to tell you the story, to try to hand over to you, as it were, its very existence, its reality — the truth disclosed in a moment of illusion.

"Cornelius broke upon it. He bolted out, vermin-like, from the long grass growing in a depression of the ground. I believe his house was rotting somewhere near by, though I've never seen it, not having been far enough in that direction. He ran towards me upon the path; his feet, shod in dirty white shoes, twinkled on the dark earth; he pulled himself up, and began to whine and cringe under a tall stove-pipe hat. His dried-up little carcass was swallowed up, totally lost, in a suit of black broadcloth. That was his costume for holidays and ceremonies, and it reminded me that this was the fourth Sunday I had spent in Patusan. All the time of my stay I had been vaguely aware of his desire to confide in me, if he only could get me all to himself. He hung about with an eager craving look on his sour yellow little face; but his timidity had kept him back as much as my natural reluctance to have anything to do with such an unsavoury creature. He would have succeeded, nevertheless, had he not been so ready to slink off as soon as you looked at him. He would slink off before Jim's severe gaze, before my own, which I tried to make indifferent, even before Tamb' Itam's surly, superior glance. He was perpetually slinking away; whenever seen he was seen moving off deviously, his face over his shoulder, with either a mis-

trustful snarl or a woe-begone, piteous, mute aspect; but no assumed expression could conceal this innate irremediable abjectness of his nature, any more than an arrangement of clothing can
conceal some monstrous deformity of the body.

"I don't know whether it was the demoralisation of my utter
defeat in my encounter with a spectre of fear less than an hour
ago, but I let him capture me without even a show of resistance.
I was doomed to be the recipient of confidences, and to be confronted with unanswerable questions. It was trying; but the
contempt, the unreasoned contempt, the man's appearance provoked, made it easier to bear. He couldn't possibly matter. Nothing mattered, since I had made up my mind that Jim, for whom
alone I cared, had at last mastered his fate. He had told me he
was satisfied . . . nearly. This is going further than most of us
dare. I — who have the right to think myself good enough —
dare not. Neither does any of you here, I suppose? . . ."

Marlow paused, as if expecting an answer. Nobody spoke.

"Quite right," he began again. "Let no soul know, since the
truth can be wrung out of us only by some cruel, little, awful
catastrophe. But he is one of us, and he could say he was satisfied . . . nearly. Just fancy this! Nearly satisfied. One could
almost envy him his catastrophe. Nearly satisfied. After this
nothing could matter. It did not matter who suspected him, who
trusted him, who loved him, who hated him — especially as it
was Cornelius who hated him.

"Yet after all this was a kind of recognition. You shall judge
of a man by his foes as well as by his friends, and this enemy of
Jim was such as no decent man would be ashamed to own, without, however, making too much of him. This was the view Jim
took, and in which I shared; but Jim disregarded him on general
grounds. 'My dear Marlow,' he said, 'I feel that if I go straight
nothing can touch me. Indeed I do. Now you have been long
enough here to have a good look round — and, frankly, don't you
think I am pretty safe? It all depends upon me, and, by Jove!
I have lots of confidence in myself. The worst thing he could
do would be to kill me, I suppose. I don't think for a moment
he would. He couldn't, you know — not if I were myself to
hand him a loaded rifle for the purpose, and then turn my back
on him. That's the sort of thing he is. And suppose he would —
suppose he could? Well — what of that? I didn't come here fly-

ing for my life — did I? I came here to set my back against the
wall, and I am going to stay here . . .'

" 'Till you are *quite* satisfied,' I struck in.

"We were sitting at the time under the roof in the stern of
his boat; twenty paddles flashed like one, ten on a side, striking
the water with a single splash, while behind our backs Tamb'
Itam dipped silently right and left, and stared right down the
river, attentive to keep the long canoe in the greatest strength
of the current. Jim bowed his head, and our last talk seemed to
flicker out for good. He was seeing me off as far as the mouth
of the river. The schooner had left the day before, working
down and drifting on the ebb, while I had prolonged my stay
overnight. And now he was seeing me off.

"Jim had been a little angry with me for mentioning Cornelius
at all. I had not, in truth, said much. The man was too insignificant to be dangerous, though he was as full of hate as he could
hold. He had called me 'honourable sir' at every second sentence,
and had whined at my elbow as he followed me from the grave
of his 'late wife' to the gate of Jim's compound. He declared
himself the most unhappy of men, a victim, crushed like a worm;
he entreated me to look at him. I wouldn't turn my head to
do so; but I could see out of the corner of my eye his obsequious
shadow gliding after mine, while the moon, suspended on our
right hand, seemed to gloat serenely upon the spectacle. He tried
to explain — as I've told you — his share in the events of the
memorable night. It was a matter of expediency. How could
he know who was going to get the upper hand? 'I would have
saved him, honourable sir! I would have saved him for eighty
dollars,' he protested in dulcet tones, keeping a pace behind me.
'He has saved himself,' I said, 'and he has forgiven you.' I heard
a sort of tittering, and turned upon him; at once he appeared
ready to take to his heels. 'What are you laughing at?' I asked,
standing still. 'Don't be deceived, honourable sir!' he shrieked,
seemingly losing all control over his feelings. '*He* save himself!
He knows nothing, honourable sir — nothing whatever. Who is
he? What does he want here — the big thief? What does he
want here? He throws dust into everybody's eyes; he throws
dust into your eyes, honourable sir; but he can't throw dust into
my eyes. He is a big fool, honourable sir.' I laughed contemptuously, and, turning on my heel, began to walk on again. He ran

up to my elbow and whispered forcibly, 'He's no more than a little child here — like a little child — a little child.' Of course I didn't take the slightest notice, and seeing the time pressed, because we were approaching the bamboo fence that glittered over the blackened ground of the clearing, he came to the point. He commenced by being abjectly lachrymose. His great misfortunes had affected his head. He hoped I would kindly forget what nothing but his troubles made him say. He didn't mean anything by it; only the honourable sir did not know what it was to be ruined, broken down, trampled upon. After this introduction he approached the matter near his heart, but in such a rambling, ejaculatory, craven fashion, that for a long time I couldn't make out what he was driving at. He wanted me to intercede with Jim in his favour. It seemed, too, to be some sort of money affair. I heard time and again the words, 'Moderate provision — suitable present.' He seemed to be claiming value for something, and he even went the length of saying with some warmth that life was not worth having if a man were to be robbed of everything. I did not breathe a word, of course, but neither did I stop my ears. The gist of the affair, which became clear to me gradually, was in this, that he regarded himself as entitled to some money in exchange for the girl. He had brought her up. Somebody else's child. Great trouble and pains — old man now — suitable present. If the honourable sir would say a word. . . . I stood still to look at him with curiosity, and fearful lest I should think him extortionate, I suppose, he hastily brought himself to make a concession. In consideration of a 'suitable present' given at once, he would, he declared, be willing to undertake the charge of the girl, 'without any other provision — when the time came for the gentleman to go home.' His little yellow face, all crumpled as though it had been squeezed together, expressed the most anxious, eager avarice. His voice whined coaxingly, 'No more trouble — natural guardian — a sum of money. . . .'

"I stood there and marvelled. That kind of thing, with him, was evidently a vocation. I discovered suddenly in his cringing attitude a sort of assurance, as though he had been all his life dealing in certitudes. He must have thought I was dispassionately considering his proposal, because he became as sweet as honey. 'Every gentleman made a provision when the time came

to go home,' he began, insinuatingly. I slammed the little gate.
'In this case, Mr. Cornelius,' I said, 'the time shall never come.'
He took a few seconds to gather this in. 'What!' he fairly
squealed. 'Why,' I continued from my side of the gate, 'haven't
you heard him say so himself? He will never go home.' 'Oh!
this is too much,' he shouted. He would not address me as 'hon-
oured sir' any more. He was very still for a time, and then without a trace of humility began very low. 'Never go — ah! He —
he — he comes here devil knows from where — comes here —
devil knows why — to trample on me till I die — ah — trample'
(he stamped softly with both feet), 'trample like this — nobody
knows why — till I die. . . .' His voice became quite extinct;
he was bothered by a little cough; he came up close to the fence
and told me, dropping into a confidential and piteous tone, that
he would *not* be trampled upon. 'Patience — patience,' he muttered, striking his breast. I had done laughing at him, but unexpectedly he treated me to a wild cracked burst of it. 'Ha!
ha! ha! We shall see! We shall see! What! Steal from me?
Steal from me everything! Everything! Everything!' His head
drooped on one shoulder, his hands were hanging before him
lightly clasped. One would have thought he had cherished the
girl with surpassing love, that his spirit had been crushed and
his heart broken by the most cruel of spoliations. Suddenly he
lifted his head and shot out an infamous word. 'Like her mother
— she is like her deceitful mother. Exactly. In her face, too. In
her face. The devil!' He leaned his forehead against the fence,
and in that position uttered threats and horrible blasphemies
in Portuguese in very weak ejaculations, mingled with miserable plaints and groans, coming out with a heave of the shoulders as though he had been overtaken by a deadly fit of sick-
ness. It was an inexpressibly grotesque and vile performance,
and I hastened away. He tried to shout something after me.
Some disparagement of Jim, I believe — not too loud though, we
were too near the house. All I heard distinctly was, 'No more
than a little child — a little child.' "

CHAPTER XXXV

"BUT next morning, at the first bend of the river shutting off the houses of Patusan, all this dropped out of my sight bodily, with its colour, its design, and its meaning, like a picture created by fancy on a canvas, upon which, after long contemplation, you turn your back for the last time. It remains in the memory motionless, unfaded, with its life arrested, in an unchanging light. There are the ambitions, the fears, the hate, the hopes, and they remain in my mind just as I had seen them — intense and as if for ever suspended in their expression. I had turned away from the picture and was going back to the world where events move, men change, light flickers, life flows in a clear stream, no matter whether over mud or over stones. I wasn't going to dive into it; I would have enough to do to keep my head above the surface. But as to what I was leaving behind, I cannot imagine any alteration. The immense and magnanimous Doramin and his little motherly witch of a wife, gazing together upon the land and nursing secretly their dreams of parental ambition; Tunju Allang, wizened and greatly perplexed; Dain Waris, intelligent and brave, with his faith in Jim, with his firm glance and his ironic friendliness; the girl, absorbed in her frightened, suspicious adoration; Tamb' Itam, surly and faithful; Cornelius, leaning his forehead against the fence under the moonlight — I am certain of them. They exist as if under an enchanter's wand. But the figure round which all these are grouped — that one lives, and I am not certain of him. No magician's wand can immobilise him under my eyes. He is one of us.

"Jim, as I've told you, accompanied me on the first stage of my journey back to the world he had renounced, and the way at times seemed to lead through the very heart of untouched wilderness. The empty reaches sparkled under the high sun; between the high walls of vegetation the heat drowsed upon the water, and the boat, impelled vigorously, cut her way through the air that seemed to have settled dense and warm under the shelter of lofty trees.

"The shadow of the impending separation had already put an immense space between us, and when we spoke it was with an effort, as if to force our low voices across a vast and increasing distance. The boat fairly flew; we sweltered side by side in the stagnant superheated air; the smell of mud, of marsh, the primeval smell of fecund earth, seemed to sting our faces; till suddenly at a bend it was as if a great hand far away had lifted a heavy curtain, had flung open an immense portal. The light itself seemed to stir, the sky above our heads widened, a far-off murmur reached our ears, a freshness enveloped us, filled our lungs, quickened our thoughts, our blood, our regrets — and, straight ahead, the forests sank down against the dark-blue ridge of the sea.

"I breathed deeply, I revelled in the vastness of the opened horizon, in the different atmosphere that seemed to vibrate with a toil of life, with the energy of an impeccable world. This sky and this sea were open to me. The girl was right — there was a sign, a call in them — something to which I responded with every fibre of my being. I let my eyes roam through space, like a man released from bonds who stretches his cramped limbs, runs, leaps, responds to the inspiring elation of freedom. 'This is glorious!' I cried, and then I looked at the sinner by my side. He sat with his head sunk on his breast and said 'Yes,' without raising his eyes, as if afraid to see writ large on the clear sky of the offing the reproach of his romantic conscience.

"I remember the smallest details of that afternoon. We landed on a bit of white beach. It was backed by a low cliff wooded on the brow, draped in creepers to the very foot. Below us the plain of the sea, of a serene and intense blue, stretched with a slight upward tilt to the thread-like horizon drawn at the height of our eyes. Great waves of glitter blew lightly along the pitted dark surface, as swift as feathers chased by the breeze. A chain of islands sat broken and massive facing the wide estuary, displayed in a sheet of pale glassy water reflecting faithfully the contour of the shore. High in the colourless sunshine a solitary bird, all black, hovered, dropping and soaring above the same spot with a slight rocking motion of the wings. A ragged, sooty bunch of flimsy mat hovels was perched over its own inverted image upon a crooked multitude of high piles the colour of ebony. A tiny black canoe put off from amongst them with

two tiny men, all black, who toiled exceedingly, striking down
at the pale water: and the canoe seemed to slide painfully on a
mirror. This bunch of miserable hovels was the fishing village
that boasted of the white lord's especial protection, and the
two men crossing over were the old headman and his son-in-
law. They landed and walked up to us on the white sand, lean,
dark-brown as if dried in smoke, with ashy patches on the skin
of their naked shoulders and breasts. Their heads were bound
in dirty but carefully folded handkerchiefs, and the old man began at once to state a complaint, voluble, stretching a lank arm,
screwing up at Jim his old bleared eyes confidently. The Rajah's people would not leave them alone; there had been some
trouble about a lot of turtles' eggs his people had collected on the
islets there — and leaning at arm's-length upon his paddle, he
pointed with a brown skinny hand over the sea. Jim listened for
a time without looking up, and at last told him gently to wait.
He would hear him by-and-by. They withdrew obediently to
some little distance, and sat on their heels, with their paddles
lying before them on the sand; the silvery gleams in their eyes
followed our movements patiently; and the immensity of the
outspread sea, the stillness of the coast, passing north and south
beyond the limits of my vision, made up one colossal Presence
watching us four dwarfs isolated on a strip of glistening sand.

" 'The trouble is,' remarked Jim, moodily, 'that for generations these beggars of fishermen in that village there had been
considered as the Rajah's personal slaves — and the old rip can't
get it into his head that . . .'

"He paused. 'That you have changed all that,' I said.

" 'Yes. I've changed all that,' he muttered in a gloomy voice.

" 'You have had your opportunity,' I pursued.

" 'Had I?' he said. 'Well, yes. I suppose so. Yes. I have got
back my confidence in myself — a good name — yet sometimes I
wish . . . No! I shall hold what I've got. Can't expect anything more.' He flung his arm out towards the sea. 'Not out
there anyhow.' He stamped his foot upon the sand. 'This is
my limit, because nothing less will do.'

"We continued pacing the beach. 'Yes, I've changed all that,'
he went on, with a sidelong glance at the two patient squatting
fishermen; 'but only try to think what it would be if I went
away. Jove! can't you see it? Hell loose. No! To-morrow I

shall go and take my chance of drinking that silly old Tunku Allang's coffee, and I shall make no end of fuss over these rotten turtles' eggs. No. I can't say — enough. Never. I must go on, go on for ever holding up my end, to feel sure that nothing can touch me. I must stick to their belief in me to feel safe and to — to' . . . He cast about for a word, seemed to look for it on the sea . . . 'to keep in touch with' . . . His voice sank suddenly to a murmur . . . 'with those whom, perhaps, I shall never see any more. With — with — you, for instance.'

"I was profoundly humbled by his words. 'For God's sake,' I said, 'don't set me up, my dear fellow; just look to yourself.' I felt a gratitude, an affection, for that straggler whose eyes had singled me out, keeping my place in the ranks of an insignificant multitude. How little that was to boast of, after all! I turned my burning face away; under the low sun, glowing, darkened and crimson, like an ember snatched from the fire, the sea lay outspread, offering all its immense stillness to the approach of the fiery orb. Twice he was going to speak, but checked himself: at last, as if he had found a formula —

" 'I shall be faithful,' he said, quietly. 'I shall be faithful,' he repeated, without looking at me, but for the first time letting his eyes wander upon the waters, whose blueness had changed to a gloomy purple under the fires of sunset. Ah! he was romantic, romantic. I recalled some words of Stein's. . . . 'In the destructive element immerse! . . . To follow the dream, and again to follow the dream — and so — always — *usque ad finem* . . .' He was romantic, but none the less true. Who could tell what forms, what visions, what faces, what forgiveness he could see in the glow of the west! . . . A small boat, leaving the schooner, moved slowly, with a regular beat of two oars, towards the sandbank to take me off. 'And then there's Jewel,' he said, out of the great silence of earth, sky, and sea, which had mastered my very thoughts so that his voice made me start. 'There's Jewel.' 'Yes,' I murmured. 'I need not tell you what she is to me,' he pursued. 'You've seen. In time she will come to understand . . .' 'I hope so,' I interrupted. 'She trusts me, too,' he mused, and then changed his tone. 'When shall we meet next, I wonder?' he said.

" 'Never — unless you come out,' I answered, avoiding his

glance. He didn't seem to be surprised; he kept very quiet for a while.

" 'Good-bye, then,' he said, after a pause. 'Perhaps it's just as well.'

"We shook hands, and I walked to the boat, which waited with her nose on the beach. The schooner, her mainsail set and jib-sheet to windward, curveted on the purple sea; there was a rosy tinge on her sails. 'Will you be going home again soon?' asked Jim, just as I swung my leg over the gunwale. 'In a year or so if I live,' I said. The forefoot grated on the sand, the boat floated, the wet oars flashed and dipped once, twice. Jim, at the water's edge, raised his voice. 'Tell them . . .' he began. I signed to the men to cease rowing, and waited in wonder. Tell who? The half-submerged sun faced him; I could see its red gleam in his eyes that looked dumbly at me. . . . 'No — nothing,' he said, and with a slight wave of his hand motioned the boat away. I did not look again at the shore till I had clambered on board the schooner.

"By that time the sun had set. The twilight lay over the east, and the coast, turned black, extended infinitely its sombre wall that seemed the very stronghold of the night; the western horizon was one great blaze of gold and crimson in which a big detached cloud floated dark and still, casting a slaty shadow on the water beneath, and I saw Jim on the beach watching the schooner fall off and gather headway.

"The two half-naked fishermen had arisen as soon as I had gone; they were no doubt pouring the plaint of their trifling, miserable, oppressed lives into the ears of the white lord, and no doubt he was listening to it, making it his own, for was it not a part of his luck — the luck 'from the word Go' — the luck to which he had assured me he was so completely equal? They, too, I should think, were in luck, and I was sure their pertinacity would be equal to it. Their dark-skinned bodies vanished on the dark background long before I had lost sight of their protector. He was white from head to foot, and remained persistently visible with the stronghold of the night at his back, the sea at his feet, the opportunity by his side — still veiled. What do you say? Was it still veiled? I don't know. For me that white figure in the stillness of coast and sea seemed to stand at the heart of a vast enigma. The twilight was ebbing fast from the sky above his head, the strip of sand had sunk already under his feet, he himself appeared no bigger than a child — then only a speck, a tiny white speck, that seemed to catch all the light left in a darkened world. . . . And, suddenly, I lost him. . . ."

CHAPTER XXXVI

WITH these words Marlow had ended his narrative, and his audience had broken up forthwith, under his abstract, pensive gaze. Men drifted off the verandah in pairs or alone without loss of time, without offering a remark, as if the last image of that incomplete story, its incompleteness itself, and the very tone of the speaker, had made discussion vain and comment impossible. Each of them seemed to carry away his own impression, to carry it away with him like a secret; but there was only one man of all these listeners who was ever to hear the last word of the story. It came to him at home, more than two years later, and it came contained in a thick packet addressed in Marlow's upright and angular handwriting.

The privileged man opened the packet, looked in, then, laying it down, went to the window. His rooms were in the highest flat of a lofty building, and his glance could travel afar beyond the clear panes of glass, as though he were looking out of the lantern of a lighthouse. The slopes of the roofs glistened, the dark broken ridges succeeded each other without end like sombre, uncrested waves, and from the depths of the town under his feet ascended a confused and unceasing mutter. The spires of churches, numerous, scattered haphazard, uprose like beacons on a maze of shoals without a channel; the driving rain mingled with the falling dusk of a winter's evening; and the booming of a big clock on a tower striking the hour, rolled past in voluminous, austere bursts of sound, with a shrill vibrating cry at the core. He drew the heavy curtains.

The light of his shaded reading-lamp slept like a sheltered pool, his footfalls made no sound on the carpet, his wandering days were over. No more horizons as boundless as hope, no more twilights within the forests as solemn as temples, in the hot quest of the Ever-undiscovered Country over the hill, across the stream, beyond the wave. The hour was striking! No more! No more! — but the opened packet under the lamp brought back the sounds, the visions, the very savour of the past — a multitude of fading faces, a tumult of low voices, dying away upon the shores of distant seas under a passionate and unconsoling sunshine. He sighed and sat down to read.

At first he saw three distinct enclosures. A good many pages closely blackened and pinned together; a loose square sheet of greyish paper with a few words traced in a handwriting he had never seen before, and an explanatory letter from Marlow. From this last fell another letter, yellowed by time and frayed on the folds. He picked it up and, laying it aside, turned to Marlow's message, ran swiftly over the opening lines, and, checking himself, thereafter read on deliberately, like one approaching with slow feet and alert eyes the glimpse of an undiscovered country.

". . . I don't suppose you've forgotten," went on the letter. "You alone have showed an interest in him that survived the telling of his story, though I remember well you would not admit he had mastered his fate. You prophesied for him the disaster of weariness and of disgust with acquired honour, with the self-appointed task, with the love sprung from pity and youth. You had said you knew so well 'that kind of thing,' its illusory satisfaction, its unavoidable deception. You said also — I call to mind — that 'giving your life up to them' (*them* meaning all of mankind with skins brown, yellow, or black in colour) 'was like selling your soul to a brute.' You contended that 'that kind of thing' was only endurable and enduring when based on a firm conviction in the truth of ideas racially our own, in whose name are established the order, the morality of an ethical progress. 'We want its strength at our backs,' you had said. 'We want a belief in its necessity and its justice, to make a worthy and conscious sacrifice of our lives. Without it the sacrifice is only forgetfulness, the way of offering is no better than the way to perdition.' In other words, you maintained that we must fight in the ranks or our lives don't count. Possibly! You ought to know — be it said without malice — you who have rushed into one or two

places single-handed and came out cleverly, without singeing
your wings. The point, however, is that of all mankind Jim had
no dealings but with himself, and the question is whether at the
last he had not confessed to a faith mightier than the laws of
order and progress.

"I affirm nothing. Perhaps you may pronounce — after you've
read. There is much truth — after all — in the common expression 'under a cloud.' It is impossible to see him clearly — especially as it is through the eyes of others that we take our last
look at him. I have no hesitation in imparting to you all I know
of the last episode that, as he used to say, had 'come to him.'
One wonders whether this was perhaps that supreme opportunity, that last and satisfying test for which I had always suspected him to be waiting, before he could frame a message to the
impeccable world. You remember that when I was leaving him
for the last time he had asked whether I would be going home
soon, and suddenly cried after me, 'Tell them!' . . . I had waited
— curious I'll own, and hopeful, too — only to hear him shout,
'No. Nothing.' That was all then — and there shall be nothing
more; there shall be no message, unless such as each of us can
interpret for himself from the language of facts, that are so often
more enigmatic than the craftiest arrangement of words. He
made, it is true, one more attempt to deliver himself; but that,
too, failed, as you may perceive if you look at the sheet of greyish foolscap enclosed here. He had tried to write; do you notice
the commonplace hand? It is headed 'The Fort, Patusan.' I suppose he had carried out his intention of making out of his house
a place of defence. It was an excellent plan: a deep ditch, an
earth wall topped by a palisade, and at the angles guns mounted
on platforms to sweep each side of the square. Doramin had
agreed to furnish him the guns; and so each man of his party
would know there was a place of safety, upon which every faithful partisan could rally in case of some sudden danger. All this
showed his judicious foresight, his faith in the future. What he
called 'my own people' — the liberated captives of the Sherif —
were to make a distinct quarter of Patusan, with their huts and
little plots of ground under the walls of the stronghold. Within
he would be an invincible host in himself. 'The Fort, Patusan.'
No date, as you observe. What is a number and a name to a
day of days? It is also impossible to say whom he had in his

mind when he seized the pen: Stein — myself — the world at large
— or was this only the aimless startled cry of a solitary man confronted by his fate? 'An awful thing has happened,' he wrote before he flung the pen down for the first time; look at the ink blot
resembling the head of an arrow under these words. After a
while he had tried again, scrawling heavily, as if with a hand
of lead, another line. 'I must now at once . . .' The pen had
spluttered, and that time he gave it up. There's nothing more;
he had seen a broad gulf that neither eye nor voice could span.
I can understand this. He was overwhelmed by the inexplicable;
he was overwhelmed by his own personality — the gift of that
destiny which he had done his best to master.

"I send you also an old letter — a very old letter. It was found
carefully preserved in his writing-case. It is from his father, and
by the date you can see he must have received it a few days before he joined the *Patna*. Thus it must be the last letter he ever
had from home. He had treasured it all these years. The good
old parson fancied his sailor-son. I've looked in at a sentence
here and there. There is nothing in it except just affection. He
tells his 'dear James' that the last long letter from him was very
'honest and entertaining.' He would not have him 'judge men
harshly or hastily.' There are four pages of it, easy morality and
family news. Tom had 'taken orders.' Carrie's husband had
'money losses.' The old chap goes on equably trusting Providence and the established order of the universe, but alive to its
small dangers and its small mercies. One can almost see him,
grey-haired and serene in the inviolable shelter of his book-lined,
faded, and comfortable study, where for forty years he had con-
scientiously gone over and over again the round of his little
thoughts about faith and virtue, about the conduct of life and
the only proper manner of dying; where he had written so many
sermons, where he sits talking to his boy, over there, on the other
side of the earth. But what of the distance? Virtue is one all
over the world, and there is only one faith, one conceivable conduct of life, one manner of dying. He hopes his 'dear James'
will never forget that 'who once gives way to temptation, in the
very instant hazards his total depravity and everlasting ruin.
Therefore resolve fixedly never, through any possible motives,
to do anything which you believe to be wrong.' There is also
some news of a favourite dog; and a pony, 'which all you boys

used to ride,' had gone blind from old age and had to be shot.
The old chap invokes Heaven's blessing; the mother and all the
girls then at home send their love. . . . No, there is nothing
much in that yellow frayed letter fluttering out of his cher-
ishing grasp after so many years. It was never answered, but
who can say what converse he may have held with all these placid,
colourless forms of men and women peopling that quiet corner
of the world as free of danger or strife as a tomb, and breathing
equably the air of undisturbed rectitude. It seems amazing that
he should belong to it, he to whom so many things 'had come.'
Nothing ever came to them; they would never be taken unawares,
and never be called upon to grapple with fate. Here they all are,
evoked by the mild gossip of the father, all these brothers and
sisters, bone of his bone and flesh of his flesh, gazing with clear unconscious eyes, while I seem to see him, returned at last, no longer
a mere white speck at the heart of an immense mystery, but of
full stature, standing disregarded amongst their untroubled shapes,
with a stern and romantic aspect, but always mute, dark — under
a cloud.

"The story of the last events you shall find in the few pages
enclosed here. You must admit that it is romantic beyond the
wildest dreams of his boyhood, and yet there is to my mind a sort
of profound and terrifying logic in it, as if it were our imagination alone that could set loose upon us the might of an overwhelming destiny. The imprudence of our thoughts recoils upon
our heads; who toys with the sword shall perish by the sword.
This astounding adventure, of which the most astounding part
is that it is true, comes on as an unavoidable consequence. Something of the sort had to happen. You repeat this to yourself
while you marvel that such a thing could happen in the year
of grace before last. But it has happened — and there is no dis-
puting its logic.

"I put it down here for you as though I had been an eyewit-
ness. My information was fragmentary, but I've fitted the pieces
together, and there is enough of them to make an intelligible
picture. I wonder how he would have related it himself. He has
confided so much in me that at times it seems as though he must
come in presently and tell the story in his own words, in his
careless yet feeling voice, with his offhand manner, a little puzzled, a little bothered, a little hurt, but now and then by a word

or a phrase giving one of these glimpses of his very own self that were never any good for purposes of orientation. It's difficult to believe he will never come. I shall never hear his voice again, nor shall I see his smooth tan-and-pink face with a white line on the forehead, and the youthful eyes darkened by excitement to a profound, unfathomable blue."

CHAPTER XXXVII

"IT ALL begins with a remarkable exploit of a man called Brown, who stole with complete success a Spanish schooner out of a small bay near Zamboanga. Till I discovered the fellow my information was incomplete, but most unexpectedly I did come upon him a few hours before he gave up his arrogant ghost. Fortunately he was willing and able to talk between the choking fits of asthma, and his racked body writhed with malicious exultation at the bare thought of Jim. He exulted thus at the idea that he had 'paid out the stuck-up beggar after all.' He gloated over his action. I had to bear the sunken glare of his fierce crow-footed eyes if I wanted to know; and so I bore it, reflecting how much certain forms of evil are akin to madness, derived from intense egoism, inflamed by resistance, tearing the soul to pieces, and giving factitious vigour to the body. The story also reveals unsuspected depths of cunning in the wretched Cornelius, whose abject and intense hate acts like a subtle inspiration, pointing out an unerring way towards revenge.

" 'I could see directly I set my eyes on him what sort of a fool he was,' gasped the dying Brown. 'He a man! Hell! He was a hollow sham. As if he couldn't have said straight out, "Hands off my plunder!" blast him! That would have been like a man! Rot his superior soul! He had me there — but he hadn't devil enough in him to make an end of me. Not he! A thing like that letting me off as if I wasn't worth a kick! . . .' Brown struggled desperately for breath. . . . 'Fraud. . . . Letting me off. . . . And so I did make an end of him after all. . . .' He choked

again. . . . 'I expect this thing'll kill me, but I shall die easy now.
You . . . you hear . . . I don't know your name — I would give
you a five-pound note if — if I had it — for the news — or my
name's not Brown. . . .' He grinned horribly. . . . 'Gentleman
Brown.'

"He said all these things in profound gasps, staring at me with
his yellow eyes out of a long, ravaged brown face; he jerked his
left arm; a pepper-and-salt matted beard hung almost into his
lap; a dirty ragged blanket covered his legs. I had found him
out in Bankok through that busybody Schomberg, the hotel-
keeper, who had, confidentially, directed me where to look. It
appears that a sort of loafing, fuddled vagabond — a white man
living amongst the natives with a Siamese woman — had considered it a great privilege to give a shelter to the last days of the
famous Gentleman Brown. While he was talking to me in the
wretched hovel, and, as it were, fighting for every minute of his
life, the Siamese woman, with big bare legs and a stupid coarse
face, sat in a dark corner chewing betel stolidly. Now and then
she would get up for the purpose of shooing a chicken away
from the door. The whole hut shook when she walked. An
ugly yellow child, naked and pot-bellied like a little heathen god,
stood at the foot of the couch, finger in mouth, lost in a profound and calm contemplation of the dying man.

"He talked feverishly; but in the middle of a word, perhaps,
an invisible hand would take him by the throat, and he would
look at me dumbly with an expression of doubt and anguish. He
seemed to fear that I would get tired of waiting and go away,
leaving him with his tale untold, with his exultation unexpressed.
He died during the night, I believe, but by that time I had nothing more to learn.

"So much as to Brown, for the present.

"Eight months before this, coming into Samarang, I went as
usual to see Stein. On the garden side of the house a Malay on
the verandah greeted me shyly, and I remembered that I had
seen him in Patusan, in Jim's house, amongst other Bugis men
who used to come in the evening to talk interminably over their
war reminiscences and to discuss State affairs. Jim had pointed
him out to me once as a respectable petty trader owning a small
seagoing native craft, who had showed himself 'one of the best
at the taking of the stockade.' I was not very surprised to see

him, since any Patusan trader venturing as far as Samarang would naturally find his way to Stein's house. I returned his greeting and passed on. At the door of Stein's room I came upon another Malay in whom I recognised Tamb' Itam.

"I asked him at once what he was doing there; it occurred to me that Jim might have come on a visit. I own I was pleased and excited at the thought. Tamb' Itam looked as if he did not know what to say. 'Is Tuan Jim inside?' I asked, impatiently. 'No,' he mumbled, hanging his head for a moment, and then with sudden earnestness, 'He would not fight. He would not fight,' he repeated twice. As he seemed unable to say anything else, I pushed him aside and went in.

"Stein, tall and stooping, stood alone in the middle of the room between the rows of butterfly cases. 'Ach! is it you, my friend?' he said, sadly, peering through his glasses. A drab sack-coat of alpaca hung, unbuttoned, down to his knees. He had a Panama hat on his head, and there were deep furrows on his pale cheeks. 'What's the matter now?' I asked, nervously. 'There's Tamb' Itam there. . . .' 'Come and see the girl. Come and see the girl. She is here,' he said, with a half-hearted show of activity. I tried to detain him, but with gentle obstinacy he would take no notice of my eager questions. 'She is here, she is here,' he repeated, in great perturbation. 'They came here two days ago. An old man like me, a stranger — *sehen Sie* — cannot do much. . . . Come this way. . . . Young hearts are unforgiving. . . .' I could see he was in utmost distress. . . . 'The strength of life in them, the cruel strength of life. . . .' He mumbled, leading me round the house; I followed him, lost in dismal and angry conjectures. At the door of the drawing-room he barred my way. 'He loved her very much,' he said, interrogatively, and I only nodded, feeling so bitterly disappointed that I would not trust myself to speak. 'Very frightful,' he murmured. 'She can't understand me. I am only a strange old man. Perhaps you . . . she knows you. Talk to her. We can't leave it like this. Tell her to forgive him. It was very frightful.' 'No doubt,' I said, exasperated at being in the dark; 'but have *you* forgiven him?' He looked at me queerly. 'You shall hear,' he said, and opening the door, absolutely pushed me in.

"You know Stein's big house and the two immense reception-rooms, uninhabited and uninhabitable, clean, full of solitude and

of shining things that look as if never beheld by the eye of man?
They are cool on the hottest days, and you enter them as you
would a scrubbed cave underground. I passed through one,
and in the other I saw the girl sitting at the end of a big mahogany table, on which she rested her head, the face hidden in her
arms. The waxed floor reflected her dimly as though it had been
a sheet of frozen water. The rattan screens were down, and
through the strange greenish gloom made by the foliage of the
trees outside, a strong wind blew in gusts, swaying the long
draperies of windows and doorways. Her white figure seemed
shaped in snow; the pendent crystals of a great chandelier clicked
above her head like glittering icicles. She looked up and watched
my approach. I was chilled as if these vast apartments had been
the cold abode of despair.

"She recognised me at once, and as soon as I had stopped,
looking down at her: 'He has left me,' she said, quietly; 'you
always leave us — for your own ends.' Her face was set. All the
heat of life seemed withdrawn within some inaccessible spot
in her breast. 'It would have been easy to die with him,' she went
on, and made a slight weary gesture as if giving up the incomprehensible. 'He would not! It was like a blindness — and yet
it was I who was speaking to him; it was I who stood before his
eyes; it was at me that he looked all the time! Ah! you are hard,
treacherous, without truth, without compassion. What makes
you so wicked? Or is it that you are all mad?'

"I took her hand; it did not respond, and when I dropped it,
it hung down to the floor. That indifference, more awful than
tears, cries, and reproaches, seemed to defy time and consolation. You felt that nothing you could say would reach the seat
of the still and benumbing pain.

"Stein had said, 'You shall hear.' I did hear. I heard it all,
listening with amazement, with awe, to the tones of her inflexible
weariness. She could not grasp the real sense of what she was
telling me, and her resentment filled me with pity for her —
for him, too. I stood rooted to the spot after she had finished.
Leaning on her arm, she stared with hard eyes, and the wind
passed in gusts, the crystals kept on clicking in the greenish
gloom. She went on whispering to herself: 'And yet he was
looking at me! He could see my face, hear my voice, hear my
grief! When I used to sit at his feet, with my cheek against his

knee and his hand on my head, the curse of cruelty and madness was already within him, waiting for the day. The day came! . . . and before the sun had set he could not see me any more — he was made blind and deaf and without pity, as you all are. He shall have no tears from me. Never, never. Not one tear. I will not! He went away from me as if I had been worse than death. He fled as if driven by some accursed thing he had heard or seen in his sleep. . . .'

"Her steady eyes seemed to strain after the shape of a man torn out of her arms by the strength of a dream. She made no sign to my silent bow. I was glad to escape.

"I saw her once again, the same afternoon. On leaving her I had gone in search of Stein, whom I could not find indoors; and I wandered out, pursued by distressful thoughts, into the gardens, those famous gardens of Stein, in which you can find every plant and tree of tropical lowlands. I followed the course of the canalised stream, and sat for a long time on a shaded bench near the ornamental pond, where some waterfowl with clipped wings were diving and splashing noisily. The branches of casuarina-trees behind me swayed lightly, incessantly, reminding me of the soughing of fir-trees at home.

"This mournful and restless sound was a fit accompaniment to my meditations. She had said he had been driven away from her by a dream, — and there was no answer one could make her — there seemed to be no forgiveness for such a transgression. And yet is not mankind itself, pushing on its blind way, driven by a dream of its greatness and its power upon the dark paths of excessive cruelty and of excessive devotion? And what is the pursuit of truth, after all?

"When I rose to get back to the house I caught sight of Stein's drab coat through a gap in the foliage, and very soon at a turn of the path I came upon him walking with the girl. Her little hand rested on his forearm, and under the broad, flat rim of his Panama hat he bent over her, greyhaired, paternal, with compassionate and chivalrous deference. I stood aside, but they stopped, facing me. His gaze was bent on the ground at his feet; the girl, erect and slight on his arm, stared sombrely beyond my shoulder with black, clear, motionless eyes. '*Schrecklich*,' he murmured. 'Terrible! Terrible! What can one do?' He seemed to be appealing to me, but her youth, the length of the days suspended over her head, appealed to me more; and suddenly, even as I realized that nothing could be said, I found myself pleading his cause for her sake. 'You must forgive him,' I concluded, and my own voice seemed to me muffled, lost in an irresponsive deaf immensity. 'We all want to be forgiven,' I added after a while.

" 'What have I done?' she asked with her lips only.

" 'You always mistrusted him,' I said.

" 'He was like the others,' she pronounced slowly.

" 'Not like the others,' I protested, but she continued evenly, without any feeling —

" 'He was false.' And suddenly Stein broke in. 'No! no! no! My poor child! . . .' He patted her hand lying passively on his sleeve. 'No! no! Not false! True! true! true!' He tried to look into her stony face. 'You don't understand. Ach! Why you do not understand? . . . Terrible,' he said to me. 'Some day she *shall* understand.'

" 'Will *you* explain?' I asked, looking hard at him. They moved on.

"I watched them. Her gown trailed on the path, her black hair fell loose. She walked upright and light by the side of the tall man, whose long shapeless coat hung in perpendicular folds from the stooping shoulders, whose feet moved slowly. They disappeared beyond that spinney (you may remember) where sixteen different kinds of bamboo grow together, all distinguishable to the learned eye. For my part, I was fascinated by the exquisite grace and beauty of that fluted grove, crowned with pointed leaves and feathery heads, the lightness, the vigour, the charm as distinct as a voice of that unperplexed luxuriating life. I remember staying to look at it for a long time, as one would linger within reach of a consoling whisper. The sky was pearly grey. It was one of those overcast days so rare in the tropics, in which memories crowd upon one, memories of other shores, of other faces.

"I drove back to town the same afternoon, taking with me Tamb' Itam and the other Malay, in whose seagoing craft they had escaped in the bewilderment, fear, and gloom of the disaster. The shock of it seemed to have changed their natures. It had turned her passion into stone, and it made the surly taciturn Tamb' Itam almost loquacious. His surliness, too, was subdued into puzzled humility, as though he had seen the failure of a potent charm in a supreme moment. The Bugis trader, a shy hesitating man, was very clear in the little he had to say. Both were evidently overawed by a sense of deep inexpressible wonder, by the touch of an inscrutable mystery."

There with Marlow's signature the letter proper ended. The privileged reader screwed up his lamp, and solitary above the billowy roofs of the town, like a lighthouse-keeper above the sea, he turned to the pages of the story.

CHAPTER XXXVIII

"It all begins, as I've told you, with the man called Brown," ran the opening sentence of Marlow's narrative. "You who have knocked about the Western Pacific must have heard of him. He was the show ruffian on the Australian coast — not that he was often to be seen there, but because he was always trotted out in the stories of lawless life a visitor from home is treated to; and the mildest of these stories which were told about him from Cape York to Eden Bay was more than enough to hang a man if told in the right place. They never failed to let you know, too, that he was supposed to be the son of a baronet. Be it as it may, it is certain he had deserted from a home ship in the early gold-digging days, and in a few years became talked about as the terror of this or that group of islands in Polynesia. He would kidnap natives, he would strip some lonely white trader to the very pyjamas he stood in, and after he had robbed the poor devil, he would as likely as not invite him to fight a duel with shot-guns on the beach — which would have been fair enough as these things go, if the other man hadn't been by that time already half-dead with fright. Brown was a latter-day buccaneer, sorry enough, like his more celebrated prototypes; but what distinguished him from his contemporary brother ruffians, like Bully Hayes or the mellifluous Pease, or that perfumed, Dundreary-whiskered, dandified scoundrel known as Dirty Dick, was the arrogant temper of his misdeeds and a vehement scorn for mankind at large

and for his victims in particular. The others were merely vulgar
and greedy brutes, but he seemed moved by some complex intention. He would rob a man as if only to demonstrate his poor
opinion of the creature, and he would bring to the shooting or
maiming of some quiet, unoffending stranger a savage and vengeful earnestness fit to terrify the most reckless of desperadoes.
In the days of his greatest glory he owned an armed barque,
manned by a mixed crew of Kanakas and runaway whalers, and
boasted, I don't know with what truth, of being financed on the
quiet by a most respectable firm of copra merchants. Later on
he ran off — it was reported — with the wife of a missionary, a
very young girl from Clapham way, who had married the mild,
flat-footed fellow in a moment of enthusiasm, and suddenly trans-
planted to Melanesia, lost her bearings somehow. It was a dark
story. She was ill at the time he carried her off, and died on
board his ship. It is said — as the most wonderful part of the tale
— that over her body he gave way to an outburst of sombre and
violent grief. His luck left him, too, very soon after. He lost
his ship on some rocks off Malaita, and disappeared for a time as
though he had gone down with her. He is heard of next at
Nuka-Hiva, where he bought an old French schooner out of
Government service. What creditable enterprise he might have
had in view when he made that purchase I can't say, but it is evident that what with High Commissioners, consuls, men-of-war,
and international control, the South Seas were getting too hot to
hold gentlemen of his kidney. Clearly he must have shifted the
scene of his operations farther west, because a year later he plays
an incredibly audacious, but not a very profitable part, in a serio-
comic business in Manila Bay, in which a peculating governor
and an absconding treasurer are the principal figures; thereafter
he seems to have hung around the Philippines in his rotten
schooner, battling with an adverse fortune, till at last, running
his appointed course, he sails into Jim's history, a blind accomplice of the Dark Powers.

"His tale goes that when a Spanish patrol cutter captured him
he was simply trying to run a few guns for the insurgents. If so,
then I can't understand what he was doing off the south coast
of Mindanao. My belief, however, is that he was blackmailing
the native villages along the coast. The principal thing is that the
cutter, throwing a guard on board, made him sail in company

towards Zamboanga. On the way, for some reason or other, both vessels had to call at one of these new Spanish settlements — which never came to anything in the end — where there was not only a civil official in charge on shore, but a good stout coasting schooner lying at anchor in the little bay; and this craft, in every way much better than his own, Brown made up his mind to steal.

"He was down on his luck — as he told me himself. The world he had bullied for twenty years with fierce, aggressive disdain, had yielded him nothing in the way of material advantage except a small bag of silver dollars, which was concealed in his cabin so that 'the devil himself couldn't smell it out.' And that was all — absolutely all. He was tired of his life, and not afraid of death. But this man, who would stake his existence on a whim with a bitter and jeering recklessness, stood in mortal fear of imprisonment. He had an unreasoning cold-sweat, nerve-shaking, blood-to-water-turning sort of horror at the bare possibility of being locked up — the sort of terror a superstitious man would feel at the thought of being embraced by a spectre. Therefore the civil official who came on board to make a preliminary investigation into the capture, investigated arduously all day long, and only went ashore after dark, muffled up in a cloak, and taking great care not to let Brown's little all clink in its bag. Afterwards, being a man of his word, he contrived (the very next evening, I believe) to send off the Government cutter on some urgent bit of special service. As her commander could not spare a prize crew, he contented himself by taking away before he left all the sails of Brown's schooner to the very last rag, and took good care to tow his two boats on to the beach a couple of miles off.

"But in Brown's crew there was a Solomon Islander, kidnapped in his youth and devoted to Brown, who was the best man of the whole gang. That fellow swam off to the coaster — five hundred yards or so — with the end of a warp made up of all the running gear unrove for the purpose. The water was smooth, and the bay dark, 'like the inside of a cow,' as Brown described it. The Solomon Islander clambered over the bulwarks with the end of the rope in his teeth. The crew of the coaster — all Tagals — were ashore having a jollification in the native village. The two shipkeepers left on board woke up suddenly and saw the devil. It had glittering eyes and leaped quick as lightning about the deck. They fell on their knees, paralysed with fear, crossing themselves and mumbling prayers. With a long knife he found in the caboose the Solomon Islander, without interrupting their orisons, stabbed first one, then the other; with the same knife he set to sawing patiently at the coir cable till suddenly it parted under the blade with a splash. Then in the silence of the bay he let out a cautious shout, and Brown's gang, who meantime had been peering and straining their hopeful ears in the darkness, began to pull gently at their end of the warp. In less than five minutes the two schooners came together with a slight shock and a creak of spars.

"Brown's crowd transferred themselves without losing an instant, taking with them their firearms and a large supply of ammunition. They were sixteen in all: two runaway blue-jackets, a lanky deserter from a Yankee man-of-war, a couple of simple, blond Scandinavians, a mulatto of sorts, one bland Chinaman who cooked — and the rest of the nondescript spawn of the South Seas. None of them cared; Brown bent them to his will, and Brown, indifferent to gallows, was running away from the spectre of a Spanish prison. He didn't give them the time to trans-ship enough provisions; the weather was calm, the air was charged with dew, and when they cast off the ropes and set sail to a faint offshore draught there was no flutter in the damp canvas; their old schooner seemed to detach itself gently from the stolen craft and slip away silently, together with the black mass of the coast, into the night.

"They got clear away. Brown related to me in detail their passage down the Straits of Macassar. It is a harrowing and desperate story. They were short of food and water; they boarded several native craft and got a little from each. With a stolen ship Brown did not dare to put into any port, of course. He had no money to buy anything, no papers to show, and no lie plausible enough to get him out again. An Arab barque, under the Dutch flag, surprised one night at anchor off Poulo Laut, yielded a little dirty rice, a bunch of bananas, and a cask of water; three days of squally misty weather from the north-east shot the schooner across the Java Sea. The yellow muddy waves drenched that collection of hungry ruffians. They sighted mailboats moving on their appointed routes; passed well-found home ships with rusty iron sides anchored in the shallow sea waiting for a change of weather or the turn of the tide; an English gunboat, white and trim, with two slim masts, crossed their bows one day in the distance; and on another occasion a Dutch corvette, black and heavily sparred, loomed upon their quarter, steaming dead slow in the mist. They slipped through unseen or disregarded, a wan, sallow-faced band of utter outcasts, enraged with hunger and hunted by fear. Brown's idea was to make for Madagascar, where he expected, on grounds not altogether illusory, to sell the schooner in Tamatave, and no questions asked, or perhaps obtain some more or less forged papers for her. Yet before he could face the long passage across the Indian Ocean food was wanted — water, too.

"Perhaps he had heard of Patusan — or perhaps he just only happened to see the name written in small letters on the chart — probably that of a largish village up a river in a native state, perfectly defenceless, far from the beaten tracks of the sea and from the ends of submarine cables. He had done that kind of thing before — in the way of business; and this now was an absolute necessity, a question of life and death — or rather of liberty. Of liberty! He was sure to get provisions — bullocks — rice — sweet-potatoes. The sorry gang licked their chops. A cargo of produce for the schooner perhaps could be extorted — and, who knows? — some real ringing coined money! Some of these chiefs and village headmen can be made to part freely. He told me he would have roasted their toes rather than be baulked. I believe him. His men believed him too. They didn't cheer aloud, being a dumb pack, but made ready wolfishly.

"Luck served him as to weather. A few days of calm would have brought unmentionable horrors on board that schooner, but with the help of land and sea breezes, in less than a week after clearing the Sunda Straits, he anchored off the Batu Kring mouth within a pistol-shot of the fishing village.

"Fourteen of them packed into the schooner's longboat (which was big, having been used for cargo-work) and started up the river, while two remained in charge of the schooner with food enough to keep starvation off for ten days. The tide and wind helped, and early one afternoon the big white boat under a ragged sail shouldered its way before the sea breeze into Patusan Reach, manned by fourteen assorted scarecrows glaring hungrily ahead, and fingering the breech-blocks of cheap rifles.

Brown calculated upon the terrifying surprise of his appearance. They sailed in with the last of the flood; the Rajah's stockade gave no sign; the first houses on both sides of the stream seemed deserted. A few canoes were seen up the reach in full flight. Brown was astonished at the size of the place. A profound silence reigned. The wind dropped between the houses; two oars were got out and the boat held on upstream, the idea being to effect a lodgment in the centre of the town before the inhabitants could think of resistance.

"It seems, however, that the headman of the fishing village at Batu Kring had managed to send off a timely warning. When the long-boat came abreast of the mosque (which Doramin had built: a structure with gables and roof finials of carved coral) the open space before it was full of people. A shout went up, and was followed by a clash of gongs all up the river. From a point above two little brass six-pounders were discharged, and the round-shot came skipping down the empty reach, spirting glittering jets of water in the sunshine. In front of the mosque a shouting lot of men began firing in volleys that whipped athwart the current of the river; an irregular, rolling fusillade was opened on the boat from both banks, and Brown's men replied with a wild, rapid fire. The oars had been got in.

"The turn of the tide at high water comes on very quick in that river, and the boat in midstream, nearly hidden in smoke, began to drift back stern foremost. Along both shores the smoke thickened also, lying below the roofs in a level streak as you may see a long cloud cutting the slope of a mountain. A tumult of war-cries, the vibrating clang of gongs, the deep snoring of drums, yells of rage, crashes of volley-firing, made an awful din, in which Brown sat confounded but steady at the tiller, working himself into a fury of hate and rage against those people who dared to defend themselves. Two of his men had been wounded, and he saw his retreat cut off below the town by some boats that had put off from Tunku Allang's stockade. There were six of them full of men. While he was thus beset he perceived the entrance of the narrow creek (the same which Jim had jumped at low water). It was then brim full. Steering the long-boat in, they landed, and, to make a long story short, they established themselves on a little knoll about 900 yards from the stockade, which,

in fact, they commanded from that position. The slopes of the
knoll were bare, but there were a few trees on the summit. They
went to work cutting these down for a breastwork, and were
fairly intrenched before dark; meantime the Rajah's boats remained in the river with curious neutrality. When the sun set
the glare of many brushwood blazes lighted on the river-front,
and between the double line of houses on the land side threw
into black relief the roofs, the groups of slender palms, the heavy
clumps of fruit-trees. Brown ordered the grass round his position to be fired; a low ring of thin flames under the slow, ascending smoke wriggled rapidly down the slopes of the knoll; here
and there a dry bush caught with a tall, vicious roar. The conflagration made a clear zone of fire for the rifles of the small
party, and expired smouldering on the edge of the forests and
along the muddy bank of the creek. A strip of jungle luxuriating in a damp hollow between the knoll and the Rajah's stockade
stopped it on that side with a great crackling and detonations
of bursting bamboo stems. The sky was sombre, velvety, and
swarming with stars. The blackened ground smoked quietly
with low creeping wisps, till a little breeze came on and blew
everything away. Brown expected an attack to be delivered as
soon as the tide had flowed enough again to enable the war-boats
which had cut off his retreat to enter the creek. At any rate
he was sure there would be an attempt to carry off his long-
boat, which lay below the hill, a dark high lump on the feeble
sheen of a wet mud-flat. But no move of any sort was made by
the boats in the river. Over the stockade and the Rajah's buildings Brown saw their lights on the water. They seemed to be
anchored across the stream. Other lights afloat were moving in
the reach, crossing and recrossing from side to side. There were
also lights twinkling motionless upon the long walls of houses up
the reach, as far as the bend, and more still beyond, others isolated inland. The loom of the big fires disclosed buildings, roofs,
black piles as far as he could see. It was an immense place. The
fourteen desperate invaders lying flat behind the felled trees raised
their chins to look over at the stir of that town that seemed to
extend up-river for miles and swarm with thousands of angry
men. They did not speak to each other. Now and then they
would hear a loud yell, or a single shot rang out, fired very far

somewhere. But round their position everything was still, dark, silent. They seemed to be forgotten, as if the excitement keeping awake all the population had nothing to do with them, as if they had been dead already."

CHAPTER XXXIX

"ALL the events of that night have a great importance, since they brought about a situation which remained unchanged till Jim's return. Jim had been away in the interior for more than a week, and it was Dain Waris who had directed the first repulse. That brave and intelligent youth ('who knew how to fight after the manner of white men') wished to settle the business off-hand, but his people were too much for him. He had not Jim's racial prestige and the reputation of invincible, supernatural power. He was not the visible, tangible incarnation of unfailing truth and of unfailing victory. Beloved, trusted, and admired as he was, he was still one of *them*, while Jim was one of *us*. Moreover, the white man, a tower of strength in himself, was invulnerable, while Dain Waris could be killed. Those unexpressed thoughts guided the opinions of the chief men of the town, who elected to assemble in Jim's fort for deliberation upon the emergency, as if expecting to find wisdom and courage in the dwelling of the absent white man. The shooting of Brown's ruffians was so far good, or lucky, that there had been half-a-dozen casualties amongst the defenders. The wounded were lying on the verandah tended by their women-folk. The women and children from the lower part of the town had been sent into the fort at the first alarm. There Jewel was in command, very efficient and high-spirited, obeyed by Jim's 'own people,' who, quitting in a body their little settlement under the stockade, had gone in to form the garrison. The refugees crowded round her; and through the whole affair, to the very disastrous last, she showed an extraordinary martial ardour. It was to her that Dain Waris had gone at once at the first intelligence of danger, for you must know that Jim was the only one in Patusan who possessed a store of gunpowder. Stein, with whom he had kept up intimate relations by letters, had obtained from the Dutch Government a special authorisation to export five hundred kegs of it to Patusan. The powder-magazine was a small hut of rough logs covered entirely with earth, and in Jim's absence the girl had the key. In the council, held at eleven o'clock in the evening in Jim's dining-room, she backed up Waris's advice for immediate and vigorous action. I am told that she stood up by the side of Jim's empty chair at the head of the long table and made a warlike impassioned speech, which for the moment extorted murmurs of approbation from the assembled headmen. Old Doramin, who had not showed himself outside his own gate for more than a year, had been brought across with great difficulty. He was, of course, the chief man there. The temper of the council was very unforgiving, and the old man's word would have been decisive; but it is my opinion that, well aware of his son's fiery courage, he dared not pronounce the word. More dilatory counsels prevailed. A certain Haji Saman pointed out at great length that 'these tyrannical and ferocious men had delivered themselves to a certain death in any case. They would stand fast on their hill and starve, or they would try to regain their boat and be shot from ambushes across the creek, or they would break and fly into the forest and perish singly there.' He argued that by the use of proper stratagems these evil-minded strangers could be destroyed without the risk of a battle, and his words had a great weight, especially with the Patusan men proper. What unsettled the minds of the townsfolk was the failure of the Rajah's boats to act at the decisive moment. It was the diplomatic Kassim who represented the Rajah at the council. He spoke very little, listened smilingly, very friendly and impenetrable. During the sitting messengers kept arriving every few minutes almost, with reports of the invaders' proceedings. Wild and exaggerated rumours were flying: there was a large ship at the mouth of the river with big guns and many more men — some white, others with black skins and of bloodthirsty appearance. They were coming with many more boats to exterminate every living thing. A sense of near, incomprehensible danger affected the common people. At one moment there was a panic in the courtyard amongst the women; shrieking; a rush; children crying — Haji Saman went out to quiet them. Then a fort sentry fired at something moving on the river, and nearly killed a villager bringing in his women-folk in a canoe together with the best of his domestic utensils and a dozen fowls. This caused more confusion. Meantime the palaver inside Jim's house went on in the presence of the girl. Doramin sat fierce-faced, heavy, looking at the speakers in turn, and breathing slow like a bull. He didn't speak till the last, after Kassim had declared that the Rajah's boats would be called in because the men were required to defend his master's stockade. Dain Waris in his father's presence would offer no opinion, though the girl entreated him in Jim's name to speak out. She offered him Jim's own men in her anxiety to have these intruders driven out at once. He only shook his head, after a glance or two at Doramin. Finally, when the council broke up it had been decided that the houses nearest the creek should be strongly occupied to obtain the command of the enemy's boat. The boat itself was not to be interfered with openly, so that the robbers on the hill should be tempted to embark, when a well-directed fire would kill most of them, no doubt. To cut the escape of those who might survive, and to prevent more of them coming up, Dain Waris was ordered by Doramin to take an armed party of Bugis down the river to a certain spot ten miles below Patusan, and there form a camp on the shore and blockade the stream with the canoes. I don't believe for a moment that Doramin feared the arrival of fresh forces. My opinion is, that his conduct was guided solely by his wish to keep his son out of harm's way. To prevent a rush being made into the town the construction of a stockade was to be commenced at daylight at the end of the street on the left bank. The old *nakhoda* declared his intention to command there himself. A distribution of powder, bullets, and percussion caps was made immediately under the girl's supervision. Several messengers were to be despatched in different directions after Jim, whose exact whereabouts were unknown. These men started at dawn, but before that time Kassim had managed to open communications with the besieged Brown.

"That accomplished diplomatist and confidant of the Rajah, on leaving the fort to go back to his master, took into his boat Cornelius, whom he found slinking mutely amongst the people in the courtyard. Kassim had a little plan of his own and wanted him for an interpreter. Thus it came about that towards morning Brown, reflecting upon the desperate nature of his position, heard from the marshy overgrown hollow an amicable, quavering, strained voice crying — in English — for permission to come up, under a promise of personal safety and on a very important errand. He was overjoyed. If he was spoken to he was no longer a hunted wild beast. These friendly sounds took off at once the awful stress of vigilant watchfulness as of so many blind men not knowing whence the deathblow might come. He pretended a great reluctance. The voice declared itself 'a white man. A poor, ruined, old man who had been living here for years.' A mist, wet and chilly, lay on the slopes of the hill, and after some more shouting from one to the other, Brown called out, 'Come on, then, but alone, mind!' As a matter of fact — he told me, writhing with rage at the recollection of his helplessness — it made no difference. They couldn't see more than a few yards before them, and no treachery could make their position worse. By-and-by Cornelius, in his week-day attire of a ragged dirty shirt and pants, barefooted, with a broken-rimmed pith hat on his head, was made out vaguely, sidling up to the defences, hesitating, stopping to listen in a peering posture. 'Come along! You are safe,' yelled Brown, while his men stared. All their hopes of life became suddenly centred in that dilapidated, mean new-comer, who in profound silence clambered clumsily over a felled tree-trunk, and shivering, with his sour mistrustful face, looked about at the knot of bearded anxious, sleepless desperadoes.

"Half an hour's confidential talk with Cornelius opened Brown's eyes as to the home affairs of Patusan. He was on the alert at once. There were possibilities, immense possibilities; but before he would talk over Cornelius's proposals he demanded that some food should be sent up as a guarantee of good faith. Cornelius went off, creeping sluggishly down the hill on the side of the Rajah's palace, and after some delay a few of Tunku Allang's men came up, bringing a scanty supply of rice, chillies, and dried fish. This was immeasurably better than nothing. Later on Cornelius returned accompanying Kassim, who stepped out with an air of perfect good-humoured trustfulness, in sandals, and muffled up from neck to ankles in dark-blue sheeting. He shook hands with Brown discreetly, and the three drew aside for a conference. Brown's men, recovering their confidence, were slapping each other on the back, and cast knowing glances at their captain while they busied themselves with preparations for cooking.

"Kassim disliked Doramin and his Bugis very much, but he

hated the new order of things still more. It had occurred to him that these whites, together with the Rajah's followers, could attack and defeat the Bugis before Jim's return. Then, he reasoned, general defection of the townsfolk was sure to follow, and the reign of the white man who protected poor people would be over. Afterwards the new allies could be dealt with. They would have no friends. The fellow was perfectly able to perceive the difference of character, and had seen enough of white men to know that these new-comers were outcasts, men without country. Brown preserved a stern and inscrutable demeanour. When he first heard Cornelius's voice demanding admittance, it brought merely the hope of a loophole for escape. In less than an hour other thoughts were seething in his head. Urged by an extreme necessity, he had come there to steal food, a few tons of rubber or gum maybe, perhaps a handful of dollars, and had found himself enmeshed by deadly dangers. Now in consequence of these overtures from Kassim he began to think of stealing the whole country. Some confounded fellow had apparently accomplished something of the kind — single-handed at that. Couldn't have done it very well though. Perhaps they could work together — squeeze everything dry and then go out quietly. In the course of his negotiations with Kassim he became aware that he was supposed to have a big ship with plenty of men outside. Kassim begged him earnestly to have this big ship with his many guns and men brought up the river without delay for the Rajah's service. Brown professed himself willing, and on this basis the negotiation was carried on with mutual distrust. Three times in the course of the morning the courteous and active Kassim went down to consult the Rajah and came up busily with his long stride. Brown, while bargaining, had a sort of grim enjoyment in thinking of his wretched schooner, with nothing but a heap of dirt in her hold, that stood for an armed ship, and a Chinaman and a lame ex-beachcomber of Levuka on board, who represented all his many men. In the afternoon he obtained further doles of food, a promise of some money, and a supply of mats for his men to make shelters for themselves. They lay down and snored, protected from the burning sunshine; but Brown, sitting fully exposed on one of the felled trees, feasted his eyes upon the view of the town and the river. There was much loot here. Cornelius, who had made himself at home in the camp, talked at his elbow, pointing out the localities, imparting advice, giving his own version of Jim's character, and commenting in his own fashion upon the events of the last three years. Brown, who, apparently indifferent and gazing away, listened with attention to every word, could not make out clearly what sort of man this Jim could be. 'What's his name? Jim! Jim! That's not enough for a man's name.' 'They call him,' said Cornelius, scornfully, 'Tuan Jim here. As you may say Lord Jim.' 'What is he? Where does he come from?' inquired Brown. 'What sort of man is he? Is he an Englishman?' 'Yes, yes, he's an Englishman. I am an Englishman, too. From Malacca. He is a fool. All you have to do is to kill him and then you are king here. Everything belongs to him,' explained Cornelius. 'It strikes me he may be made to share with somebody before very long,' commented Brown half aloud. 'No, no. The proper way is to kill him the first chance you get, and then you can do what you like,' Cornelius would insist earnestly. 'I have lived for many years here, and I am giving you a friend's advice.'

"In such converse and in gloating over the view of Patusan, which he had determined in his mind should become his prey, Brown whiled away most of the afternoon, his men, meantime, resting. On that day Dain Waris's fleet of canoes stole one by one under the shore farthest from the creek, and went down to close the river against his retreat. Of this Brown was not aware, and Kassim, who came up the knoll an hour before sunset took good care not to enlighten him. He wanted the white man's ship to come up the river, and this news, he feared, would be discouraging. He was very pressing with Brown to send the 'order,' offering at the same time a trusty messenger, who for greater secrecy (as he explained) would make his way by land to the mouth of the river and deliver the 'order' on board. After some reflection Brown judged it expedient to tear a page out of his pocket-book, on which he simply wrote, 'We are getting on. Big job. Detain the man.' The stolid youth selected by Kassim for that service performed it faithfully, and was rewarded by being suddenly tipped, head first, into the schooner's empty hold by the ex-beachcomber and the Chinaman, who thereupon hastened to put on the hatches. What become of him afterwards Brown did not say."

CHAPTER XL

"Brown's object was to gain time by fooling with Kassim's diplomacy. For doing a real stroke of business he could not help thinking the white man was the person to work with. He could not imagine such a chap (who must be confoundedly clever after all to get hold of the natives like that) refusing a help that would do away with the necessity for slow, cautious, risky cheating, that imposed itself as the only possible line of conduct for a single-handed man. He, Brown, would offer him the power. No man could hesitate. Everything was in coming to a clear understanding. Of course they would share. The idea of there being a fort — all ready to his hand — a real fort, with artillery (he knew this from Cornelius), excited him. Let him only once get in and . . . He would impose modest conditions. Not too low, though. The man was no fool, it seemed. They would work like brothers till . . . till the time came for a quarrel and a shot that would settle all accounts. With grim impatience of plunder he wished himself to be talking with the man now. The land already seemed to be his to tear to pieces, squeeze, and throw away. Meantime Kassim had to be fooled for the sake of food first — and for a second string. But the principal thing was to get something to eat from day to day. Besides, he was not averse to begin fighting on that Rajah's account, and teach a lesson to those people who had received him with shots. The lust of battle was upon him.

"I am sorry that I can't give you this part of the story, which of course I have mainly from Brown, in Brown's own words. There was in the broken, violent speech of that man, unveiling before me his thoughts with the very hand of Death upon his throat, an undisguised ruthlessness of purpose, a strange vengeful attitude towards his own past, and a blind relief in the righteousness of his will against all mankind, something of that feeling which could induce the leader of a horde of wandering cutthroats to call himself proudly the Scourge of God. No doubt the natural senseless ferocity which is the basis of such a char-

acter was exasperated by failure, ill-luck, and the recent privations, as well as by the desperate position in which he found
himself; but what was most remarkable of all was this, that while
he planned treacherous alliances, had already settled in his own
mind the fate of the white man, and intrigued in an overbearing,
offhand manner with Kassim, one could perceive that what he
had really desired, almost in spite of himself, was to play havoc
with that jungle town which had defied him, to see it strewn
over with corpses and enveloped in flames. Listening to his pitiless, panting voice, I could imagine how he must have looked at
it from the hillock, peopling it with images of murder and rapine.
The part nearest to the creek wore an abandoned aspect, though
as a matter of fact every house concealed a few armed men on
the alert. Suddenly beyond the stretch of waste ground, inter-
spersed with small patches of low dense bush, excavations, heaps
of rubbish, with trodden paths between, a man, solitary and
looking very small, strolled out into the deserted opening of the
street between the shut-up, dark, lifeless buildings at the end.
Perhaps one of the inhabitants, who had fled to the other bank
of the river, coming back for some object of domestic use. Evidently he supposed himself quite safe at that distance from the
hill on the other side of the creek. A light stockade, set up hastily, was just round the turn of the street, full of his friends. He
moved leisurely. Brown saw him, and instantly called to his side
the Yankee deserter, who acted as a sort of second in command.
This lanky, loose-jointed fellow came forward, wooden-faced,
trailing his rifle lazily. When he understood what was wanted
from him a homicidal and conceited smile uncovered his teeth,
making two deep folds down his sallow, leathery cheeks. He
prided himself on being a dead shot. He dropped on one knee,
and taking aim from a steady rest through the unlopped branches
of a felled tree, fired, and at once stood up to look. The man,
far away, turned his head to the report, made another step forward, seemed to hesitate, and abruptly got down on his hands
and knees. In the silence that fell upon the sharp crack of the
rifle, the dead shot, keeping his eyes fixed upon the quarry,
guessed that 'this there coon's health would never be a source of
anxiety to his friends any more.' The man's limbs were seen to
move rapidly under his body in an endeavour to run on all-fours.
In that empty space arose a multitudinous shout of dismay and

surprise. The man sank flat, face down, and moved no more. 'That showed them what we could do,' said Brown to me. 'Struck the fear of sudden death into them. That was what we wanted. They were two hundred to one, and this gave them something to think over for the night. Not one of them had an idea of such a long shot before. That beggar belonging to the Rajah scouted down-hill with his eyes hanging out of his head.'

"As he was telling me this he tried with a shaking hand to wipe the thin foam on his blue lips. 'Two hundred to one. Two hundred to one . . . strike terror . . . terror, terror, I tell you. . . .' His own eyes were starting out of their sockets. He fell back, clawing the air with skinny fingers, sat up again, bowed and hairy, glared at me sideways like some man-beast of folklore, with open mouth in his miserable and awful agony before he got his speech back after that fit. There are sights one never forgets.

"Furthermore, to draw the enemy's fire and locate such parties as might have been hiding in the bushes along the creek, Brown ordered the Solomon Islander to go down to the boat and bring an oar, as you send a spaniel after a stick into the water. This failed, and the fellow came back without a single shot having been fired at him from anywhere. 'There's nobody,' opined some of the men. It is 'onnatural,' remarked the Yankee. Kassim had gone, by that time, very much impressed, pleased, too, and also uneasy. Pursuing his tortuous policy, he had despatched a message to Dain Waris warning him to look out for the white men's ship, which, he had had information, was about to come up the river. He minimised its strength and exhorted him to oppose its passage. This double-dealing answered his purpose, which was to keep the Bugis forces divided and to weaken them by fighting. On the other hand, he had in the course of that day sent word to the assembled Bugis chiefs in town, assuring them that he was trying to induce the invaders to retire; his messages to the fort asked earnestly for powder for the Rajah's men. It was a long time since Tunku Allang had had ammunition for the score or so of old muskets rusting in their arm-racks in the audience-hall. The open intercourse between the hill and the palace unsettled all the minds. It was already time for men to take sides, it began to be said. There would soon be much bloodshed, and thereafter great trouble for many people. The social fabric of orderly, peaceful life, when every man was sure of to-morrow, the edifice raised by Jim's hands, seemed on that evening ready to collapse into a ruin reeking with blood. The poorer folk were already taking to the bush or flying up the river. A good many of the upper class judged it necessary to go and pay their court to the Rajah. The Rajah's youths jostled them rudely. Old Tunku Allang, almost out of his mind with fear and indecision, either kept a sullen silence or abused them violently for daring to come with empty hands: they departed very much frightened; only old Doramin kept his countrymen together and pursued his tactics inflexibly. Enthroned in a big chair behind the improvised stockade, he issued his orders in a deep veiled rumble, unmoved, like a deaf man, in the flying rumours.

"Dusk fell, hiding first the body of the dead man, which had been left lying with arms outstretched as if nailed to the ground, and then the revolving sphere of the night rolled smoothly over Patusan and came to a rest, showering the glitter of countless worlds upon the earth. Again, in the exposed part of the town big fires blazed along the only street, revealing from distance to distance upon their glares the falling straight lines of roofs, the fragments of wattled walls jumbled in confusion, here and there a whole hut elevated in the glow upon the vertical black stripes of a group of high piles; and all this line of dwellings, revealed in patches by the swaying flames, seemed to flicker tortuously away up-river into the gloom at the heart of the land. A great silence, in which the looms of successive fires played without noise, extended into the darkness at the foot of the hill; but the other bank of the river, all dark save for a solitary bonfire at the river-front before the fort, sent out into the air an increasing tremor that might have been the stamping of a multitude of feet, the hum of many voices, or the fall of an immensely distant waterfall. It was then, Brown confessed to me, while, turning his back on his men, he sat looking at it all, that notwithstanding his disdain, his ruthless faith in himself, a feeling came over him that at last he had run his head against a stone wall. Had his boat been afloat at the time, he believed he would have tried to steal away, taking his chances of a long chase down the river and of starvation at sea. It was very doubtful whether he would have succeeded in getting away. However, he didn't try this. For an-

other moment he had a passing thought of trying to rush the
town, but he perceived very well that in the end he would find
himself in the lighted street, where they would be shot down like
dogs from the houses. They were two hundred to one — he
thought, while his men, huddling round two heaps of smouldering embers, munched the last of the bananas and roasted the few
yams they owed to Kassim's diplomacy. Cornelius sat amongst
them dozing sulkily.

"Then one of the whites remembered that some tobacco had
been left in the boat, and, encouraged by the impunity of the
Solomon Islander, said he would go to fetch it. At this all the
others shook off their despondency. Brown applied to, said, 'Go,
and be d—d to you,' scornfully. He didn't think there was any
danger in going to the creek in the dark. The man threw a leg
over the tree-trunk and disappeared. A moment later he was
heard clambering into the boat and then clambering out. 'I've
got it,' he cried. A flash and a report at the very foot of the hill
followed. 'I am hit,' yelled the man. 'Look out, look out — I am
hit,' and instantly all the rifles went off. The hill squirted fire
and noise into the night like a little volcano, and when Brown
and the Yankee with curses and cuffs stopped the panic-stricken
firing, a profound, weary groan floated up from the creek, succeeded by a plaint whose heart-rending sadness was like some
poison turning the blood cold in the veins. Then a strong voice
pronounced several distinct incomprehensible words somewhere
beyond the creek. 'Let no one fire,' shouted Brown. 'What does
it mean?' . . . 'Do you hear on the hill? Do you hear? Do you
hear?' repeated the voice three times. Cornelius translated, and
then prompted the answer. 'Speak,' cried Brown, 'we hear.' Then
the voice, declaiming in the sonorous inflated tone of a herald,
and shifting continually on the edge of the vague waste-land,
proclaimed that between the men of the Bugis nation living in
Patusan and the white men on the hill and those with them, there
would be no faith, no compassion, no speech, no peace. A bush
rustled; a haphazard volley rang out. 'Dam' foolishness,' muttered the Yankee, vexedly grounding the butt. Cornelius translated. The wounded man below the hill, after crying out twice,
'Take me up! take me up!' went on complaining in moans. While
he had kept on the blackened earth of the slope and afterwards
crouching in the boat, he had been safe enough. It seems that in

his joy at finding tobacco he forgot himself and jumped out on her off-side, as it were. The white boat, lying high and dry, showed him up; the creek was no more than seven yards wide in that place, and there happened to be a man crouching in the bush on the other bank.

"He was a Bugis of Tondano only lately come to Patusan, and a relation of the man shot in the afternoon. That famous long shot had indeed appalled the beholders. The man in utter security had been struck down, in full view of his friends, dropping with a joke on his lips, and they seemed to see in the act an atrocity which had stirred a bitter rage. That relation of his, Si-Lapa by name, was then with Doramin in the stockade only a few feet away. You who know these chaps must admit that the fellow showed an unusual pluck by volunteering to carry the message, alone, in the dark. Creeping across the open ground, he had deviated to the left and found himself opposite the boat. He was startled when Brown's man shouted. He came to a sitting position with his gun to his shoulder, and when the other jumped out, exposing himself, he pulled the trigger and lodged three jagged slugs point-blank into the poor wretch's stomach. Then, lying flat on his face, he gave himself up for dead, while a thin hail of lead chopped and swished the bushes close on his right hand; afterwards he delivered his speech shouting, bent double, dodging all the time in cover. With the last word he leaped sideways, lay close for a while, and afterwards got back to the houses unharmed, having achieved on that night such a renown as his children will not willingly allow to die.

"And on the hill the forlorn band let the two little heaps of embers go out under their bowed heads. They sat dejected on the ground with compressed lips and downcast eyes, listening to their comrade below. He was a strong man and died hard, with moans now loud, now sinking to a strange confidential note of pain. Sometimes he shrieked, and again, after a period of silence, he could be heard muttering deliriously a long and unintelligible complaint. Never for a moment did he cease.

"'What's the good?' Brown had said unmoved once, seeing the Yankee, who had been swearing under his breath, prepare to go down. 'That's so,' assented the deserter, reluctantly desisting. 'There's no encouragement for wounded men here. Only his noise is calculated to make all the others think too much of the hereafter, cap'n.' 'Water!' cried the wounded man in an extraordinarily clear vigorous voice, and then went off moaning feebly. 'Ay, water. Water will do it,' muttered the other to himself, resignedly. 'Plenty by-and-by. The tide is flowing.'

"At last the tide flowed, silencing the plaint and the cries of pain, and the dawn was near when Brown, sitting with his chin in the palm of his hand before Patusan, as one might stare at the unscalable side of a mountain, heard the brief ringing bark of a brass six-pounder far away in town somewhere. 'What's this?' he asked of Cornelius, who hung about him. Cornelius listened. A muffled roaring shout rolled down-river over the town; a big drum began to throb, and others responded, pulsating and droning. Tiny scattered lights began to twinkle in the dark half of the town, while the part lighted by the loom of fires hummed with a deep and prolonged murmur. 'He has come,' said Cornelius. 'What? Already? Are you sure?' Brown asked. 'Yes! yes! Sure. Listen to the noise.' 'What are they making that row about?' pursued Brown. 'For joy,' snorted Cornelius; 'he is a very great man, but all the same, he knows no more than a child, and so they make a great noise to please him, because they know no better.' 'Look here,' said Brown, 'how is one to get at him?' 'He shall come to talk to you,' Cornelius declared. 'What do you mean? Come down here strolling as it were?' Cornelius nodded vigorously in the dark. 'Yes. He will come straight here and talk to you. He is just like a fool. You shall see what a fool he is.' Brown was incredulous. 'You shall see; you shall see,' repeated Cornelius. 'He is not afraid — not afraid of anything. He will come and order you to leave his people alone. Everybody must leave his people alone. He is like a little child. He will come to you straight.' Alas! he knew Jim well — that 'mean little skunk,' as Brown called him to me. 'Yes, certainly,' he pursued with ardour, 'and then, captain, you tell that tall man with a gun to shoot him. Just you kill him, and you shall frighten everybody so much that you can do anything you like with them afterwards — get what you like — go away when you like. Ha! ha! ha! Fine. . . .' He almost danced with impatience and eagerness; and Brown, looking over his shoulder at him, could see, shown up by the pitiless dawn, his men drenched with dew, sitting amongst the cold ashes and the litter of the camp, haggard, cowed, and in rags."

CHAPTER XLI

"To THE very last moment, till the full day came upon them with a spring, the fires on the west bank blazed bright and clear; and then Brown saw in a knot of coloured figures motionless between the advanced houses a man in European clothes, in a helmet, all white. 'That's him; look! look!' Cornelius said excitedly. All Brown's men had sprung up and crowded at his back with lustreless eyes. The group of vivid colours and dark faces with the white figure in the midst were observing the knoll. Brown could see naked arms being raised to shade the eyes and other brown arms pointing. What should he do? He looked around, and the forests that faced him on all sides walled the cock-pit of an unequal contest. He looked once more at his men. A contempt, a weariness, the desire of life, the wish to try for one more chance — for some other grave — struggled in his breast. From the outline the figure presented it seemed to him that the white man there, backed up by all the power of the land, was examining his position through binoculars. Brown jumped up on the log, throwing his arms up, the palms outwards. The coloured group closed round the white man, and fell back twice before he got clear of them, walking slowly alone. Brown remained standing on the log till Jim, appearing and disappearing between the patches of thorny scrub, had nearly reached the creek; then Brown jumped off and went down to meet him on his side.

"They met, I should think, not very far from the place, perhaps on the very spot, where Jim took the second desperate leap of his life — the leap that landed him into the life of Patusan, into the trust, the love, the confidence of the people. They faced each other across the creek, and with steady eyes tried to understand each other before they opened their lips. Their antagonism must have been expressed in their glances; I know that Brown hated Jim at first sight. Whatever hopes he might have had vanished at once. This was not the man he had expected to see. He hated him for this — and in a checked flannel shirt with

273

sleeves cut off at the elbows, grey bearded, with a sunken, sun-
blackened face — he cursed in his heart the other's youth and
assurance, his clear eyes and his untroubled bearing. That fellow had got in a long way before him! He did not look like a
man who would be willing to give anything for assistance. He
had all the advantages on his side — possession, security, power;
he was on the side of an overwhelming force! He was not hungry and desperate, and he did not seem in the least afraid. And
there was something in the very neatness of Jim's clothes, from
the white helmet to the canvas leggings and the pipe-clayed shoes,
which in Brown's sombre irritated eyes seemed to belong to
things he had in the very shaping of his life contemned and
flouted.

" 'Who are you?' asked Jim at last, speaking in his usual voice.
'My name's Brown,' answered the other, loudly; 'Captain Brown.
What's yours?' and Jim after a little pause went on quietly, as if
he had not heard: 'What made you come here?' 'You want to
know,' said Brown, bitterly. 'It's easy to tell. Hunger. And
what made you?'

" 'The fellow started at this,' said Brown, relating to me the
opening of this strange conversation between those two men,
separated only by the muddy bed of a creek, but standing on the
opposite poles of that conception of life which includes all mankind — 'The fellow started at this and got very red in the face.
Too big to be questioned, I suppose. I told him that if he looked
upon me as a dead man with whom you may take liberties, he
himself was not a whit better off really. I had a fellow up there
who had a bead drawn on him all the time, and only waited for
a sign from me. There was nothing to be shocked at in this.
He had come down of his own freewill. "Let us agree," said I,
"that we are both dead men, and let us talk on that basis, as
equals. We are all equal before death," I said. I admitted I was
there like a rat in a trap, but we had been driven to it, and even
a trapped rat can give a bite. He caught me up in a moment.
"Not if you don't go near the trap till the rat is dead." I told him
that sort of game was good enough for these native friends of
his, but I would have thought him too white to serve even a rat
so. Yes, I had wanted to talk with him. Not to beg for my life,
though. My fellows were — well — what they were — men like
himself, anyhow. All we wanted from him was to come on in

the devil's name and have it out. "God d—n it," said I, while
he stood there as still as a wooden post, "you don't want to come
out here every day with your glasses to count how many of us
are left on our feet. Come. Either bring your infernal crowd
along or let us go out and starve in the open sea, by God! You
have been white once, for all your tall talk of this being your
own people and you being one with them. Are you? And what
the devil do you get for it; what is it you've found here that is
so d—d precious? Hey? You don't want us to come down here
perhaps — do you? You are two hundred to one. You don't want
us to come down into the open. Ah! I promise you we shall
give you some sport before you've done. You talk about me
making a cowardly set upon unoffending people. What's that
to me that they are unoffending when I am starving for next to
no offence? But I am not a coward. Don't you be one. Bring
them along or, by all the fiends, we shall yet manage to send half
your unoffending town to heaven with us in smoke!" '

"He was terrible — relating this to me — this tortured skeleton
of a man drawn up together with his face over his knees, upon
a miserable bed in that wretched hovel, and lifting his head to
look at me with malignant triumph.

" 'That's what I told him — I knew what to say,' he began
again, feebly at first, but working himself up with incredible
speed into a fiery utterance of his scorn. 'We aren't going into
the forest to wander like a string of living skeletons dropping one
after another for ants to go to work upon us before we are fairly
dead. Oh, no! . . . "You don't deserve a better fate," he said.
"And what do you deserve," I shouted at him, "you that I find
skulking here with your mouth full of your responsibility, of innocent lives, of your infernal duty? What do you know more
of me than I know of you? I came here for food. D'ye hear?
— food to fill our bellies. And what did *you* come for? What
did you ask for when you came here? We don't ask you for
anything but to give us a fight or a clear road to go back whence
we came. . . ." "I would fight with you now," says he, pulling
at his little moustache. "And I would let you shoot me, and welcome," I said. "This is as good a jumping-off place for me as
another. I am sick of my infernal luck. But it would be too
easy. There are my men in the same boat — and, by God, I am
not the sort to jump out of trouble and leave them in a d—d

lurch," I said. He stood thinking for a while and then wanted to know what I had done ("out there," he says, tossing his head down-stream) to be hazed about so. "Have we met to tell each other the story of our lives?" I asked him. "Suppose you begin. No? Well, I am sure I don't want to hear. Keep it to yourself. I know it is no better than mine. I've lived — and so did you though you talk as if you were one of those people that should have wings so as to go about without touching the dirty earth. Well — it is dirty. I haven't got any wings. I am here because I was afraid once in my life. Want to know what of? Of a prison. That scares me, and you may know it — if it's any good to you. I won't ask you what scared you into this infernal hole, where you seem to have found pretty pickings. That's your luck and this is mine — the privilege to beg for the favour of being shot quickly, or else kicked out to go free and starve in my own way."' . . .

"His debilitated body shook with an exultation so vehement, so assured, and so malicious that it seemed to have driven off the death waiting for him in that hut. The corpse of his mad self-love uprose from rags and destitution as from the dark horrors of a tomb. It is impossible to say how much he lied to Jim then, how much he lied to me now — and to himself always. Vanity plays lurid tricks with our memory, and the truth of every passion wants some pretence to make it live. Standing at the gate of the other world in the guise of a beggar, he had slapped this world's face, he had spat on it, he had thrown upon it an immensity of scorn and revolt at the bottom of his misdeeds. He had overcome them all — men, women, savages, traders, ruffians, missionaries — and Jim — that beefy-faced beggar. I did not begrudge him this triumph *in articulo mortis*, this almost posthumous illusion of having trampled all the earth under his feet. While he was boasting to me, in his sordid and repulsive agony, I couldn't help thinking of the chuckling talk relating to the time of his greatest splendour when, during a year or more, Gentleman Brown's ship was to be seen, for many days on end, hovering off an islet befringed with green upon azure, with the dark lot of the mission-house on a white beach; while Gentleman Brown, ashore, was casting his spells over a romantic girl for whom Melanesia had been too much, and giving hopes of a remarkable conversion to her husband. The poor man, some time or other, had been heard to express the intention of winning 'Captain Brown to a better way of life.' . . . 'Bag Gentleman Brown for Glory' — as a leery-eyed loafer expressed it once — 'just to let them see up above what a Western Pacific trading skipper looks like.' And this was the man, too, who had run off with a dying woman, and had shed tears over her body. 'Carried on like a big baby,' his then mate was never tired of telling, 'and where the fun came in may I be kicked to death by diseased Kanakas if *I* know. Why, gents! she was too far gone when he brought her aboard to know him; she just lay there on her back in his bunk staring at the beam with awful shining eyes — and then she died. Dam' bad sort of fever, I guess. . . .' I remembered all these stories while, wiping his matted lump of a beard with a livid hand, he was telling me from his noisome couch how he got round, got in, got home, on that confounded, immaculate, don't-you-touch-me sort of fellow. He admitted that he couldn't be scared, but there was a way, 'as broad as a turnpike, to get in and shake his twopenny soul around and inside out and upside down — by God!' "

CHAPTER XLII

"I DON'T think he could do more than perhaps look upon that straight path. He seemed to have been puzzled by what he saw, for he interrupted himself in his narrative more than once to exclaim, 'He nearly slipped from me there. I could not make him out. Who was he?' And after glaring at me wildly he would go on, jubilating and sneering. To me the conversation of these two across the creek appears now as the deadliest kind of duel on which Fate looked on with her cold-eyed knowledge of the end. No, he didn't turn Jim's soul inside out, but I am much mistaken if the spirit so utterly out of his reach had not been made to taste to the full the bitterness of that contest. These were the emissaries with whom the world he had renounced was pursuing him in his retreat. White men from 'out there' where he did

not think himself good enough to live. This was all that came
to him — a menace, a shock, a danger to his work. I suppose it
is this sad, half-resentful, half-resigned feeling, piercing through
the few words Jim said now and then, that puzzled Brown so
much in the reading of his character. Some great men owe most
of their greatness to the ability of detecting in those they destine
for their tools the exact quality of strength that matters for their
work, and Brown, as though he had been really great, had a
satanic gift of finding out the best and the weakest spot in his
victims. He admitted to me that Jim wasn't of the sort that can
be got over by truckling, and accordingly he took care to show
himself as a man confronting without dismay ill-luck, censure,
and disaster. The smuggling of a few guns was no great crime, he
pointed out. As to coming to Patusan, who had the right to
say he hadn't come to beg? The infernal people here let loose
at him from both banks without staying to ask questions. He
made the point brazenly, for, in truth, Dain Waris's energetic
action had prevented the greatest calamities; because Brown told
me distinctly that, perceiving the size of the place, he had re-
solved instantly in his mind that as soon as he had gained a footing he would set fire right and left, and begin by shooting down
everything living in sight, in order to cow and terrify the population. The disproportion of forces was so great that this was
the only way giving him the slightest chance of attaining his
ends — he argued in a fit of coughing. But he didn't tell Jim this.
As to the hardships and starvation they had gone through, these
had been very real; it was enough to look at his band. He made,
at the sound of a shrill whistle, all his men appear standing in a
row on the logs in full view, so that Jim could see them. For the
killing of the man, it had been done — well, it had — but was not
this war, bloody war — in a corner? and the fellow had been
killed cleanly, shot through the chest, not like that poor devil of
his lying now in the creek. They had to listen to him dying for six
hours, with his entrails torn with slugs. At any rate this was a
life for a life. . . . And all this was said with the weariness, with
the recklessness of a man spurred on and on by ill-luck till he
cares not where he runs. When he asked Jim, with a sort of
brusque despairing frankness, whether he himself — straight now
— didn't understand that when 'it came to saving one's life in
the dark, one didn't care who else went — three, thirty, three

hundred people' — it was as if a demon had been whispering advice in his ear. 'I made him wince,' boasted Brown to me. 'He very soon left off coming the righteous over me. He just stood there with nothing to say, and looking as black as thunder — not at me — on the ground.' He asked Jim whether he had nothing fishy in his life to remember that he was so damnedly hard upon a man trying to get out of a deadly hole by the first means that came to hand — and so on, and so on. And there ran through the rough talk a vein of subtle reference to their common blood, an assumption of common experience; a sickening suggestion of common guilt, of secret knowledge that was like a bond of their minds and of their hearts.

"At last Brown threw himself down full length and watched Jim out of the corners of his eyes. Jim on his side of the creek stood thinking and switching his leg. The houses in view were silent, as if a pestilence had swept them clean of every breath of life; but many invisible eyes were turned, from within, upon the two men with the creek between them, a stranded white boat, and the body of the third man half sunk in the mud. On the river canoes were moving again, for Patusan was recovering its belief in the stability of earthly institutions since the return of the white lord. The right bank, the platforms of the houses, the rafts moored along the shores, even the roofs of bathing-huts, were covered with people that, far away out of earshot and almost out of sight, were straining their eyes towards the knoll beyond the Rajah's stockade. Within the wide irregular ring of forests broken in two places by the sheen of the river there was a silence. 'Will you promise to leave the coast?' Jim asked. Brown lifted and let fall his hand, giving everything up as it were — accepting the inevitable. 'And surrender your arms?' Jim went on. Brown sat up and glared across. 'Surrender our arms! Not till you come to take them out of our stiff hands. You think I am gone crazy with funk? Oh, no! That and the rags I stand in is all I have got in the world, besides a few more breechloaders on board; and I expect to sell the lot in Madagascar, if I ever get so far — begging my way from ship to ship.'

"Jim said nothing to this. At last, throwing away the switch he held in his hand, he said, as if speaking to himself, 'I don't know whether I have the power.' . . . 'You don't know! And you wanted me just now to give up my arms! That's good, too,'

cried Brown. 'Suppose they say one thing to you, and do the
other thing to me.' He calmed down markedly. 'I daresay you
have the power, or what's the meaning of all this talk?' he continued. 'What did you come down here for? To pass the time
of day?'

" 'Very well,' said Jim, lifting his head suddenly after a long
silence. 'You shall have a clear road or else a clear fight.' He
turned on his heel and walked away.

"Brown got up at once, but he did not go up the hill till he
had seen Jim disappear between the first houses. He never set
his eyes on him again. On his way back he met Cornelius slouch-
ing down with his head between his shoulders. He stopped before Brown. 'Why didn't you kill him?' he demanded in a sour,
discontented voice. 'Because I could do better than that,' Brown
said with an amused smile. 'Never! never!' protested Cornelius
with energy. 'Couldn't. I have lived here for many years.'
Brown looked up at him curiously. There were many sides to
the life of that place in arms against him; things he would never
find out. Cornelius slunk past dejectedly in the direction of the
river. He was now leaving his new friends; he accepted the dis-
appointing course of events with a sulky obstinacy which seemed
to draw more together his little yellow old face; and as he went
down he glanced askant here and there, never giving up his
fixed idea.

"Henceforth events move fast without a check, flowing from
the very hearts of men like a stream from a dark source, and we
see Jim amongst them, mostly through Tamb' Itam's eyes. The
girl's eyes had watched him, too, but her life is too much en-
twined with his: there is her passion, her wonder, her anger, and,
above all, her fear and her unforgiving love. Of the faithful servant, uncomprehending as the rest of them, it is the fidelity alone
that comes into play; a fidelity and a belief in his lord so strong
that even amazement is subdued to a sort of saddened acceptance
of a mysterious failure. He has eyes only for one figure, and
through all the mazes of bewilderment he preserves his air of
guardianship, of obedience, of care.

"His master came back from his talk with the white men,
walking slowly towards the stockade in the street. Everybody
was rejoiced to see him return, for while he was away every
man had been afraid not only of him being killed, but also of

what would come after. Jim went into one of the houses, where old Doramin had retired, and remained alone for a long time with the head of the Bugis settlers. No doubt he discussed the course to follow with him then, but no man was present at the conversation. Only Tamb' Itam, keeping as close to the door as he could, heard his master say, 'Yes. I shall let all the people know that such is my wish; but I spoke to you, O Doramin, before all the others, and alone; for you know my heart as well as I know yours and its greatest desire. And you know well also that I have no thought but for the people's good.' Then his master, lifting the sheeting in the doorway, went out, and he, Tamb' Itam, had a glimpse of old Doramin within, sitting in the chair with his hands on his knees, and looking between his feet. Afterwards he followed his master to the fort, where all the principal Bugis and Patusan inhabitants had been summoned for a talk. Tamb' Itam himself hoped there would be some fighting. 'What was it but the taking of another hill?' he exclaimed regretfully. However, in the town many hoped that the rapacious strangers would be induced, by the sight of so many brave men making ready to fight, to go away. It would be a good thing if they went away. Since Jim's arrival had been made known before daylight by the gun fired from the fort and the beating of the big drum there, the fear that had hung over Patusan had broken and subsided like a wave on a rock, leaving the seething foam of excitement, curiosity, and endless speculation. Half of the population had been ousted out of their homes for purposes of defence, and were living in the street on the left side of the river, crowding round the fort, and in momentary expectation of seeing their abandoned dwellings on the threatened bank burst into flames. The general anxiety was to see the matter settled quickly. Food, through Jewel's care, had been served out to the refugees. Nobody knew what their white man would do. Some remarked that it was worse than in Sherif Ali's war. Then many people did not care; now everybody had something to lose. The movements of canoes passing to and fro between the two parts of the town were watched with interest. A couple of Bugis war-boats lay anchored in the middle of the stream to protect the river, and a thread of smoke stood at the bow of each; the men in them were cooking their midday rice when Jim, after his interviews with Brown and Doramin, crossed the river and entered by the water-

gate of his fort. The people inside crowded round him so that
he could hardly make his way to the house. They had not seen
him before, because on his arrival during the night he had only
exchanged a few words with the girl, who had come down to the
landing-stage for the purpose, and had then gone on at once to
join the chiefs and the fighting men on the other bank. People
shouted greetings after him. One old woman raised a laugh by
pushing her way to the front madly and enjoining him in a
scolding voice to see to it that her two sons, who were with
Doramin, did not come to harm at the hands of the robbers. Several of the bystanders tried to pull her away, but she struggled
and cried, 'Let me go. What is this, O Muslims? This laughter
is unseemly. Are they not cruel, bloodthirsty robbers bent on
killing?' 'Let her be,' said Jim, and as a silence fell suddenly, he
said slowly, 'Everybody shall be safe.' He entered the house before the great sigh, and the loud murmurs of satisfaction, had
died out.

"There's no doubt his mind was made up that Brown should
have his way clear back to the sea. His fate, revolted, was forcing his hand. He had for the first time to affirm his will in the
face of out-spoken opposition. 'There was much talk, and at
first my master was silent,' Tamb' Itam said. 'Darkness came, and
then I lit the candles on the long table. The chiefs sat on each
side, and the lady remained by my master's right hand.'

"When he began to speak the unaccustomed difficulty seemed
only to fix his resolve more immovably. The white men were
now waiting for his answer on the hill. Their chief had spoken
to him in the language of his own people, making clear many
things difficult to explain in any other speech. They were erring
men whom suffering had made blind to right and wrong. It is
true that lives had been lost already, but why lose more? He
declared to his hearers, the assembled heads of the people, that
their welfare was his welfare, their losses his losses, their mourning his mourning. He looked round at the grave listening faces
and told them to remember that they had fought and worked
side by side. They knew his courage . . . Here a murmur interrupted him . . . And that he had never deceived them. For
many years they had dwelt together. He loved the land and the
people living in it with a very great love. He was ready to answer with his life for any harm that should come to them if the

white men with beards were allowed to retire. They were evil-doers, but their destiny had been evil, too. Had he ever advised them ill? Had his words ever brought suffering to the people? he asked. He believed that it would be best to let these whites and their followers go with their lives. It would be a small gift. 'I whom you have tried and found always true ask you to let them go.' He turned to Doramin. The old *nakoda* made no movement. 'Then,' said Jim, 'call in Dain Waris, your son, my friend, for in this business I shall not lead.' "

CHAPTER XLIII

"Tamb' Itam behind his chair was thunderstruck. The declaration produced an immense sensation. 'Let them go because this is best in my knowledge which has never deceived you,' Jim insisted. There was a silence. In the darkness of the courtyard could be heard the subdued whispering, shuffling noise of many people. Doramin raised his heavy head and said that there was no more reading of hearts than touching the sky with the hand, but — he consented. The others gave their opinion in turn. 'It is best,' 'Let them go,' and so on. But most of them simply said that they 'believed Tuan Jim.'

"In this simple form of assent to his will lies the whole gist of the situation; their creed, his truth; and the testimony to that faithfulness which made him in his own eyes the equal of the impeccable men who never fall out of the ranks. Stein's words, 'Romantic! — Romantic!' seem to ring over those distances that will never give him up now to a world indifferent to his failing and his virtues, and to that ardent and clinging affection that refuses him the dole of tears in the bewilderment of a great grief and of eternal separation. From the moment the sheer truthfulness of his last three years of life carries the day against the ignorance, the fear, and the anger of men, he appears no longer to me as I saw him last — a white speck catching all the dim light left upon a sombre coast and the darkened sea — but greater and more pitiful in the loneliness of his soul, that remains even for her who loved him best a cruel and insoluble mystery.

"It is evident that he did not mistrust Brown; there was no reason to doubt the story, whose truth seemed warranted by the rough frankness, by a sort of virile sincerity in accepting the morality and the consequences of his acts. But Jim did not know the almost inconceivable egotism of the man which made him, when resisted and foiled in his will, mad with the indignant and revengeful rage of a thwarted autocrat. But if Jim did not mistrust Brown, he was evidently anxious that some misunderstanding should not occur, ending perhaps in collision and bloodshed. It was for this reason that directly the Malay chiefs had gone he asked Jewel to get him something to eat, as he was going out of the fort to take command in the town. On her remonstrating against this on the score of his fatigue, he said that something might happen for which he would never forgive himself. 'I am responsible for every life in the land,' he said. He was moody at first; she served him with her own hands, taking the plates and dishes (of the dinner-service presented him by Stein) from Tamb' Itam. He brightened up after a while; told her she would be again in command of the fort for another night. 'There's no sleep for us, old girl,' he said, 'while our people are in danger.' Later on he said jokingly that she was the best man of them all. 'If you and Dain Waris had done what you wanted, not one of these poor devils would be alive to-day.' 'Are they very bad?' she asked, leaning over his chair. 'Men act badly sometimes without being much worse than others,' he said after some hesitation.

"Tamb' Itam followed his master to the landing-stage outside the fort. The night was clear, but without a moon, and the middle of the river was dark, while the water under each bank reflected the light of many fires 'as on a night of Ramadan,' Tamb' Itam said. War-boats drifted silently in the dark lane or, anchored, floated motionless with a loud ripple. That night there was much paddling in a canoe and walking at his master's heels for Tamb' Itam: up and down the street they tramped, where the fires were burning, inland on the outskirts of the town where small parties of men kept guard in the fields. Tuan Jim gave his orders and was obeyed. Last of all they went to the Rajah's stockade, which a detachment of Jim's people manned on that

night. The old Rajah had fled early in the morning with most
of his women to a small house he had near a jungle village on a
tributary stream. Kassim, left behind, had attended the council
with his air of diligent activity to explain away the diplomacy
of the day before. He was considerably cold-shouldered, but
managed to preserve his smiling, quiet alertness, and professed
himself highly delighted when Jim told him sternly that he pro-
posed to occupy the stockade on that night with his own men.
After the council broke up he was heard outside accosting this
and that departing chief, and speaking in a loud, gratified tone
of the Rajah's property being protected in the Rajah's absence.

"About ten or so Jim's men marched in. The stockade commanded the mouth of the creek, and Jim meant to remain there
till Brown had passed below. A small fire was lit on the flat,
grassy point outside the wall of stakes, and Tamb' Itam placed
a little folding-stool for his master. Jim told him to try and
sleep. Tamb' Itam got a mat and lay down a little way off; but
he could not sleep, though he knew he had to go on an important journey before the night was out. His master walked to
and fro before the fire with bowed head and with his hands
behind his back. His face was sad. Whenever his master approached him Tamb' Itam pretended to sleep, not wishing his
master to know he had been watched. At last his master stood
still, looking down on him as he lay, and said softly, 'It is time.'

"Tamb' Itam arose directly and made his preparations. His
mission was to go down the river, preceding Brown's boat by
an hour or more, to tell Dain Waris finally and formally that the
whites were to be allowed to pass out unmolested. Jim would
not trust anybody else with that service. Before starting Tamb'
Itam, more as a matter of form (since his position about Jim
made him perfectly known), asked for a token. 'Because, Tuan,'
he said, 'the message is important, and these are thy very words
I carry.' His master first put his hand into one pocket, then into
another, and finally took off his forefinger Stein's silver ring,
which he habitually wore, and gave it to Tamb' Itam. When
Tamb' Itam left on his mission, Brown's camp on the knoll was
dark but for a single small glow shining through the branches
of one of the trees the white men had cut down.

"Early in the evening Brown had received from Jim a folded
piece of paper on which was written, 'You get the clear road.

Start as soon as your boat floats on the morning tide. Let your men be careful. The bushes on both sides of the creek and the stockade at the mouth are full of well-armed men. You would have no chance, but I don't believe you want bloodshed.' Brown read it, tore the paper into small pieces, and, turning to Cornelius, who had brought it, said jeeringly, 'Good-bye, my excellent friend.' Cornelius had been in the fort, and had been sneaking around Jim's house during the afternoon. Jim chose him to carry the note because he could speak English, was known to Brown, and was not likely to be shot by some nervous mistake of one of the men as a Malay, approaching in the dusk, perhaps might have been.

"Cornelius didn't go away after delivering the paper. Brown was sitting up over a tiny fire; all the others were lying down. 'I could tell you something you would like to know,' Cornelius mumbled crossly. Brown paid no attention. 'You did not kill him,' went on the other, 'and what do you get for it? You might have had money from the Rajah, besides the loot of all the Bugis houses, and now you get nothing.' 'You had better clear out from here,' growled Brown, without even looking at him. But Cornelius let himself drop by his side and began to whisper very fast, touching his elbow from time to time. What he had to say made Brown sit up at first, with a curse. He had simply informed him of Dain Waris's armed party down the river. At first Brown saw himself completely sold and betrayed, but a moment's reflection convinced him that there could be no treachery intended. He said nothing, and after a while Cornelius remarked, in a tone of complete indifference, that there was another way out of the river which he knew very well. 'A good thing to know, too,' said Brown, pricking up his ears; and Cornelius began to talk of what went on in town and repeated all that had been said in council, gossiping in an even undertone at Brown's ear as you talk amongst sleeping men you do not wish to wake. 'He thinks he has made me harmless, does he?' mumbled Brown very low. . . . 'Yes. He is a fool. A little child. He came here and robbed me,' droned on Cornelius, 'and he made all the people believe him. But if something happened that they did not believe him any more, where would he be? And the Bugis Dain who is waiting for you down the river there, captain, is the very man who chased you up here when you first came.' Brown observed nonchalantly that it would be just as well to avoid him, and with the same detached, musing air Cornelius declared himself acquainted with a backwater broad enough to take Brown's boat past Waris's camp. 'You will have to be quiet,' he said as an afterthought, 'for in one place we pass close behind his camp. Very close. They are camped ashore with their boat hauled up.' 'Oh, we know how to be as quiet as mice; never fear,' said Brown. Cornelius stipulated that in case he were to pilot Brown out, his canoe should be towed. 'I'll have to get back quick,' he explained.

"It was two hours before the dawn when word was passed to the stockade from outlying watchers that the white robbers were coming down to their boat. In a very short time every armed man from one end of Patusan to the other was on the alert, yet the banks of the river remained so silent that but for the fires burning with sudden blurred flares the town might have been asleep as if in peace-time. A heavy mist lay very low on the water, making a sort of illusive grey light that showed nothing. When Brown's long-boat glided out of the creek into the river, Jim was standing on the low point of land before the Rajah's stockade — on the very spot where for the first time he put his foot on Patusan shore. A shadow loomed up, moving in the greyness, solitary, very bulky, and yet constantly eluding the eye. A murmur of low talking came out of it. Brown at the tiller heard Jim speak calmly: 'A clear road. You had better trust to the current while the fog lasts; but this will lift presently.' 'Yes, presently we shall see clear,' replied Brown.

"The thirty or forty men standing with muskets at ready outside the stockade held their breath. The Bugis owner of the prau, whom I saw on Stein's verandah, and who was amongst them, told me that the boat, shaving the low point close, seemed for a moment to grow big and hang over it like a mountain. 'If you think it worth your while to wait a day outside,' called out Jim, 'I'll try to send you down something — bullock, some yams — what I can.' The shadow went on moving. 'Yes. Do,' said a voice, blank and muffled out of the fog. Not one of the many attentive listeners understood what the words meant; and then Brown and his men in their boat floated away, fading spectrally without the slightest sound.

"Thus Brown, invisible in the mist, goes out of Patusan elbow to elbow with Cornelius in the sternsheets of the long-boat. 'Perhaps you shall get a small bullock,' said Cornelius. 'Oh, yes. Bullock. Yam. You'll get it if *he* said so. He always speaks the truth. He stole everything I had. I suppose you like a small bullock better than the loot of many houses.' 'I would advise you to hold your tongue, or somebody here may fling you overboard into this damned fog,' said Brown. The boat seemed to be standing still; nothing could be seen, not even the river alongside, only the water-dust flew and trickled, condensed, down their beards and faces. It was weird, Brown told me. Every individual man of them felt as though he were adrift alone in a boat, haunted by an almost imperceptible suspicion of sighing, muttering ghosts. 'Throw me out, would you? But I would know where I was,' mumbled Cornelius, surlily. 'I've lived many years here.' 'Not long enough to see through a fog like this,' Brown said, lolling back with his arm swinging to and fro on the useless tiller. 'Yes. Long enough for that,' snarled Cornelius. 'That's very useful,' commented Brown. 'Am I to believe you could find that backway you spoke of blindfold, like this?' Cornelius grunted. 'Are you too tired to row?' he asked after a silence. 'No, by God!' shouted Brown suddenly. 'Out with your oars there.' There was a great knocking in the fog, which after a while settled into a regular grind of invisible sweeps against invisible thole-pins. Otherwise nothing was changed, and but for the slight splash of a dipped blade it was like rowing a balloon car in a cloud, said Brown. Thereafter Cornelius did not open his lips except to ask querulously for somebody to bale out his canoe, which was towing behind the long-boat. Gradually the fog whitened and became luminous ahead. To the left Brown saw a darkness as though he had been looking at the back of the departing night. All at once a big bough covered with leaves appeared above his head, and ends of twigs, dripping and still, curved slenderly close alongside. Cornelius, without a word, took the tiller from his hand."

CHAPTER XLIV

~~~~~~

"I DON'T think they spoke together again. The boat entered
a narrow by-channel, where it was pushed by the oar-blades set
into crumbling banks, and there was a gloom as if enormous black
wings had been outspread above the mist that filled its depth to
the summits of the trees. The branches overhead showered big
drops through the gloomy fog. At a mutter from Cornelius,
Brown ordered his men to load. 'I'll give you a chance to get
even with them before we're done, you dismal cripples, you,'
he said to his gang. 'Mind you don't throw it away — you
hounds.' Low growls answered that speech. Cornelius showed
much fussy concern for the safety of his canoe.

Meantime Tamb' Itam had reached the end of his journey.
The fog had delayed him a little, but he had paddled steadily,
keeping in touch with the south bank. By-and-by daylight came
like a glow in a ground glass globe. The shores made on each
side of the river a dark smudge, in which one could detect hints
of columnar forms and shadows of twisted branches high up.
The mist was still thick on the water, but a good watch was
being kept, for as Tamb' Itam approached the camp the figures
of two men emerged out of the white vapour, and voices spoke
to him boisterously. He answered, and presently a canoe lay
alongside, and he exchanged news with the paddlers. All was
well. The trouble was over. Then the men in the canoe let go
their grip on the side of his dug-out and incontinently fell out
of sight. He pursued his way till he heard voices coming to him
quietly over the water, and saw, under the now lifting, swirling
mist, the glow of many little fires burning on a sandy stretch,
backed by lofty thin timber and bushes. There again a look-out
was kept, for he was challenged. He shouted his name as the two
last sweeps of his paddle ran his canoe up on the strand. It was
a big camp. Men crouched in many knots under a subdued murmur of early morning talk. Many thin threads of smoke curled
slowly on the white mist. Little shelters, elevated above the
ground, had been built for the chiefs. Muskets were stacked in

small pyramids, and long spears were stuck singly into the sand
near the fires.

"Tamb' Itam, assuming an air of importance, demanded to be
led to Dain Waris. He found the friend of his white lord lying
on a raised couch made of bamboo, and sheltered by a sort of
shed of sticks covered with mats. Dain Waris was awake, and
a bright fire was burning before his sleeping-place, which resembled a rude shrine. The only son of Nakhoda Doramin
answered his greeting kindly. Tamb' Itam began by handing
him the ring which vouched for the truth of the messenger's
words. Dain Waris, reclining on his elbow, bade him speak and
tell all the news. Beginning with the consecrated formula, 'The
news is good,' Tamb' Itam delivered Jim's own words. The
white men, departing with the consent of all the chiefs, were
to be allowed to pass down the river. In answer to a question
or two Tamb' Itam then reported the proceedings of the last
council. Dain Waris listened attentively to the end, toying with
the ring which ultimately he slipped on the forefinger of his
right hand. After hearing all he had to say he dismissed Tamb'
Itam to have food and rest. Orders for the return in the afternoon were given immediately. Afterwards Dain Waris.lay down
again, open-eyed, while his personal attendants were preparing
his food at the fire, by which Tamb' Itam also sat talking to
the men who lounged up to hear the latest intelligence from the
town. The sun was eating up the mist. A good watch was kept
upon the reach of the main stream where the boat of the whites
was expected to appear every moment.

"It was then that Brown took his revenge upon the world
which, after twenty years of contemptuous and reckless bullying, refused him the tribute of a common robber's success. It
was an act of cold-blooded ferocity, and it consoled him on his
deathbed like a memory of an indomitable defiance. Stealthily
he landed his men on the other side of the island opposite to the
Bugis camp, and led them across. After a short but quite silent
scuffle, Cornelius, who had tried to slink away at the moment of
landing, resigned himself to show the way where the undergrowth was most sparse. Brown held both his skinny hands together behind his back in the grip of one vast fist, and now and
then impelled him forward with a fierce push. Cornelius remained as mute as a fish, abject but faithful to his purpose, whose

accomplishment loomed before him dimly. At the edge of the patch of forest Brown's men spread themselves out in cover and waited. The camp was plain from end to end before their eyes, and no one looked their way. Nobody even dreamed that the white men could have any knowledge of the narrow channel at the back of the island. When he judged the moment come, Brown yelled, 'Let them have it,' and fourteen shots rang out like one.

"Tamb' Itam told me the surprise was so great that, except for those who fell dead or wounded, not a soul of them moved for quite an appreciable time after the first discharge. Then a man screamed, and after that scream a great yell of amazement and fear went up from all the throats. A blind panic drove these men in a surging swaying mob to and fro along the shore like a herd of cattle afraid of the water. Some few jumped into the river then, but most of them did so only after the last discharge. Three times Brown's men fired into the ruck, Brown, the only one in view, cursing and yelling, 'Aim low! aim low!'

"Tamb' Itam says that, as for him, he understood at the first volley what had happened. Though untouched he fell down and lay as if dead, but with his eyes open. At the sound of the first shots Dain Waris, reclining on the couch, jumped up and ran out upon the open shore, just in time to receive a bullet in his forehead at the second discharge. Tamb' Itam saw him fling his arms wide open before he fell. Then, he says, a great fear came upon him — not before. The white men retired as they had come — unseen.

"Thus Brown balanced his account with the evil fortune. Notice that even in this awful outbreak there is a superiority as of a man who carries right — the abstract thing — within the envelope of his common desires. It was not a vulgar and treacherous massacre; it was a lesson, a retribution — a demonstration of some obscure and awful attribute of our nature which, I am afraid, is not so very far under the surface as we like to think.

"Afterwards the whites depart unseen by Tamb' Itam, and seem to vanish from before men's eyes altogether; and the schooner, too, vanishes after the manner of stolen goods. But a story is told of a white long-boat picked up a month later in the Indian Ocean by a cargo-steamer. Two parched, yellow, glassy-eyed, whispering skeletons in her recognised the authority of a third, who declared that his name was Brown. His schooner, he reported, bound south with a cargo of Java sugar, had sprung a bad leak and sank under his feet. He and has companions were the survivors of a crew of six. The two died on board the steamer which rescued them. Brown lived to be seen by me, and I can testify that he had played his part to the last.

"It seems, however, that in going away they had neglected to cast off Cornelius's canoe. Cornelius himself Brown had let go at the beginning of the shooting, with a kick for a parting benediction. Tamb' Itam, after arising from amongst the dead, saw the Nazarene running up and down the shore amongst the corpses and the expiring fires. He uttered little cries. Suddenly he rushed to the water, and made frantic efforts to get one of the Bugis boats into the water. 'Afterwards, till he had seen me,' related Tamb' Itam, 'he stood looking at the heavy canoe and scratching his head.' 'What became of him?' I asked. Tamb' Itam, staring at me, made an expressive gesture with his right arm. 'Twice I struck, Tuan,' he said. 'When he beheld me approaching he cast himself violently on the ground and made a great outcry, kicking. He screeched like a frightened hen till he felt the point; then he was still, and lay staring at me while his life went out of his eyes.'

"This done, Tamb' Itam did not tarry. He understood the importance of being the first with the awful news at the fort. There were, of course, many survivors of Dain Waris's party; but in the extremity of panic some had swum across the river, others had bolted into the bush. The fact is that they did not know really who struck that blow — whether more white robbers were not coming, whether they had not already got hold of the whole land. They imagined themselves to be the victims of a vast treachery, and utterly doomed to destruction. It is said that some small parties did not come in till three days afterwards. However, a few tried to make their way back to Patusan at once, and one of the canoes that were patrolling the river that morning was in sight of the camp at the very moment of the attack. It is true that at first the men in her leaped overboard and swam to the opposite bank, but afterwards they returned to their boat and started fearfully upstream. Of these Tamb' Itam had an hour's advance."

CHAPTER XLV

"When Tamb' Itam, paddling madly, came into the town-reach, the women, thronging the platforms before the houses, were looking out for the return of Dain Waris's little fleet of boats. The town had a festive air; here and there men, still with spears or guns in their hands, could be seen moving or standing on the shore in groups. Chinamen's shops had been opened early; but the market-place was empty, and a sentry, still posted at the corner of the fort, made out Tamb' Itam, and shouted to those within. The gate was wide open. Tamb' Itam jumped ashore and ran in headlong. The first person he met was the girl coming down from the house.

"Tamb' Itam, disordered, panting, with trembling lips and wild eyes, stood for a time before her as if a sudden spell had been laid on him. Then he broke out very quickly: 'They have killed Dain Waris and many more.' She clapped her hands, and her first words were, 'Shut the gates.' Most of the fortmen had gone back to their houses, but Tamb' Itam hurried on the few who remained for their turn of duty within. The girl stood in the middle of the courtyard while the others ran about. 'Doramin,' she cried despairingly, as Tamb' Itam passed her. Next time he went by he answered her thought rapidly, 'Yes. But we have all the powder in Patusan.' She caught him by the arm, and, pointing at the house, 'Call him out,' she whispered, trembling.

"Tamb' Itam ran up the steps. His master was sleeping. 'It is I, Tamb' Itam,' he cried at the door, 'with tidings that cannot wait.' He saw Jim turn over on the pillow and open his eyes, and he burst out at once. 'This, Tuan, is a day of evil, an accursed day.' His master raised himself on his elbow to listen — just as Dain Waris had done. And then Tamb' Itam began his tale, trying to relate the story in order, calling Dain Waris Panglima, and saying: 'The Panglima then called out to the chief of his own boatmen, "Give Tamb' Itam something to eat"' — when his master put his feet to the ground and looked at him with such a discomposed face that the words remained in his throat.

"'Speak out,' said Jim. 'Is he dead?' 'May you live long,' cried Tamb' Itam. 'It was a most cruel treachery. He ran out at the first shots and fell. . . . His master walked to the window and with his fist struck at the shutter. The room was made light; and then in a steady voice, but speaking fast, he began to give him orders to assemble a fleet of boats for immediate pursuit, go to this man, to the other — send messengers; and as he talked he sat down on the bed, stooping to lace his boots hurriedly, and suddenly looked up. 'Why do you stand here?' he asked very red-faced. 'Waste no time.' Tamb' Itam did not move. 'Forgive me, Tuan, but . . . but,' he began to stammer. 'What?' cried his master aloud, looking terrible, leaning forward with his hands gripping the edge of the bed. 'It is not safe for thy servant to go out amongst the people,' said Tamb' Itam, after hesitating a moment.

"Then Jim understood. He had retreated from one world, for a small matter of an impulsive jump, and now the other, the work of his own hands, had fallen in ruins upon his head. It was not safe for his servant to go out amongst his own people! I believe that in that very moment he had decided to defy the disaster in the only way it occurred to him such a disaster could be defied; but all I know is that, without a word, he came out of his room and sat before the long table, at the head of which he was accustomed to regulate the affairs of his world, proclaiming daily the truth that surely lived in his heart. The dark powers should not rob him twice of his peace. He sat like a stone figure. Tamb' Itam, deferential, hinted at preparations for defence. The girl he loved came in and spoke to him, but he made a sign with his hand, and she was awed by the dumb appeal for silence in it. She went out on the verandah and sat on the threshold, as if to guard him with her body from dangers outside.

"What thoughts passed through his head — what memories? Who can tell? Everything was gone, and he who had been once unfaithful to his trust had lost again all men's confidence. It was then, I believe, he tried to write — to somebody — and gave it up. Loneliness was closing on him. People had trusted him with their lives — only for that; and yet they could never, as he had said, never be made to understand him. Those without did not hear him make a sound. Later, towards the evening, he came to the door and called for Tamb' Itam. 'Well?' he asked. 'There is much weeping. Much anger, too,' said Tamb' Itam. Jim looked up at him. 'You know,' he murmured. 'Yes, Tuan,' said Tamb' Itam. 'Thy servant does know, and the gates are closed. We shall have to fight.' 'Fight! What for?' he asked. 'For our lives.' 'I have no life,' he said. Tamb' Itam heard a cry from the girl at the door. 'Who knows?' said Tamb' Itam. 'By audacity and cunning we may even escape. There is much fear in men's hearts, too.' He went out, thinking vaguely of boats and of open sea, leaving Jim and the girl together.

"I haven't the heart to set down here such glimpses as she had given me of the hour or more she has passed in there wrestling with him for the possession of her happiness. Whether he had any hope — what he expected, what he imagined — it is impossible to say. He was inflexible, and with the growing loneliness of his obstinacy his spirit seemed to rise above the ruins of his existence. She cried 'Fight!' into his ear. She could not understand. There was nothing to fight for. He was going to prove his power in another way and conquer the fatal destiny itself. He came out into the courtyard, and behind him, with streaming hair, wild of face, breathless, she staggered out and leaned on the side of the doorway. 'Open the gates,' he ordered. Afterwards, turning to those of his men who were inside, he gave them leave to depart to their homes. 'For how long, Tuan?' asked one of them timidly. 'For all life,' he said, in a sombre tone.

"A hush had fallen upon the town after the outburst of wailing and lamentation that had swept over the river, like a gust of wind from the opened abode of sorrow. But rumours flew in whispers, filling the hearts with consternation and horrible doubts. The robbers were coming back, bringing many others with them, in a great ship, and there would be no refuge in the land for any one. A sense of utter insecurity as during an earthquake pervaded the minds of men, who whispered their suspicions, looking at each other as if in the presence of some awful portent.

"The sun was sinking towards the forests when Dain Waris's body was brought into Doramin's *campong*. Four men carried it in, covered decently with a white sheet which the old mother had sent out down to the gate to meet her son on his return. They laid him at Doramin's feet, and the old man sat still for a long time, one hand on each knee, looking down. The fronds of palms swayed gently, and the foliage of fruit-trees stirred above his head. Every single man of his people was there, fully armed, when the old *nakhoda* at last raised his eyes. He moved them slowly over the crowd, as if seeking for a missing face. Again his chin sank on his breast. The whispers of many men mingled with the slight rustling of the leaves.

"The Malay who had brought Tamb' Itam and the girl to Samarang was there, too. 'Not so angry as many,' he said to me, but struck with a great awe and wonder at the 'suddenness of men's fate, which hangs over their heads like a cloud charged with thunder.' He told me that when Dain Waris's body was uncovered at a sign of Doramin's, he whom they often called the white lord's friend was disclosed lying unchanged with his eyelids a little open as if about to wake. Doramin leaned forward a little more, like one looking for something fallen on the ground. His eyes searched the body from its feet to its head, for the wound maybe. It was in the forehead and small; and there was no word spoken while one of the bystanders, stooping, took off the silver ring from the cold stiff hand. In silence he held it up before Doramin. A murmur of dismay and horror ran through the crowd at the sight of that familiar token. The old *nakhoda* stared at it, and suddenly let out one great fierce cry, deep from the chest, a roar of pain and fury, as mighty as the bellow of a wounded bull, bringing great fear into men's hearts, by the magnitude of his anger and his sorrow that could be plainly discerned without words. There was a great stillness afterwards for a space, while the body was being borne aside by four men. They laid it down under a tree, and on the instant, with one long shriek, all the women of the household began to wail together; they mourned with shrill cries; the sun was setting, and in the intervals of screamed lamentations the high singsong voices of two old men intoning the Koran chanted alone.

"About this time Jim, leaning on a gun-carriage, looked at the river, and turned his back on the house; and the girl, in the doorway, panting as if she had run herself to a standstill, was looking at him across the yard. Tamb' Itam stood not far from his master, waiting patiently for what might happen. All at once Jim, who seemed to be lost in quiet thought, turned to him and said, 'Time to finish this.'

" 'Tuan?' said Tamb' Itam, advancing with alacrity. He did not know what his master meant, but as soon as Jim made a movement the girl started, too, and walked down into the open space. It seems that no one else of the people of the house was in sight. She tottered slightly, and about half-way down called out to Jim, who had apparently resumed his peaceful contemplation of the river. He turned round, setting his back against the gun. 'Will you fight?' she cried. 'There is nothing to fight for,' he said; 'nothing is lost.' Saying this he made a step towards her. 'Will you fly?' she cried again. 'There is no escape,' he said, stopping short, and she stood still also, silent, devouring him with her eyes. 'And you shall go?' she said, slowly. He bent his head. 'Ah!' she exclaimed, peering at him as it were, 'you are mad or false. Do you remember the night I prayed you to leave me, and you said that you could not? That it was impossible! Impossible! Do you remember you said you would never leave me? Why? I asked you for no promise. You promised unasked — remember.' 'Enough, poor girl,' he said. 'I should not be worth having.'

"Tamb' Itam said that while they were talking she would laugh loud and senselessly like one under the visitation of God. His master put his hands to his head. He was fully dressed as for every day, but without a hat. She stopped laughing suddenly, 'For the last time,' she cried, menacingly, 'will you defend yourself?' 'Nothing can touch me,' he said in a last flicker of superb egoism. Tamb' Itam saw her lean forward where she stood, open her arms, and run at him swiftly. She flung herself upon his breast and clasped him round the neck.

" 'Ah! but I shall hold thee thus,' she cried. . . . 'Thou art mine!'

"She sobbed on his shoulder. The sky over Patusan was blood-red, immense, streaming like an open vein. An enormous sun nestled crimson amongst the treetops, and the forest below had a black and forbidding face.

"Tamb' Itam tells me that on that evening the aspect of the heavens was angry and frightful. I may well believe it, for I knew that on that very day a cyclone passed within sixty miles of the coast, though there was hardly more than a languid stir of air in the place.

"Suddenly Tamb' Itam saw Jim catch her arms, trying to unclasp her hands. She hung on them with her head fallen back;

her hair touched the ground. 'Come here!' his master called, and Tamb' Itam helped to ease her down. It was difficult to separate her fingers. Jim, bending over her, looked earnestly upon her face, and all at once ran to the landing-stage. Tamb' Itam followed him, but turning his head, he saw that she had struggled up to her feet. She ran after them a few steps, then fell down heavily on her knees. 'Tuan! Tuan!' called Tamb' Itam, 'look back;' but Jim was already in a canoe, standing up paddle in hand. He did not look back. Tamb' Itam had just time to scramble in after him when the canoe floated clear. The girl was then on her knees, with clasped hands, at the water-gate. She remained thus for a time in a supplicating attitude before she sprang up. 'You are false!' she screamed out after Jim. 'Forgive me,' he cried. 'Never! Never!' she called back.

"Tamb' Itam took the paddle from Jim's hands, it being unseemly that he should sit while his lord paddled. When they reached the other shore his master forbade him to come any farther; but Tamb' Itam did follow him at a distance, walking up the slope to Doramin's *campong*.

"It was beginning to grow dark. Torches twinkled here and there. Those they met seemed awestruck, and stood aside hastily to let Jim pass. The wailing of women came from above. The courtyard was full of armed Bugis with their followers, and of Patusan people.

"I do not know what this gathering really meant. Were these preparations for war, or for vengeance, or to repulse a threatened invasion? Many days elapsed before the people had ceased to look out, quaking, for the return of the white men with long beards and in rags, whose exact relation to their own white man they could never understand. Even for those simple minds poor Jim remains under a cloud.

"Doramin, alone, immense and desolate, sat in his arm-chair with the pair of flintlock pistols on his knees, faced by an armed throng. When Jim appeared, at somebody's exclamation, all the heads turned round together, and then the mass opened right and left, and he walked up a lane of averted glances. Whispers followed him; murmurs: 'He has worked all the evil.' 'He hath a charm.' . . . He heard them — perhaps!

"When he came up into the light of torches the wailing of the women ceased suddenly. Doramin did not lift his head, and Jim stood silent before him for a time. Then he looked to the left, and moved in that direction with measured steps. Dain Waris's mother crouched at the head of the body, and the grey dishevelled hair concealed her face. Jim came up slowly, looked at his dead friend, lifting the sheet, then dropped it without a word. Slowly he walked back.

" 'He came! He came!' was running from lip to lip, making a murmur to which he moved. 'He hath taken it upon his own head,' a voice said aloud. He heard this and turned to the crowd. 'Yes. Upon my head.' A few people recoiled. Jim waited awhile before Doramin, and then said gently, 'I am come in sorrow.' He waited again. 'I am come ready and unarmed,' he repeated.

"The unwieldy old man, lowering his big forehead like an ox under a yoke, made an effort to rise, clutching at the flintlock pistols on his knees. From his throat came gurgling, choking, inhuman sounds, and his two attendants helped him from behind. People remarked that the ring which he had dropped on his lap fell and rolled against the foot of the white man, and that poor Jim glanced down at the talisman that had opened for him the door of fame, love, and success within the wall of forests fringed with white foam, within the coast that under the western sun looks like the very stronghold of the night. Doramin, struggling to keep his feet, made with his two supporters a swaying, tottering group; his little eyes stared with an expression of mad pain, of rage, with a ferocious glitter, which the bystanders noticed; and then, while Jim stood stiffened and with bared head in the light of torches, looking him straight in the face, he clung heavily with his left arm round the neck of a bowed youth, and lifting deliberately his right, shot his son's friend through the chest.

"The crowd, which had fallen apart behind Jim as soon as Doramin had raised his hand, rushed tumultuously forward after the shot. They say that the white man sent right and left at all those faces a proud and unflinching glance. Then with his hand over his lips he fell forward, dead.

"And that's the end. He passes away under a cloud, inscrutable at heart, forgotten, unforgiven, and excessively romantic. Not in the wildest days of his boyish visions could he have seen the alluring shape of such an extraordinary success! For it may very well be that in the short moment of his last proud and unflinching glance, he had beheld the face of that opportunity which, like an Eastern bride, had come veiled to his side.

"But we can see him, an obscure conqueror of fame, tearing himself out of the arms of a jealous love at the sign, at the call of his exalted egoism. He goes away from a living woman to celebrate his pitiless wedding with a shadowy ideal of conduct. Is he satisfied — quite, now, I wonder? We ought to know. He is one of us — and have I not stood up once, like an evoked ghost, to answer for his eternal constancy? Was I so very wrong after all? Now he is no more, there are days when the reality of his existence comes to me with an immense, with an overwhelming force; and yet upon my honour there are moments, too, when he passes from my eyes like a disembodied spirit astray amongst the passions of this earth, ready to surrender himself faithfully to the claim of his own world of shades.

"Who knows? He is gone, inscrutable at heart, and the poor girl is leading a sort of soundless, inert life in Stein's house. Stein has aged greatly of late. He feels it himself, and says often that he is 'preparing to leave all this; preparing to leave . . .' while he waves his hand sadly at his butterflies."

September 1899 — July 1900.

THE END

ADDENDUM

The biography of Conrad, of which a sketch is given here on pp. xxxix–xliv, still offers numerous problems to his biographers, and research on these is only now advancing into documentary certainty. In 1940 John Dozier Gordan laid the basis of our present knowledge of Conrad's experiences in the East and on the Congo journey of 1890 in his *Joseph Conrad: The Making of a Novelist*, but he gave few details on Conrad's first seventeen years in Poland or his four years in southern France, 1874–78. The Polish years have thus far been most fully treated by G. Jean-Aubry in his *Joseph Conrad: Life and Letters* (1927), pp. 1–27, and his *Vie de Conrad* (1947), pp. 15–51 (English translation, *The Sea Dreamer*, 1957, pp. 17–54); by Gustav Morf in *The Polish Heritage of Joseph Conrad* (c. 1929); and by Jozef Ujejski in *O Konradzie Korzeniowskim* (1936; French translation, Paris, 1939, pp. 13–65), with further material given in other Polish studies by Zbigniew Grabowski (1927), Roman Dybowski (1932 and 1933), Piotr Grzegorozyk (1933), Jan Perlowski (1937), Zdzislaw Najder (1956), among others. Conrad's own account of his Polish origins and background was given in *A Personal Record* (originally *Some Reminiscences*, 1912), Chapters II and III (*The Mirror of the Sea*, 1906, includes nothing on the Polish years), but these are intimate memories or impressions, without documentation.

The four years at Marseilles, 1874–78, set for Conrad's biographer what Mr. Jocelyn Baines has recently called "his most knotty problem" ("The Affair at Marseilles," *The London Magazine*, November 1957, pp. 41–46). Conrad himself laid the basis of our knowledge of this crucial passage in his career in 1906 in *The Mirror of the Sea*, Chapters XL–XLV, with their account of the *Tremolino* venture, of Dominic Cervoni, of the Carlist cause, of "Doña Rita's" part in it, and of J. M. K. B[lunt]; but this account was impressionistic and highly dramatized, and only slightly reinforced by a short passage on the Delestang circle at Marseilles in *A Personal Record*, Chapters VI–VII. His novel of 1919, *The Arrow of Gold*, was based on these episodes and persons, but in a fictional form which has never been available to documentary use. Jean-Aubry discovered some of the relevant facts but without exactly identifying Doña Rita de Lastaola, Blunt, Cervoni, or other personages who appear in the novel.

What is here called a "revised account" of this episode rests chiefly on the letter written by Conrad's uncle Tadeusz Bobrowski to Stefan Buszczynski of March 24, 1879, first described by Maria Dynowska in the *Kurjer Warszawski* (Warsaw), June 13, 1937, again reported in the *New York Times*, August 15, 1937, but first printed (in translation) by Mr. Baines in *The Times Literary Supplement* (London), December 6, 1957, p. 748. While I have followed the evidence of this letter, as well as Mr. Baines's tracing of discrepancies in the connection of the *Tremolino's* smuggling activities with the Carlist agitation in Spain, it must, as Mr. Baines says, "be borne in mind that [Tadeusz] Bobrowski was relating wnat Conrad and his friends had told him, which did not necessarily correspond with the facts," and that it is "possible that there was another, or additional, reason for [Conrad's] action, and that this was connected with the mysterious 'Rita de Lastaola.'" "But," he adds, "this is mere guesswork." Mr. Baines's forthcoming biography of Conrad, announced for 1958, will enlarge upon the episode and the evidence.

In her recent biography of Conrad, *The Thunder and the Sunshine* (New York: G. P. Putnam's Sons, 1958), Miss Jerry Allen makes less allowance for guesswork. She has done important research on the Marseilles episode (pp. 61–168). Through documents in the Jagellon and Pan libraries in Cracow and the Narodowa library in Warsaw, and through several French sources, she has discovered new facts on Conrad's Polish and French years; has traced the Carlist activity in detail; and has for the first time identified Rita de Lastaola of *The Arrow of Gold* as Paula de Somoggy (or Somogyi), mistress of the Spanish pretender Don Carlos (*l'amie du Roi*) and partner in Conrad's youthful liaison at Marseilles. She accepts as fact Conrad's duel with Blunt as given in *The Arrow of Gold*, and takes Tadeusz Bobrowski's account of Conrad's attempted suicide in the letter of 1879 as "the confused myth Conrad had woven to camouflage his romance." Unfortunately Miss Allen, apart from her bibliographical references, leaves so much of her account without specific documentation, and employs so many fictional or imaginative devices in her book generally, that it is difficult, in spite of her remarkable findings and speculations, to take her version as final. Conrad's biography, and this Marseilles and Carlist part of it especially, must therefore remain in large part speculative, and the account given here must be considered tentative until further documentation appears. Mr. Baines's biography will doubtless present the evidence in the most complete form thus far available.

M. D. Z.